FOURTH EDITION

Computer Concepts

BASICS

Dr. Dolores Wells
Professor, Computer Science
Hillsborough Community College
Tampa, FL

 COURSE TECHNOLOGY
CENGAGE Learning™

Australia • Brazil • Japan • Korea • Mexico • Singapore • Spain • United Kingdom • United States

COURSE TECHNOLOGY
CENGAGE Learning™

Computer Concepts BASICS, 4th Edition
Dolores Wells

Executive Editor: Donna Gridley

Product Manager: Allison O'Meara

Development Editor: Lisa Ruffolo

Associate Product Manager: Amanda Lyons

Editorial Assistant: Michelle Camisa

Content Project Manager: Catherine G. DiMassa

Marketing Manager: Valerie Lauer

Director of Manufacturing: Denise Powers

Text Designer: Shawn Girsberger

Photo Researcher: Abigail Reip

Manuscript Quality Assurance Lead: Jeff Schwartz

Manuscript Quality Assurance Reviewers:
    John Freitas, Danielle Shaw, Susan Whalen

Copy Editor: Harry Johnson

Proofreader: Kim Kosmatka

Indexer: Rich Carlson

Art Director: Kun-Tee Chang

Cover Designer: Hanh L. Luu

Compositor: GEX Publishing Services

For product information and technology assistance, contact us at
Cengage Learning Academic Resourse Center, 1-800-423-0563

For permission to use material from this text or product, submit all requests online at **www.cengage.com/permissions**
Further permissions questions can be emailed to
permissionrequest@cengage.com

Hardcover
ISBN-13: 978-1-423-90461-8
ISBN-10: 1-423-90461-3

Softcover
ISBN-13: 978-1-423-90462-5
ISBN-10: 1-423-90462-1

Course Technology
20 Channel Center Street
Boston, Massachusetts 02210
USA

Cengage Learning is a leading provider of customized learning solutions with office locations around the globe, including Singapore, the United Kingdom, Australia, Mexico, Brazil, and Japan. Locate your local office at:
international.cengage.com/region

Cengage Learning products are represented in Canada by Nelson Education, Ltd.

To learn more about Course Technology, visit **www.cengage.com/coursetechnology**
To learn more about Cengage Learning, visit **www.cengage.com**.

Any fictional data related to persons or companies or URLs used throughout this book is intended for instructional purposes only. At the time this book was printed, any such data was fictional and not belonging to any real persons or companies.

Printed in the United States of America
1 2 3 4 5 6 7 12 11 10 09

ABOUT THIS BOOK

Computer Concepts BASICS, Fourth Edition, is a brief introduction to computers that puts computer literacy information at your fingertips. This text covers computer hardware, software, application skills, the Internet, networking, and more. It can be used in any class on business applications, technology, or computer applications. This textbook, along with the instructor's materials, is all that is needed for a brief course on computer concepts and the Internet and can be used for 35 or more hours of instruction. It is assumed in this course that students have no prior experience with computer concepts. After completing these materials, the student should have a basic understanding of computers and the importance of technology in the world we live in today.

When partnered with a tutorial on a software application, this text provides a complete course on computer concepts—with hands-on applications. The textbook can also be used to supplement a mathematics, science, language arts, or social studies class through the integrated end-of-lesson and workbook activities and exercises.

To complete all Lessons and End-of-Lesson material, this book will require approximately 35 to 45 hours of classroom contact hours. Hours required for end-of-lesson activities and reviews vary depending on the number and type of activity selected. Examples for end-of-chapter and unit review activities are as follows:

Example 1 – End-of-lesson activities—approximately two hours required per Lesson:
Complete Review Questions
Complete two Cross-Curricular Projects
Complete either Web Project or Teamwork Project

Example 2 – End-of-lesson activitiess—approximately two and one-half hours required per Lesson:
Complete Review Questions
Complete two Cross-Curricular Projects
Complete either Web Project or Teamwork Project
Complete Google Online Project

Example 3 – End-of-lesson activities—approximately three hours required per Lesson:
Complete Review Questions
Complete two Cross-Curricular Projects
Complete both Web Project and Teamwork Project
Complete Google Online Project

Example 4 – Unit Review—approximately three hours required:
Complete Review Questions
Complete two projects and either Web Project or Teamwork Project
Complete Google Project
Complete one of the Simulations

Start-up Checklist

Hardware

- 500 megahertz (MHz) processor or higher
- 256 megabyte (MB) RAM or higher1
- 1.5 gigabyte (GB) hard disk
- CD-ROM or DVD drive
- Display 1024 x 768 or higher resolution monitor
- 10-20 MB USB Drive
- Enhanced keyboard
- Mouse or pen pointer
- Internet connection
- Printer

Software

- Windows Vista and Microsoft Office 2007
- Text editor such as Windows Notepad or WordPad

INSIDE THE BASICS SERIES

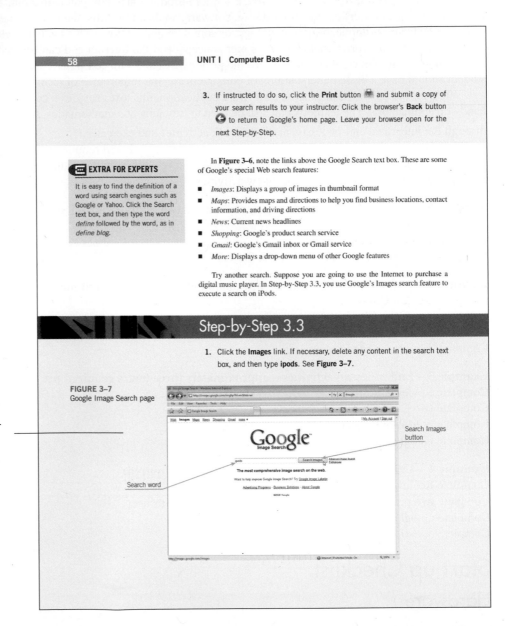

Step-by-Step Exercises offer "hands-on practice" of the material just learned. Each exercise uses a data file or requires you to create a file from scratch.

Lesson opener elements include the **Objectives** and **Suggested Completion Time**.

End of Lesson elements include the **Summary**, **Vocabulary Review**, **Review Questions**, **Lesson Projects**, and **Critical Thinking Activities**.

Instructor Resources Disk

ISBN-13: 9780324598940
ISBN-10: 0324598947

The Instructor Resources CD or DVD contains the following teaching resources:

The Data and Solution files for this course.

ExamView® tests for each lesson. ExamView is a powerful testing software package that allows instructors to create and administer printed, computer (LAN-based), and Internet exams.

Instructor's Manual that includes lecture notes for each lesson and references to the end-of-lesson activities and Unit Review projects.

Answer Keys that include solutions to the lesson and unit review questions.

Copies of the figures that appear in the student text.

Suggested Syllabus with block, two quarter, and 18-week schedule.

Annotated Solutions and Grading Rubrics.

PowerPoint presentations for each lesson.

ExamView®

This textbook is accompanied by ExamView, a powerful testing software package that allows instructors to create and administer printed, computer (LAN-based), and Internet exams. ExamView includes hundreds of questions that correspond to the topics covered in this text, enabling students to generate detailed study guides that include page references for further review. The computer-based and Internet testing components allow students to take exams at their computers, and save the instructor time by grading each exam automatically.

Online Companion

This book uses an Online Companion Web site that contains valuable resources to help enhance your learning. Go to www.cengage.com/coursetechnology and enter this book's ISBN to find the link to the Online Companion.

- Key terms and definitions for each lesson
- Student data files to complete text projects and activities
- PowerPoint presentations in both Microsoft Office 2003 and Office 2007 formats
- Crossword puzzles to review important concepts and vocabulary terms
- Fast Checks that include True/False and Multiple Choice quizzes for each unit
- Net Fun projects and additional Google projects that include Web site and Google activities
- Video projects on innovations in computers and technology
- Keyboarding drills reinforce keyboarding skills
- Link to CourseCasts

SAM

SAM 2007 helps bridge the gap between the classroom and the real world by allowing students to train and test on important computer skills in an active, hands-on environment.

SAM 2007's easy-to-use system includes powerful interactive exams, training or projects on critical applications such as Word, Excel, Access, PowerPoint, Outlook, Windows, the Internet, and much more. SAM simulates the application environment, allowing students to demonstrate their knowledge and think through the skills by performing real-world tasks.

SAM 2007 includes built-in page references so students can print helpful study guides that match the textbooks used in class. Powerful administrative options allow instructors to schedule exams and assignments, secure tests, and run reports with almost limitless flexibility.

CourseCasts

CourseCasts—Learning on the Go. Always Available…Always Relevant.

Want to keep up with the latest technology trends relevant to you? Visit our site to find a library of podcasts, CourseCasts, featuring a "CourseCast of the Week," and download them to your mp3 player at http://coursecasts.course.com.

Our fast-paced world is driven by technology. You know because you're an active participant—always on the go, always keeping up with technological trends, and always learning new ways to embrace technology to power your life.

Ken Baldauf, a faculty member of the Florida State University Computer Science Department, is responsible for teaching technology classes to thousands of FSU students each year. He knows what you want to know; he knows what you want to learn. He's also an expert in the latest technology and will sort through and aggregate the most pertinent news and information so you can spend your time enjoying technology, rather than trying to figure it out.

Visit us at **http://coursecasts.course.com** to learn on the go!

ACKNOWLEDGMENTS

This book is dedicated to my son, Bryan Pusins.

Special thanks go to Lisa Ruffolo and to Cathie DiMassa, Amanda Lyons, and Allison O'Meara for their patience and assistance.

Bring Your Course Back To the BASICS

Developed with the needs of new learners in mind, the **BASICS** series is ideal for lower-level courses covering basic computer concepts, Microsoft Office, programming, and more. Introductory in nature, these texts are comprehensive enough to cover the most important features of each application.

Computer Literacy Basics: Microsoft Office 2007 Companion
ISBN-13: 978-1-4239-0431-1
ISBN-10: 1-4239-0431-1
This companion edition from our BASICS series provides coverage of Internet and Computing Core Certification (IC3), using Microsoft Office 2007. This book works both as a companion to *Computer Literacy BASICS* and as a standalone Introductory Office text. Key skills for word processing, spreadsheets, presentation graphics, and databases are covered, making this text appropriate for any computer literacy course as well as those course preparing students for IC3 certification.

CONTENTS

UNIT I   COMPUTER BASICS

UNIT II   USING THE COMPUTER

CONTENTS

UNIT III   COMPUTERS AND SOCIETY

UNIT I

COMPUTER BASICS

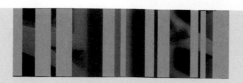

LESSON 1

Computers and Computer Literacy

■ OBJECTIVES

Upon completion of this lesson, you should be able to:

- Discuss the history of computers.
- Define the term computer and describe a computer system.
- Define the different computer classification categories.
- Describe the two types of computer software.
- Describe communications and networks.
- Identify how we use computers and technology in our daily lives.

Introducing Computers

The computer is one of the most important inventions of the past century. The widespread use of computers affects us individually and as a society. You can see computers in use almost everywhere! For instance, consider the following:

- Educational institutions use computers to enhance instruction in all disciplines and to provide online instruction.
- Video game systems transport you to an imaginary world.
- Using ATMs, you can withdraw money from your bank account from almost any location in the world.
- On television and at the movies, you can see instant replays in sports or amazing special effects that take you to outer space.
- Mobile computing, text messaging, e-mail, and online audio/video conferencing allow you to communicate with people at almost any location.

As indicated by these examples, computers and computer technology are pervasive throughout our society—from businesses and financial organizations, to home

■ VOCABULARY

clients

computer

data

desktop computer

electronic communication

embedded computer

extranet

hardware

icon

information

Internet

intranet

mobile devices

network

nodes

personal computers

servers

software

supercomputer

users

. . .

electronics and appliances, and to personal applications such as clothing embedded with iPod controls.

The importance of the computer is not surprising. Many people consider the computer to be the single most important invention of the 20th century! This technology affects all aspects of our daily lives. Computers are no longer bulky machines that sit on our desktops. Computers come in every shape and size and are found everywhere. As more powerful and special-purpose computers become available, society will find more ways to use this technology to enhance our lives. See **Figure 1–1**.

FIGURE 1–1   A group of students playing an online video game

A Brief History of the Computer

Computers have been around for more than 60 years. The first computers were developed in the late 1940s and early 1950s. They were massive, special-purpose machines with names like *UNIVAC* and *ENIAC* and were designed initially for use by the military and government. These early computers had less processing power than today's iPhone, occupied small buildings or entire city blocks, and cost millions of dollars. Computers in the mid-1950s through early 1970s were somewhat smaller and more powerful, but still were limited in what they could do. They remained expensive, so only major companies and government organizations could afford these systems. See **Figure 1–2**.

FIGURE 1–2 Early computers

In 1971, Dr. Ted Hoff developed the microprocessor. Visionaries like Steve Jobs and Steve Wozniak saw a future for the microprocessor and its application to personal computers. Jobs and Wozniak built the first Apple computer in 1976. Shortly thereafter, they released a second version, the Apple II. It became an immediate success, especially in schools. In 1980, Bill Gates worked with IBM to develop the disk operating system (DOS) for the IBM PC. This computer, introduced in 1981, quickly became the PC of choice for businesses. See **Figure 1–3**.

FIGURE 1–3 The Apple II and IBM PC

Computers and Computer Systems

Throughout a normal workday, millions of people interact globally using computers and other digital devices, often without even knowing it. Doctors, lawyers, warehouse workers, store clerks, homemakers, teachers, musicians, and students, to name a few examples, constantly depend on computers to perform part of their daily duties.

So, what exactly is a computer? What does it really do? A *computer* is an electronic device that receives data (*input*), processes data, stores data, and produces a result (*output*).

UNIT I Computer Basics

▶ VOCABULARY
hardware
software
data
information
users

A *computer system* includes hardware, software, data, and people. The actual machine—wires, transistors, and circuits—is called *hardware*. Peripheral devices such as printers and monitors also are hardware. *Software* consists of instructions or programs for controlling the computer. *Data* is text, numbers, sound, images, or video. The computer receives data through an input device, processes the data, stores the data on a storage device, and produces output or *information*. The *users*, the people who use computers, also are part of the system. See **Figure 1–4**.

FIGURE 1–4 Using a mobile computer to process data into information

Compare the description of a computer system with examples of ways a store clerk might use a computer at a hardware rental store.

- *Receives data*: The store clerk enters the customer's name and scans the bar code of a rented tool into the computer through input devices, such as the keyboard or digital scanner.

- *Processes data*: The computer uses stored instructions to process the data into information.

- *Stores data*: The data and information are stored in temporary memory and then on a permanent storage device, such as a hard disk drive.

- *Outputs information*: An output device, such as a monitor or a printer, displays the information.

This series of steps often is referred to as the *information processing cycle*. See **Figure 1–5**.

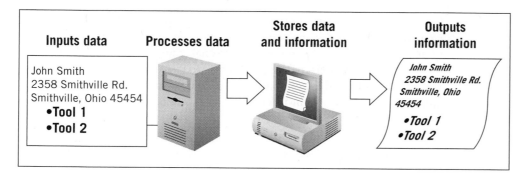

FIGURE 1–5 Information processing cycle

This brief overview of a computer and the listing of some of the tasks you can accomplish with a computer might appear to imply that the computer is a very complicated device. A computer, however, performs only two operations:

- Arithmetic computations such as addition, subtraction, multiplication, and division, and comparisons such as greater than, less than, or equal to

- Logical operations using logical operators, such as AND, OR, and NOT

You will learn more about these operations, how a computer works, and how data is transformed into information in Lesson 4.

How Computers Work

Today's computers are available in a variety of shapes and sizes. Computers are not intelligent and do only what we ask them to do. The benefits of a computer are possible because a computer has the advantage of speed, reliability, accuracy, storage, and communications.

- *Speed*: Some computers can perform billions of calculations per second.
- *Reliability*: The electronic components are dependable.
- *Accuracy*: If data is entered correctly, computers generate error-free results.
- *Storage*: Computers can store and retrieve volumes of data and information.
- *Communications*: Computers communicate and share resources with other computers.

 **EXTRA FOR EXPERTS**

A computer won a World Chess Championship game playing against a human.

Along with most advantages, however, come disadvantages. Some of the more common disadvantages are environmental impact and pollution, violation of privacy, identity theft, health risks, and outsourcing of jobs to foreign countries.

Classifying Computers

Computers today come in all shapes and sizes, with specific types being especially suited for specific tasks. Computers are considered special purpose or general purpose. *Special-purpose computers* are used mostly to control something else. Tiny chips are embedded in devices, such as a dishwasher, bathroom scale, or airport radar system, and these chips control the particular devices.

General-purpose computers are divided into categories, based on their physical size, function, cost, and performance.

- Desktop and notebook computers are today's most widely used *personal computers (PCs)*. A *desktop computer* is designed so that all components fit on or under a desk. Two popular types of personal computers are the PC (based on the original IBM personal computer design) and the Apple Macintosh. *Notebook computers* (also called laptop computers) are small personal computers that contain the monitor with a built-in keyboard. They are designed to be carried from one location to another.

- *Mobile devices* generally can fit into the palm of your hand. Examples of mobile devices are handheld devices such as PDAs, calculators, smart phones, electronic organizers, handheld games, and other similar tools. Many mobile devices can connect wirelessly to the Internet.

- The *server* (sometimes called a minicomputer) is used by small to medium-size companies and generally supports hundreds of users. A company would choose to use minicomputers rather than personal computers if they have many users and large amounts of data.

- The modern *mainframe computer* is a large, expensive computer, capable of supporting hundreds or even thousands of users. This type of computer is big compared to personal computers. Large companies use these to perform processing tasks for hundreds or thousands of users.

- A *supercomputer* is the fastest type of computer. Government agencies and large corporations use these computers for specialized applications to process enormous amounts of data. The cost of a supercomputer can be as much as several million dollars.

- *Embedded computers* perform specific tasks and can be found in a range of devices such as a digital watch, an MP3 player, or as a system controller for a nuclear power plant.

Today's small personal and handheld computers are more powerful than the mainframes and supercomputers of yesteryear. **Figure 1–6** shows examples of different types of computers.

FIGURE 1–6 1. Desktop computer 2. Mobile device 3. Contains embedded computer 4. Mainframe 5. Supercomputer

Computer Software

Two basic types of software (also called programs) are *application software* and *system software*. Application software is a set of programs that performs specific tasks for users, such as word processing, spreadsheets, and databases. System software is a set of programs that controls the operations of the computer and its devices. Most microcomputers use either the Windows or the Mac operating system software.

Most software has a *graphical user interface* (*GUI*, pronounced "gooey"). If you are using a PC, almost everything you do within the GUI environment requires working with windows and icons. An *icon* is a small image that represents a file, command, or another computer function. You execute the associated command by clicking or double-clicking the icon. For an introduction to Windows Vista, Step-by-Step 1.1 illustrates how to start Windows, display the desktop, open and close an application (Notepad), and then shut down the system. In later lessons, you learn how to save and print your documents.

The Step-by-Step exercises in this book use Windows Vista. The menus and screens for earlier versions of Windows are similar. Please make appropriate adjustments if you are using a different Windows version or working on a network. To start Windows is as simple as turning on your computer.

▶ VOCABULARY
icon

Step-by-Step 1.1

1. Turn on the computer. If your computer is on a network, you might be prompted to enter your username and a password. Your instructor will provide you with this information.

2. Click the **Start** button 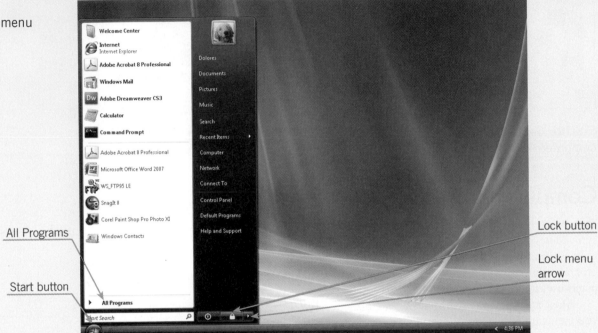 on the taskbar. The Start menu opens. The Windows Vista Start menu is shown in **Figure 1–7**. Your Start menu and the Start menu in earlier versions of Windows will look similar.

FIGURE 1–7
Windows Start menu

All Programs

Start button

Lock button

Lock menu arrow

3. Point to **All Programs**, click **Accessories**, and then point to **Notepad**. See **Figure 1–8**.

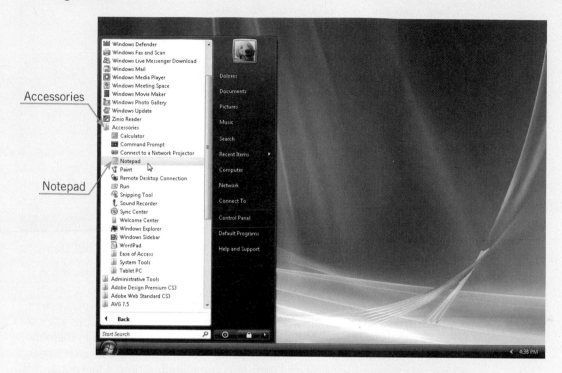

Accessories

Notepad

FIGURE 1–8
Starting Notepad

4. Click **Notepad**. The Notepad window opens.

5. Type a sentence or two about your favorite movie. See **Figure 1–9**.

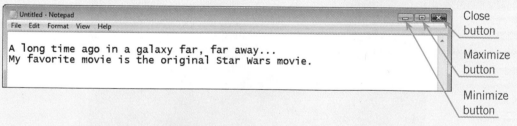

A long time ago in a galaxy far, far away...
My favorite movie is the original Star Wars movie.

Close button

Maximize button

Minimize button

FIGURE 1–9
Working in Notepad

6. Click the **Close** button ![X].

7. A dialog box is displayed, asking if you want to save the changes. See **Figure 1–10**.

FIGURE 1–10
Notepad dialog box

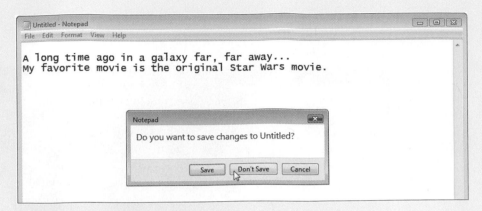

8. Click the **Don't Save** button. The Notepad window closes, and you are returned to the Windows desktop.

9. Click the **Start** button 🪟 on the taskbar, point to the Lock menu arrow ▶ to the right of the Lock button 🔒, and then point to **Shut Down**.

Pointing to the arrow to the right of the Lock button also displays other options. The Switch User option is for changing users without logging off or closing the computer; Log Off closes any open programs and logs off; Lock temporarily locks the computer and prevents others from viewing your work or accessing the system; Sleep saves programs and open documents to memory and then puts the computer into a low-power state; and Hibernate saves open documents to your hard disk and then puts the computer into a low-power state. See **Figure 1–11**.

FIGURE 1–11
Shutting down
the computer

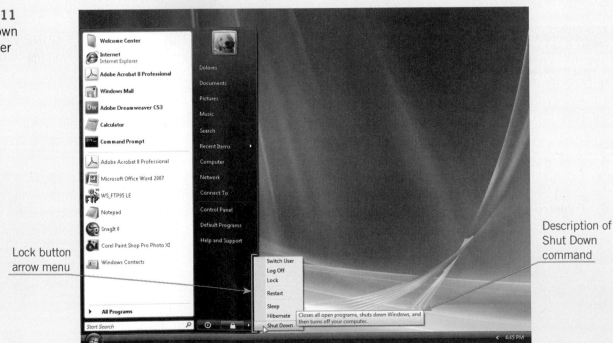

Lock button
arrow menu

Description of
Shut Down
command

10. Click **Shut Down**. Windows Vista turns off the computer.

If you are using a school computer and the logoff procedure is different, follow your school's logoff procedure.

Communications and Networks

Electronic communication is the technology that enables computers to communicate with each other and other devices. It is the transmission of text, numbers, voice, and video from one computer or device to another. Electronic communication has changed the way the world does business and the way we live our lives.

When computers were developed in the 1950s, they did not communicate with each other. This all changed in 1969. ARPANET was established and served as a testing ground for new networking technologies. ARPANET was a large wide-area network created by the United States Defense Advanced Research Project Agency (ARPA). On Labor Day in 1969, the first message was sent via telephone lines from a computer at UCLA to another computer at Stanford Research Institute. This was the beginning of the Internet and electronic communication as we know it today.

Electronic communication requires the following four components:

- *Sender*: The computer sending the message
- *Receiver*: The computer receiving the message
- *Channel*: The media that carries or transports the message; this could be telephone wire, coaxial cable, radio signal, microwave signal, or fiber-optic cable
- *Protocol*: The rules that govern the transfer of data

This technology has made it possible to communicate around the globe using tools such as the Internet, electronic mail (e-mail), faxes, e-commerce, and electronic banking. See **Figure 1–12**.

▶ VOCABULARY
electronic communication
network
nodes
clients
servers

FIGURE 1–12 Transmitting a message from sender to receiver

Networks

A *network* is a group of two or more computer systems linked together via communications devices. This connection enables the computers to share resources such as printers, data, information, and programs. A network can consist of two computers or millions of computers and other devices and can connect all categories of computers, including mobile devices, personal computers, mid-range servers, mainframes, and even supercomputers.

Computers on a network are called *nodes* or *clients*. *Servers* are computers that allocate resources on a network. Networks are covered in detail in Lesson 7. See **Figure 1–13** for a networking representation.

EXTRA FOR EXPERTS

Use Google to search for **biomedical clothing** and learn how dry-electrode technology is used to monitor body signals, such as heart rate.

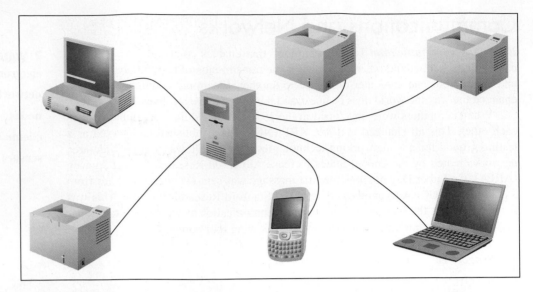

FIGURE 1–13 A network connecting users through various communications devices

Intranets and Extranets

▶ VOCABULARY
intranet
extranet
Internet

Many companies have implemented intranets within their organizations. An *intranet* is a network for the exclusive use of workers within an organization and contains company information. Company manuals, handbooks, and newsletters are just a few of the types of documents distributed via an intranet. Online forms also are a popular intranet feature. The major advantages of using an intranet are reliability and security—which are possible because the organization controls access.

Extranets are systems that allow outside organizations to access a company's internal information system. Access is controlled tightly and is usually reserved for suppliers and customers.

The Internet

The *Internet*, the world's largest network, evolved from ARPANET. Following the first historic message between two computers in 1969, ARPANET quickly grew into a global network consisting of hundreds of military and university sites. In 1990, ARPANET was disbanded and the Internet was born. Today, billions of users surf the Internet and the World Wide Web, one of the more popular segments of the Internet. Other Internet services are e-mail, chat rooms, instant messaging, mailing lists, blogging, RSS, conferencing, and newsgroups. The Internet and World Wide Web are covered in detail in Lesson 2. **Figure 1–14** shows an illustration of the Internet.

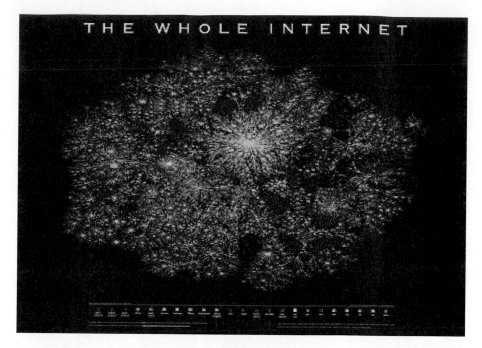

FIGURE 1–14   A graphical representation of the Internet

Technology for Everyday Life

Technology affects our lives every day and has dramatically changed the way we live. Without computers and computerized devices, the world as we know it today would come to a sudden halt. They have become necessary tools in almost every type of activity and in almost every type of business. Think of the many ways computers affect you every day. For example:

- In school, instruction is enhanced and information is accessible from anywhere in the world.
- Obtaining a high school or college degree via distance learning is possible.
- Electronic security systems protect our homes and workplaces.
- In game rooms, simulations transport you to an imaginary world.
- In government research operations, computer systems guide satellites through space.
- At home, our appliances are computerized.
- On television, we can watch an instant replay of a tackle in a football game.

In most everyday activities in which you participate, you benefit from the variety of applications and ways in which computers and technology are used.

Computers in Our Future

It is a fair assumption that computers of the future will be more powerful and less expensive. It also is a fair assumption that almost every type of job will somehow involve a computer. With long-distance connectivity, more people will work full-time or part-time from home. See **Figure 1–15**.

FIGURE 1–15   Working from home

One of the major areas of change in the evolution of computers is connectivity, or the ability to connect with other computers. Wireless and mobile devices will become the norm. Computer literacy, which is the knowledge and understanding of computers and their uses, will become even more important.

SUMMARY

In this lesson, you learned:

■ Computers have been around for more than 60 years.

■ A computer is an electronic device that receives data, processes data, produces information, and stores the data and information.

■ A computer derives its power from its speed, reliability, accuracy, storage, and communications capability.

■ Computer classifications include personal computers (desktop and notebook), mobile devices, servers, mainframes, supercomputers, and embedded computers.

■ The two basic types of software are application software and system software.

■ Electronic communication enables computers to communicate with each other and other devices.

■ A network is a group of two or more connected computers, an intranet is a closed network within an organization, and an extranet is a closed network for an organization and its customers and suppliers.

■ The Internet is the world's largest network.

■ Computers and technology affect almost every facet of our daily lives.

■ Computers in our future are likely to be more powerful and less expensive.

■ Computer literacy is the ability to use a computer and its software to accomplish practical tasks.

■ VOCABULARY REVIEW

Define the following terms:

clients	hardware	nodes
computer	icon	personal computers
data	information	servers
desktop computer	Internet	software
electronic communication	intranet	supercomputer
embedded computer	mobile devices	users
extranet	network	

■ REVIEW QUESTIONS

MULTIPLE CHOICE

Select the best response for the following statements.

1. A(n) _____ is a small image that represents a file, command, or another computer function.

   A. server   C. frown

   B. icon   D. field

2. A(n) _____ consists of hardware, software, data, and users.

   A. client   C. mobile device

   B. node   D. computer system

3. A(n) _____ generally can fit into the palm of your hand.

   A. mainframe computer   C. supercomputer

   B. mid-range server   D. mobile device

4. The world's largest network is _____.

   A. an extranet   C. the Internet

   B. an intranet   D. the World Wide Web

5. A(n) _____ is a group of two or more linked computers.

   A. client   C. network

   B. server   D. icon

TRUE / FALSE

Circle T if the statement is true or F if the statement is false.

T   F   **1.**   Information is processed data.

T   F   **2.**   Small businesses and companies rarely use computers.

T   F   **3.**   Data is stored in temporary memory and on a permanent storage device.

T   F   **4.**   A notebook computer can fit in the palm of your hand.

T   F   **5.**   The majority of computers are very unreliable.

FILL IN THE BLANK

1. A(n) _____ is the fastest type of computer.

2. Computer equipment that can be seen or touched is called _____.

3. The computer on the network that manages the network resources is called a(n) _____.

4. _____ is data that has been organized and processed.

5. A(n) _____ is a computer on a network that is not acting as a server.

■ PROJECTS

CROSS-CURRICULAR—MATHEMATICS

Use the Internet and other resources to search for information on a famous woman mathematician. Use the keywords *women mathematician* with one or two search engines, such as *www.google.com*, *www.yahoo.com*, or *www.ask.com*. Prepare a two-page report on what you discover.

CROSS-CURRICULAR—SCIENCE

Use the Internet and other resources to find information about wireless technology and computers of the future. Prepare a two-page report describing what you found. Use *www.ask.com* to locate resources for this report.

CROSS-CURRICULAR—SOCIAL STUDIES

Visit the Web site *www.mrnussbaum.com/gamescode.htm#social* and click the Social Studies link. Play at least three of the social studies games. Prepare a one-page report describing the games you played, why you selected those games, and then list three new facts you learned from this exercise.

CROSS-CURRICULAR—LANGUAGE ARTS

The computer has influenced the ways in which we communicate. Use the Internet and other resources to find information on different methods of communication. Prepare a two-page report on your findings.

WEB PROJECT

You are a member of a special group exploring the history of computers. Your instructor has asked you to investigate the history of computing and report your findings to the class. You are to research and report on significant contributors/contributions to the evolution of computing, using the Internet and other resources. The Web site located at *www.computerhistory.org* is a good starting point.

TEAMWORK PROJECT

Assume that your classroom has an existing network with six computers and an old, out-of-date printer. Your classroom has just received five new computers and a new printer. One of the computers is a server. Your teacher has asked that you and three of your fellow students create a work plan and blueprint to implement the new computers into the existing network.

She would like answers to the following questions: What information and resources can be shared? Will any other special hardware be required? Prepare a report on your findings. Include any other information about networks you think will be helpful. Start by using *www.about.com* or *http://en.wikipedia.org* and search for *computer networks*.

◼ CRITICAL THINKING

The computer has influenced the ways in which we communicate. Use the Internet and other resources to locate information on how the computer has affected our methods of communication. What other communication changes do you think could occur in the future? Explain how mobile devices could become more popular and how you think these devices might influence our society. Write a two-page report on your findings.

◼ EXPLORING GOOGLE

Gmail is a free Web mail service provided through Google. To create an account, complete the following steps:

1. Open your browser and type **http://mail.google.com/mail/help/open.html** in the Address bar.

2. When the Welcome to Gmail screen is displayed, read the information provided on the page.

3. Click the **Create an account** link.

4. Type your first and last name and desired login name. Click the **check availability** button to verify that the name is available.

5. When selecting a password, Google assists with a Password strength level—poor, fair, or strong. Your goal is to create a strong password, which must be a minimum of eight characters. Be sure to write down your password or send the password to yourself in an e-mail message.

6. If you are using a school computer or a computer other than your own, *do not* select the "Remember me on this computer" or the "Enable Web History" check boxes.

7. Select a Security Question that you are sure to remember. E-mail the answer to yourself.

8. If you have another e-mail address, you can enter it into the Secondary e-mail text box. However, this is not necessary or required.

9. For Word Verification, type the characters displayed on the form.

10. Read the Terms of Service, and then click the **I Accept. Create my account.** button.

11. An Introduction to Gmail page is displayed. Read the information on the page and then click the **I'm ready – show me my account.** link.

12. Click the **Compose Mail** link and send a message to your instructor or another classmate. Print a copy of your message and submit it to your instructor.

For additional information, see *http://mail.google.com/support*.

LESSON 2

The Internet and the World Wide Web

■ OBJECTIVES

Upon completion of this lesson, you should be able to:

- Explain the origin of the Internet and describe how the Internet works.
- Explain the difference between the World Wide Web and the Internet.
- Describe the major features of the Internet.
- Explain how to connect to the Internet.
- Describe a browser.
- Identify browser features.
- Apply and use browser features.
- Describe other Internet features.

Each day millions of people "surf," or explore, the information superhighway. The "information superhighway" refers to the Internet. It is compared to a highway system because it functions much like a network of interstate highways. People use the Internet to research information, to shop, to go to school, to communicate with family and friends, to read the daily newspaper, to make airplane and hotel reservations, and so on. They use the Internet at work, at home, and while traveling. Anyone with access to the Internet can connect with and communicate with anyone else in the world that also has Internet access.

■ VOCABULARY

Address bar

browser

domain name

home page

host computer

host node

hyperlink

Hypertext Markup Language (HTML)

Hypertext Transfer Protocol (HTTP)

Internet service provider (ISP)

online service provider (OSP)

protocol

Transmission Control Protocol and Internet Protocol (TCP/IP)

Uniform Resource Locator (URL)

Web 2.0

Web page

World Wide Web

...

Evolution of the Internet

Even though no one person or organization can claim credit for creating the Internet, its origins can be traced to the 1960s and the United States Department of Defense. The birth of the Internet is tied closely to a computer-networking project started by a governmental division called the Advanced Research Projects Agency (ARPA). The goal was to create a network that would allow scientists to share information on military and scientific research.

The original name for the Internet was ARPANET. In 1969, ARPANET was a wide area network with four main host node computers. A *host node* is any computer directly connected to the network. These computers were located at the University of California at Santa Barbara, the University of California at Los Angeles, the Stanford Research Institute, and the University of Utah.

Over the next several years, the Internet grew steadily but quietly. Some interesting details are as follows:

▶ **VOCABULARY**

host node

browser

- The addition of e-mail in 1972 spurred some growth.

- By 1989, more than 100,000 host computers were linked to ARPANET.

- In 1990, ARPANET ceased to exist, but few noticed because its functions continued.

- The real growth began when the World Wide Web came into being in 1992.

- The thousands of interconnected networks were called an Inter-Net-Network and became known as the Internet, or a network of networks.

- In 1993, the world's first browser, Mosaic, was released. A *browser* is a software program that provides a graphical interface for the Internet. Mosaic made it so easy to access the Internet that there was a 340 percent growth in the number of Internet users in this one year.

- The Internet is still growing at an unprecedented rate. See **Figure 2–1**.

FIGURE 2–1   Global Internet map

The Internet's Impact on Society

The use of the Internet in American homes has spread quickly among all demographic groups and across geographic regions. This increase is fueled by expanding computer use in schools and workplaces. In mid-2007, over 70 percent of all Americans, nearly 220 million people, used the Internet at home, work, or school.

The benefits of the Internet are so numerous and widespread that its value is almost incalculable. Businesses have automated record-keeping tasks that previously required countless hours, freeing workers for more productive activities. Marketers instantaneously send information via the Internet to prospective customers anywhere in the world. Shoppers can compare products, prices, and services offered by dozens or even hundreds of possible sellers, all without making a single phone call.

People who have difficulty moving around physically now can conduct many activities through the Internet that previously would not have been possible. The Internet is creating new opportunities every day—to learn and research, to keep in touch with distant friends and family members, to stay informed about political developments and make views known to government officials, and to nurture relationships that bridge and break down national, ethnic, and cultural barriers in an increasingly interconnected world.

Internet Basics

Recall from Lesson 1 that a network is a group of two or more computers linked together. The Internet is a loose association of thousands of networks and millions of computers across the world that all work together to share information. It is transitory and is constantly changing, reshaping, and remolding itself. The beauty of this network of networks is that all brands, models, and makes of computers can communicate with each other. This is called *interoperability*.

So how do we communicate across the Internet? Consider our postal service. If you want to send someone a letter anywhere in the world, you can do that—as long as you know the address. The Internet works in a similar fashion. From your computer, you can connect with any other networked computer anywhere in the world—as long as you know the address or know how to find the address.

Computers on the Internet communicate with each other using a set of protocols known as *TCP/IP* or *Transmission Control Protocol and Internet Protocol*. A *protocol* is a standard format for transferring data between two devices. TCP/IP is the agreed-upon international standard for transmitting data. It is considered the language of the Internet and supports nearly all Internet applications. The TCP protocol enables two host computers to establish a connection and exchange data. A *host computer* is a computer that you access remotely from your computer. The IP protocol works with the addressing scheme. It allows you to enter an address and send it to another computer; from there the TCP protocol takes over and establishes a connection between the two computers. Returning to the postal service analogy, this is similar to what happens when you take a letter to the post office. You deliver the letter to the post office and then the post office takes over and delivers the letter to the recipient. See **Figure 2–2**.

▶ **VOCABULARY**

interoperability

Transmission Control Protocol and Internet Protocol (TCP/IP)

protocol

host computer

FIGURE 2–2 Data travels the Internet using TCP/IP

▶ **VOCABULARY**
domain name
World Wide Web
Hypertext Transfer Protocol (HTTP)

Postal addresses usually contain numbers and street names. Likewise, when we access another computer on the Internet, we are accessing it via a number. We do not need to remember or type the number. Instead, we can type the domain name. The ***domain name*** identifies a site on the Internet. For example, the domain name in the Web address *www.microsoft.com* is *microsoft.com*. If you want to access Microsoft Corporation's computers that are connected to the Internet, you can open your Web browser and type the domain name into the browser's Address box. Browsers are discussed later in this lesson.

The World Wide Web

The Internet is made up of many services. Some of the more popular of these services include blogs, chat rooms, e-mail, FTP (file transfer protocol), instant messaging, mailing lists, newsgroups and bulletin boards, online conferencing, and Voice over Internet Protocol (VoIP). These services are discussed later in this lesson. One of the more popular Internet services is the World Wide Web.

Many people use the terms ***World Wide Web***, or *Web* for short, and *Internet* interchangeably. In reality, they are two different things. The Web is a subset or an application that makes use of the Internet. The Internet can exist without the Web, but the Web cannot exist without the Internet. The Web actually began in 1990, when Dr. Tim Berners-Lee, who currently is the director of the World Wide Web Consortium, wrote a small computer program for his own personal use. This program, referred to as the ***Hypertext Transfer Protocol (HTTP)***, became the language computers would use to communicate hypertext documents over the Internet. Dr. Berners-Lee next designed a scheme to give documents addresses on the Internet, and then created a text-based program that permitted pages to be linked through a formatting process

▶ **VOCABULARY**
Hypertext Markup Language (HTML)

Web 2.0

Web server

known as *Hypertext Markup Language (HTML)*. Clicking a linked word or image transfers you from one Web page to another or to another part of the same Web page. Dr. Berners-Lee's contributions were a step forward, but they were not the catalyst that made the Web what it is today.

In 1993, the number of people using the Web greatly increased. This increase occurred when Marc Andreessen, working for the National Center for Supercomputing Applications at the University of Illinois, released Mosaic. Mosaic was the first graphical browser. See **Figure 2–3**.

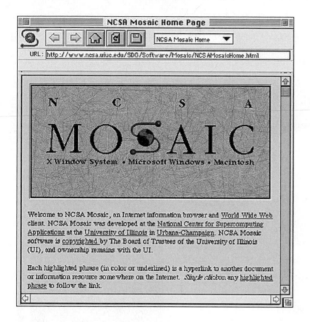

FIGURE 2–3   Mosaic Web page

In 1994, Andreessen co-founded Netscape Communications. With the introduction of Mosaic and the Web browsers that followed, the Web became a communications tool for a much wider audience. Currently, the most popular Web browser is Internet Explorer. Some other popular browsers include Firefox, Mozilla, Netscape, Safari, and Opera.

In 2004, the phrase **Web 2.0** was coined. Also called the *participatory Web*, this term has several definitions, although the most popular definition refers to Web sites where users can modify the content. This includes a new generation of Web-based services such as *blogs*, social-networking sites, *wikis*, and application software built into the site. Because of these enhancements, the Web is one of the more widely used services on the Internet.

Web Protocols—HTTP

The Web has several underlying protocols. One of these protocols, mentioned earlier, is HTTP, or Hypertext Transfer Protocol. This protocol or standard defines how pages are transmitted. You can send and receive Web pages over the Internet because Web servers and Web browsers both understand HTTP. When you enter a Web site address in your browser, for instance, this sends an HTTP command to the Web server to tell it to locate and transmit the requested Web page. A **Web server** is a computer that delivers, or serves up, Web pages. By installing special software, any computer can become a Web server. Every Web server has its own IP address and most have a domain name.

> **VOCABULARY**
> Uniform Resource Locator (URL)

The Web page address often is referred to as the *URL*, or *Uniform Resource Locator*. Every Web page on the Internet has its own unique address. The first part of the address indicates what protocol to use, and the second part specifies the IP address or the domain name where the resource is located. For example, in the URL *http://smithsonianmag.com* the *http* protocol indicates that this is a Web page and that the domain name is *smithsonian*. See **Figure 2–4**. The *.com* at the end of the name indicates that this is a commercial, business, or organization site. **Table 2–1** contains a list of popular top-level domain abbreviations; however, many other infrequently used domain abbreviations also exist.

FIGURE 2–4   Smithsonian Magazine Web page

TABLE 2–1   Top-level domain name abbreviations

TOP-LEVEL DOMAIN ABBREVIATIONS	TYPE OF ORGANIZATION
com	Commercial businesses, companies, and organizations
edu	Educational institutions
gov	Government institutions, such as the IRS
mil	Military organizations, such as the U.S. Army
net	Network providers
mobi	Mobile Internet devices
org	Associations and organizations

Web Protocols—HTML

A second protocol or standard that controls how the World Wide Web works is HTML, or Hypertext Markup Language. This computer language determines how Web pages are formatted and displayed and allows the users to exchange text, images, sound, video, and multimedia files. Hypertext is a text-based link to other text-based documents and often referred to as a *link*, which is short for **hyperlink**. The location can be within the same document, in another document on the same Web server, or on a Web server on the other side of the world. You click the link and are transported to the Web page. A *hypermedia* link combines text-based links with audio, graphic, and video links. Links allow the user to surf the Web using a nonlinear method.

A **Web page** is nothing more than an ordinary text page that is coded with HTML markup tags and then displayed within a browser. Markup tags consist of a set of text commands that are interpreted by the browser. Different browsers might interpret HTML tags differently or might not support all HTML tags. Thus, the same Web page can be displayed differently when viewed in different browsers. Altogether, three items determine how a Web page is displayed:

- The type and version of the browser displaying the Web page
- The HTML markup tags used to code the page
- The user's monitor and monitor resolution

Hundreds of markup tags exist that can be used within a document. All Web pages, however, have a minimum basic requirement. Lesson 16 contains instructions on how to create a Web page.

Accessing the Internet

Before you can begin to access the Internet, you have to be connected and become part of a network. If you connect to the Internet through an organization such as a school or business, you probably are connecting through a local area network. A *local area network (LAN)* connects computers and devices within a limited geographical area. You connect to the Internet using a *network interface card (NIC)*. This is a special card inside your computer that allows the computer to be networked. A direct connection is made from the local area network to a high-speed connection line from a local, regional, or national Internet service provider.

Home users generally connect to the Internet using one of the following methods: a dial-up modem and a telephone line, a cable modem, a digital subscriber line (high-speed digital telephone line), fiber optics, satellite, or wireless.

The next step is learning how to use the Web browser.

Getting Connected

Connecting to the Internet is a simple process, but you first must complete a few steps:

- **Step 1**: The first step is to locate an *Internet service provider (ISP)*, an *online service provider (OSP)*, or a *wireless Internet service provider (WISP)*. There are thousands of ISPs. Many are small, local companies. Their service is primarily an Internet connection. OSPs are large national and international companies such as America Online (AOL) and Microsoft Network (MSN). WISPs provide service to mobile devices such as smartphones, PDAs, and notebook computers with built-in wireless capabilities. Generally, the local ISP is less expensive than the OSP or WISP, but many people use an OSP or WISP because of the additional information and services offered.

> ▶ **VOCABULARY**
> hyperlink
> Web page
> local area network (LAN)
> network interface card (NIC)
> Internet service provider (ISP)
> online service provider (OSP)
> wireless Internet service provider (WISP)

> **EXTRA FOR EXPERTS**
>
> Broadband is high-speed Internet access; almost 60 percent of Internet users in the United States have broadband access.

- **Step 2**: Once you decide which service provider to use, you must install some type of communication software. This software enables your computer to connect to another computer. Most likely, your ISP, OSP, or WISP will provide this software.

- **Step 3**: You will need to install a Web browser to use the Web. The most popular browser is Microsoft's Internet Explorer. Some OSPs, such as AOL, provide their own browser versions.

After you contract with your ISP and install your software, you are ready to connect to the Internet. This is the easy part. You may have to give instructions to your computer to dial a local telephone number if you are using a dial-up modem. This connects you to your ISP's computer, which in turn connects you to the Internet. If you are using a cable connection, DSL, fiber optics, or a wireless service, you automatically are connected when you turn on your computer.

Browser Basics

Recall that a browser is the software program you use to retrieve documents from the Web and to display them in a readable format. The Web is the graphical portion of the Internet. The browser functions as an interface between you and the Web. Using a browser, you can display both text and images. Newer versions of most browsers also support multimedia information, including sound, animation, and video. Companies constantly update browsers to support the latest information the Web has to offer. It is important to keep your browser software updated to the most recent version your computer can handle.

The browser sends a message to the Web server to retrieve your requested Web page. Then the browser renders the HTML code to display the page. Recall that HTML is the language used to create documents for the Web. You navigate the Web by using your mouse to point to and click hyperlinks displayed in the browser window. As previously discussed, a hyperlink is a highlighted word or image within a hypertext document which, when clicked, takes you to another place within that document or to another Web page.

Browser Terminology and Browser Basics

Understanding browser terminology is the key to using a browser effectively. Although most browsers have similar features, the menu options to select these features might be somewhat different. The major differences are special built-in tools. These tools include programs for mail, chat, viewing and listening to multimedia, and so on. This book uses Internet Explorer, version 7.

Tabbed browsing is a new feature added to Internet Explorer 7. When you start Internet Explorer, the page you have designated as the home page opens in the first tab. To view other pages within the same window, point to then click the New Tab button on the tab row and then, in the Address bar, type the address of the site that you want to visit. Your home page remains open in the first tab. To close a page, click the Close button that is displayed on the right side of the selected tab. If you have several tabs open, use the Quick Tabs button to locate the site in which you are interested or to close sites with which you are finished. See **Figure 2–5** and **Table 2–2**.

FIGURE 2–5   Internet Explorer browser window

TABLE 2–2   Parts of the Internet Explorer window

COMPONENT	DEFINITIONS
Address bar	Contains the URL or address of the active Web page; also, where you type the location for the Web page you want to visit
Back button	Displays the page you previously viewed prior to the current page displayed in the browser window
Command bar	A horizontal toolbar located on the right side of the window; provides a selection of options used to execute common commands; the buttons on the Command bar are described in Table 2–4
Document window	Displays the active Web page
Forward button	Displays the next page in the series of pages you previously have viewed; this button is not active until the Back button has been clicked at least one time
Menu bar	Lists menu commands if you select the option to display the menu bar
New Tab button	Opens a new window
Quick Tabs button	Locates a previous site or closes sites
Refresh button	Refreshes or reloads the current Web page
Scroll bar	Lets you scroll vertically or horizontally if the Web page is too long or too wide to fit within one screen
Search box	Lets you search for Web pages containing information that you specify
Status bar	Located at the bottom of the browser; shows the progress of Web page transactions
Tab	Lets you open multiple Web pages within the same browser window
Title bar	The bar on top of the window that contains the name of the document

Launching the Browser

In this lesson, it is assumed that you have an Internet connection—either a dial-up or direct connection. If you have a dial-up modem, most likely you will have to start a program that dials the Internet connection. If you have a direct high-speed or a wireless connection, however, you simply will start your Web browser to access the Internet. In most instances, you can double-click the browser icon located on your computer's desktop. If the icon is not available, open the browser from the Start menu.

If you want to visit a specific Web site, you need to know the address. The *Address bar*, located near the top of the browser window, is where you enter the address or URL of the Web site you want to visit (see **Figure 2–5**). As discussed earlier in this lesson, a unique URL identifies each Web page and tells the browser where to locate the page. The first part of the URL indicates the protocol and the second part specifies the domain name. To visit a specific Web site, type the address of the Web site you want to visit in the Address bar. Press Enter after typing the address to link to and display the Web page.

Toolbars

The menu bar is located on the left side of the Internet Explorer window and the Command bar is located on the right side of the window below the menu bar. If the menu bar is not displayed, right-click the Command bar, and then click Menu Bar on the shortcut menu. See **Figure 2–6**.

► **VOCABULARY**

Address bar

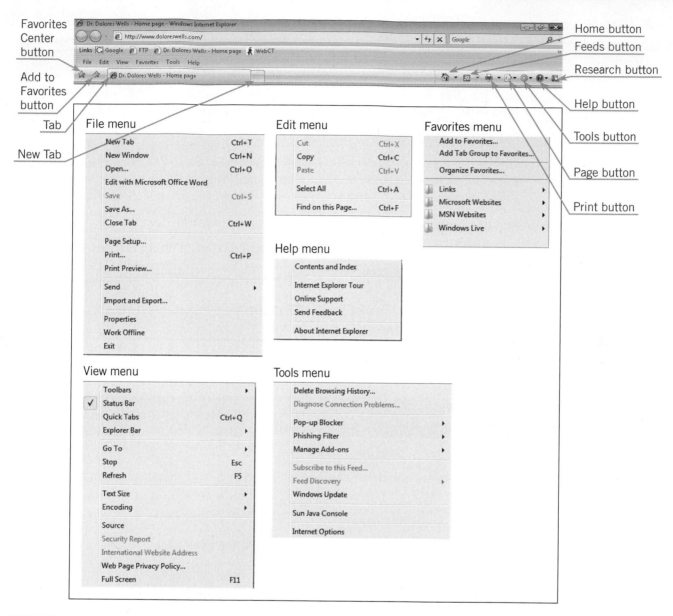

FIGURE 2–6   Internet Explorer menu bar and Command bar

Tables 2–3 and **2–4** provide an overview of the menu bar options and Command bar buttons. (The buttons on your Command bar might differ slightly from those described here.)

TABLE 2–3   Menu bar options

MENU	COMMANDS
File	New Tab, New Window, Open, Edit, Save, Save As, Close Tab, Page Setup, Print, Print Preview, Send, Import and Export, Properties, Work Offline, and Exit
Edit	Cut, Copy, Paste, Select All, and Find on this Page
View	Toolbars, Status Bar, Quick Tabs, Explorer Bar, Go To, Stop, Refresh, Text Size, Encoding, Source, Security Report, International Website Address, Web Page Privacy Policy, and Full Screen
Favorites	Add to Favorites, Add Tab Group to Favorites, and Organize Favorites
Tools	Delete Browsing History, Diagnose Connection Problems, Pop-up Blocker, Phishing Filter, Manage Add-ons, Subscribe to this Feed, Feed Discovery, Windows Update, Sun Java Console, and Internet Options
Help	Contents and Index, Internet Explorer Tour, Online Support, Send Feedback, and About Internet Explorer

TABLE 2–4   Command bar options

BUTTON	COMMANDS
Home	Displays the home page (also called start page)
Feeds	Displays frequently updated content published by a Web site; also known as RSS feeds
Print	Prints the current Web page
Page	Displays a menu of commands for working with the open page
Tools	Displays a menu of commands
Help	Displays content and index help for Windows Explorer
Research	Opens a pane within the existing window that includes a list of reference books and Web sites

Some other browser features are as follows:

- *AutoComplete*: Keeps track of and saves previous entries you have made for Web addresses, forms, and passwords
- *Address List*: Displays previously visited Web pages; click the Address bar list arrow to view these (see **Figure 2–7**)

Address bar
list arrow

Previously
visited
Web sites

FIGURE 2–7   Internet Explorer browser list of previously visited Web sites

To explore various methods of navigating through a Web site, complete the following exercise using the Web page shown in **Figure 2–8**. Web pages are updated and change over time. If the Web page used in this exercise has changed, see your instructor for additional information.

Find A Park By State

List of links

FIGURE 2–8   National Park Service (*nps.gov*) Web page

Step-by-Step 2.1

1. Start your Internet browser. The first page you see is your home page.

2. Type **www.nps.gov** in the Address bar, and then press **Enter**. The National Park Service home page opens.

3. You can navigate through the pages of this site using several navigation tools:

   a. Notice the list of links on the left side of the home page below the topic heading *NPS Home*. Click a link of your choice and review the information on the page to which you linked. Click the browser's **Back** button ⬅ to return to the NPS home page.

    b. Click the **Site Index** link. Review the information on the page to which you linked. Click the browser's **Back** button ⬅ to return to the NPS home page.

    c. Below the topic heading *Find A Park By State*, click your state on the displayed map. You link to a page for your state. The page contains links to the different parks for the state you chose.

    d. Click one of the park links. Review the information you find.

4. Click the browser's **Back** button ⬅ the number of times necessary to return to the nps.gov home page.

5. Click the **Home** button 🏠 on the Command bar to return to your browser's home page. Leave your browser open for the next Step-by-Step.

Your Home Page

When your browser is installed, a default home page is selected. The ***home page*** is the first page that is displayed when you start your browser. The Address bar located near the top of the browser window contains the address of the current page. In Step-by-Step 2.2, you use the Internet Options dialog box to change the default home page to *nps.gov* and then return it to its original default.

▶ **VOCABULARY**
home page

Step-by-Step 2.2

1. In the Internet Explorer Address bar, if necessary, type **nps.gov**.

2. Press **Enter**.

3. Click **Tools** on the Command bar, and then click **Internet Options**. The Internet Options dialog box is displayed. Click the **General** tab, if necessary. See **Figure 2–9**.

FIGURE 2–9
Internet Options dialog box

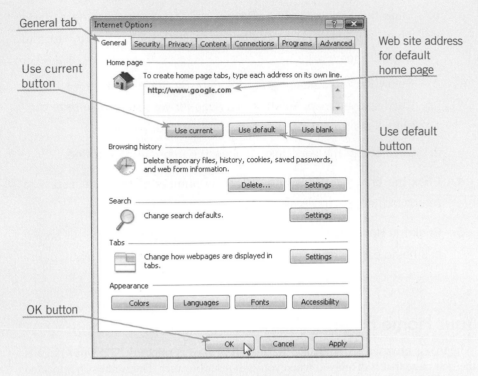

General tab

Use current button

Web site address for default home page

Use default button

OK button

4. In the Home page section, click **Use current** and then click **OK**. Close your browser.

5. Start your browser. Note that it now opens to nps.gov. Click **Tools** on the Command bar, click **Internet Options**, and, if necessary, click the **General** tab. Return the home page to its original settings by clicking **Use default**. (This is the original default page that was selected when your system was purchased. Verify with your instructor if another home page should be selected.)

6. Click the **OK** button to close the Internet Options dialog box. Leave your browser open for the next Step-by-Step.

Searching

▶ **VOCABULARY**
AutoSearch

Internet Explorer has a special feature called *AutoSearch* that makes it easy for you to locate your desired information quickly. You type a common term in the Address bar and press the Enter key. For example, suppose that you are saving your money for a new car, and you would like to have additional information about a Chevrolet Corvette. Launch your browser, type *Chevrolet Corvette*, and press Enter. Internet Explorer displays the Live Search page with links to over 20 million Chevrolet Corvette Web pages, as shown in **Figure 2–10**. Additional searching techniques are discussed in Lesson 3.

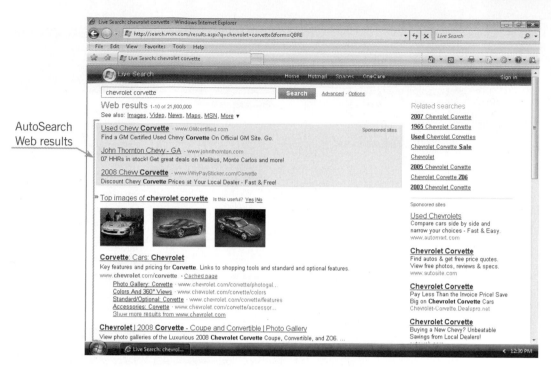

AutoSearch
Web results

FIGURE 2–10   AutoSearch Web results

History

The Back and Forward buttons take you to sites you have visited in your current session. What if, however, you want to return to that Web page you found last week, and you cannot remember the URL? Then the History button is for you.

In Internet Explorer, click the Favorites Center button, and then click the History button. The Favorites pane opens on the left side of the window and displays a list of options from 3 Weeks Ago to Today. This is a record of all the sites you have visited in the past three weeks or 20 days. The number of days (20) is the default. You can change the number of days through options on the Tools menu. To make it easier to find the site for which you are searching, you can click the History button arrow to sort the list by date, by site, by most visited, and by order visited today. You also can search the list for a keyword in a site name. See **Figure 2–11**.

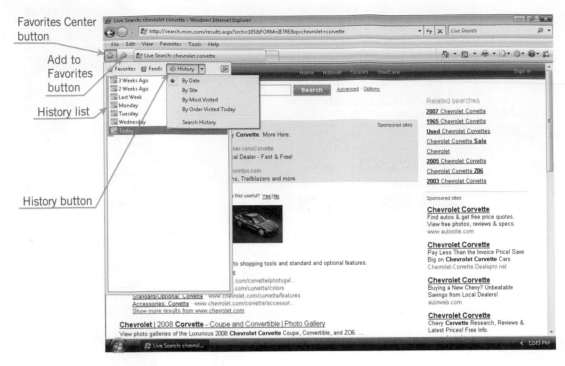

FIGURE 2–11   History list

To clear the History list, click Tools on the Command bar, and then click Internet Options to display the Internet Options dialog box. Click the General tab and then click the Delete button in the Browsing history section.

Favorites

The Web has so much to offer that it is very likely you are going to find some Web sites you really like and want to return to often. It is easy to keep these sites just a mouse click away by adding them to your *Favorites* list.

To add a site to your list of favorite sites:

▶ **VOCABULARY**
Favorites

- Go to the site you want to add.
- Click the Add to Favorites button.
- To revisit any of the Favorites, just click the Favorites Center button, and then select the shortcut to the site.

As your list begins to grow, you can organize it by creating folders. You can organize by topics in much the same way you would organize files in a file drawer. In Step-by-Step 2.3, you create a folder within the Favorites list.

Step-by-Step 2.3

1. Type **Chevrolet Corvette** in the Address bar, and then press **Enter**.

2. Click the Add to Favorites button ⊕, and then click Organize Favorites. The Organize Favorites dialog box opens, as shown in **Figure 2–12**.

Organize
Favorites
dialog box

Delete
button

New Folder
button

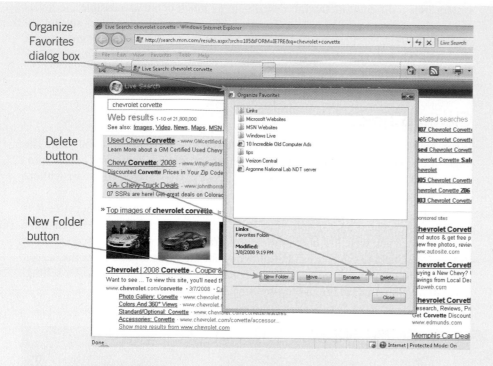

FIGURE 2–12
Organize Favorites dialog box

3. Click the **New Folder** button, type a name of your choice for the folder, and then press **Enter**.

4. Now, if indicated by your instructor, delete the folder. Click the folder name, and then click the **Delete** button. When the Delete Folder dialog box opens, click the **Yes** button.

5. Click the **Close** button. Leave your browser open for the next Step-by-Step.

Controlling Access

The *Content Advisor* in Internet Explorer provides some control over what content can be viewed on the Internet. It enables you to:

- Control access to settings through a password.
- View and adjust the ratings settings to reflect what you think is appropriate content.
- Adjust what types of content other people can view with or without your permission.
- Set up a list of Web sites that other people can never view and a list of Web sites other people can always view.
- Set up a list of Web sites that other people can always view, regardless of how the sites' contents are rated.

Web site publishers voluntarily rate their pages. The Internet rating standard is known as PICS: Platform for Internet Content Selection. The Content Advisor uses two independent PICS-compliant ratings systems—RSACi and SafeSurf. Each

▶ **VOCABULARY**
Content Advisor

system uses a different method to describe in as much detail as possible the levels of offensive content on Web pages. To use the Content Advisor requires setting the supervisor password. You can find step-by-step instructions by clicking the Internet Explorer Help button, clicking Contents and Index, and then typing *content advisor* in the Search Help box.

Cleanup Time

▶ VOCABULARY
disk cache

When you explore the Web, your browser keeps a record of the sites you visit. The pages are stored in temporary folders on your hard drive in your ***disk cache*** (pronounced *cash*). This process enables you to view the saved pages offline or without being connected to the Internet.

If you return to a cached Web page, that page will load faster because it is loading from cache. This can sometimes be a problem because the page might have changed since you were last at the site. The Refresh button was mentioned earlier in this lesson. Clicking the Refresh button will load the current page from the server. Another option is to change the *Check for newer versions of stored pages* setting. You will explore this setting in Step-by-Step 2.4.

ETHICS IN TECHNOLOGY

Internet Security

If you have accessed the Internet recently, you know that you can purchase just about any item you want, from a Mercedes Benz to Uncle Bill's Jam and Jellies. You can have your purchase shipped to you and pay for it when it arrives, or you can use a credit card. The question is, how safe do you feel about transmitting credit card and other financial information over the Internet?

When you provide your credit card number, it travels through several computers before it reaches its final destination. To ensure that your credit card number is not stolen easily, companies use a technology called encryption. Encryption software acts somewhat similarly to the cable converter box on your television. The data is scrambled with a secret code so that no one can interpret it while it is being transmitted. When the data reaches its destination, the same software unscrambles the information.

Not all Web sites use security measures. One way to identify a secure site is to check the status bar at the bottom of your Web browser. There you will see a small icon—usually a lock. When the lock is closed, it indicates that the site is using security technology.

Step-by-Step 2.4

1. Click **Tools** on the Command bar, and then click **Internet Options**. The Internet Options dialog box is displayed.

2. Click the **General** tab, if necessary. In the Browsing history section, click the **Settings** button to display the Temporary Internet Files and History Settings dialog box (see **Figure 2–13**). In the *Check for newer versions of stored pages* section, you have four options:

   ■ Every time I visit the webpage

   ■ Every time I start Internet Explorer

- Automatically
- Never

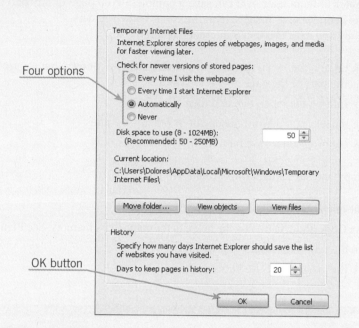

Four options

OK button

3. Select the option that is best for you and your individual requirements. The first option, *Every time I visit the webpage*, can slow down browsing time between pages. The *Never* option provides the fastest browsing time.

4. Click **OK** and then click **OK** again to return to Internet Explorer. Leave your browser open for the next step-by-step.

ETHICS IN TECHNOLOGY

Hackers

Computer security violation is one of the biggest problems experienced on computer networks. People who break into computer systems are called hackers. The reasons they do this are many and varied. Some of more common reasons are as follows:

- *Theft of services*: Many password-protected services charge a fee for usage. A hacker finds a way to bypass the password and uses the service without paying for it.

- *Theft of information*: A hacker may break into a system to steal credit card numbers, test data, or even national security data.

- *Hatred and vengeance*: Many people have groups or companies that they do not like. They may hack into the system to destroy files or to steal information to sell to opposing groups.

- *For the thrill of it*: Some hackers break into sites just to see if they can do it. The thrill for them is in breaking the code.

Copy and Save Text, Web Pages, and Images

As you view pages on the Web, you will find things you would like to save so that you can refer to them later. You can save a complete Web page or any part of a Web page. This includes text, images, hyperlinks, and other objects.

To copy and save text using Internet Explorer:

- Click Edit on the menu bar, and then click Select All or use your mouse to select a specific part of the page.
- Click Edit on the menu bar, and then click Copy.
- Paste the text into a Word document or other program.
- Click the program's Save button.

To copy and save a hyperlink from a Web page:

- Right-click the link to display the shortcut menu.
- Select Copy Shortcut to copy the link into the computer's memory. See **Figure 2–14**.
- Paste the link into another document.
- Click the program's Save button.

FIGURE 2–14   Copying a hyperlink

To save an entire Web page:

- Click Page on the Command bar, and then click Save As.
- Select the drive and folder into which you want to save the page.
- In the File name box, use the default name or type a name for the page.
- Click the Save as type button, and then select the *Web Page, complete (*.htm;*.html)* option. This option saves all of the files needed to display this page in its original format. This includes images and any other Web page elements. See **Figure 2–15**.
- Click the Save button.

FIGURE 2–15   Saving a Web page

To save an image:

- Right-click the image to display the shortcut menu.
- On the shortcut menu, select Save Picture As to display the Save Picture dialog box.
- Select the location and the folder into which you want to save the image.
- Type the name for the image.
- Click the Save button.

If you need a printed copy of a Web page, right-click the page to display the shortcut menu and then click Print.

Download and Install a Program

As you browse the Internet, you eventually will find a program you want to download. To *download* means to transfer from a Web server or another computer to your computer. The program could be a plug-in or enhancement for your browser, a utility program to help you better manage your computer system, a shareware game, and so on. Many companies that sell software allow you to download trial versions or offer an option to pay for a new program online and then download the program directly from their site. Before completing Step-by-Step 2.5 and downloading a program, obtain permission from your instructor.

> **VOCABULARY**
> **download**

Step-by-Step 2.5

1. Create a separate folder on your USB drive or hard drive for your downloaded programs.

2. Go to the Web site providing the program you want to download.

3. Follow the Web site's download instructions. These will vary from site to site, but most sites have some type of Download Now button. If a File Download – Security Warning dialog box is displayed, verify with your instructor that it is safe to download the file. Then click the Save button. The Save As dialog box is displayed.

4. Select the folder on your computer where you want to store the downloaded program. See **Figure 2–16**.

FIGURE 2–16
Save As dialog box

Save As
dialog box

Folder on local
computer

File name

Save button

5. Click the **Save** button to start the downloading process. A downloading box is displayed, indicating the estimated download time and transfer rate.

6. Wait while the download takes place. When the download is completed, click the **Close** button.

7. Next, most likely, you need to install the program. Using a folder window, locate the file you downloaded and double-click the filename. Follow the installation instructions as provided by the program.

8. Close your browser and turn off your computer if instructed to do so.

Other Internet Features

Blog or Web Log

A *blog* (short for Web log) is a Web page that serves as a publicly accessible journal or log. Blogs cover many topics. A blog may consist of the recorded ideas of one person, or it could be a complex collaboration open to anyone. For example, it could focus on the daily activities of an individual (a sort of diary) or it could be an alliance open to the general public. The theme could be on a mixture of subjects or center on one topic. Generally, the blog is updated periodically, normally in reverse order, showing the newest postings first.

▶ **VOCABULARY**

blog

chat room

File Transfer Protocol (FTP)

Chat Rooms

You can call someone through the Internet and "talk" to them the way you do on the phone, only you are writing and reading on your computer rather than talking and listening with a phone in your hand. You are using the computer to create real-time communication between yourself and another user or a group of users. This is referred to as a *chat room*. To participate in a chat, you enter a virtual chat room. Once a chat is initiated, users enter text by typing on the keyboard, and the message appears on the monitor of the other participants. Chat rooms provide an opportunity for people with a common interest to talk together about the subject, although many chat rooms are more general in nature and provide a place for people to meet and talk. You should always be cautious in chat rooms and not give away information of a personal nature.

E-Mail

E-mail, or electronic mail, was one of the original Internet services and continues to be one of the more popular services. Using e-mail, you can create, send, forward, print, save, and delete e-mail messages. Microsoft Outlook and Windows Mail (formerly Outlook Express) are two of the more popular e-mail programs.

File Transfer Protocol

At one time or another, you might have been on the Internet, tried to access a special feature such as an audio file, and received a message that a plug-in was required. A plug-in is an add-on software application that adds a specific feature to your Web browser or other programs. You click a link, and the plug-in is downloaded or transmitted to your computer. You most likely used *File Transfer Protocol (FTP)*. This is an Internet standard that allows users to download and upload files from and to other computers on the Internet.

Many FTP servers are connected to the Internet. Some of these require user IDs and passwords. Others permit anonymous FTP access. This means that anyone can upload and download files from the server. The files on the server can be any type of file. Some examples are software updates for your printer, a revised instruction manual, or a new program that is being tested.

▶ **VOCABULARY**
instant messaging
mailing list
LISTSERV
newsgroup
online conferencing

Instant Messaging

Instant messaging allows you to maintain a list of people with whom you want to interact in real time. You can send messages to any person on your list, often called a buddy list or contact list, as long as that person is online. Sending a message opens up a window where you and your friend can type messages that both of you can see.

Mailing Lists

A *mailing list* is a group of people with a shared interest. Their e-mail addresses are collected into a group, and this group is identified by a single name. Whenever you send a message, everyone on the list receives a copy. Some mailing lists are called *LISTSERVs*, named after a mailing list software program. There are mailing lists for every imaginable topic. Many professional groups and associations use mailing lists as an effective way of communicating with members and potential members. You can subscribe to a mailing list just as you would subscribe to a magazine. A list owner is the person who manages the list.

Newsgroups and Bulletin Boards

A *newsgroup* is a discussion forum or a type of bulletin board. Each board is dedicated to a discussion on a particular topic. The difference between a newsgroup and a mailing list is that with a newsgroup you can select the topics you want to read. These messages are stored on a news server, which is a computer that contains the necessary newsgroup. Software messages or information sent to the group generally are read and reviewed by a moderator. The moderator determines whether the information is appropriate and relevant and, in some cases, might edit the material before posting to the group.

Online Conferencing

Technology now provides business people, students taking online classes, members of a national organization, and even far-flung family members with the hardware and software needed to connect online to discuss issues, earn degrees, or just have a reunion. Freeware and commercial versions of software such as Adobe Connect, GoToMeeting, Microsoft Live Meeting, and WebEx are available that provide a chat setting with audio and video. Hardware requirements for *online conferencing* include a microphone and speakers for audio and a digitizing camera for video. Video and audio on the Internet require high-speed connections.

Voice over Internet Protocol

Voice over Internet Protocol (VoIP) uses a high-speed Internet connection instead of a regular (analog) telephone line. The voice is converted to and transmitted as a digital signal. If you are calling an analog number, then the signal is converted before it reaches the destination. Many VoIP providers permit the user to call anywhere for a fixed monthly fee.

SUMMARY

In this lesson, you learned:

- No one person or organization can claim credit for creating the Internet.
- Origins of the Internet can be traced to the United States Department of Defense.
- The original name for the Internet was ARPANET.
- Mosaic was the Internet's first graphical interface.
- To connect to the Internet from a business, school, or other organization, you probably have a direct connection via a local area network and a network interface card.
- Types of Internet connections include modem and telephone line, DSL, cable modem, wireless, and fiber optics.
- To connect to the Internet, you need an Internet connection, telecommunications software, and a browser for the Web.
- Interoperability means that all brands, models, and makes of computers can communicate with each other.
- A protocol is a standard format for transferring data between two devices.
- TCP/IP is the agreed upon international standard for transmitting data.

- The domain name identifies a site on the Internet.
- The Internet is made up of many services.
- The Web is an application that makes use of the Internet.
- Web pages can be linked through hyperlinks.
- Microsoft Internet Explorer is a popular Web browser.
- The HTTP protocol defines how Web messages are formatted and transmitted.
- A Web site address is referred to as the URL, or Universal Resource Locator.
- Every Web page on the Internet has its own unique address.
- HTML is a coding language that controls how Web pages are formatted and displayed.
- A Web page is coded with HTML markup tags.
- Other Internet services include blogs, chat rooms, e-mail, File Transfer Protocol, instant messaging, mailing lists, newsgroups and bulletin boards, online conferencing, and Voice over Internet Protocol.

■ VOCABULARY REVIEW

Define the following terms:

Address bar
browser
domain name
home page
host computer
host node

hyperlink
Hypertext Markup Language (HTML)
Hypertext Transfer Protocol (HTTP)
Internet service provider (ISP)
online service provider (OSP)
protocol

Transmission Control Protocol and
    Internet Protocol (TCP/IP)
Uniform Resource Locator (URL)
Web 2.0
Web page
World Wide Web

■ REVIEW QUESTIONS

MULTIPLE CHOICE

Select the best response for the following statements.

1. A Web site address also is referred to as a(n) _____.

   A.   Location bar
   B.   URL
   C.   Address bar
   D.   toolbar

2. The _____ identifies the IP address.

   A.   domain name
   B.   history window
   C.   content advisor
   D.   disk cache

3. The first graphical browser was named _____.

    A.   Internet Explorer   C.   Microsoft

    B.   Navigator   D.   Mosaic

4. A(n) _____ serves as a publicly accessible journal or log.

    A.   instant message   C.   newsgroup

    B.   blog   D.   protocol

5. A _____ displays a record of all the sites you have visited recently.

    A.   discussion board   C.   favorites list

    B.   blog   D.   history list

TRUE/FALSE

Circle T if the statement is true or F if the statement is false.

T   F   **1.**   Fiber optics is a type of Internet connection.

T   F   **2.**   VoIP always uses traditional telephone lines.

T   F   **3.**   Microsoft's Web site is the first page that always is displayed when you start your browser.

T   F   **4.**   You can use AutoSearch to locate Web pages on the Internet.

T   F   **5.**   Web pages cannot be saved to an individual's computer.

FILL IN THE BLANK

Complete the following sentences by writing the correct word or words in the blanks provided.

1. The original name for the Internet was _____.

2. _____ is a computer language that determines how Web pages are formatted and displayed.

3. To _____ a file means to transfer it from the Web server to your computer.

4. The _____ bar is the bar on top of the Internet Explorer window that contains the name of the document.

5. _____ lets the user open multiple Web pages within the same browser window.

◼ PROJECTS

CROSS-CURRICULAR— MATHEMATICS

Access the Answer Math Web site at *www.answermath.com/tips/general.htm* and complete at least two of the mental math activities. Prepare a report on the activities you completed. Include a definition of mental math. Do you think these activities are important? Explain why or why not.

CROSS-CURRICULAR—SCIENCE

The World Weather Watch is an interactive cross-curricular Internet project. To participate in the project, you collect weather data once a week for a specified time period. Your group can register to participate in the project, or you can post your data and use it for comparison discussions. The Web site is located at *www.cyberbee.com/weatherwatch.*

CROSS-CURRICULAR—SOCIAL STUDIES

Who's who in the Internet world? Visit the Web site *www.wiwiw.org/pioneers* and learn about the pioneers who made the Internet what it is today. Select one or two of the pioneers and prepare a report. Include a picture of the people you select.

CROSS-CURRICULAR—LANGUAGE ARTS

Complete a research project on blogs. Include at least three blogs in which you would be interested. Assume you want to start your own blog. What software would you use? What would be the main topic? List the steps necessary to start your own blog.

WEB PROJECT

Internet etiquette is an important topic for someone who uses the Internet for e-mail, newsgroups, and other Internet features. Do an Internet search and locate information on Internet etiquette. Prepare a report on your findings. The following are some URLs to get you started:

http://en.wikipedia.org/wiki/Netiquette

www.albury.net.au/new-users/netiquet.htm

www.google.com/Top/Computers/Internet/Etiquette

 TEAMWORK PROJECT

Your instructor is impressed with your knowledge of the Internet. She has asked you to coordinate a project with at least two other students. The Internet connection at your school is very slow. Your instructor wants to convince the principal that a high-speed Internet connection would be a vital enhancement for your class and for the entire school. Your goal is to create a persuasive presentation or report for your instructor that she can present to the principal. Include the address of the Web sites where you find your information.

 CRITICAL THINKING

Do you think the government will ever be able to regulate the Internet? That is, will any agency ever be able to control and limit what someone uploads online? Use your word-processing program and write a page on your thoughts about this issue.

 EXPLORING GOOGLE

Google has a feature that focuses solely on blog searching. This feature, called Blog Search, is located at *www.google.com/blogsearch*. Frequently Asked Questions about Blog Search can be found at *www.google.com/help/about_blogsearch.html*. Access this Web site and then write a one-page report on what you learned. Google also has *www.blogger.com*—a Web site where you can start your own blog. Recruit two or three teammates and start your own blog about your class activities.

LESSON 3

The Internet and Research

■ OBJECTIVES

Upon completion of this lesson, you should be able to:

- List reasons for searching the Internet.
- Describe different search approaches.
- Define a search engine.
- Explain how search engines work.
- Identify some of the more popular search engines.
- List some of the specialty search engines.
- Describe some search tips and tricks.
- Describe the subject directory search approach.
- Describe the invisible Web.

The Internet contains a wealth of information. In fact, you can find information on just about any topic you can imagine. The problem is that the Internet contains so much information it can be difficult to locate just what you need. In this lesson, you learn Internet search techniques to help you locate the specific information you seek.

Why Search the Internet?

You might ask yourself, "Why would I want to search the Internet? What information does it contain that can help me?" The reasons people search the Internet are varied and many. The following are just a few examples:

- You need to do research for the term paper due in your English class next week.
- Your grandmother is losing her hearing and has asked you to help her find some information on hearing aids.

■ VOCABULARY

Boolean logic

concept searching

database

hits (results)

index (indexer)

invisible Web (Deep Web)

keyword

math symbols

MP3

related search

search engine

search engine math

spider

stemming

subject directories

truncation

wildcard character

...

- You lost the manual for your DVD player and need a replacement.
- You plan to take a trip to Australia this summer and would like information on some of the hotels.

As you can see from these examples, you might have hundreds of reasons to conduct an Internet search. See **Figure 3–1**.

FIGURE 3–1   Searching the Internet

The Key to a Successful Search

We live in the information age, and information continues to grow at an ever-spiraling rate. To conduct an effective online search on a particular topic can be a challenge. You easily can be overwhelmed by the abundance of raw data. With the right tools, however, the task becomes easier. One key to a successful Internet search is an understanding of the many search tools that are available. Learning to use and apply the different tools will help you devise a better search strategy.

Two of the more popular tools available for online searches are search engines and subject directories. You use a search engine to search for keywords. You use a directory to find specialized topics. The primary difference between these two search tools is that people assemble directories and organize Web sites into categories, while search engines are automated. Some search sites, such as *yahoo.com*, are hybrids and offer both types of searches. Search engines are discussed in the first part of this lesson, and an overview of directories is covered in the second part.

Search Engines

A *search engine* is a software program that lets you search the Internet using key-words. A *keyword* (also called a search term) is a descriptive word within the Web document. The Internet contains hundreds of search engines. Each search engine might work a little differently, but most of them have some common search features. For example, all search engines support keyword searches. Although keyword searches might not be the most effective way to search, this is the search method that most people use.

Some search engines support an additional enhancement called *concept searching*. The search engine tries to determine what you mean and displays links to Web sites that relate to the keywords. If you search for "video games," for example, the search engine also might return results on sites that contain Nintendo and PlayStation.

Another feature supported by some search engines is *stemming* or *truncation*. When you search for a word, the search engine also includes the stem of the word. For example, you enter the search word "player," and you might receive results for play, plays, and playing.

How Does a Search Engine Work?

As indicated previously, a search engine is a software program. In addition to the software component, the search engine contains two other programmed elements: spiders and the index.

The *spider* (or crawler) is a search engine robot that searches the Internet for the keywords. It is called a spider because it "crawls" the Web continually, examining Web sites and finding and looking for links. Every month or so, it might return to a previous Web site to look for changes.

The third part of the search engine is the *index* or *indexer*. When the spider finds a page, it feeds the data to the index. After a Web page is indexed, it becomes part of the search engine's database and is available to anyone using that search engine. A *database* is a collection of organized information.

> ▶ **VOCABULARY**
>
> search engine
>
> keyword
>
> concept searching
>
> stemming
>
> truncation
>
> spider
>
> index (indexer)
>
> database

> **EXTRA FOR EXPERTS**
>
> When typing a Web site address in the browser text box, do not include the period that marks the end of the sentence.

NET BUSINESS

Search Engine Optimization

When Web site developers register their sites with search engines, they normally provide a list of keywords to help get their site on a user's search results list. Web site owners often can improve their site rankings (or where they appear in the list) by employing cutting-edge Web marketing technology. For example, several organizations offer search engine optimization services to Web site entrepreneurs. These services can include analyzing keywords that people use while searching, designing banner ads and buttons to be placed on the search engine Web site, and so on.

In addition, you can use a service such as Wordtracker to find out what keywords are used most often to find products or services similar to yours. Also available are several "pay-per-click" search engines. With this type of search engine, Web site owners bid on keywords. When a person uses the keywords in a search, the links in the search results list appear in order from highest to lowest bid on the keywords. The owner of the Web site pays the search engine the per-click fee when someone clicks the link to the site.

Some search engines index only Web page titles, while some search engines claim to index all words, even the articles "a," "an," and "the." Other search engines index all words, except articles and stop words such as "www," "but," "or," "nor," "for," "so," or "yet." Some search engines index all words without reference to capitalization. Other engines differentiate uppercase from lowercase.

Most Web sites contain *meta tags*. These tags describe the content of a Web page and are part of the document source code. Meta tags convey information about the document and are not displayed when a Web page is viewed in a browser. The two more common meta tags are description and keywords. If your hobby is bird watching, for instance, you might include the following tags in your Web site source code:

<META name="description" content="Everything you wanted to know about bird watching.">

<META name="keywords" content="bird watching, nesting, bird house, wild birds, types of birds">

When you type a keyword or keywords into a search engine's Search text box, your input is checked against the index of all the Web pages in the engine's database. The relevant sites are returned to you as hits, ranked in order with the best results at the top. *Hits*, or *results*, are the number of returns or hyperlinked Web site addresses displayed based on your keyword(s). Recall from Lesson 2 that a hyperlink is a highlighted word(s) or image within a hypertext document, which, when clicked, takes you to another location within the same Web page or to a different document.

To search using keywords, the process is as follows:

- Start your Web browser and display a search engine Web site.

- Type your keyword or keywords into the Search text box. These keywords describe the information you are trying to locate.

- Click the Search button.

- The search engine matches as many keywords as possible by searching its own database.

- The search engine returns a hyperlinked list of Web site addresses where the keywords are found. You click the hyperlinks to display and view the Web sites.

- If you are unable to find the information for which you are searching within these hyperlinked sites, you can revise your keywords and submit a new request.

One of the more popular search engines is Google. In Step-by-Step 3.1, you use Google to find out more about keywords and how they are used in Web searches.

▶ **VOCABULARY**

hits (results)

⌨ EXTRA FOR EXPERTS

Many search engines have banner ads, which are advertisements using text or graphics. Most major search engines carry paid placement listings. Companies and organizations pay to guarantee their site a high ranking, usually in relation to desired words. The exact position of these listings can vary.

Step-by-Step 3.1

1. Start your browser. Type **google.com** in the Address bar and press **Enter**.

2. Type **keywords Web pages** in the Google Search text box. See **Figure 3–2**.

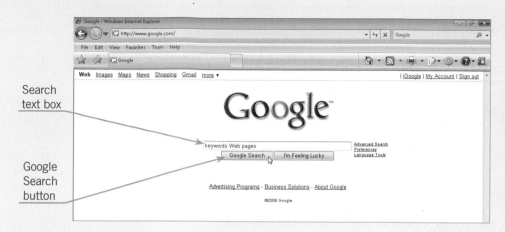

FIGURE 3–2
Google search engine Web page

Search
text box

Google
Search
button

3. Click the **Google Search** button. Within a few seconds, Google displays the results of your search. Your search results most likely will be different from those shown in **Figure 3–3**.

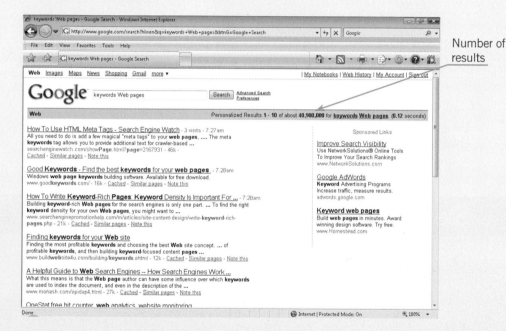

FIGURE 3–3
Google search results

Number of
results

4. Click one of the links and see if you can find a definition for keywords (see **Figure 3–4**). If the first link does not provide the information, click the browser's **Back** button ⬅ and then try another link.

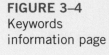

FIGURE 3–4
Keywords
information page

Back button

Keywords
information
page

Print button

5. If instructed to do so, click the **Back** button to return to your Search results, click the **Print** button 🖨 and submit a copy of your search results to your instructor. Leave your browser open for the next step-by-step.

Google also has several special features; one is called Definitions. You can use Google's Definitions feature to expand your knowledge of how search engines work. Other special features are discussed later in this lesson. Complete Step-by-Step 3.2 to find additional information about search engines using Google's Definitions tool.

Step-by-Step 3.2

1. Click the browser's **Back** button ⬅ to return to the Google home page. Type **define:search engines** in the Google Search text box. See **Figure 3–5**.

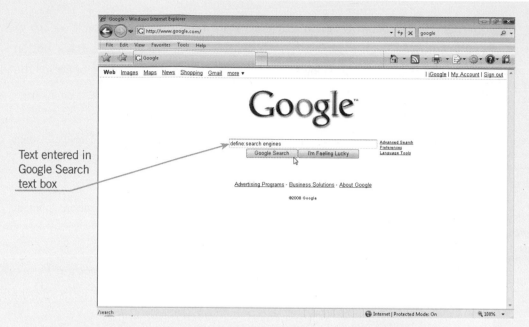

FIGURE 3–5
Searching for a definition

Text entered in
Google Search
text box

2. Click the **Google Search** button. Within a few seconds, Google displays
   the results. Scroll the page and read the various search engine definitions. Your search results most likely will be different from those shown
   in **Figure 3–6**.

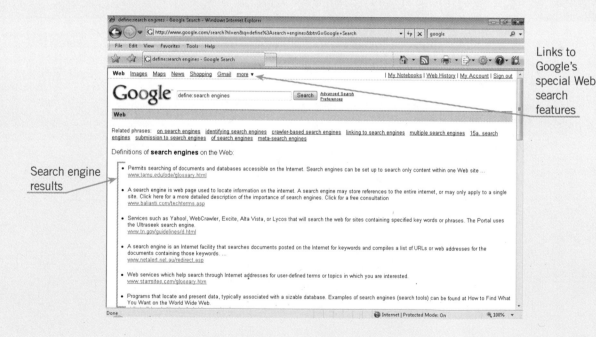

FIGURE 3–6
Google search
engine definitions
Web page

Links to
Google's
special Web
search
features

Search engine
results

3. If instructed to do so, click the **Print** button 🖶 and submit a copy of your search results to your instructor. Click the browser's **Back** button ⬅ to return to Google's home page. Leave your browser open for the next Step-by-Step.

In **Figure 3–6**, note the links above the Google Search text box. These are some of Google's special Web search features:

- *Images*: Displays a group of images in thumbnail format
- *Maps*: Provides maps and directions to help you find business locations, contact information, and driving directions
- *News*: Current news headlines
- *Shopping*: Google's product search service
- *Gmail*: Google's Gmail inbox or Gmail service
- *More*: Displays a drop-down menu of other Google features

Try another search. Suppose you are going to use the Internet to purchase a digital music player. In Step-by-Step 3.3, you use Google's Images search feature to execute a search on iPods.

Step-by-Step 3.3

1. Click the **Images** link. If necessary, delete any content in the search text box, and then type **ipods**. See **Figure 3–7**.

FIGURE 3–7
Google Image Search page

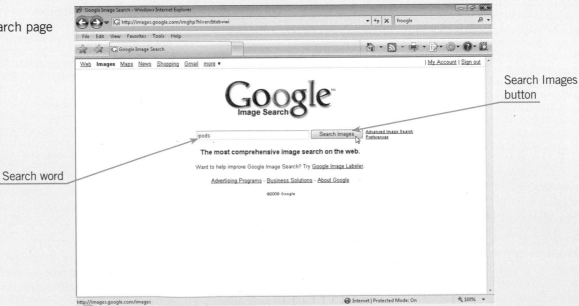

Search word

Search Images button

2. Click the **Search Images** button. See **Figure 3–8**.

FIGURE 3–8
Google Image Search results

3. Scroll down and review the results. Your results most likely will be different from those displayed in **Figure 3–8**.

4. Click the browser's Back button ⬅ to return to Google's Image Search page. Leave your browser open for the next step-by-step.

As you see from these examples, the number of results sometimes can be a bit overwhelming. At this point, you have several options:

- You can click any of the links and review the information at the linked site.
- You can redefine your keywords search term.
- You can use another search engine.

If you do not locate the information for which you are searching in the first 20 or so hits, the third option—use another search engine—could be your next best choice. It is impossible for any one search engine to index every page on the Web. Each search engine use its own technique to index Web sites. Using a different engine, therefore, might provide a different list of hits. Many popular search engine sites exist, and you might need to try several before you find the information you are seeking. Some of the more well-known search engines are the following:

- Yahoo at *yahoo.com*
- Live Search at *msn.com*
- AOL/Netscape at *netscape.aol.com*
- Ask at *ask.com*

Specialty Search Engines

So far in this lesson, we have discussed general search engines. There are, however, many specialized search engines on the Internet. These search engines sometimes are called *category-oriented search* tools. They generally focus on a particular topic. If you are looking for information in a particular format, your best bet is to search a site that specializes in indexing and retrieving that particular information. Some examples of uses for specialty search engines are as follows:

- You are looking for a former classmate or a long-lost cousin—try Yahoo's people search at *people.yahoo.com*.

- You want to download a free card game—try the Download.com site at *download.com*.

- You want to do online jewelry shopping or item comparison—try Shop.com at *www.shop.com* or Bottom Dollar at *www.bottomdollar.com*.

- You are thinking about your future and what career options you might have—try CareerBuilder at *www.careerbuilder.com*.

- You are considering taking classes at an online college or university—try Guide to Online Schools at *guidetoonlineschools.com*.

The preceding are just a few examples of the many hundreds of specialty Web sites. If you are looking for a particular information source, but you are not sure where to look, try the New Mexico State University site at *http://lib.nmsu.edu/ instruction/specialtysearch.htm*. This site contains links to dozens of specialty search engines, including the "invisible Web." See **Figure 3–9**.

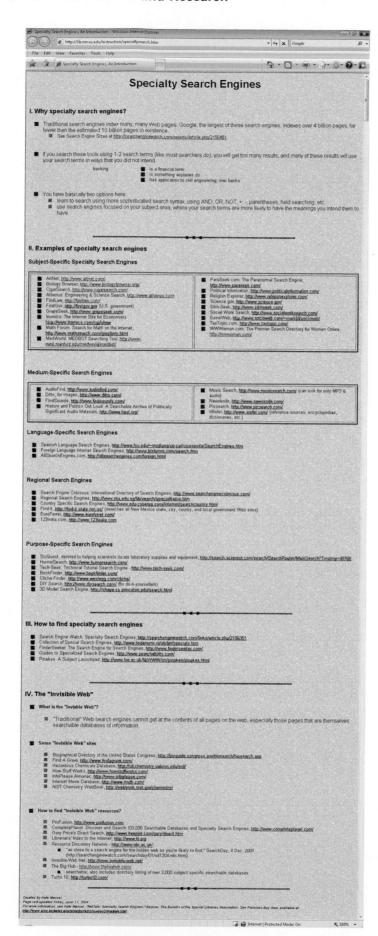

FIGURE 3–9 New Mexico State University Specialty Search Engines Web page

To view a list of the most popular search engines worldwide, access the Wikipedia site at *http://en.wikipedia.org/wiki/Web_Search_engine*. Scroll to the "See also" section near the bottom of the page, and then click the List of search engines link. You will find links to hundreds of search engines and desktop search tools. **Table 3–1** lists some popular specialty search engines.

TABLE 3–1   Some popular specialty search engines

MAPS & TRAVEL	PEOPLE & INFORMATION	COMPANIES & CAREERS	WORLD DATA
Microsoft's *www.expedia.com*	People finder at *www.usa-people-search.com*	Occupational Outlook Handbook at *www.bls.gov/oco*	World Health Organization at *www.who.int*
www.mapquest.com	Yellow Pages Search Power at *www.yellow.com*	America's Job Bank at *www.ajb.dni.us*	CIA World Factbook at *www.cia.gov/cia/publications/factbook*
Worldwide Online Reservations at *www.orbitz.com*	Toll-free numbers at *www.inter800.com*	Monster job bank at *www.monster.com*	World Bank at *www.worldbank.org*
Great Outdoors at *www.gorp.com*	U.S. Gov Web Portal at *www.usa.gov*	Career Resource Center *at www.careers.org*	World Data Center at *www.ngdc.noaa.gov/wdc/wdcmain.html*

Multimedia Search Engines

Are you interested in finding graphics, video clips, animation, and even MP3 music files? If so, a multimedia search engine is an option to consider. For music and MP3, you might want to try the Lycos Entertainment search engine at *http://music.lycos.com/* or *www.kazaa.com*. **MP3** is a file format that allows audio compression at near-CD quality.

▶ **VOCABULARY**
MP3

Other multimedia search engines include the following: Corbis at *www.corbis.com* boasts of "the world's largest collection of fine art and photography." AltaVista at *www.altavista.com* has a special tab for images, MP3/audio, and video. Or, try *www.classroomclipart.com*, a Web site that features free clip art, clip art pictures, and illustrations.

Meta-Search Engines

Have you searched and searched for the right information—going from search engine to search engine—and still not found what you need? If so, you might want to try a meta-search engine. This type of search engine searches several major engines at one time. These search engines do not have their own databases. Instead, they act as a "middle person." They send the query to major search engines and then return the results or hits. Meta-search engines generally work best with simple searches. Two popular meta-search engines are Dogpile at *www.dogpile.com* and MetaCrawler at *www.metacrawler.com*.

Search Engine Tools and Techniques

In the previous Step-by-Step exercises, you used a keyword approach to search for your topic. As the Internet continues to expand, however, and more and more pages are added, effective searching requires new approaches and strategies. The more specific your search, the more likely you will find what you want. To find relevant information, you must use a variety of tools and techniques.

Phrase Searching

If you want to search for words that must appear next to each other, then phrase searching is your best choice. Enter a phrase using double quotation marks, and phrase searching matches only those words that appear adjacent to each other and in the order you specify. For example, if you are searching for baseball cards, enter the phrase *"baseball cards"* in double quotation marks. The results will contain Web sites with the words *baseball cards* next to each other. Without the quotation marks, the search engine would find Web pages that contain the words *baseball* and *cards* anywhere within each page.

   If you are searching for more than one phrase, you can separate multiple phrases or proper names with a comma. For example, to find Mickey Mantle baseball cards, you would enter *"baseball cards", "Mickey Mantle"*. It is always a good idea to capitalize proper nouns because some search engines distinguish between uppercase and lowercase letters. On the other hand, if you capitalize a common noun such as *Bread*, you will get fewer returns than if you typed *bread*.

Search Engine Math

Practically all the major search engines and directories support **search engine math**. You use **math symbols** to enter a formula to filter out unwanted listings. For example:

- Put a plus sign (+) before words that must be displayed (also called an *inclusion operator*).

- Put a minus sign (–) before words that you do not want to display (also called an *exclusion operator*).

- Words without qualifiers do not have to be displayed, but still are involved in sorting your search.

   Suppose you are making cookies and would like to try some new recipes. Your search words are *+cookie+recipes*. Only pages that contain both words would appear in your results. Now suppose you want recipes for chocolate cookies. Your search words are *+cookie+recipe+chocolate*. This would display pages with all three words.

   To take this a step further, suppose you do not like coconut. You therefore do not want any recipes that contain the word *coconut*. The minus (–) symbol is helpful for reducing the number of unrelated results. You would type your search phrase as *+cookie+recipe+chocolate-coconut*. This tells the search engine to find pages that contain *cookie*, *recipe*, and *chocolate*, and then to remove any pages that contain the word *coconut*. To extend this idea and to get chocolate cookie recipes without coconut and honey, your search phrase would be *+cookie+recipe+chocolate-coconut-honey*. Simply begin subtracting terms you know are not of interest, and you will get better results. You also can use math symbols with most directories. Directories are discussed later in this lesson.

EXTRA FOR EXPERTS

Recall that a meta tag is a special HTML tag that provides information about a Web page. Meta tags do not affect how the page is displayed. They provide information such as the title, description, and keywords. Many search engines use this information when creating their index.

VOCABULARY

search engine math

math symbols

EXTRA FOR EXPERTS

Google has a special calculator feature. To use Google's built-in calculator function, enter the calculation in the search box, and then click the Google Search button.

Boolean Searching

When you search for a topic on the Internet, you are not going from server to server and viewing documents on that server. Instead, you are searching databases. Recall that a database is a collection of organized information. **Boolean logic** is another way that you can search databases. This works on a principle similar to search engine math, but has a little more power. Boolean logic consists of three logical operators:

- AND
- NOT
- OR

Returning to our cookie example, you are interested in a relationship between cookies and recipes. So you might search for *"cookies AND recipes"*. The more terms you combine with AND, the fewer returns you will receive. Or, you want chocolate cookie recipes without coconut. You would search for *"cookies AND recipes AND chocolate NOT coconut"*.

OR logic is more commonly used to search for similar terms or concepts. For example, you search for *"cookies AND recipes OR chocolate"* to retrieve results containing one term or the other, or both. The more terms you combine in a search with OR logic, the more results you receive from your search.

The power of the Boolean search is the use of multiple parameters, which is not possible with the math symbols. For instance, you can create a search on *"cookies AND recipes NOT (coconut OR honey OR spinach)"*.

Some search engines provide forms to assist you with search engine math and logical searching. For example, if you access the AltaVista search engine, clicking the Advanced Search link opens a form. Using this form, you can specify the language, words, and phrases to include and to omit, and even specify a time period. In addition, AltaVista provides a Boolean expression text box option. Keep in mind that some search engines do not support Boolean logic. Check the search engine Help feature to determine if Boolean logic is supported.

Complete Step-by-Step 3.4 to build a query using AltaVista's Advanced Web Search form.

▶ **VOCABULARY**
Boolean logic

EXTRA FOR EXPERTS

Some search engines, such as AltaVista, will translate your search results into another language.

Step-by-Step 3.4

1. Type **altavista.com** in the browser Address bar and then press **Enter** (see **Figure 3–10**). Your screen might look somewhat different.

FIGURE 3–10
AltaVista search engine Web page

2. Click the Advanced Search link. AltaVista's Advanced Web Search page appears.

3. In the all of these words text box, type cookie recipes chocolate.

4. In the *and none of these words* text box, type **coconut honey** (see **Figure 3–11**).

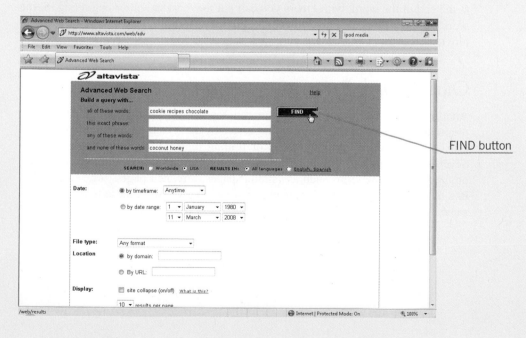

FIGURE 3–11
AltaVista Advanced Web Search page

5. Click the **FIND** button to display the results of your query (see **Figure 3–12**). Leave your browser open for the next Step-by-Step.

FIGURE 3–12
AltaVista query results

Query results

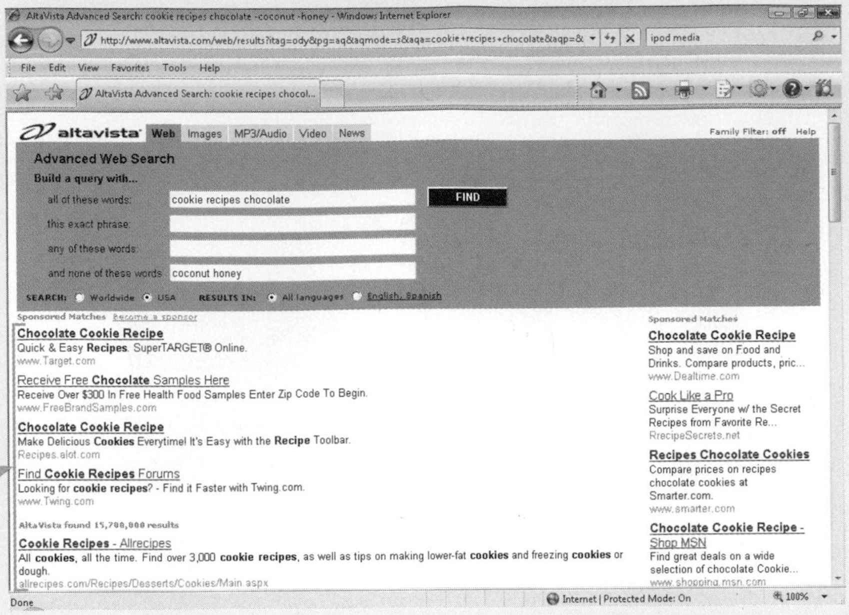

Wildcard Searching

VOCABULARY
wildcard character
related search

The * symbol, or asterisk, is considered a ***wildcard character***. If you do not know the spelling of a word or you want to search plurals or variations of a word, use the wildcard character. For example, you want to search for *"baseball cards and Nolan Ryan"* but you are not sure how to spell *Nolan*. You can construct your search using a wildcard—*"baseball cards"* and *"N* Ryan"*. Some search engines permit the * only at the end of the word; with others you can put the * at the end or beginning. Some search engines do not support wildcard searches. Check the search engine Help feature to determine if wildcard searches are supported.

Other Search Features

Another feature provided by several search engines is a ***related search***. These are preprogrammed queries or questions suggested by the search engine. A related search can dramatically improve your odds of finding the information you are seeking. Several search engines offer this feature, although they might use different terminology. You might see terms such as "similar pages," "related pages," or "more pages like this." WebCrawler and Google use "Similar pages." All of these terms mean the same thing. See **Figure 3–13**.

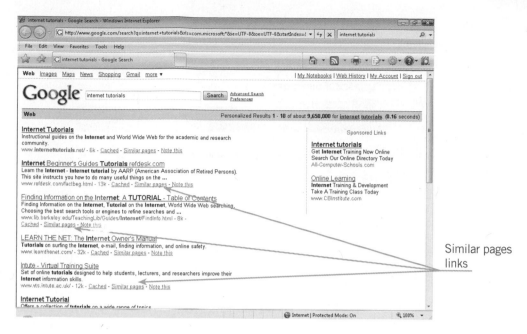

FIGURE 3–13   Google uses the term "Similar pages"

Subject Directory Searching

Recall that earlier in this lesson we discussed the primary difference between a search engine and a directory. Search engines use software programs to index sites; people assemble directories. Subject experts carefully check a Web site to make sure it meets a particular set of standards before the site is included in a directory. Then they add the URL for the Web site to the database.

Most *subject directories* are organized by subject categories, with a collection of links to Internet resources. These resources are arranged by subject and then displayed in a series of menus. To access a particular topic, you start from the top and "drill down" through the different levels—going from the general to the specific. This is similar to a traditional card catalog or the telephone yellow pages.

Suppose you want to visit the Great Smoky Mountains National Park. You can use a search engine and keywords to try to locate information, or you can use a subject directory search tool. The Yahoo! Directory provides a list and links to approximately 14 subject directories. See **Figure 3–14**.

▶ **VOCABULARY**
subject directories

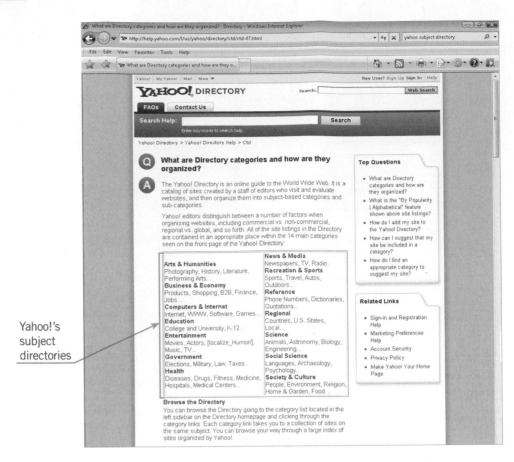

FIGURE 3–14   Yahoo! subject directories

ETHICS IN TECHNOLOGY

Spamming

You probably have heard of spam. No, not the luncheon meat that comes in a can. We are talking about Internet spam. Internet spam has several definitions. It is defined as electronic junk mail or junk newsgroup postings, or even unsolicited e-mail. The unsolicited e-mail most likely is some type of advertising or get-rich scheme, similar to the junk mail you receive almost every day. With traditional junk mail, however, the people who send the mail pay a fee to distribute their materials.

Spam, in contrast, is similar to receiving a postage-due letter. Even though you do not pay the postage as it arrives in your electronic mailbox, you still pay for it indirectly. The charges are in the form of disk space, connect time, and sometimes long-distance Internet connections.

Spam is not illegal, but several groups are trying to stop it. Numerous services exist to which you can submit a complaint or report a spam provider. Also available are spam-blocking and filtering services, as well as services and programs that hide your e-mail address from potential spammers. Visit *spam.abuse.net* to learn more about spam.

Complete Step-by-Step 3.5 to learn how to use a directory and search for information on the Great Smoky Mountains National Park.

Step-by-Step 3.5

1. Type **dir.yahoo.com** in the browser Address bar, and then press **Enter**. This takes you to the Yahoo! Directory Web site shown in **Figure 3–15**. (The content you see on this site most likely will differ from that shown in **Figure 3–15**.)

Outdoors link

FIGURE 3–15
Yahoo! Directory Web page

2. Click the **Outdoors** link below the Recreation & Sports category. This drills down one level and takes you to the Outdoors page, as shown in **Figure 3–16**. Now a list of Activities categories is displayed. Within this list is a link to Parks and Public Lands. Notice the number in parentheses to the right of each link. This is the number of links in that category.

FIGURE 3-16
Yahoo! Directory—Outdoors
Web page

Outdoors
level

Parks and
Public Lands

Number of
links

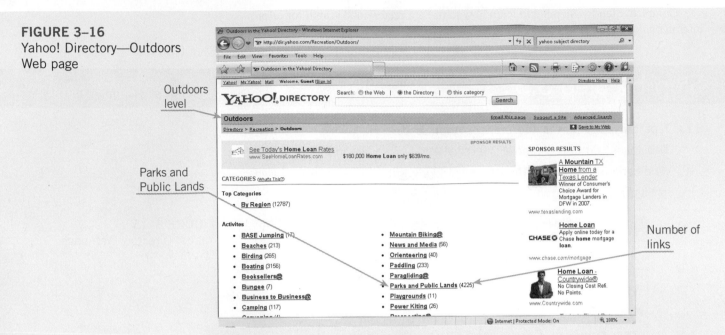

3. Remember that you are looking for the Great Smoky Mountains National Park, so click **Parks and Public Lands** to move to the next level—the Parks and Public Lands page. You have moved down one level where all of the categories relate to parks and public lands. The United States is one of the top categories. Click **United States** to move down to the next level—Parks and Public Lands>United States. See **Figure 3-17**.

FIGURE 3-17
Yahoo! Directory—Parks and
Public Lands>United States

Parks and
Public Lands
>United
States

National
Parks link

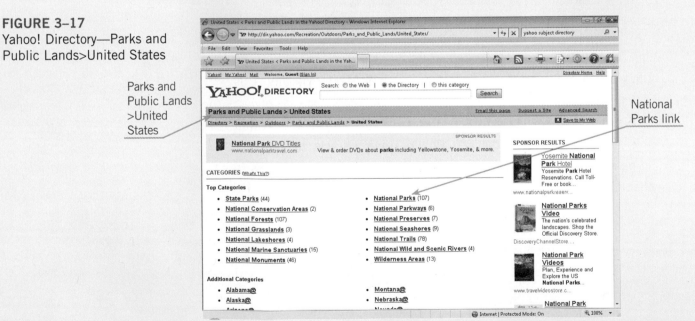

4. At this level, you find that National Parks is one of your Top Categories selections. Click **National Parks** to move to the next level.

5. You are getting closer to your goal—the National Parks Web page contains a link to the Great Smoky Mountains National Park. Scroll down if necessary to find the link. See **Figure 3–18**.

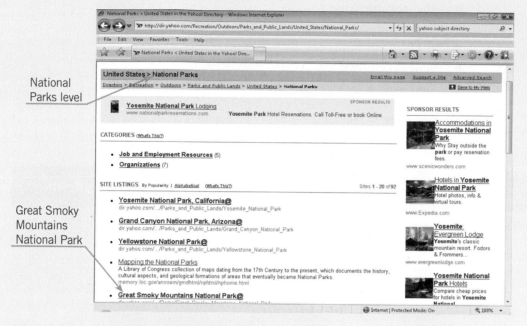

FIGURE 3–18
United States National Parks

6. Click the **Great Smoky Mountains National Park** link to display the Web page and links to several related sites. Note that the Web page contains an option to sort the sites by popularity or alphabetically. See **Figure 3–19**. Click one or two of the links and review the content. When you are done, close your browser.

FIGURE 3–19
Yahoo! Directory—links to the Great Smoky Mountains National Park

As you can see from this exercise, drilling down through a subject directory is a more guided approach than entering keywords into a search engine. Additional benefits of directories are as follows:

- They are easy to use.
- You are not searching the entire Web.
- The Web sites have been handpicked and evaluated.
- Most links include some type of description.
- They produce better quality hits on searches for common items.

See **Table 3–2** for a list of some other popular subject directories.

TABLE 3–2   Some popular subject directories

DIRECTORY NAME	DESCRIPTION	PHRASE SEARCHING*
The Librarian's Internet Index at *www.lii.org*	High quality; compiled by public librarians	Yes
About at *about.com*	Annotations created by guides and experts	Yes
Galaxy at *www.galaxy.com*	Good annotations; good quality	No
Infomine at *http://infomine.ucr.edu/*	Scholarly Internet resources	Yes
*Requires that the phrase be enclosed in double quotation marks		

The Invisible Web

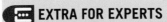
EXTRA FOR EXPERTS

Some search engines automatically include plurals; others do not. To be on the safe side, include the plural. For example, if you are searching for *squirrels*, use keywords such as *"squirrel"* or *"squirrels."*

Searching for information online can be deceptive. Search engines such as Google and MSN make it appear easy. And, sometimes it is easy. You type your keywords, click the Search button, and hundreds or even thousands of links are displayed—links to Web sites that are part of the *visible* Web. The visible Web, however, is only one part of the Internet. A great deal more information is available freely in databases and waiting to be found. The problem, however, is that the spidering technology of the general search engines does not search every single database. These additional searchable databases are part of the **invisible Web** (also called the **Deep Web**). The content quality of the invisible Web is purported to be superior. One of the better invisible Web resources is *www.completeplanet.com*. This Web site contains links to over 70,000 searchable databases and specialty search engines. The Intute Web site at *www.intute.ac.uk* provides links to Web resources for education and research.

As you learn more about Internet searching, keep in mind that no single organization indexes the Internet the way the Library of Congress catalogs books. So how many ways can you search? There are dozens of primary search engines and hundreds of specialty search engines. New ones are added on a continual basis. In many instances, it is almost like looking for the needle in the haystack. With a little effort, however, you probably will find that special Web page that contains the information for which you are searching.

SUMMARY

In this lesson, you learned:

- Search engines and directories are two basic tools that you can use to find information on the Web.

- People assemble directories; search engines are automated.

- A search engine is a software program.

- Most search engines support keyword searches.

- Concept-based searching occurs when the search engine returns hits that relate to keywords.

- Stemming relates to the search engine's capability to find variations of a word.

- Meta tags are special tags embedded in a Web page; many search engines use the tags to create their indexes.

- Keywords describe the information you are trying to locate within a Web page.

- Search engines contain a database of organized information.

- Some search engines use natural language.

- A search engine has three main parts: the search engine software, a spider that searches for keywords, and an index.

- Stop words, such as *www*, *but*, *or*, and so forth, are not indexed by many search engines.

- A search engine uses an algorithm to index Web sites.

- Specialized search engines focus on a particular topic.

- Multimedia search engines focus on video, animation, graphics, and music.

- Subject directories are organized by subject categories.

- Subject experts check the Web sites that are part of a subject directory's database.

- Use double quotation marks around a set of words for phrase searching.

- Use the plus and minus signs for inclusion and exclusion of words within a search.

- Boolean searching uses the three logical operators OR, AND, and NOT.

- The * symbol is used for wildcard searching.

- No single organization indexes the entire Internet.

■ VOCABULARY REVIEW

Define the following terms:

Boolean logic

concept searching

database

hits (results)

index (indexer)

invisible Web (Deep Web)

keyword

math symbols

MP3

related search

search engine

search engine math

spider

stemming

subject directories

truncation

wildcard character

■ REVIEW QUESTIONS

MULTIPLE CHOICE

Select the best response for the following statements.

1. _____ occurs when the search engine links to Web sites that relate to the keywords.

   A. Concept searching   C. Truncation

   B. Stemming   D. Natural language

2. The _____ is a search engine robot that roams the Internet looking for keywords.

   A. index   C. spider

   B. searcher   D. warthog

3. A(n) _____ is a collection of organized information.

   A. database

   B. stem

   C. indexer

   D. URL

4. If you were looking for video and music resources, you might use a _____ search engine.

   A. multimedia

   B. sports

   C. phrase

   D. spider

5. Searchable databases are part of the _____.

   A. index

   B. invisible Web

   C. subject directories

   D. stop words

TRUE/FALSE

Circle T if the statement is true or F if the statement is false.

T   F   **1.** All search engines index all words in a Web page.

T   F   **2.** Keywords describe the information you are trying to locate.

T   F   **3.** Subject directories are organized by categories.

T   F   **4.** The invisible Web also is called the Deep Web.

T   F   **5.** Boolean searches and math symbol searches are identical.

FILL IN THE BLANK

Complete the following sentences by writing the correct word or words in the blanks provided.

1. A preprogrammed _____ or question suggested by a search engine is a related search.

2. Use a(n) _____ search engine to find video clips, graphics, animation and music files.

3. Web pages for _____ directories are reviewed by people.

4. _____ are the number of returns or hyperlinked Web site addresses displayed based on your keywords.

5. To search for words that must appear next to each other, use _____ searching.

■ PROJECTS

CROSS-CURRICULAR— MATHEMATICS

1. Use Google or another search engine of your choice. Use search engine math and math symbols to create searches for the following:

   A. Carnivals and circuses in Australia, but not in New Zealand

   B. Skateboard and roller skating parks in California

2. Use Boolean logic and the same search engine to search for the same topics as in 1A and 1B above.

3. Compare your findings and then prepare a report listing the similarities and differences between the two methods of searching.

CROSS-CURRICULAR—SCIENCE

Your instructor has assigned a research project. You are to select a type of butterfly and provide information about the life and habits of the type you selected. Create a "Search Strategy" form that your fellow classmates can use to search the Internet. Within the form, list possible search tools and ways in which to search. Include at least one image in your project, and include the Web site address for any suggested search engines or directory Web sites.

CROSS-CURRICULAR—SOCIAL STUDIES

One infamous question that most of us have heard throughout our lives is "Why did the chicken cross the road?" Use the search engine Ask located at *www.ask.com* to find the answer to this question. How many links did you find? Describe the three best answers that you found. Prepare a report on your findings and present it to your class.

CROSS-CURRICULAR—LANGUAGE ARTS

Create a Boolean search on your favorite search engine to locate information about your two favorite bands or music groups. Prepare a one-page report on your findings. Include within the report: which search engine you used and why; how many results were returned; and how you were able to narrow the search.

WEB PROJECT

You want to learn more about how the invisible Web works. Your instructor thinks this is a great idea and has asked you to prepare a report and share your findings with the class. Your report should include Web searching methodologies and Web-based resources.

 TEAMWORK PROJECT

Your teamwork project is to provide a detailed description of how MP3 technology works, how to download this music, what the copyright issues are for downloading music, what kind of MP3 hardware is available, and what type of player and encoder you would use. You and your team are to put together a two-page report containing this information and any other relevant information you might find. Include a list of all links you used as a reference source. A good place to start searching is *www.kazaa.com*.

 # CRITICAL THINKING

Select a topic of your choice to research on the Web. Consider something original such as "What is utopia?" or "Who wrote the first opera?" Search for information using three different search engines. Use the same search techniques (keywords, Boolean operators, or related searches) for all three search engines. Create a table with a separate column for each search engine. Under the column headings, list the top 10 sites that the search engine locates. Determine which engine provided you with the highest-quality results.

 # EXPLORING GOOGLE

Create your own search engine? Google's Custom Search Engine lets you do just that. Access the Google Custom Search Engine at *www.google.com/coop/cse*. Review the featured examples and describe one or two of these search engines. What would be your focus if you were to create a personal search engine? If you were to create one for your school?

LESSON 4

How a Computer Processes Data

■ OBJECTIVES

Upon completion of this lesson, you should be able to:

- Identify computer system components.
- Explain how the CPU works.
- Differentiate between RAM and ROM.
- Describe how data is represented.

   With today's technology, a little knowledge about what is inside a computer can make you a more effective user and help you select the right computer for the job you need it to do. In this lesson, you learn how the CPU processes data and turns it into information. You also learn about some of the basic components contained on the computer's motherboard.

Computer Systems

We use computers for all kinds of tasks—to predict weather, to fly airplanes, to control traffic lights, to play games, to access the Internet, to send e-mail, and so on. You might wonder how a machine can do so many things.

   To appreciate how a computer really operates requires knowledge of calculus, probability, and statistics—all of which are needed to understand physics and circuit analysis. Most of us, however, do not need this level of comprehension. Instead, we need a fundamental understanding. This lesson presents the fundamentals on how a computer operates.

■ VOCABULARY

arithmetic/logic unit (ALU)

bit

Bluetooth

byte

cache memory

computer system

control unit

controller

dual-core processor

execution cycle (E-cycle)

expansion slot

FireWire

instruction cycle (I-cycle)

machine cycle

memory

modem

motherboard

multi-core processor

port

processor

random access memory (RAM)

read-only memory (ROM)

serial

Small Computer System Interface (SCSI)

Universal Serial Bus (USB)

...

UNIT I Computer Basics

Just about all computers, regardless of size, take raw data and change it into information. The procedure involves input, processing, output, and storage (IPOS). For example:

■ You input programs and data with some type of input device.

■ The computer uses instructions to process the data and to turn it into information.

■ You output the information to some type of output device.

■ You store it for later retrieval.

Input, output, and processing devices grouped together represent a *computer system*. In this lesson, we look at the components that the computer uses to process data. These components are contained within the system case. See **Figure 4–1**.

FIGURE 4–1   Computer system components

System Components

The PC system case is the metal and plastic case that houses the main system components of the computer. Central to all of this is the ***motherboard*** or system board that mounts into the case. The motherboard is a circuit board that contains many integral components. A ***circuit board*** is simply a thin plate or board that contains electronic components. See **Figure 4–2**. Some of the most important of these components are as follows:

- Central processing unit
- Memory
- Basic controllers
- Expansion ports and expansion slots

▶ **VOCABULARY**
motherboard
circuit board
processor

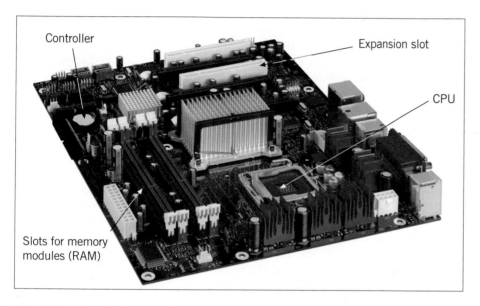

Controller

Expansion slot

CPU

Slots for memory modules (RAM)

FIGURE 4–2   Motherboard

The Processor

The ***processor***, also called the microprocessor, central processor, or the central processing unit (CPU), is the brains of the computer. The processor is housed on a tiny silicon chip similar to that shown in **Figure 4–3**. This chip contains millions of switches and pathways that help your computer make important decisions. The switches control the flow of the electricity as it travels across the miles of pathways. The processor knows which switches to turn on and which to turn off because it receives its instructions from computer programs. Recall from Lesson 1 that programs are a set of special instructions, written by programmers, which control the activities of the computer. Programs also are known as software.

FIGURE 4–3   Microprocessor

Some chip manufacturers now offer dual-core and multi-core processors. A *dual-core processor* ia a single chip that contains two separate processors, and a *multi-core processor* is an expansion that provides for more than two separate processors. These processors do not necessarily double the processing speed of a single-core processor, but do provide increased performance when running multiple programs simultaneously.

The CPU has two primary sections: the arithmetic/logic unit and the control unit.

The Arithmetic/Logic Unit

The *arithmetic/logic unit* (*ALU*) performs arithmetic computations and logical operations. The arithmetic computations include addition, subtraction, multiplication, and division. The logical operations involve comparisons—asking the computer to determine if two numbers are equal or if one number is greater than or less than another number. These might seem like simple operations. However, by combining these operations, the ALU can execute complex tasks. For example, a video game uses arithmetic operations and comparisons to determine what appears on your screen.

The Control Unit

The *control unit* is the boss, so to speak, and coordinates all of the processor's activities. Using programming instructions, it controls the flow of information through the processor by controlling what happens inside the processor.

We communicate with the computer through programming languages. You might have heard of programming languages called Java, COBOL, C++, or Visual Basic. These are just a few of the many languages we can use to give instructions to a computer. For example, we might have a programming statement such as *Let X = 2 + 8*. With this statement, we are using a programming language to ask the computer to add 2 and 8 and assign the calculated value to X. However, when we input this instruction, something else has to happen. The computer does not understand our language. It understands only machine language, or *binary*, which is ones and zeros. This is where the control unit takes over.

Ethnicity Code
904318

Crystal_miller@ddouglas.

K12.or.rs

The control unit reads and interprets the program instruction and changes the instruction into machine language. Recall that earlier we discussed the processor and pathways and switches. It is through these pathways and the turning on and off of switches that the processor represents the ones and zeros. When electricity is present, it represents a one. The absence of electricity represents a zero. After changing the instructions into machine language (binary), the control unit then sends out the necessary messages to execute the instructions.

To view an example of a binary number, complete Step-by-Step 4.1.

Step-by-Step 4.1

1. Click the **Start** button on the taskbar, point to **All Programs**, click **Accessories**, and then click **Calculator**. The Standard calculator is displayed (see **Figure 4–4**).

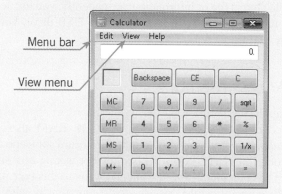

Menu bar

View menu

FIGURE 4–4
Windows Standard calculator

2. Click **View** on the menu bar and then click **Scientific**. The Scientific calculator is displayed (see **Figure 4–5**).

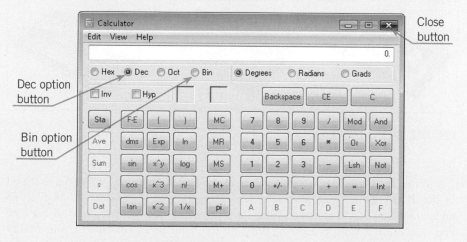

Dec option button

Bin option button

Close button

FIGURE 4–5
Windows Scientific calculator

3. If necessary, click the **Dec** (decimal) option button. Enter **30** by clicking the calculator numeric buttons. Click the **Bin** (binary) option button. The number 11110 is displayed.

4. Click the **Dec** option button and convert the following decimal number to binary: **4545**. The number 1000111000001 is displayed. Convert **1112** to binary. The number 10001011000 is displayed.

5. What decimal number is equal to 101101 in the binary system? What decimal number is equal to 1111011? When you are finished, close the calculator by clicking the **Close** button [X] in the upper-right corner.

Memory

Memory also is found on the motherboard. Sometimes understanding memory can be confusing because it can mean different things to different people. The easiest way to understand memory is to think of it as either "short term" or "long term." When you want to store a file or information permanently, you use secondary storage devices such as the computer's hard disk drive or a USB drive. You might think of this as long term.

Random Access Memory

You can think about the memory on the motherboard as short term. This type of memory is called *random access memory*, or *RAM*. RAM also is referred to as *main memory* and *primary memory*. You might have heard someone ask, "How much memory is in your computer?" Most likely, they are asking how much RAM is in your computer. The computer can read from and write to this type of memory. Data, information, and program instructions are stored temporarily within the CPU on a RAM chip or a set of RAM chips such as those shown in **Figure 4–6**.

FIGURE 4–6 RAM chips

When the computer is turned off or otherwise loses power, whatever is stored in the RAM memory chips disappears. Therefore, it is considered volatile. To understand how RAM works and how the computer processes data, think about how you would use a word processing program to create an address list of your family and friends.

1. First, you start your word processing program. The computer then loads your word processing program instructions into RAM.

2. You input the names, addresses, and telephone numbers (your data). Your data also is stored in RAM.

3. Next, you give your word processing program a command to process your data by arranging it in a special format, such as alphabetical order. This command and your processed data, or information, are also now stored in RAM.

4. You then click the Print button. Instructions to print are transmitted to RAM, and your document is sent to your printer.

5. Then, you click the Save button. Instructions to provide you with an opportunity to name and save your file are loaded into RAM. Once you save your file, you exit your word processing program and turn off the computer.

6. All instructions, data, and information that you used to create your address list are erased from RAM.

This process is known as the *instruction cycle* or *I-cycle* and the *execution cycle* or *E-cycle*. When the CPU receives an instruction to perform a specified task, the instruction cycle is the amount of time it takes to retrieve the instruction and complete the command. The execution cycle refers to the amount of time it takes the CPU to execute the instruction and store the results in RAM. Together, the instruction cycle and one or more execution cycles create a *machine cycle*.

For every instruction, a processor repeats a set of four basic operations, which comprise a machine cycle: (1) fetching, (2) decoding, (3) executing, and, if necessary, (4) storing (see **Figure 4–7**). *Fetching* is the process of obtaining a program instruction or data item from RAM. The term *decoding* refers to the process of translating the instruction into signals the computer can execute. *Executing* is the process of carrying out the commands. *Storing*, in this context, means writing the result to memory (not to a storage medium).

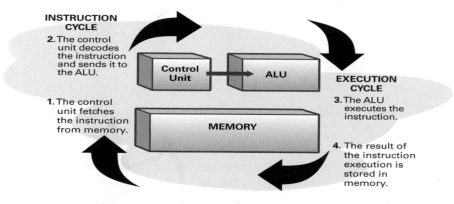

FIGURE 4–7 Processing cycle

Machine cycles are measured in microseconds (millionths of a second), nanoseconds (billionths of a second), and even picoseconds (trillionths of a second) in some of the larger computers. The faster the machine cycle, the faster your computer processes data. The speed of the processor has a lot to do with the speed of the machine cycle. However, the amount of RAM in your computer also can help increase the speed with which the computer processes data. The more RAM you have, the faster the computer processes data. See **Figure 4–8**.

▶ **VOCABULARY**
instruction cycle (I-cycle)
execution cycle (E-cycle)
machine cycle

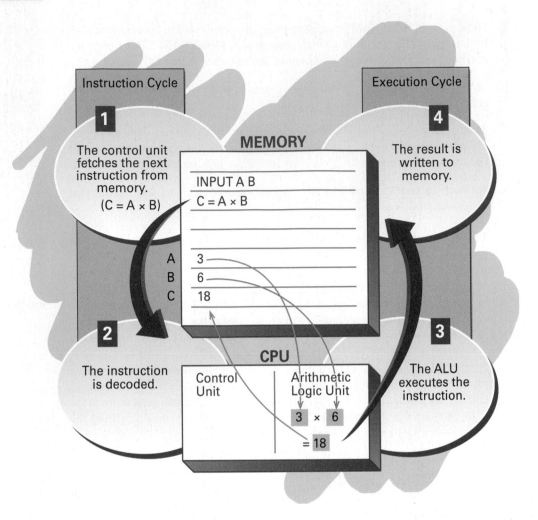

FIGURE 4–8   Machine cycle

Read-Only Memory

Another type of memory you will find on the motherboard is ***read-only memory***, or ***ROM***. ROM chips are found throughout a computer system. The computer manufacturer uses this type of chip to store specific instructions that are needed for the computer operations. This type of memory is nonvolatile. These instructions remain on the chip even when the power is turned off. The more common of these is the ***BIOS ROM***. The computer uses instructions contained on this chip to boot or start the system when you turn on your computer. A computer can read from a ROM chip, but cannot write or store data on the chip.

EXTRA FOR EXPERTS

Cache memory is another type of memory. This high-speed RAM is used to increase the speed of the processing cycle.

PC Support Specialist

The PC support specialist provides support for application software and related hardware via telephone and/or site visits to all workstation users.

As a PC support specialist, you need to be knowledgeable about current software and have good oral communication and organizational skills. You will be required to interact with all departments within the company and with users who have various skill levels ranging from novice to expert. You must be willing to learn other areas of Management Information Systems (MIS) such as networking, printer maintenance, and e-mail.

A bachelor's degree is preferred for most of these jobs; however, impressive experience also is accepted. Experience performing actual hands-on hardware and software upgrades is important.

Basic Controllers

The motherboard also contains several controllers. A *controller* is a device that controls the transfer of data from the computer to a peripheral device and vice-versa. Examples of common *peripheral devices* are keyboards, monitors, printers, and the mouse. Controllers generally are stored on a single chip. When you purchase a computer, all the necessary controllers for the standard devices are contained on the motherboard. See **Figure 4–2**.

Ports and Connectors

A *port,* also called a jack, is an interface by which a peripheral device attaches to or communicates with the system unit. We use devices such as *serial* and *parallel ports* to connect our peripheral devices to the computer. Serial devices transmit data one bit at a time. Parallel devices transfer eight bits at a time. A *bit* is represented by a zero or one. Typically, eight bits make one *byte*. Most computers traditionally have at least one parallel port and one serial port. In older computers, you likely will find a printer connected to a parallel port and perhaps a mouse connected to a serial port. A *modem* is a device that allows one computer to talk to another.

The *Universal Serial Bus (USB)* port can connect up to 127 different peripherals with a single connector and supports data transfer rates of up to 200 million bits per second (Mbps). USB is replacing the standard serial and parallel ports on newer computers. Today's personal computers typically have four to eight USB ports either on the front or back of the system unit. Using a daisy-chain arrangement or a *USB hub*, you can use a single USB port to connect up to 127 peripheral devices. A USB hub is a device that plugs into a USB port and contains multiple USB ports into which cables from USB devices can be plugged. USB also supports plug-and-play and hot plugging. *Plug-and-play* refers to the ability of a computer system to configure expansion boards and other devices automatically. *Hot plugging* is the ability to add and remove devices to a computer while the computer is running and have the operating system automatically recognize the change. *USB 2.0* is the more recent and advanced version of USB technology, and can support data transfer rates of up to 470 Mbps.

▶ **VOCABULARY**

controller

peripheral devices

port

serial port

parallel port

bit

byte

modem

Universal Serial Bus (USB)

USB 2.0

UNIT I   Computer Basics

Another type of external bus is *FireWire*, also known as *IEEE 1394* and *IEEE 1394b*. The IEEE 1394 bus standard supports data transfer rates of up to 400 Mbps and can connect up to 63 external devices; IEEE 1394b provides speeds up to 3200 Mbps. **Figure 4–9** shows an example of some of the ports traditionally used for a mouse, speakers, and other peripherals, and examples of FireWire and USB ports.

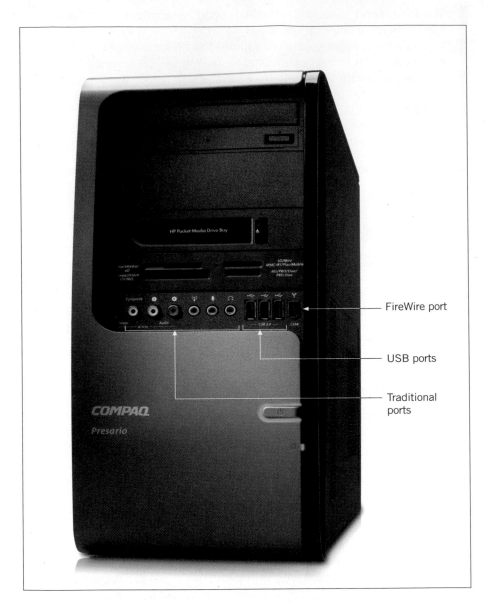

FIGURE 4–9   Traditional, FireWire, and USB ports

In addition to the above described ports, you might find three special-purpose ports on various computing devices. These special-purpose ports are as follows:

SCSI—An abbreviation for ***Small Computer System Interface, SCSI*** (pronounced *skuzzy*) is a standard interface for connecting peripherals such as disk drives and printers.

IrDA—A wireless standard that allows data to be transferred between devices using infrared light instead of cables is called *IrDA*. Both the computer and the device must have an IrDA port, and the IrDA port on the device must align with the IrDA port on the computer.

Bluetooth—**Bluetooth** uses radio waves and provides wireless short-range communications of data and voice between both mobile and stationary devices. See **Figure 4–10**. This technology does not require alignment; it is an alternative to IrDA.

IrDA and Bluetooth are discussed in more detail in Lesson 7.

▶ VOCABULARY
Bluetooth

expansion slots

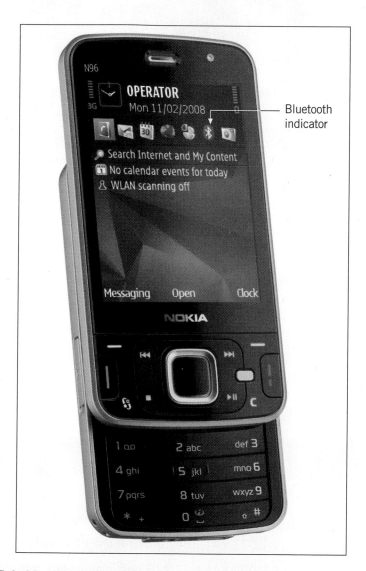

FIGURE 4–10   Bluetooth device

Expansion slots are openings on the motherboard where an *expansion board*, also called an *adapter card*, can be inserted. Expansion boards enhance functions of a component of the system unit and/or provide connections through a port or other connectors to peripheral devices. Expansion boards also are called expansion cards, add-ins, and add-ons. See **Figure 4–11**.

FIGURE 4–11   Expansion slots and card

Traditionally, ports have been located on the back of the system unit. With the introduction of portable devices, such as digital cameras and pocket PCs, many newer computers also include ports on the front of the system unit. This provides for easier access.

Windows provides several options to determine what hardware you have in your computer system. In Step-by-Step 4.2, you learn how to view this information. When you view this information, most likely you will see abbreviations such as MB or GB. **Table 4–1** defines these measurement terms.

TABLE 4–1   Measurement terms

TERM	ABBREVIATION	NUMBER OF BYTES
Kilobyte	K or KB	1024 (approximately 1000)
Megabyte	MB	1,048,576 (approximately 1 million)
Gigabyte	GB	1,073,741,824 (approximately 1 billion)
Terabyte	TB	1,099,511,627,776 (approximately 1 trillion)

Complete Step-by-Step 4.2 to display information about your computer.

Step-by-Step 4.2

1. Click the **Start** button 🪟 on the taskbar, and then click **Computer**. The Computer window appears, as shown in **Figure 4–12**.

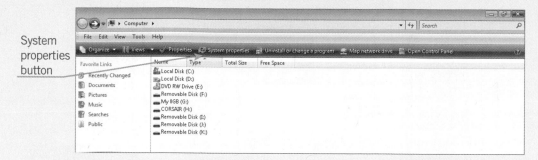

FIGURE 4–12
Computer window

2. Click the **System properties** button on the Command bar. The System window is displayed. See **Figure 4–13**. Most likely, your System window will display different system information from **Figure 4–13**.

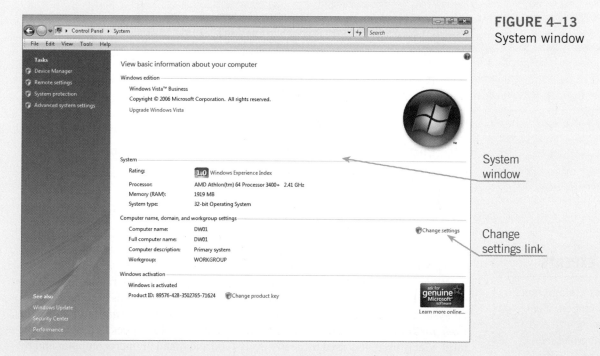

FIGURE 4–13
System window

3. What Microsoft Windows edition is listed for your computer? What processor does your computer contain? How much memory (RAM) is in your computer? What description and name are assigned to your computer?

4. Click the **Change settings** link. If a User Account Control dialog box is displayed, click the **Continue** button. The System Properties dialog box is displayed (see **Figure 4–14**).

FIGURE 4–14
System Properties dialog box

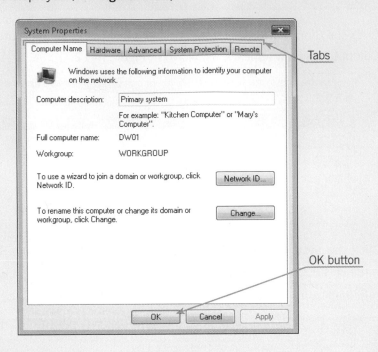

5. Click each of the tabs and read the information contained on each tab. If directed by your instructor, use Notepad or your word-processing program and write an overview of the features contained within the System Properties dialog box.

6. Click the **OK** button to close the System Properties dialog box, and then close the System window.

Data Representation

Earlier in this lesson, you read about binary, and learned that a bit is either a zero or a one. You might wonder, though, exactly how the computer determines what combination of zeros and ones represent the letter A or the number 1. It is really very simple. This is accomplished through standardized coding systems. The most popular system is called *ASCII* (pronounced AS-kee) and stands for *American Standard Code for Information Interchange*. There are other standard codes, but ASCII is the most widely used. It is used by nearly every type and brand of microcomputer and by many large computers.

As noted earlier in this lesson, eight bits are called a byte, or character, which is the basic unit of information. Each capital letter, lowercase letter, number, punctuation mark, and symbol has its own unique combination of eight ones and zeros.

Another type of standard code is called *Extended Binary Coded Decimal Interchange Code*, or *EBCDIC* (pronounced EB-si-dik). This code mostly is used in very large computers.

EXTRA FOR EXPERTS

Music and pictures are different from letters and numbers. For the computer to recognize and work with music and pictures, these objects must be digitized—converted to a digital format represented by 0s and 1s.

SUMMARY

In this lesson, you learned:

- Just about all computers perform the same general functions: input, processing, output, and storage.

- Input, output, and processing devices grouped together represent a computer system.

- The motherboard is the center of all processing.

- The motherboard contains the CPU, memory, and basic controllers. It also contains ports and expansion slots.

- The processor is the brains of the computer.

- The computer is given instructions through computer programs.

- The CPU has two main sections—the arithmetic/logic unit (ALU) and the control unit. All calculations and comparisons take place in the ALU. The control unit coordinates the CPU activities.

- The motherboard contains different types of memory.

- The machine cycle is made up of the instruction cycle and the execution cycle.

- Random access memory is volatile and is used to store instructions, data, and information temporarily.

- Read-only memory is nonvolatile and is used to store permanent instructions needed for computer operations.

- A controller is used to control the transfer of data between the computer and peripheral devices.

- Expansion slots contain expansion boards. Expansion boards are used to connect specialized peripheral devices or to add more memory to the computer.

- Peripheral devices are connected to the computer through serial and parallel ports.

- The Universal Serial Bus standard is expected to replace serial and parallel ports.

- FireWire is a type of external bus that can connect up to 63 external devices.

- SCSI, IrDA, and Bluetooth are special-purpose ports.

- The ASCII and EBCDIC codes are used to represent the alphabet, numbers, symbols, and punctuation marks.

■ VOCABULARY REVIEW

Define the following terms:

arithmetic/logic unit (ALU)	dual-core processor	motherboard
bit	execution cycle (E-cycle)	multi-core processor
Bluetooth	expansion slot	port
byte	FireWire	processor
cache memory	instruction cycle (I-cycle)	random access memory (RAM)
computer system	machine cycle	read-only memory (ROM)
control unit	memory	serial
controller	modem	Small Computer System Interface (SCSI)
		Universal Serial Bus (USB)

■ REVIEW QUESTIONS

MULTIPLE CHOICE

Select the best response for the following statements.

1. Eight _____ make one character.

   A. characters   C. bytes

   B. bits   D. codes

3. A _____ is approximately 1 trillion bytes.

   A. kilobyte   C. gigabyte

   B. megabyte   D. terabyte

5. A printer would be considered a(n) _____.

   A. controller   C. input device

   B. peripheral device   D. USB

2. _____ is a special port that uses radio waves.

   A. Bluetooth   C. FireWire

   B. IrDA   D. SCSI

4. Random access memory is _____.

   A. permanent   C. nonvolatile

   B. volatile   D. the same as ROM

TRUE / FALSE

Circle T if the statement is true or F if the statement is false.

T   F   **1.** For every instruction, a processor repeats a set of four basic operations.

T   F   **2.** The EBCDIC code is the most widely used standardized coding system.

T   F   **3.** The faster the machine cycle, the faster your computer processes data.

T   F   **4.** The two primary sections of the CPU are the ALU and the control unit.

T   F   **5.** Read-only memory (ROM) is volatile.

FILL IN THE BLANK

Complete the following sentences by writing the correct word or words in the blanks provided.

1. You can think of RAM as _____-term memory.

2. The instruction cycle and the execution cycle create a(n) _____ cycle.

3. The _____ the machine cycle, the faster your computer.

4. A(n) _____ controls the transfer of data from the computer to a peripheral device.

5. A device that plugs into a USB port and contains multiple USB ports is called a(n) _____.

■ PROJECTS

CROSS-CURRICULAR— MATHEMATICS

Access the Dell computer Web site at *www.dell.com*. Select either the Home and Office laptops or Home and Office Desktops category. Using a spreadsheet program or paper and pencil, create a comparison table. Include the following elements: processor speed, amount of RAM, number of expansion slots, number of USB ports, other ports, and price. Write a short paragraph explaining which computer you would purchase and why.

CROSS-CURRICULAR—SCIENCE

Using Google or another search engine, find an image of a computer system with the case removed. Print a copy of the image. Look for the motherboard and the components connected it. Count the number of available expansion slots. Locate the RAM chips. See if you can find the CPU. Can you see the chip itself? What other elements are visible? Using your printed copy, label each element you locate.

CROSS-CURRICULAR—SOCIAL STUDIES

The "digital divide theory" is described as the gap between those people who can access and make effective use of information technology and those who cannot. Research the digital divide theory and create a report expressing your opinion. Do you feel there is a digital divide? Explain why or why not.

CROSS-CURRICULAR—LANGUAGE ARTS

Using the Internet or other resources, research the history of computers. See if you can answer the following questions: (1) What was the name of the first commercially available electronic digital computer? (2) In what year was the IBM PC introduced? (3) What software helped Bill Gates become one of the richest men in the world? (4) In what year did Apple introduce the Macintosh computer? Use your word-processing program to answer each of these questions and/or to provide additional historical facts.

WEB PROJECT

Who invented the first microprocessor? Launch your Web browser and type the following URL: *www.wikipedia.org*. When the Web site opens, type "microprocessor" in the Search text box. Scroll down and click the History link. Use a presentation program (such as Microsoft Office PowerPoint) to create a presentation on what you found. Find an image of a microprocessor to add to your presentation. Share your presentation with your class.

TEAMWORK PROJECT

Some people say you should leave your computer on at all times— that turning the computer on and off creates stress on the components. Others argue that computers use a lot of energy and should be turned off when not in use. Your computer operating system, however, includes power-management settings. Work with your team to investigate these options. Use Windows Help and Support. Prepare a report on these power-management options and how you can create a power plan. Describe the steps to modify Sleep mode.

■ CRITICAL THINKING

Think about what you have read in this lesson. Your goal is to purchase a computer. Where would you shop—online, local computer dealer, retail store, or other? What type of processor would you purchase? How much memory would you need? Would you purchase a desktop, notebook, or other type of computer? Write a one-page report answering these questions and outlining your thoughts on what other technologies you would include. Explain why you made these selections.

■ EXPLORING GOOGLE

Google Web Accelerator is a free download that works with your browser to help display Web pages faster. To access Google Web Accelerator, type *http://webaccelerator.google.com* in your browser's Address bar. When the Speed Up the Web page is displayed, click the Learn more link. Describe this application and how it works. What are the computer system requirements? Do you think this would be a valuable tool to have on your computer? Explain why or why not.

LESSON 5

Input, Output, and Storage

■ OBJECTIVES

Upon completion of this lesson, you should be able to:

- Identify and describe the most common input devices.
- Identify and describe the most common output devices.
- Identify and describe storage devices.
- Identify and describe how input and output devices are connected to the computer.

We can agree that when it comes to processing data, it is the computer that does all of the work! However, it needs help. *Input*, which is data or instructions, must be entered into the computer. After the data is entered and processed, it has to be "presented" to the user. We use special devices for these tasks and refer to them as input and output devices.

Input devices enable you to input data and commands into the computer, and *output devices* enable the computer to give you the results of the processed data. Some devices perform both input and output functions. The fax machine and modem are examples. You use these devices to send (output) and receive (input) data over communications media.

■ VOCABULARY

audio input

biometrics

hard disk

inkjet printer

input

input devices

keyboard

laser printer

monitor

mouse

optical storage

output

output devices

pointing device

solid-state storage

USB flash drive

video input

...

Input Devices

The type of input device used is determined by the task to be completed. An input device can be as simple as the keyboard or as sophisticated as those used for specialized applications such as voice or retinal recognition.

Keyboard

The *keyboard* is the most commonly used input device for entering numeric and alphabetic data into a computer. If you are going to use the computer efficiently, it is important that you learn to type. Most of the keyboards used with desktop computers are enhanced. An enhanced keyboard has 12 function keys along the top, two Alt keys, two Ctrl keys, and a set of directional/arrow keys between the typing area and the numeric keypad.

Some keyboards, such as the one shown in **Figure 5–1**, have multimedia hot keys that enable you to access e-mail and the Internet, adjust speaker volume, and have other features such as a *zoom slider*. This device makes it easy to zoom in for a closer look at documents, spreadsheets, pictures, maps, and Web pages.

Zoom slider

Multimedia hot keys

FIGURE 5–1 Enhanced keyboards

A wide variety of keyboards are available. Some popular types of keyboards include:

- *Ergonomic*: a keyboard designed to provide users with more natural, comfortable hand, wrist, and arm positions
- *Cordless or wireless*: a battery-powered keyboard that transmits data using wireless technology
- *Specialized*: a keyboard with specialized keys that represent items such as those used in fast-food restaurants
- *Security*: a keyboard that provides security features such as a biometric fingerprint reader and magnetic stripe and smart card readers. See **Figure 5–2a**.
- *Foldable or flexible*: an easily transported keyboard primarily used with PDA and pocket PC-type devices; it has a soft touch and is water resistant. See **Figure 5–2b**.

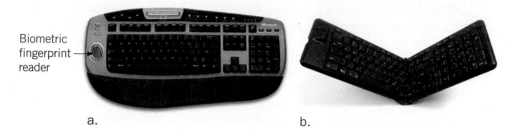

Biometric
fingerprint
reader

a.   b.

FIGURE 5–2   (a) Keyboard with fingerprint reader (b) Foldable keyboard

Pointing Devices

A *pointing device* is an input device that allows a user to position the *pointer* on the screen. The pointer can have several shapes, but the most common is an arrow. You use a pointing device to move the pointer and to select objects, such as text or graphics, and click buttons, icons, menu items, and links. The following sections discuss several different pointing devices.

Mouse

The *mouse* is the most commonly used pointing device for personal computers. It moves around on a flat surface and controls the pointer on the screen. The mouse fits conveniently in the palm of your hand. A description of four types of mice follows:

- *Mechanical*: This type of mouse has a ball located on the bottom that rolls on a flat surface as the mouse is moved. Sensors inside the mouse determine the direction and distance of the movement. A mouse pad generally is used with a mechanical mouse.

- *Optomechanical*: This mouse is the same as a mechanical mouse, but uses optical sensors to detect motion of the ball.

- *Optical*: An optical mouse uses a laser to detect the mouse's movement. See **Figure 5–3a**. Optical mice have no mechanical moving parts. They respond more quickly and precisely than mechanical and opto-mechanical mice.

- *Wireless*: A wireless mouse is a battery-powered device that relies on infrared or radio waves to communicate with the computer. See **Figure 5–3b**.

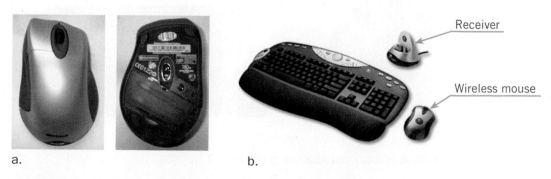

Receiver

Wireless mouse

a.   b.

FIGURE 5–3   (a) Optical mouse (b) Wireless mouse and receiver

Most of these devices have two or three buttons; some have a wheel. You use the left button for most mouse operations. Generally, clicking the right button displays a context menu. After you place the on-screen pointer where you want it, press a button on the mouse. This will cause some type of action to take place in the computer; the type of action depends on the program. Use the wheel to scroll or zoom a page.

You use the mouse to accomplish the following techniques in most software programs and Web pages:

- *Pointing*: placing the on-screen pointer at a designated location
- *Clicking*: pressing and releasing the mouse button to select a specific location within a document
- *Dragging*: pressing down the mouse button and moving the mouse while continuing to hold down the button to highlight a selected portion of text
- *Double-clicking*: pressing and releasing the mouse button two times in rapid succession to select a word
- *Triple-clicking*: pressing and releasing the mouse button three times in rapid succession to select a paragraph
- *Right-clicking*: pressing the right mouse button to display a menu
- *Rotate wheel*: rotating the rotate wheel on the mouse forward or backward to scroll vertically through a document on the screen
- *Tilt wheel*: pressing the mouse's rotate wheel right or left to scroll horizontally

Except for the wireless mouse, mice connect to personal computers through a port. A wireless mouse communicates through a receiver connected to a port. Ports were discussed in Lesson 4.

Trackball

The *trackball* is a pointing device that works like a mouse turned upside down; the ball is on top of the device. See **Figure 5–4a**. You use your thumb and fingers to operate the ball, thus controlling the pointer on the screen. A trackball is a stationary device and is a good alternative to the mouse when the user has limited desktop space. Some trackballs are built into the keyboard. See **Figure 5–4b**.

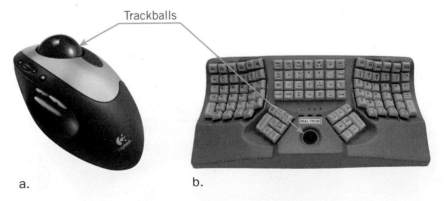

Trackballs

a.   b.

FIGURE 5–4   (a) Trackball on a mouse (b) Trackball on a keyboard

Joystick and Wheel

The joystick and wheel also are pointing devices. Joysticks and wheels, such as the ones shown in **Figure 5–5**, most often are used for games. The *joystick* consists of a plastic or metal rod mounted on a base. You can move the rod in any direction. Some joysticks have switches or buttons that can input data in an on/off response. A *wheel* is a steering-wheel type of device used to simulate driving a vehicle. Most wheels also include foot pedals used for braking and acceleration actions.

▶ **VOCABULARY**
joystick
wheel
pointing stick

a.   b.

FIGURE 5–5   (a) Joystick (b) Wheel

Pointing Stick

Many notebook computers contain a *pointing stick*—a pressure-sensitive device that looks like a pencil eraser. It is located on the keyboard, generally between the G, H, and B keys. See **Figure 5–6**. It is moved with the forefinger, while the thumb is used to press related keys. In a confined space, a lot of people find a pointing stick more convenient than a mouse. IBM popularized this device by introducing the TrackPoint on its ThinkPad notebooks.

Pointing stick

FIGURE 5–6   Pointing stick

Other Input Devices

A variety of other input devices also are available, most of which are used for special applications. The following section describes these input devices.

graphics tablet

touch display screen

stylus

digital pen

Graphics Tablet

A *graphics tablet*, also called a digitizing tablet, is a flat drawing surface on which the user can draw figures or write something freehand. Architects, engineers, artists, mapmakers, and designers use these tablets to create precise drawings. After the drawing is created and saved, it can be manipulated like a regular graphic.

Touch Display Screen

The *touch display screen*, as shown in **Figure 5–7**, is a special screen with pictures or shapes. You use your fingers to "point" to the desired object to make a selection. You can find these screens in many public establishments such as airports, hotels, banks, libraries, delivery services, and fast-food restaurants. Many mobile devices (discussed in Lesson 1) have touch screens.

FIGURE 5–7   Touch screen on a handheld device

Stylus

A *stylus* and *digital pen* are pen-like writing instruments. See **Figure 5–8**. These devices allow the user to input information by writing on a PDA or other mobile devices or to use the pen as a pointer.

FIGURE 5–8   Stylus for mobile device

Audio Input

Audio input is the process of inputting sound into the computer. This could include speech, sound effects, and music. Audio input devices include microphones, CD/DVD players, radios, and other devices such as electronic keyboards.

  Voice input is a category of audio input. *Voice recognition* devices are used to "speak" commands into the computer and to enter text. These devices usually are microphones. The computer must have some type of voice recognition software installed before you can use a voice recognition device. Directory assistance is a type of voice recognition technology. Voice recognition technology also has made it possible for disabled persons to command wheelchairs and other objects that make them more mobile.

Touchpad

A *touchpad* is an input device commonly used in laptop computers. To move the pointer, slide your fingertip across the surface of the pad. To imitate mouse operations, such as clicking, tap or double-tap the surface of the touchpad.

Scanner

A *scanner* is a device that can change images into codes for input to the computer. Scanners are available in various sizes and types, including the following:

- *Image scanners*: These devices convert images into an electronic form that can be stored in a computer's memory. The image then can be manipulated.
- *Bar code scanners*: This type of scanner reads bar lines that are printed on products (for example, in a grocery store or department store). See **Figure 5–9a**.

▶ **VOCABULARY**
audio input
voice input
voice recognition
touchpad
scanner

EXTRA FOR EXPERTS

Microsoft has a text-only version of Internet Explorer, and Mozilla has a version of its Firefox browser that incorporates voice recognition capabilities in an effort to assist visually impaired users.

- *Magnetic scanners*: These devices read encoded information on the back of credit cards. The magnetic strip on the back of the cards contains the encoded user's account number. See **Figure 5–9b**.
- *Optical character recognition (OCR)* and *Optical mark recognition (OMR) scanners*: These devices use a light source to read characters, marks, and codes; the data then is converted into digital data. Banks use OCR technology to scan checks. Commonly known as Scantrons, schools and other organizations use OMR for testing purposes.

 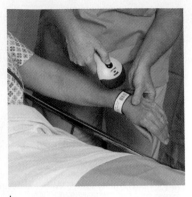

a.   b.

FIGURE 5–9   (a) Optical scanner (b) Bluetooth scanner

Digital Cameras

The pictures taken with a ***digital camera*** are stored digitally and then transferred to the computer's memory. Digital cameras use a variety of mobile storage media to store the images, including flash memory card, memory stick, USB, and mini-disc. The *Solid-State Storage Media* section later in this lesson discusses digital cameras and other solid-state storage devices. After the pictures are transferred to the computer, they can be viewed quickly and any imperfections can be edited with photo-editing software.

Video Input

Video input is the process of capturing full-motion images with a type of video camera and then saving the video on a storage medium such as a hard drive, CD, or DVD. After the video is saved, you can view and edit it. Some example video input devices are as follows:

- A digital video (DV) camera records video as digital signals; some cameras also capture still images. Some are just a little larger than a credit card. See **Figure 5–10**. A PC video camera is a type of digital video camera that allows the user to send live images over the Internet, make video telephone calls, and send e-mail messages with video attachments.
- A Web camera (or Webcam) is a real-time camera that displays images through the World Wide Web.

FIGURE 5-10   Miniaturized digital video camera

Biometric Input

Consider the following scenario: You are going on a two-week vacation to Tahiti and Bora Bora—you are packed and ready to go, but you do not need a wallet or credit cards. You use your fingerprint as an input device to pay for all of your expenses.

In information technology, ***biometrics*** is an authentication technique using automated methods of recognizing a person based on a physiological or behavioral characteristic. Biometric devices consist of a reader or scanning device, and software that converts the scanned information into a digital format. The scanned information then is compared to a database of stored biometric data.

Several types of biometric identification techniques exist. Some of the more common are the fingerprint, face, handwriting, and voice. Other less common techniques are retina (analysis of the capillary vessels located at the back of the eye), iris (analysis of the colored ring surrounding the eye's pupil), hand geometry (analysis of the shape of the hand and length of the fingers), and vein (analysis of the pattern of veins on the back of the hand and the wrist).

The process or the way in which biometric technology works, however, basically is the same for all identification techniques:

- *Enrollment*: The user enrolls in the system by establishing a baseline measurement for comparison.
- *Submission*: The user presents biological proof of his or her identify to the capture system.
- *Verification*: The system compares the submitted sample with the stored sample.

Privacy and civil liberties advocates, however, are concerned about the widespread adoption of biometric systems. They argue that using biometric data, third parties can access the data of an individual without their consent, and link it to other information, resulting in secondary uses of the information. This erodes the individual's personal control over the uses of his or her information. On the other hand, biometrics also can be applied to private security. For example, several companies now offer biometric computer keyboards and USB flash drives with fingerprint authentication that can be used for personal applications. Flash drives are discussed later in this lesson. See **Figure 5-11**.

▶ **VOCABULARY**
biometrics

a.   b.

FIGURE 5–11   (a) Biometric keyboard scanner (b) Fingerprint scanner

Virtual Devices

Virtual devices use the synchronized positioning of light emitting and sensing devices to detect user input. **Figure 5–12a** shows a virtual computer keyboard and **Figure 5–12b** shows a virtual piano keyboard.

a.   b.

FIGURE 5–12   (a) Virtual computer keyboard (b) Virtual piano keyboard

Touch-Sensitive Pads

The *touch-sensitive pad* on a portable device, such as an iPod, enables the user to scroll through and adjust the volume, play music, view videos or pictures, and customize settings.

In Step-by-Step 5.1, you examine the settings for sound output in Windows Vista. You will need a speaker or headphones to complete this Step-by-Step.

Step-by-Step 5.1

1. Click the **Start** button ⊞ on the taskbar, and then click **Control Panel**. If necessary, click **Classic View**. If necessary, press the **Alt** key to display the menu bar. If the Control Panel appears in a view different from that shown in **Figure 5–13**, click **View** on the menu bar, and then click **Medium Icons**. Most likely the Control Panel on your computer will display different options.

Control
Panel

Classic
View
selected

Sound tool

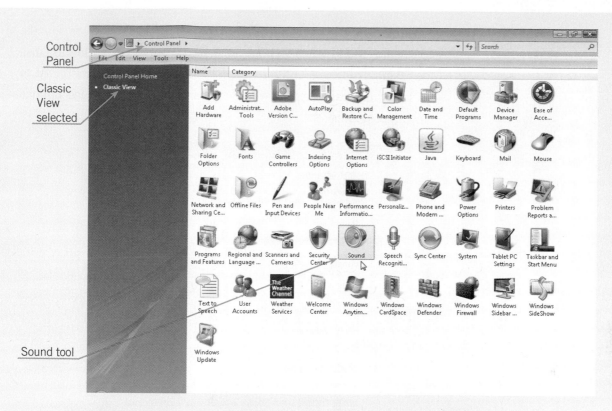

FIGURE 5–13
Windows Vista
Control Panel

2. Double-click **Sound**. The Sound dialog box is displayed. See **Figure 5–14**.
    Click the Sounds tab.

Sound dialog box

Sounds tab

Asterisk sound

OK button

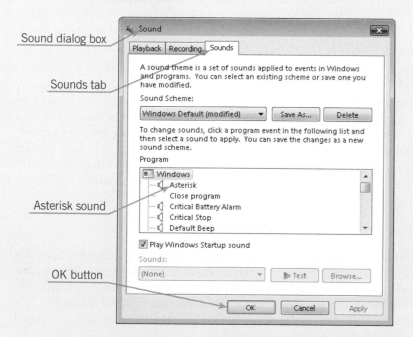

FIGURE 5–14
Sounds tab in the Sound dialog box

3. Click **Asterisk** in the Program events list. Next, click the **Test** button to lis-
    ten to the sound.

4. Scroll through the list of Program events and listen to various sounds. See **Figure 5–15**. When you are finished, click the **OK** button to close the Sound dialog box, and then close the Control Panel. If instructed to do so, write a paragraph on what you learned about the sound options on your computer.

FIGURE 5–15
Testing Program sounds

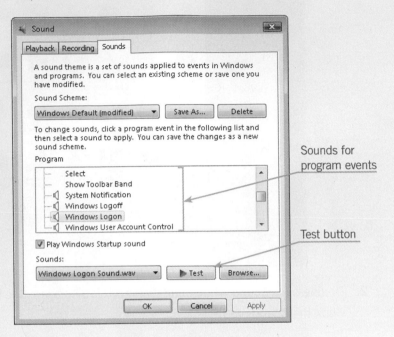

Sounds for program events

Test button

Storage Devices

As data is entered in the computer and processed, it is stored in RAM (temporary memory). If you want to keep a permanent copy of the data, you must store it on some type of storage medium. The more popular types of storage medium technology are USB drives, hard disks, CD and DVD, solid-state storage, and tape. Storage devices are categorized by the method they use to store data. The categories include magnetic technology, optical technology, and solid-state storage media.

Magnetic Storage Devices

Magnetic storage devices use oxide-coated plastic storage media called Mylar. As the disk rotates in the computer, an electromagnetic read/write head stores or retrieves data in circles called *tracks*. The number of tracks on a disk varies with the type of disk. The tracks are numbered from the outside to the inside. As data is stored on the disk, it is stored on a numbered track. Each track is labeled and the location is kept in a special log on the disk called a *file allocation table* (*FAT*).

The most common types of magnetic storage media are floppy disk, hard drives, and magnetic tape.

▶ **VOCABULARY**
tracks

file allocation table (FAT)

Floppy Disk

A *floppy disk*, usually just called a disk, is a flat circle of iron oxide-coated plastic enclosed in a hard plastic case. Most floppy disks are 3½ inches in diameter, although you might see other sizes. They have a capacity to hold 1.44 MB or more of data. See **Figure 5–16**. To protect unwanted data from being added to or removed from a disk, write protection is provided. To write-protect a disk, open the write-protect window on the disk. Since the introduction of USB drives and solid-state storage media, floppy disks are becoming obsolete.

FIGURE 5–16   Parts of a floppy disk

Hard Disk

Most **hard disks** (also called hard disk drives) are used to store data inside the computer, although removable hard disks also are available. They provide two advantages: speed and capacity. Accessing data is faster and the amount of data that can be stored is much larger than what can be stored on a floppy disk. The size of the hard drive is measured in megabytes or gigabytes, and one hard drive can consist of several disks. See **Figure 5–17**.

FIGURE 5–17   Hard disk

Magnetic Tape

Companies and other organizations use *magnetic tape* mostly for making backup copies of large volumes of data. This is a very slow process and therefore is not used for regularly saving data. The tape can be used to replace data that might have been lost from the hard drive.

Optical Storage Devices

Optical storage devices use laser technology to read and write data on silver platters. See **Figure 5–18**. The term *disc* is used for optical media. CDs and DVDs are a type of optical storage media. Most computers today come equipped with some type of optical storage—a CD drive or a DVD drive. The technology for CDs and DVDs is similar, but storage capacities are quite different and several variations exist. These storage devices come in several formats, as follows:

FIGURE 5–18   A laser reads data on a CD or DVD

- *CD-DA*: The Compact Disc Digital Audio format also is known as an audio CD; it is the industry-wide standard for music publishing and distribution.

- *CD-R*: The Compact Disc Recordable format makes it possible for you to create your own compact discs that can be read by any CD-ROM drive. After information is written to this type of disc, it cannot be changed.

- *CD-ROM*: The Compact Disc Read-Only Memory format can store up to 680 MB. This is the equivalent of about 450 floppy disks! You can read data from the CD; you cannot store data on a CD unless you are using a writable CD.

- *CD-RW*: The Compact Disc Read Writable is a type of compact disc that enables you to write onto it multiple times. Not all CD players can read CD-RWs.

- *DVD-ROM*: The Digital Versatile Disc Read-Only Memory is a read-only DVD format commonly used for distribution of movies and computer games; its capacity ranges from 4.7 GB to 17 GB.

- *DVD-R*: The Digital Versatile Disc Recordable is similar to the CD-R except it has a much larger capacity; after information is written to this type of disc, it cannot be changed.

- *DVD-RW*: The Digital Versatile Disc Read Writable stores data using technology similar to that of a CD-RW, but with a much larger capacity.

- *HD-DVD*: The High Density DVD, originally introduced as a more expensive DVD, was an optical storage device, now replaced by the Blu-ray disc. The single-layer HD-DVD provided up to 15 gigabytes of storage capacity and the double-layer disc provided up to 30 GB.

- *Blu-ray*: This disc has 100 GB of storage capacity and is expected to provide 200 GB of storage capacity in the near future. This format is predicted to replace conventional DVD. (A still higher-capacity holographic storage medium called HVD (holographic versatile disc) is on the horizon.) Blu-ray technology is backward compatible with DVD and CD formats, whereas HD-DVD was backward compatible with DVD formats.

 EXTRA FOR EXPERTS

DVD also is called Digital Video Disc and is backward-compatible with CD-ROMs.

Solid-State Storage Media

Solid-state storage is a nonvolatile, removable medium that uses integrated circuits. The main advantage of this type of storage medium is that everything is processed electronically, and it contains no mechanical parts. Several types of solid-state storage are available. Miniature mobile media, for example, are popular solid-state storage devices for cameras, PDAs, music players, and other such electronics. **Figure 5–19** contains an assortment of miniature mobile media, most of which are no larger than a postage stamp.

FIGURE 5–19   Miniature mobile storage media

Another popular solid-state storage medium is the ***USB flash drive***. This small removable data storage device comes in a variety of configurations, such as those shown in **Figure 5–20**. It uses a USB connector to connect to your computer's USB port or other electronic device. Flash drives also are known by other names such as a keydrive, thumb drive, jump drive, USB flash memory drive, and USB stick.

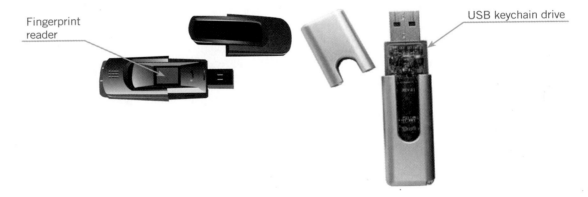

Fingerprint reader

USB keychain drive

FIGURE 5–20   Examples of USB flash drives

Caring for Storage Media

Removable storage media require special care if the data stored is to remain undamaged. Here are some safeguards that should be taken:

- Keep away from magnetic fields such as those contained in televisions and computer monitors (magnetic media).
- Avoid extreme temperatures.
- Remove media from drives and store them properly when not in use.
- When handling CDs and other optical discs, hold them at the edges.
- Never try to remove the media from a drive when the drive indicator light is on.
- Keep disks in a sturdy case when transporting.

Output Devices

Output is data that has been processed into a useful format. Examples of output are printed text, spoken words, music, pictures, video, or graphics. The most common output devices are monitors and printers. Output devices display information.

Monitors

Desktop computers typically use a *monitor* as their display device. The screen is part of the monitor, which also includes the housing for its electrical components. Screen output is called *soft copy* because it is temporary.

Computer monitors come in many varieties. The *cathode ray tube* (*CRT*) was one of the earliest types of monitors. This type of monitor is similar to a standard television and can be either monochrome or color. A monochrome monitor screen has a one-color display. It could be white, green, or amber. Color monitors display thousands of colors. Most of today's monitors are color. CRT monitors are available in various sizes, with the more common being 17-, 19-, and 21-inch. See **Figure 5–21a**.

Flat-panel monitors come in two varieties: liquid crystal display (LCD) and gas plasma. Both types of monitors are more expensive than CRT monitors. They take up less space, however, and are much lighter in weight.

LCD panels produce an image by manipulating light within a layer of liquid crystal cells. See **Figure 5–21b**. Until recently, LCD panels were used primarily on notebook computers and other mobile devices such as cell phones and PDAs. In 1997, several manufacturers started producing full-size LCD panels as alternatives to CRT monitors.

Gas plasma technology consists of a tiny amount of gas that is activated by an electrical charge. See **Figure 5–21c**. The gas illuminates miniature colored fluorescent lights arranged in a panel-like screen. These monitors have a brilliant color display and are available in sizes up to 60 inches or more.

▶ **VOCABULARY**

output

monitor

soft copy

cathode ray tube (CRT)

LCD panel

gas plasma

ETHICS IN TECHNOLOGY

Computer Viruses

The word "virus" can put fear into anyone who uses the Internet or exchanges disks. How can such a small word cause such fear? It is because a virus can cause tremendous damage to your computer files!

A virus is a computer program that is written intentionally to attach itself to other programs or disk boot sectors and duplicates itself whenever those programs are executed or the infected disks are accessed. A virus can wipe out all of the files that are on your computer.

Viruses can sit on your computer for weeks or months and not cause any damage until a predetermined date or time code is activated. Not all viruses cause damage. Some are just pranks; maybe your desktop will display some silly message. Other viruses cripple computer systems and cause millions of dollars worth of damage. The motivation for creating and distributing a virus varies. People might create viruses to gain recognition for their computer expertise, to maliciously destroy data or services, or to illegally access data or financial reward.

To protect your computer from virus damage, install an antivirus software program on your computer and keep it running at all times so that it can continuously scan for viruses.

FIGURE 5–21   (a) CRT (b) LCD display (c) Gas plasma display

Printers

Printers are used to produce a paper or hard copy of the processing results. Several types of printers are available, with tremendous differences in speed, print quality, price, and special features.

When selecting a printer, consider the following features:

- *Speed*: Printer speed is measured in pages per minute (ppm). The number of pages a printer can print per minute varies for text and for graphics. Graphics print more slowly than regular text.
- *Print quality*: Print quality is measured in dots per inch (dpi). The more dpi, the higher the resolution or print quality.
- *Price*: The price includes the original cost of the printer as well as what it costs to maintain the printer. A good-quality printer can be purchased very inexpensively; a high-output system can cost thousands of dollars. The ink cartridges and toners need to be replaced periodically.

The two more popular types of printers are laser and inkjet. Printers are classified as either impact or nonimpact. *Impact printers* use a mechanism that actually strikes the paper to form letters and images. Dot matrix printers are impact printers. *Nonimpact printers* form characters without striking the paper. Laser printers and inkjet printers are examples of nonimpact printers.

Laser Printers

A *laser printer* produces images using the same technology as copier machines. The image is made with a type of powder called toner. A laser printer produces high-quality output. The cost of a laser printer has decreased substantially in recent years. Color laser printers, however, are quite expensive, some costing thousands of dollars. See **Figure 5–22**.

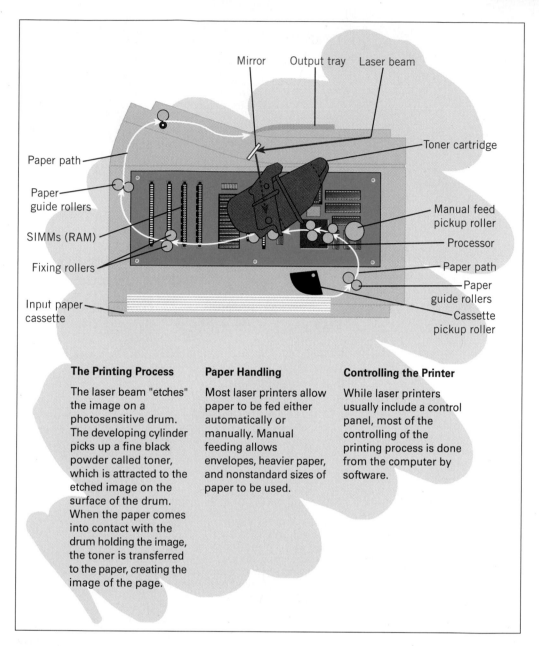

Mirror   Output tray   Laser beam

Paper path

Paper guide rollers

SIMMs (RAM)

Fixing rollers

Input paper cassette

Toner cartridge

Manual feed pickup roller

Processor

Paper path

Paper guide rollers

Cassette pickup roller

The Printing Process

The laser beam "etches" the image on a photosensitive drum. The developing cylinder picks up a fine black powder called toner, which is attracted to the etched image on the surface of the drum. When the paper comes into contact with the drum holding the image, the toner is transferred to the paper, creating the image of the page.

Paper Handling

Most laser printers allow paper to be fed either automatically or manually. Manual feeding allows envelopes, heavier paper, and nonstandard sizes of paper to be used.

Controlling the Printer

While laser printers usually include a control panel, most of the controlling of the printing process is done from the computer by software.

FIGURE 5–22   How a laser printer works

Inkjet Printers

An *inkjet printer* provides good quality color printing for less expense. See **Figure 5–23**. As a nonimpact printer, the color is sprayed onto the paper. Inkjet printers also print on other materials, such as iron-on t-shirt transfers, card stock for greeting cards, labels, and transparencies. Unlike earlier versions of the inkjet printer, newer versions can also use regular photocopy paper. The quality of an inkjet printer is determined by its resolution, which is measured by the number of dots per inch (dpi) a printer can print.

▶ **VOCABULARY**
inkjet printer

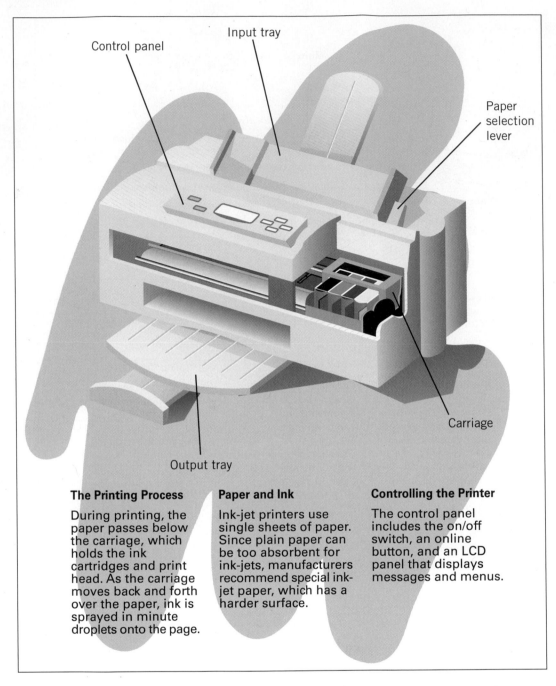

Control panel
Input tray
Paper selection lever
Carriage
Output tray

The Printing Process

During printing, the paper passes below the carriage, which holds the ink cartridges and print head. As the carriage moves back and forth over the paper, ink is sprayed in minute droplets onto the page.

Paper and Ink

Ink-jet printers use single sheets of paper. Since plain paper can be too absorbent for ink-jets, manufacturers recommend special ink-jet paper, which has a harder surface.

Controlling the Printer

The control panel includes the on/off switch, an online button, and an LCD panel that displays messages and menus.

FIGURE 5–23   How an inkjet printer works

Other Types of Printers

Impact printers, such as the dot matrix and line printer, have been around for a long time. *Dot matrix printers* print by transferring ink to the paper by striking a ribbon with pins. The higher the number of pins (dpi), the better the resolution or output. The mechanism that actually does the printing is called a *printhead*. The speed of the dot matrix printer is measured in characters per second (cps). With the reduction in cost of laser and inkjet printers, dot matrix printers are used less often today. A variation of the dot matrix printer is the *line printer*. This type of high-speed printer is attached primarily to large computers such as mainframes or mid-range servers.

▶ **VOCABULARY**

dot matrix printer

printhead

line printer

Several other types of specialty printers are available. Some examples are as follows:

- *Thermal*: A ***thermal printer*** forms characters by heating paper. The printer requires special heat-sensitive paper.

- *Mobile*: A ***mobile printer*** is a small, battery-powered printer, primarily used to print from a notebook computer.

- *Label and postage*: A ***label printer*** prints labels of various types and sizes on an adhesive-type paper; a postage printer is a special type of label printer. This type of printer contains a built-in digital scale and prints postage stamps.

- *Plotters/large-format*: Engineers, architects, and graphic artists use ***plotters*** and ***large-format printers*** for drawings and drafting output.

Other Output Devices

In addition to printers, other types of output devices exist. Some examples are as follows:

- *Speakers and headsets*: ***Speakers*** generate sound, such as music or instructions on how to complete a tutorial. Individuals use headsets or earphones to hear the music or other voice output privately.

- *Fax machines and fax modems*: A ***fax machine*** and ***fax modem*** transmit and receive documents over a telephone line or through a computer.

- *Multifunction peripherals*: A ***multifunctional peripheral*** provides a combination of various output options such as printing, scanning, copying, and faxing.

- *Data projectors*: A ***data projector*** projects the computer image onto a screen; mostly used for presentations.

Complete Step-by-Step 5.2 to view the devices on your computer.

▶ **VOCABULARY**

thermal printer

mobile printer

label printer

plotter

large-format printer

speaker

fax machine

fax modem

multifunctional peripheral

data projector

Step-by-Step 5.2

1. Click the **Start** button ⊞ on the taskbar, right-click **Computer** to display the shortcut menu, and point to **Properties**, as shown in **Figure 5–24**.

FIGURE 5–24
Computer shortcut menu

2. Click **Properties**. The System window opens. See **Figure 5–25**. In the System window, click the **Device Manager** link. If the User Account Control dialog box is displayed, click the **Continue** button.

FIGURE 5–25
System window

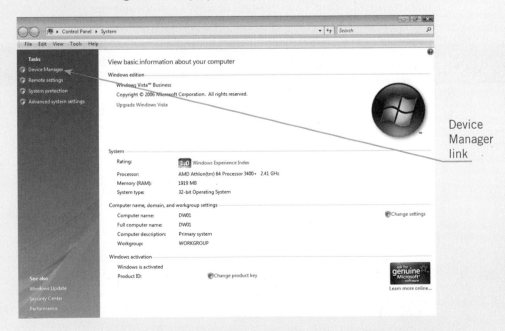

3. A list of hardware device categories appears. See **Figure 5–26**. Your lists and devices most likely will be different from those shown in **Figure 5–26** and the other figures in this exercise.

Disk drives
plus sign

FIGURE 5–26
Device Manager dialog box

4. Click the **plus sign** to the left of Disk drives. See **Figure 5–26**. How many disk drives are displayed? See **Figure 5–27**.

FIGURE 5–27
Device Manager showing disk drives

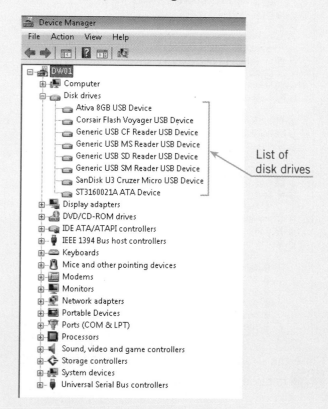

List of
disk drives

5. Click the **plus sign** to the left of Display adapters. What type of display adapter do you have?

6. Click the **plus signs** to the left of the following (if available) and review the information that is displayed: **DVD/CD-ROM drives**, **Keyboards**, **Mice and other pointing devices**, **Monitors**, **Ports (COM & LPT)**, **Sound, video and game controllers**, and **Universal Serial Bus controllers**. See **Figure 5–28**. If requested to do so, make a list of the displayed items and give your printout to your instructor.

FIGURE 5–28
Displaying input and output devices

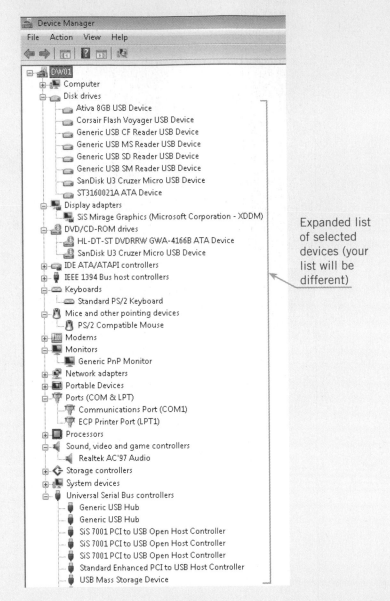

Expanded list of selected devices (your list will be different)

7. Close the Device Manager dialog box, and then click the **Close** button to close the System window.

Connecting Input/Output (I/O) Devices to the Computer

Input and output devices must be connected to the computer. Some devices connect to the computer through a physical connection, such as a port. For instance, you can plug the cable for a physical device into an existing port located on the back or front of the computer. Some monitors also have ports. See Lesson 4 for a discussion on ports. Wireless devices connect through infrared or radio waves.

SUMMARY

In this lesson, you learned:

- Input devices enable you to input data and commands into the computer.

- The most common input devices are the keyboard and mouse.

- Other types of input devices include the trackball, joystick and wheel, pointing stick, graphics tablet, touch display screen, stylus, voice recognition devices, touchpad, scanner, digital camera, video input, and biometric input.

- To maintain a permanent copy of data, you should store it on some type of storage medium.

- The three categories of storage media are magnetic storage, optical storage, and solid-state storage.

- Monitors and printers are examples of output devices.

- Monitors produce soft copy.

- Printers are used to produce a paper or hard copy of the processed result.

- Criteria for selecting a printer include speed, print quality, and cost.

- Input and output devices must be connected to the computer.

- Some I/O devices communicate with the computer through a physical connection.

- Wireless devices communicate with the computer through infrared or radio waves.

■ VOCABULARY REVIEW

Define the following terms:

audio input	keyboard	output devices
biometrics	laser printer	pointing device
hard disk	monitor	solid-state storage
inkjet printer	mouse	USB flash drive
input	optical storage	video input
input devices	output	

■ REVIEW QUESTIONS

MULTIPLE CHOICE

Select the best response for the following statements.

1. Laser, inkjet, and dot matrix are types of _____.

   A. monitors   C. storage devices

   B. printers   D. input devices

2. Which of the following is not considered an input device?

   A. keyboard   C. mouse

   B. scanner   D. monitor

3. A keyboard that requires fingerprint identification is an example of a(n) _____ input device.

   A. biometric   C. SCSI

   B. USB   D. MIDI

4. As data is entered in the computer and processed, it is stored _____.

   A. in RAM   C. on a magnetic device

   B. in ROM   D. on an optical device

5. Solid-state storage _____.

   A. is volatile   C. contains mechanical parts

   B. is not volatile   D. is the same as RAM

TRUE / FALSE

Circle T if the statement is true or F if the statement is false.

T   F   **1.**   A DVD-RW disc is an example of optical media.

T   F   **2.**   When data is stored on a disk, it is stored in circles called tracks.

T   F   **3.**   Input and output devices perform the same function.

T   F   **4.**   Digital cameras use only one type of storage medium.

T   F   **5.**   Some devices can function as both input and output devices.

FILL IN THE BLANK

Complete the following sentences by writing the correct word or words in the blanks provided.

1. A(n) _____ is the most widely used device for entering data into the computer.

2. A(n) _____ is a pointing device that works like an upside-down mouse.

3. Hard disks and floppy disks are types of _____ storage devices.

4. _____ is data or instructions, which is entered into the computer.

5. Input and output devices are connected to computers through _____.

■ PROJECTS

CROSS-CURRICULAR—MATHEMATICS

Your goal is to become a robotic engineer. Use appropriate research sources to locate information on education requirements. How would you prepare for this career? What challenges would you face? How much education would you need? Is this a job that is heavily in demand? Prepare a presentation to show your findings.

CROSS-CURRICULAR—SCIENCE

There are many styles of keyboards for computers. Many of the designs were developed to address various health issues related to keyboard use. Use appropriate research sources to locate information on various keyboard designs and report on the theory on which they are designed. You also may visit retail stores that sell computers to obtain information and sales documents. Prepare a written report outlining the information you locate.

CROSS-CURRICULAR—SOCIAL STUDIES

Biometric technology is the automated method of recognizing a person based on a physiological or behavioral characteristic. Use the Internet and other sources to research this topic. Make a list of the pros and cons that relate to this technology. Include your personal opinion about this topic.

CROSS-CURRICULAR— LANGUAGE ARTS

Prepare a written report describing at least five input devices. Include a table in your report listing the input device, describing how it could be used, and explaining the device's advantages and disadvantages.

WEB PROJECT

You want to learn more about optical storage devices. Your instructor thinks this is a great idea and has asked you to prepare a report and share your findings with the class. Your report should include the Web searching methodologies used and the Web-based resources. A minimum of three Web sites should be used.

TEAMWORK PROJECT

This exercise is a student role-playing activity. Students are given a specific task and a set of rules. They then role-play parts of a computer to accomplish the task. Student roles include: a processor, main memory, storage devices, and input/output devices. Some task examples are as follows: a) inputting pictures from a digital camera, modifying and viewing the pictures, and outputting and printing the pictures; b) using word processing software to create a report on a specified school topic, adding pictures to the report, and then printing copies for all students in the class; c) using a spreadsheet program to create a worksheet and chart and then print copies for all students in the class; d) using a presentation program such as PowerPoint to create and display in class a presentation with text, images, and video.

 ## CRITICAL THINKING

Review the section in this lesson on solid-state storage devices. Research the Internet and other resources to learn more about this technology. Prepare a report indicating if you think this technology eventually will replace magnetic and optical storage media. Explain why you think this will or will not happen.

EXPLORING GOOGLE

Google Docs is a free, Web-based word processor, spreadsheet, and presentation application located at *docs.google.com*. Users can create and edit documents online while collaborating in real time with other users. Take a tour of Google Docs at *www.google.com/google-d-s/tour1.html*. Then sign in to your Google account and create a word processing document describing your school. Next, invite other classmates (collaborators) to join in and to edit and view your document. Print a copy of the final report and submit it to your instructor.

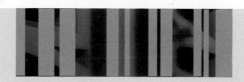

LESSON 6

Operating Systems and Software

■ OBJECTIVES

Upon completion of this lesson, you should be able to:

■ Distinguish between software and hardware.

■ Describe the difference between applications software and system software.

■ Describe the three categories of system programs.

■ Describe operating systems for microcomputers.

■ Describe network operating systems.

Over the last 50 years, computer technology has changed the world. Thirty or so years ago, only a few workers would have used computers. Customers would not have had ID cards that could be scanned. Accounting was done using ledgers. Online banking was not available. And, the Internet and World Wide Web did not exist. Computers have changed our society drastically.

When most of us think about computers, we think of hardware and how the hardware has changed—that computers have become smaller and faster. If we look at the history of computers, however, we find that the early computers were little more than high-speed calculators. This alone would not have had such a major influence on our culture and economy. The reason that computers have had such an impact is through the vision and desire of software developers. These software creators came up with hundreds of ideas and ways in which to use computers. They created programs that affect us in every aspect of our lives.

■ VOCABULARY

applications software

basic input/output system (BIOS)

booting

graphical user interface (GUI)

language translator

Linux

Mac OS

MS-DOS

multitasking

network operating system (NOS)

operating system (OS)

system software

UNIX

user interface

utility program

Windows

Windows Embedded CE

Windows Mobile

. . .

Hardware and Software

You probably have heard the words *software* and *hardware* many times. Sometimes it is difficult to distinguish between these two terms. As was discussed in Lesson 1, hardware refers to the tangible, physical computer equipment that can be seen and touched. This includes objects such as the keyboard, mouse, monitor, printer, chips, disks, disk drives, and DVD/CD recorders. Software is a set of instructions issued to the computer so that specific tasks are performed. You cannot touch software because it has no substance. Another word for software is *program*.

For example, a computer programmer might write a program that lets the user download music from the Internet. Or suppose a bookkeeper has a problem with his computer. You might hear him say, "The problem lies in the software," or "it's a software problem." This means there is a problem with the program or data, and not with the computer or hardware itself. A good analogy is a book. The book, including the pages and the ink, is the hardware. The words and ideas on the pages are the software. One has little value without the other. The same is true of computer software and hardware.

Types of Software

The computer uses two basic types of software: applications software and system software. Applications software helps you perform a specific task. System software refers to the operating system and the utility programs that manage computer resources at a low level. Figuratively speaking, applications software sits on top of system software. Without the operating system and system utilities, the computer cannot run any applications program.

Applications Software

Applications software often is referred to as productivity software. Applications software is designed for an end user. Some of the more commonly used application programs are word processors, database systems, presentations, spreadsheets, and desktop publishing programs. Some other applications categories are as follows:

- *Education, home, and personal software*—reference, entertainment, personal finance, calendars, e-mail, and browsers
- *Multimedia software*—authoring, animation, music, video and sound capturing and editing, virtual reality, and Web site development
- *Workgroup computing software*—calendars and scheduling, e-mail, browsers, electronic conferencing, and project management

Applications software is covered in detail in Lessons 9 through 13.

System Software

System software is a group of programs that coordinate and control the resources and operations of a computer system. System software enables the many components of the computer system to communicate and is made up of three categories: operating systems, utilities, and language translators.

Operating Systems

An *operating system (OS)* provides an interface between the user or application program and the computer hardware. See **Figure 6–1**. Several brands and versions of operating system software exist. Each of these is designed to work with one or more particular processors. For example, an operating system such as Windows is designed to work with a processor made by Intel or Advanced Micro Devices (AMD). Many IBM PC-compatible computers contain this brand of processor. Most Macintosh computers contain a processor manufactured by Motorola. Generally, the Windows operating system does not work with this Motorola processor. Recently, however, Microsoft and Apple have released operating systems for use on both types of processors.

▶ **VOCABULARY**
operating system (OS)
utility program

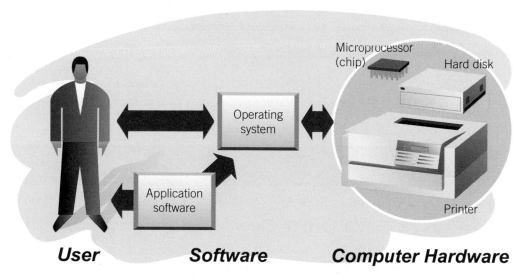

User   Software   Computer Hardware

FIGURE 6–1 Operating system: an interface between users and computers

Utilities

Utility programs help you perform housekeeping chores. You use these programs to complete specialized tasks related to managing the computer's resources, files, and so on. Some utility programs are part of the operating system, and others are self-contained programs. Some examples of utility program functions are as follows:

- You format a disk—a disk formatting utility provides the instructions to the computer on how to do this.

- You copy a file from the hard drive to a USB drive—the file management utility provides the instructions to the computer.

- You back up the hard drive—a backup utility provides the instructions to the computer.

- You want to consolidate fragmented files—a defragmentation utility provides the instructions to the computer. See **Figure 6–2**.

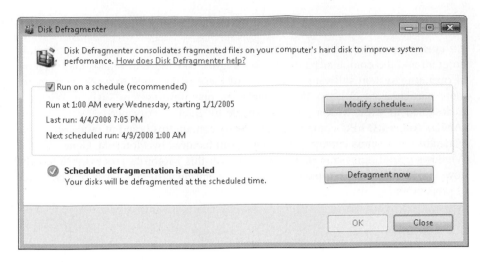

FIGURE 6–2   Disk Defragmenter utility

See **Table 6–1** for a list of the more commonly used utilities and their purpose.

TABLE 6–1   Utility programs

TYPE OF UTILITY	PURPOSE
Backup	Makes a duplicate copy of the contents of a secondary storage device
Built-in diagnostic	Provides detailed information about the computer system and attempts to locate problems
Disk compression	Frees storage space on a disk by compressing the existing files
Disk defragmentation	Attempts to place the segments of each file on the hard disk as close to one another as possible
File conversion	Converts a file from one format to another
File manager	Allows the user to perform tasks such as copying, moving, and deleting files
File recovery	Attempts to recover a file that has been deleted
Firewall	Protects the computer system from viruses such as worms, and from other threats such as Trojan horses, spyware, and so on
Search	Helps to locate files quickly
Uninstaller	Removes an application that is no longer needed

Some of the previously listed utilities are incorporated into the operating system. Other utility programs, such as antivirus programs, also are sold as stand-alone programs.

Language Translators

Language translators convert English-like software programs into machine language that the computer can understand. For instance, a company hires a programmer to write a software program to inventory all of the items in the store. The programmer writes the program statements using a high-level programming language such as Microsoft Visual Basic. A program statement directs the computer to perform a specified action.

The computer, however, cannot read the Visual Basic programming statements because they are written in a language that we understand. This is where the language translator takes over. The translator changes each of the Visual Basic programming statements into machine language. A single statement in a high-level language can represent several machine-language instructions. Now the statements can be executed and the company's inventory can be processed.

Microcomputer Operating Systems

All computers, big and small, have operating systems. For most of us, however, the computer we most often use is a microcomputer. Our primary focus in this lesson is on microcomputer operating systems. Users interact with the computer through the user interface.

The *user interface* is the part of the operating system with which we are most familiar. This is the part of the operating system with which we interact when using our computer. Two types of user interfaces are command-line interfaces and graphical interfaces.

Several popular operating systems are available for microcomputers. If you are using a Macintosh, you most likely will be using a version of the Mac OS.

If your computer is what is commonly referred to as a PC, you most likely are using one of these three operating systems:

- DOS
- A combination of DOS and Windows
- A stand-alone version of Windows

Command-Line Interfaces

All early computers used command-line interfaces instead of a graphical interface such as Windows. With this type of interface, you must type the exact command you want to execute. One of the most widely used command-line interfaces for microcomputers is MS-DOS.

DOS

IBM introduced its first IBM PC in 1981. With the introduction of this new microcomputer came a new operating system. This system was called DOS (Disk Operating System). IBM referred to this operating system as *PC-DOS*. They licensed this software from a small start-up company called Microsoft. But as agreements go, Microsoft retained the rights to market its own version of the OS. Microsoft called their version *MS-DOS*. This OS was the catalyst that launched Microsoft into the multibillion-dollar company it is today.

DOS is a character-based operating system. The user interacts with the system by typing commands. DOS is a single-user or single-tasking operating system because the user can run only one program at a time. DOS still is accessible in all Windows OS versions.

EXTRA FOR EXPERTS

If you have a computer, you should have an emergency boot disk. Sooner or later, your computer might not boot from the hard drive. You can use your emergency boot disk to get your computer started. Each operating system has its own way of creating a boot disk. Check your operating system help files for information on how to create this disk. Then be sure to store it in an easy-to-find and safe place.

▶ **VOCABULARY**

language translators

user interface

PC-DOS

MS-DOS

Using DOS, suppose you want to look at a list of files on your computer's hard drive. You type the DOS command *dir* and press Enter. In **Figure 6–3**, the *Ping* command is used. This command is used to determine Web site addresses as well as to determine and assist in resolving network issues.

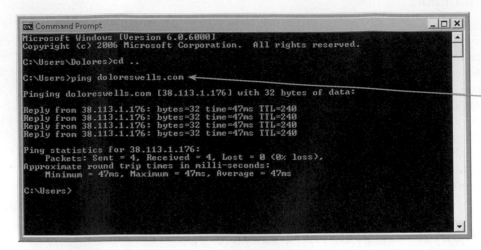

Ping command used to determine Web site address

FIGURE 6–3   Command-line interface showing an example of the Ping command

This type of interface is not considered very user friendly. You must memorize the commands and type them without any spelling errors. Otherwise, they do not work.

It is occasionally helpful to know some DOS commands. For instance, suppose you are trying to delete a file that is responsible for a computer virus. If you are using Windows, after the file loads into the computer's memory, it is difficult, if not impossible, to delete it. You can, however, load DOS and delete the file. To see a list of DOS commands, open a Command Prompt window, and then type Help at the command prompt.

TECHNOLOGY CAREERS

Software Developer

A software developer maintains and helps develop new applications and operating system programs. When you see a job listing for software developer, it could include many requirements.

A company might be looking for someone to develop software using a particular programming language such as Java, Visual Basic, C, or C++. Or a company might be looking for someone to develop add-ons to operating system programs. This could include enhancements to utility programs, updates to language translators, or new additions to the operating system itself. Many companies seek employees with skills in operating system programs such as UNIX and Windows.

If you look for software developer jobs online, you will find that many of them refer to Oracle, a large information technology software company. Oracle products support database technology, data design and modeling, Web applications, and much more.

Salaries and educational requirements for software developers vary. Salaries can range from $25,000 to $100,000 plus. Educational requirements range from some college to a bachelor's or master's degree or maybe even a Ph.D. Generally, but not always, the more education you have, the higher the starting salary. Most companies require some experience, but a few have entry-level positions.

To open a Command Prompt window:

1. Click the Start button.

2. Type Command Prompt in the search box.

3. Click Command Prompt in the list of results.

Graphical User Interfaces

As microcomputer technology developed, so did the operating system interface. *Menus* represented the next step in this progression. The user could choose commands from a list.

The big breakthrough in ease of use came with the development of *graphical user interfaces (GUIs)*. When the user turns on the computer and starts the operating system, a symbolic desktop is displayed. On this desktop are various objects, or icons. These graphical symbols represent files, disks, programs, and other objects. GUIs permit the user to manipulate these on-screen icons. Most people use a pointing device such as a mouse to click the icons and execute the commands. **Figure 6–4** shows an example of the Windows Vista graphical user interface.

VOCABULARY

graphical user interfaces (GUIs)

Mac OS

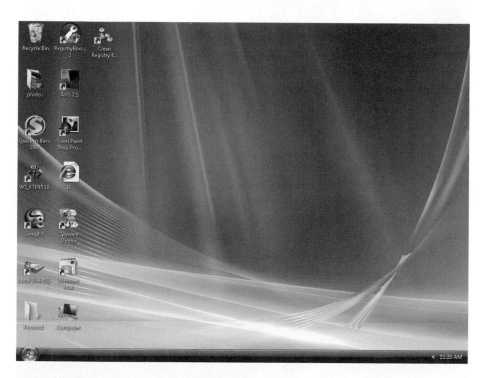

FIGURE 6–4 Graphical user interface

Mac OS

Macintosh's operating system, the *Mac OS*, is used with Apple's Macintosh computers. The Macintosh was introduced in 1984. One of the main features of this new computer was a GUI. The GUI was called the Finder and contained icons or symbols that represented documents, software, disks, and so forth. To activate the icon, the user clicked it with a mouse. This operating system also was the first OS to provide on-screen help or instructions. In 2005, Macintosh released OS X Tiger, with over 200 new features. The most recent release is the Mac OS X version 10.5 Leopard, which was released in October 2007. See **Figure 6–5**.

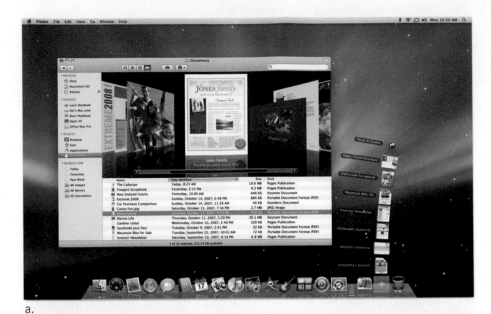

a.

b.

FIGURE 6–5 (a) Desktop (b) Macintosh widgets

Windows

In response to the competition from the Macintosh, Microsoft introduced its own GUI. This OS was called *Windows*. Following is an overview of Windows history, from the first version through the most recent version.

- Microsoft first began development of the Interface Manager, subsequently called Windows, in 1981. On November 10, 1983, Microsoft announced Windows as an extension of the MS-DOS operating system that would provide a graphical operating environment for PC users.

- The first versions of Windows (versions 1 and 2) contained a graphical shell and were called *operating environments* because they worked in combination with DOS. The different applications installed on a computer appeared as icons. The user activated the icons by clicking them with a mouse.

- The versions of Windows following the first two versions were consecutively numbered beginning with Windows 3.0, Windows 3.1, and so on.

Windows 95 was Microsoft's first true multitasking operating system. *Multitasking* allows a single user to work on two or more applications that reside in memory at the same time. Some advantages of Windows 95 included the following:

▶ **VOCABULARY**
multitasking

- The graphical interface was improved.

- Programs ran faster than with earlier Windows versions.

- The software included support for networking, which allowed a group of two or more computers to be linked.

- It used Plug and Play technology, the goal of which is just to plug in a new device and immediately be able to use it, without complicated setup maneuvers.

Windows 98 was released in June of 1998. Integrated Web browsing and the Active Desktop provided a browser-like interface. Windows 98 was easier to use than Windows 95 and had some additional features, such as Internet integration, a Web browser-look option for Windows Explorer, faster system startup and shutdown, and support for the Universal Serial Bus.

Windows 2000 was an update to the Windows 98 and Windows NT operating systems. Windows NT was Microsoft's platform for high-end systems. It was intended for use on network servers, workstations, and software development machines.

Windows XP, which provided increased stability and improved device recognition, followed Windows 2000 in 2001. As in previous versions, this version included utilities to show how much space is available on a storage media device and an error-checking program. Windows XP was designed to work with more than 12,000 hardware devices.

Microsoft's newest operating system is called Windows Vista. This new version is available in five editions:

- *Home Basic*—This edition is ideal for basic computing needs, is easy to set up and maintain, and provides a secure environment.

- *Home Premium*—This is the preferred edition for home desktop and mobile PCs; it includes Windows Media Center and a new level of security and reliability.

- *Ultimate*—This edition offers all of the features found in Windows Vista Home Premium, plus security, data protection, and support for new mobility features.

- *Business*—This edition is designed specifically to meet the needs of small businesses.

- *Enterprise*—This edition is designed specially to meet the needs of large global organizations.

Some of Windows Vista's more popular new and updated features are as follows:

- Built-in accessibility settings help people with visual difficulties, hearing loss, and pain in their hands or arms.
- Clicking the Power button on the Start menu initiates the Fast Sleep and Resume feature, which saves your current session to memory and then goes into a low power state; to return to your session, just press the hardware power button on your PC.
- Live icons display a thumbnail image of the actual contents of every file, making it easier to select a given item.
- Windows updating is faster and easier and occurs in the background. Windows Update can determine which updates are necessary for your computer. If your computer contains the correct settings, the updates are downloaded and installed.
- Windows Firewall can protect your computer from many types of viruses. The firewall automatically is turned on when Vista is installed.

Vista requires two gigabytes of hard drive space to install and is designed to work with more than 12,000 hardware devices. Many older computers, however, do not have the hardware to support Vista.

Even though the Windows versions have changed, some features remain consistent, such as the Start menu, taskbar, and desktop.

In Step-by-Step 6.1, you have an opportunity to examine some Windows Vista features and commands relating to defragmentation of a drive. Defragmentation generally is used with hard drives and can improve the drive performance by rearranging the order of the files so that each file is represented in a physically continuous segment. You can use these same steps to examine any storage media device, including the computer's hard drive.

Step-by-Step 6.1

1. Insert your USB drive into a USB port on your computer. Click the **Start** button 🏵 and then click **Computer**. The Computer window is displayed. See **Figure 6–6**. Your window, most likely, will display different drives.

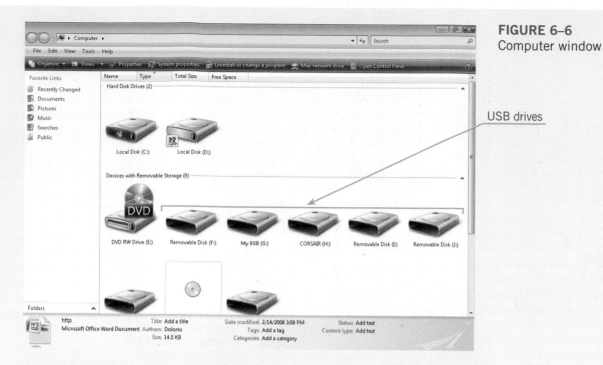

FIGURE 6–6
Computer window

2. Right-click your **USB drive** to display its shortcut menu and then point to **Properties**. See **Figure 6–7**. Most likely the menu options on your shortcut menu will be different from those in **Figure 6–7**.

FIGURE 6–7
Shortcut menu for a USB drive

3. Click **Properties** to open the Properties dialog box for the removable disk, and then click the **General** tab, if necessary. See **Figure 6–8**. What is the drive capacity? How much space has been used and how much free space is available?

FIGURE 6–8
Removable Disk (H:) Properties
dialog box

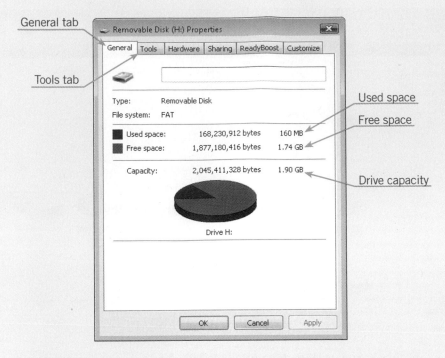

General tab

Tools tab

Used space

Free space

Drive capacity

4. Click the **Tools** tab to display three buttons: Check Now, Defragment Now, and Backup Now. See **Figure 6–9**. If instructed to do so, click the **Check Now** button, click the **Continue** button if asked for permission to continue, make sure only the "Automatically fix file system errors" check box is selected, and then click the **Start** button to let Windows Vista check your disk for errors, if possible. When Windows Vista is finished, close any dialog boxes related to the disk check, click the **Defragment Now** button in the Properties dialog box for your USB flash drive, click the **Continue** button if asked for permission to continue, read the information in the Disk Defragmenter dialog box, and then click the **Close** button.

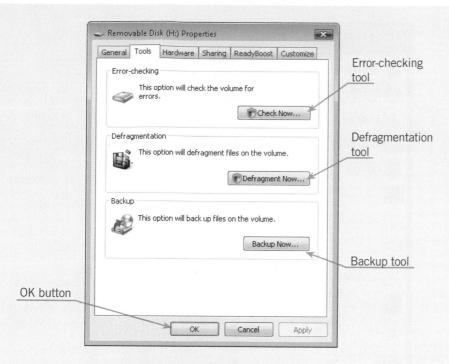

FIGURE 6–9
Tools tab

5. Click the **OK** button to return to the Computer window and then close the window.

When turning off your computer, be sure to follow the proper procedure. If Windows Vista is not shut down correctly, when you restart the computer, you may encounter error messages or the system might not start at all.

One of the fastest and easiest ways to turn off the computer is to click the Start button and then click the Power button in the lower-right corner of the Start menu. Using this method saves your data, keeps your computer more secure, and saves energy. Also, the computer will start quickly the next time you use it. To restart your computer, press the power button, press the Spacebar, or click the mouse. Windows quickly restarts.

Step-by-Step 6.2 gives you practice using the Power button on the Start menu.

Step-by-Step 6.2

1. If necessary, start your computer and open one or two programs, such as your word processing program and your e-mail program.

2. Click the **Start** button ⊕ and then click the **Power** button [⏻]. See **Figure 6–10**. The monitor turns off and the computer fan stops. Generally a light on your computer case turns yellow or blinks. This indicates the computer is in sleep mode.

FIGURE 6-10
Power button on the Start menu

3. Now move the mouse, press the **Spacebar**, or press the computer's power button. The computer quickly restarts and returns to its previous state.

In addition to using the Power button on the Start menu to turn off the computer, Windows Vista provides four other shutdown options. See **Figure 6–11**. Pressing the Lock arrow button displays this menu.

FIGURE 6-11   Shut down options

- *Restart*—This option closes all programs and all open windows, logs off any users, and powers down the computer. Then the computer restarts and Windows Vista reloads. Any programs that were opened previously do not reopen.

- *Sleep*—Sleep is a power-saving option and works the same as the Power button.

- *Hibernate*—Also a power-saving option; when Hibernate is selected, your work is saved on disk and the computer is turned off. When the computer is turned on, your desktop is restored to its previous state.

- *Shut Down*—Shut Down closes all programs, logs off the user, and then turns off the power.

Note the three other options in **Figure 6–11**: Switch User, Log Off, and Lock. The Switch User option primarily is used for guest accounts. Logging off closes all your open programs, but does not turn off the computer. Log Off usually is used when more than one user has access to the same system.

Embedded Operating Systems

An *embedded operating system* includes technologies and tools that enable developers to create a broad range of devices. This operating system, which resides on a ROM chip, is used on small handheld computers and wireless communication devices. Several embedded operating systems exist, but three of the more popular are as follows:

- *Windows Embedded CE* (Consumer Electronics) is a scaled-down Windows operating system, designed for including or embedding in service-oriented devices such as bar-code scanners, digital picture frames, fuel pumps, and global positioning devices.

- *Windows Mobile* works on most types of PDAs such as Pocket PC and smartphones. Both types of devices enable the user to store and retrieve e-mail, contacts, and appointments, play multimedia files and games, exchange text messages, browse the Web, and more. In addition, the user can exchange and synchronize information with a desktop computer. See **Figure 6–12**.

> **VOCABULARY**
> **embedded operating system**
> **Windows Embedded CE**
> **Windows Mobile**

FIGURE 6–12   Smartphone with Windows Mobile

■ *Palm OS* is a competing operating system with Windows Mobile and runs on Palm handhelds and other third-party devices. Some of the more common built-in applications include an address book, calculator, datebook/calendar, expense list, memo and notepad, to-do list, and the capability to hot sync or integrate with the user's PC.

UNIX

Still another operating system is *UNIX*. This operating system frequently is used by scientists and programmers. UNIX was developed by a group of programmers for AT&T, and is considered a multitasking, portable operating system. This means it can run on just about any hardware platform. Some versions of UNIX have a command-line interface similar to DOS, but most versions provide a graphical user interface such as that shown in **Figure 6–13**. There are several variants of the language, such as *Linux* and IBM's AIX.

FIGURE 6–13   Linux desktop

Both the IBM AIX system and Linux are based on UNIX. Linux, however, is an open source program that is free and one that programmers and developers can use or modify as they like. Linux has a reputation of being stable and rarely crashing. One Linux user interface is called GNOME (pronounced gah-NOHM) and allows the user to select a desktop similar to Windows or Macintosh. GNOME also includes software applications such as word processing, spreadsheet, database, presentation, e-mail, and a Web browser. Even with these included applications, however, the number of available application programs is far fewer than those for Windows or the Mac OS.

Loading the Operating System

Booting is the process of starting a computer. When you start your computer, operating system commands are loaded into memory. Each operating system boots or starts the computer in its own way. Understanding the boot process is the key to diagnosing many computer startup problems.

The steps in this example are based on the Windows operating system. Keep in mind, however, that the boot process is similar for all operating systems.

1. Turn on your computer. The first thing that happens is that the *basic input/output system (BIOS)* is activated. Next is POST, an acronym for Power-on Self Test. This is a series of diagnostic tests to check RAM and to verify that the keyboard, disk drives, and other devices you have are physically connected to the computer.

2. Next, the BIOS searches for the boot record—sometimes first on drive A, then on drive C or the CD drive. The BIOS is built-in software that normally is placed on a ROM chip. It contains all of the code that controls the most common devices connected to your computer. This includes the monitor, keyboard, disk drives, and other components. This chip comes with your computer when you purchase it.

3. Now the boot record is loaded into RAM. The boot record contains several files. These files contain programming configuration instructions for hardware devices and software applications that are installed on your computer.

4. Software drivers are the next thing loaded. Drivers are what enable you to use your printer, modem, scanner, or other devices. Generally, when you add a new device to your system, you install drivers for that device.

5. After the software drivers are loaded, the GUI is loaded. In this instance, the GUI is Windows. When loading the GUI, the operating system reads the commands for your desktop configuration. It also loads whatever programs you previously have specified in the Windows Startup folder.

6. If everything goes as it should, the GUI appears and the computer is ready to use.

EXTRA FOR EXPERTS

Sometimes Windows does not boot properly. Instead, a dialog box indicating that you are in safe mode is displayed on the screen. This means that something did not function properly during the boot process. Safe mode provides functionality so you or an expert user can do diagnostic testing.

Sharing Files on Different Operating Systems

In many business and educational settings, it is necessary to share files across operating system platforms. A business might have workers using both Macintosh and Windows computers, depending on the task: often artists and designers use Macintosh computers, while accountants and writers might have PCs. In the classroom, all of the computers might be the same type, but students might have different kinds of computers at home for doing homework. These situations require the ability to read disks and share files created on different operating systems. It might even be necessary to run programs on one system that were written only for another system. Hardware and software solutions are available for these problems.

One type of hardware solution is an emulation card that is added to the motherboard of the computer. These cards provide the ability for the computer to run a program that was designed for a different operating system. For example, a card can be added to a Macintosh that will allow it to run Windows programs. Software emulation programs also are available to provide this capability for some programs.

Macintosh computers have software installed that allows them to read disks that were formatted on PCs. Additional software finds a compatible program to run a PC file after the user double-clicks the file's icon.

Another solution to the file-sharing issue is to save files in a format that is readable on different operating systems. One example for word processing documents is the basic text format (.txt). This format usually is readable by most word-processing programs on different systems. However, documents saved as .txt do not retain complicated formatting. Another text format, called Rich Text Format (.rtf), does retain more formatting commands, such as paragraph breaks, fonts, and styles such as bold and italic. To save a file in Rich Text Format, you use the Save As command in your word processing program and select Rich Text Format as the file type.

Network Operating Systems

> VOCABULARY
network operating system (NOS)

Networks require a multiuser operating system because many users access the server at one time. All networks have some type of network server that manages resources. A *network operating system* (*NOS*) resides on a network server and is designed specifically to support a network. See **Figure 6–14**. The NOS program allows a group of computers (also called clients) to be connected and to share resources. One of the main goals of the operating system is to make the resources appear as though they are running from the client computer. Several brands of network operating systems exist. Examples of network operating systems include Windows Server 2008, Novell NetWare, UNIX, and Linux. Networks are discussed in detail in Lesson 7.

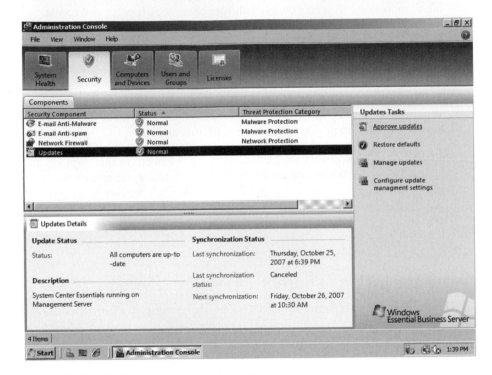

FIGURE 6–14   Network operating system

ETHICS IN TECHNOLOGY

What Is Computer Ethics?

Ethics is the branch of philosophy concerned with evaluating human action, and a system or code of morals of a particular religion, group, or profession.

Ethical judgments are no different in the area of computing than they are in any other area. The use of computers can raise many issues of privacy, copyright, theft, and power, to name just a few. In 1990, the Institute of Electrical and Electronics Engineers created a code of ethics. Many businesses and organizations have adopted this code as their code. Remember that this is just a code—not a law. People choose to follow it voluntarily. You can view this code by visiting *www.ieee.org* and searching for "code of ethics."

SUMMARY

In this lesson, you learned:

- Hardware refers to the tangible, physical computer equipment that can be seen and touched.

- Software is a set of instructions that tells the computer what to do; software also is called a program.

- The two basic types of computer software are applications software and system software.

- Applications software also is known as productivity software.

- System software coordinates and controls the resources and operations of a computer system.

- Three major categories of system software are operating systems, utilities, and language translators.

- Operating systems provide an interface between the user and application program and the computer hardware.

- Utility programs help users complete specialized tasks such as file management.

- Language translators convert English-like software programs into machine language.

- A programmer uses a programming language to write program statements.

- All computers have operating systems.

- The user interface is the part of the operating system with which we are most familiar.

- The two most common user interfaces are command-line interfaces and graphical user interfaces.

- The Mac operating system is used with Apple's Macintosh computers.

- Icons are symbols that represent documents, software programs, disks, and so forth.

- DOS was introduced with the IBM PC in 1981 and is a character-based operating system.

- Microsoft introduced the first version of Windows in 1983; this was an operating environment.

- Windows 95 was Microsoft's first true multitasking operating system.

- Windows Embedded CE is a scaled-down Windows operating system used for small handheld computers.

- UNIX and Linux are portable operating systems.

- Network operating systems allow a group of two or more microcomputers to be connected.

- Several methods are available for sharing files on different operating systems.

■ VOCABULARY REVIEW

Define the following terms:

applications software	MS-DOS	user interface
basic input/output system (BIOS) booting	multitasking	utility program
graphical user interfaces (GUIs)	network operating system (NOS)	Windows
language translators	operating system (OS)	Windows Embedded CE
Linux	system software	Windows Mobile
Mac OS	UNIX	

■ REVIEW QUESTIONS

MULTIPLE CHOICE

Select the best response for the following statements.

1. Which is another word for software?

   A. hardware

   B. program

   C. programming statement

   D. interface

2. Which are the two basic types of computer software?

   A. program, applications

   B. productivity, applications

   C. applications, systems

   D. systems, networking systems

3. A group of programs that coordinate and control the resources of a computer system is called _____.

    A.   system software
    C.   language translator

    B.   applications software
    D.   utility program

4. The part of the operating system with which we are most familiar is the _____.

    A.   formatting utility
    C.   language translator

    B.   programming statement
    D.   user interface

5. DOS was first introduced with the _____.

    A.   Apple Macintosh
    C.   UNIX operating system

    B.   IBM PC
    D.   Windows operating system

TRUE/FALSE

Circle T if the statement is true or F if the statement is false.

T   F   **1.**   The first version of Windows was a true operating system.

T   F   **2.**   The computer cannot run any applications without an operating system.

T   F   **3.**   Apple Computer developed the first GUI for a PC.

T   F   **4.**   Computer software is anything you can touch.

T   F   **5.**   When you turn on a computer, the boot record loads into ROM.

FILL IN THE BLANK

Complete the following sentences by writing the correct word or words in the blanks provided.

1. An embedded operating system resides on a(n) _____ chip.

2. A spreadsheet program is an example of _____ software.

3. The _____ operating system is an open-source program.

4. Windows Mobile is a type of _____ operating system.

5. DOS is a(n) _____ -user operating system.

■ PROJECTS

CROSS-CURRICULAR— MATHEMATICS

Windows Disk Cleanup utility helps you free space on your computer by deleting unnecessary files. Use Windows Help and Support and research this utility program. Explain the purpose of this utility and provide an example of how you would access the program and then apply it.

CROSS-CURRICULAR—SCIENCE

Operating systems have come a long way in the last few years. They are much easier to use and support many more features. If you were going to design an operating system for computers for the year 2012, what features would you include? How would your operating system be different from those that are currently available?

Use your word-processing program to write a report or give an oral report to the class.

CROSS-CURRICULAR—SOCIAL STUDIES

The more recent versions of operating systems include accessibility options for people with visual or hearing disabilities. Research the operating system on your computer, list the accessibility options, and then include a description of each item.

CROSS-CURRICULAR—LANGUAGE ARTS

You have been hired to create an icon to represent a new software program that has just been developed. This is an interactive encyclopedia. It also contains games to help reinforce the topics presented in the encyclopedia. Think about the icons on your computer's desktop or that you see in the figures throughout this lesson. Using graph paper or a computer drawing program, create an icon for this new interactive encyclopedia.

WEB PROJECT

Access the Web site *www.howstuffworks.com* and then type "setting up a wireless network" in the Search HowStuffWorks text box. Provide an overview of how you would set up a home-based network. Explain why a wireless network is an easier and less-expensive way to create a home network. What negatives are involved with a wireless network?

TEAMWORK PROJECT

You and two team members have been given the responsibility for purchasing new computers for your company's front office. One team member wants to purchase an Apple Macintosh with the latest version of the Mac OS and the latest software suite; another wants to purchase a PC with the latest version of the Windows OS; and the third wants to purchase a PC with the UNIX OS. The manager has requested that your team do some research and present her with a report so that she can make the best choice. Your report should include the positives and negatives for each of these operating systems.

CRITICAL THINKING

Assume you are a member of a team and your objective is to present three ideas on how the Windows Vista operating system can be improved. Provide a thorough explanation of why you think your ideas would make the operating system better and easier to use.

EXPLORING GOOGLE

Google Mobile provides several options that are designed especially for mobile devices such as Search, Maps, Gmail, News, and more. To view these options, go to *www.google.com/mobile*. Which mobile devices are listed? What are the popular Google items that are listed on this Web site? Next, click the All Products link. List and describe at least three different items that you would like to access through your mobile phone. How would you access any of these mobile options?

LESSON 7

Networks

■ OBJECTIVES

Upon completion of this lesson, you should be able to:

- Describe the benefits and disadvantages of networks.
- List and describe the types of networks.
- List and describe communications hardware.
- List and describe communications media.
- Describe the different network topologies.
- Describe network architecture and protocols.

Telephony, which is the technology associated with the electronic transmission of voice, fax, or other information between distant parties, is nothing new. Early forays into telephony such as the telegraph and telephone have evolved into more complicated devices; now a computer can be networked to the Internet, another PC, or even a home stereo. In this lesson, we look at how networks function and the components necessary to make them function.

Network Building Blocks

When most people think of networks, they envision something fairly complicated. At the lowest level, networks are not that complex. In fact a network, as discussed in Lesson 1, is simply a group of two or more computers linked together. As the size of a network increases and more devices are added, installation of devices and management of the network do become more technical. Even so, networking concepts and terminology basically remain the same regardless of size.

■ VOCABULARY

baseband
broadband
bus topology
client/server network
client
communications channel
data communications
Ethernet
local area network (LAN)
modem
peer-to-peer network
ring topology
router
server
star topology
token ring
topology
transmission media
wide area network (WAN)
...

UNIT I **Computer Basics**

Most organizations today rely on computers and the data stored on them. In addition, more people work and communicate from home. Many times, organizations and individuals find that they need to transmit data or communicate from one location to another. The transmission of data from one location to another is known as *data communications*. Communications devices are discussed in detail later in this chapter. Transmittal of data requires the following components, as shown in **Figure 7–1**:

- A sending device, which generally is a computer
- A communications device that converts the computer signal into signals supported by the communications channel
- A communications channel or path, such as telephone lines, fiber, or cable, over which the signals are sent
- A receiving device that accepts the incoming signal, which generally is a computer
- Communications software

▶ **VOCABULARY**
telephony

data communications

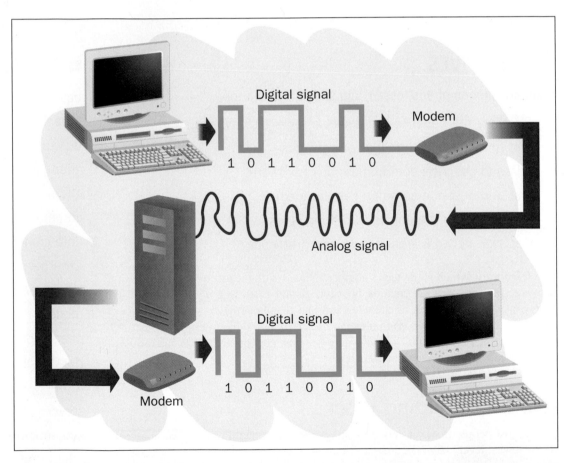

FIGURE 7–1 Communications components using dial-up modem and telephone lines

Network Benefits and Disadvantages

To consider the topic of network benefits, you first might think about the biggest network of all—the Internet. Consider some of the many changes that have occurred in our society because of the Internet. Perhaps the most profound of all of these changes is electronic mail. A network provides almost instant communication, and e-mail messages are delivered almost immediately. Other network benefits include the following:

- *Information sharing*: Authorized users can access computers on the network to share information and data. This could include special group projects and news groups, databases, blogs, fax, FTP, Internet telephony, instant messaging, and chat rooms. Many of these services are discussed in Chapter 2.

- *Hardware sharing*: It is not necessary to purchase a printer or a scanner or other frequently used peripherals for each computer. Instead, one device connected to a network can serve the needs of many users.

- *Software sharing*: Instead of purchasing and installing a software program on every single computer, it can be installed on the server. All of the users then can access the program from this one central location. This also saves money because companies can purchase a site license for the number of users. This is less expensive than purchasing individual software packages, and updating software on the server is much easier and more efficient than updating on individual computers.

- *Collaborative environment*: A shared environment enables users to work together on group projects by combining the power and capabilities of diverse equipment and software.

As with any technology, disadvantages also exist. For instance, data security—the vulnerability to unauthorized access—is a primary weakness with many networks. Hackers can access and steal or delete data. Some other disadvantages are as follows:

- *Malicious code*: Networks are more vulnerable than stand-alone computers to viruses, worms, Trojan horses, and spyware.

- *Network faults*: Network equipment problems can result in loss of data or resources.

- *Setup and management costs*: Setting up a network requires an investment in hardware and software; ongoing maintenance and management of the network requires the care and attention of an IT professional or professionals.

Network Types

As discussed in Lesson 1, a network is a group of two or more computer systems linked together via communications devices. Several types of networks exist, but the two most common types are local area networks (LANs) and wide area networks (WANs). Other types of networks are metropolitan area networks (MANs), personal area network (PANs), home area networks (HANs), and campus area networks (CANs).

Local Area Networks

Most *local area networks (LANs)* connect personal computers, workstations, and other devices such as printers and scanners in a limited geographical area, such as an office building, a school, or a home. Each device on the network is called a *node* and generally shares resources such as a printer, programs, and other hardware. A *wireless LAN (WLAN)* is similar to a LAN, but uses no physical wires. To communicate on a WLAN, the computer and other devices that access the WLAN must contain a wireless device such as a network card, flash card, PC Card, or a USB network adapter or some type of built-in wireless capability.

Wide Area Networks

A *wide area network (WAN)* covers a large geographical area. See **Figure 7–2**. This area might be as large as a state or a country or even the world. The largest WAN is the Internet. Most WANs consist of two or more LANs that are connected by routers. Communications channels can include telephone systems, fiber optics, satellites, microwaves, or any combination of these.

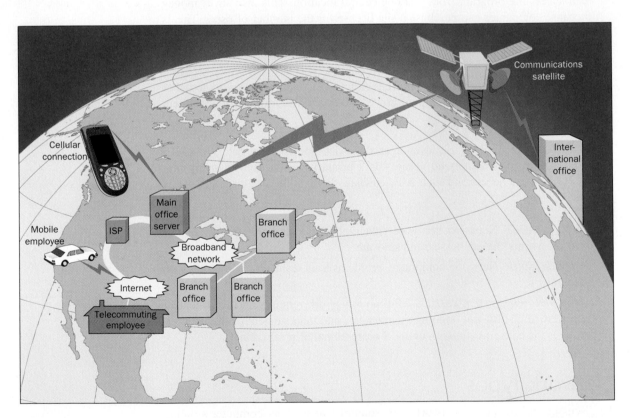

FIGURE 7–2   Wide area network

Two variations on a WAN are intranets and extranets. An intranet is designed for the exclusive use of people within an organization. Many businesses have implemented intranets within their own organizations. On such intranets, employees can access files such as handbooks and employee manuals, newsletters, and employment forms.

ETHICS IN TECHNOLOGY

Risks of Networked Computing

The security of a computer network is challenged every day by equipment malfunctions, system failures, computer hackers, and virus attacks.

Equipment malfunctions and system failures can be caused by a number of factors, including natural disasters such as floods or storms, fires, and electrical disturbances, such as a brownout or blackout. Server malfunctions or failures mean users lose temporary access to network resources, such as printers, drives, and information.

As mentioned in Chapter 2, computer hackers and viruses present a great risk to networked environments. Hackers are people who break into computer systems to steal services and information, such as credit card numbers, passwords, test data, and even national security information. Other people threaten networks and data by creating viruses and other malicious software, which are very dangerous to networked computers—they are usually designed to sabotage shared files.

An extranet is similar to an intranet, but it allows specified users outside the organization to access internal information systems. Like the Internet, intranets and extranets use and support Web technologies, such as hyperlinks and Web pages coded in hypertext markup language (HTML).

MANs, PANs, HANs, and CANs

Other types of networks have been developed to connect specific regions and users. The following list describes some of the more common networks:

- *Metropolitan area network (MAN)*: A MAN interconnects users with computer resources in a geographic area or region larger than that covered by a large local area network, but smaller than the area covered by a wide area network.

- *Personal area network (PAN)*: A PAN interconnects personal digital devices within a range of about 30 feet—generally in a small office. Wireless technologies such as Bluetooth (discussed later in this lesson) let the users wirelessly connect electronic devices including mobile phones, PCs, handheld devices, and printers.

- *Home area network (HAN)*: A HAN is contained within a user's home. This network connects digital devices such as computers, telephones, DVD players, televisions, video game players, security systems, smart appliances, and other such equipment.

- *Campus area network (CAN)*: A CAN is a collection of local area networks within a limited geographical space, such as a university campus or a military base. A CAN also is referred to as controller area networks and cluster area networks.

Network Architectures

The two popular types of LANs are client/server and peer-to-peer. The basic difference between the two is how the network is managed and where the data is stored.

▶ **VOCABULARY**

client/server network

server

client

peer-to-peer network

internet peer-to-peer

- ▪ *Client/server network*: In this type of architecture, one or more computers on the network act as a *server*. The server manages network resources. Depending on the size of the network, several different servers might be connected. For example, a print server manages the printing, and a database server manages a large database. In most instances, the server(s) is a high-speed computer with considerable storage space. The network operating system software and network versions of software applications are stored on the server. All of the other computers on the network are called *clients*. They share the server resources and other peripherals such as hubs, firewalls, and routers. Users access the server through a username and password. See **Figure 7–3**.

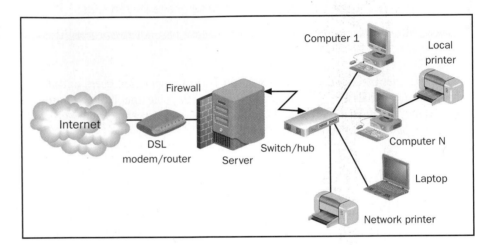

FIGURE 7–3   Client/server local area network

- ▪ *Peer-to-peer network*: In this type of network, all of the computers are equals. No computer is designated as the server. People on the network each determine what files on their computer they will share with others on the network. This type of network is much easier to set up and manage. Many small offices use peer-to-peer networks. See **Figure 7–4a**.

- ▪ *Internet peer-to-peer*: Also called P2P, this type of network is a variation of the peer-to-peer network. Users connect directly to each others' storage media and exchange files over the Internet. See **Figure 7–4b**.

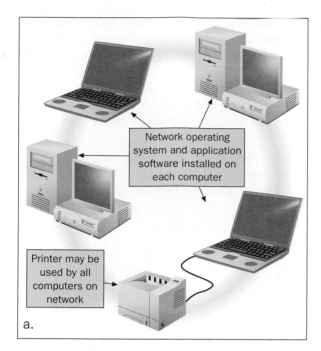

FIGURE 7–4   (a) Peer-to-peer network (b) Internet peer-to-peer network

Network Hardware

As indicated previously, the purpose of a network is to share hardware and software resources. Most networks consist of one or more network servers, client computers, a printer, and other peripheral devices. In addition to these hardware components, communications and transmission software also is required to accomplish the connections between the various devices.

Communications Devices

Communications devices facilitate the transmitting and receiving of data, instructions, and information. When we think about communications hardware, the first thing that generally comes to mind is the desktop computer and some type of modem. However, many other devices send and receive data. Some examples include large computers such as supercomputers, mainframe computers, and minicomputers; handheld and laptop computers; and even fax machines and digital cameras. The following list describes common communications devices:

- *Dial-up modem*: The word *modem* is an acronym for *modulate-demodulate*, which means to convert analog signals to digital and vice versa. A *dial-up modem* enables a computer to transmit data over analog telephone lines. Computer information is stored digitally, whereas information sent over telephone lines is transmitted in the form of analog waves. Both the sending and receiving users must have a modem. The sending modem converts the computer's digital signal into an analog signal, and the receiving modem converts the analog signal into a digital signal. See **Figure 7–5a**.

▶ **VOCABULARY**
communications device
modem
dial-up modem

> **VOCABULARY**

DSL (digital subscriber line) modem

ISDN (integrated services digital network) modem

cable modem

wireless modem

network interface card (NIC)

gateway

router

- *DSL and ISDN modems*: **DSL** (*digital subscriber line*) and **ISDN** (*integrated services digital network*) **modems** connect your computer to the Internet. These modems are designed to allow digital transmission of voice and data over ordinary telephone copper wires.

- *Cable modem*: A **cable modem** uses coaxial cable to send and receive data. This is the same type of cable used for cable TV. The bandwidth, which determines the amount of data that can be sent at one time, is much greater with a cable modem. See **Figure 7–5b**.

- *Wireless modem*: Many mobile devices such as notebook computers, smartphones, and PDAs contain a **wireless modem**. This type of modem contains a built-in antenna and is available as a flash card, a PC Card, or ExpressCard.

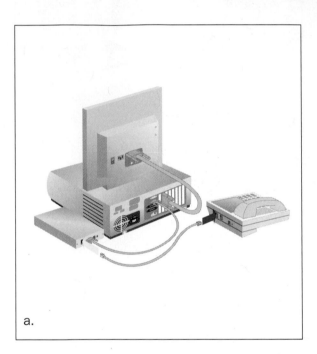

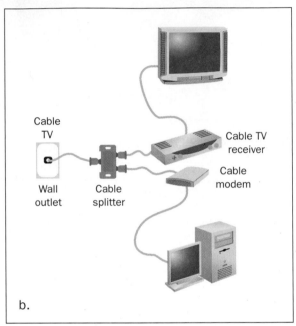

FIGURE 7–5 (a) Computer with dial-up modem attached (b) Computer with cable modem attached

- *Network interface card*: A **network interface card (NIC)** is an add-on card for either a desktop PC or a laptop computer. Each computer on a network must have a NIC. This card enables and controls the sending and receiving of data between the computers in a network. Most computers now come with a network interface built on the motherboard.

- *Gateway*: A **gateway** is a combination of software and hardware that links two different types of networks that use different protocols. For instance, gateways between electronic mail systems permit users on different systems to exchange messages.

- *Router*: A **router** is like a traffic policeman—this intelligent device directs network traffic. When you send data through a network, it is divided into small packets. All packets do not travel the same route; instead one might go in one direction and another in a different direction. When the packets reach their final destination, they are reassembled into the original message. A router connects multiple networks and determines the fastest available path to send these packets of data on their way to their correct destination. Just like our traffic policeman, in the event of a partial network failure, the router can redirect the traffic over alternate paths.

■ *Wireless access point*: A ***wireless access point*** (***WAP*** or ***AP***) is a device that connects wireless communications devices together to create a wireless network. See **Figure 7–6a**. The WAP generally is connected to a wired network and can relay data between devices on each side. Many WAPs can be connected together to create a larger network that allows roaming.

■ *Hub*: A ***hub*** is a place of convergence where data arrives from one or more directions and is forwarded in one or more other directions. A network hub connects multiple wired network devices. See **Figure 7–6b**.

a.

b.

FIGURE 7–6   (a) Wireless access point (b) Network hub

Communications Media

To transfer data from one computer to another requires some type of link through which the data can be transmitted. This link is known as the ***communications channel***. The worldwide telephone network is an important part of this channel. The telephone system is actually a collection of the world's telephone networks, including cellular, local, long-distance, and communications satellite networks. Although it originally was designed to handle voice communications, it is now used to transmit data, including fax transmissions, computer-to-computer communications such as e-mail, and live video from the Web. ***Bandwidth*** is the transmission capacity of a communications channel. High bandwidth media, such as cable, fiber, and DSL, generally are referred to as ***broadband***, whereas a standard telephone line generally is referred to as ***baseband***.

▶ VOCABULARY
wireless access point (WAP or AP)
hub
communications channel
bandwidth
broadband
baseband

At one end of the communications channel, you have a sending device, such as a computer or fax machine. A communications device, such as a modem, connected to the sending device converts the signal from the sender to a form that transmits over a standard dial-up telephone line or a dedicated line. A dial-up line provides a "temporary" connection, meaning each time a call is placed, the telephone company selects the line over which to transmit it. A dedicated line, on the other hand, provides a permanent or constant connection between the sending and receiving communications devices. The transmission is moved or "switched" from one wire or frequency to another. A *switch* is a device located at the telephone company's central office that establishes a link between a sender and receiver of data communications. At the receiving end, another modem converts the signal back into a format that the receiving device can understand.

To send the data through the channel requires some type of *transmission media*, which may be either physical or wireless.

Physical Media

Several types of physical media are used to transmit data. These include the following:

- *Twisted-pair cable* is the least expensive type of cable and is the same type used for many telephone systems. It consists of two independently insulated copper wires twisted around one another. One of the wires carries the signal and the other wire is grounded to absorb signal interference. See **Figure 7–7**.

> ▶ **VOCABULARY**
> switch
> transmission media
> twisted-pair cable

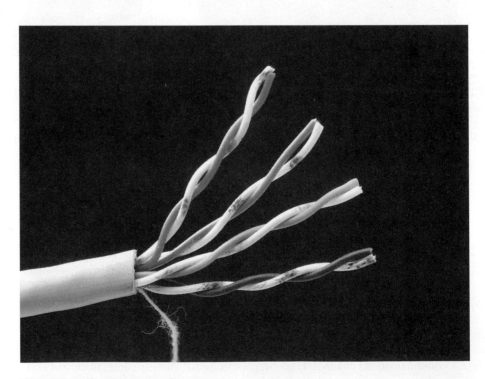

FIGURE 7–7   Twisted-pair cable

LESSON 7   Networks

153

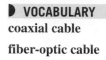
VOCABULARY
coaxial cable
fiber-optic cable

■ *Coaxial cable* is the primary type of cable used by the cable television industry, and it is also widely used for computer networks. Because the cable is heavily shielded, it is much less prone to interference than twisted-pair cable. However, it is more expensive than twisted-pair. See **Figure 7–8**.

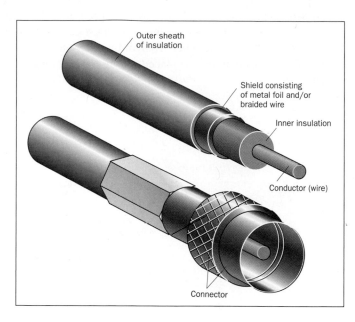

FIGURE 7–8   Coaxial cable

■ *Fiber-optic cable* is made from thin, flexible glass tubing. Fiber-optic cables have several advantages over traditional metal communications lines. The bandwidth is much greater, so it can carry more data; it is much lighter than metal wires; and is much less susceptible to interference. The main disadvantage of fiber optics is that it is fragile and expensive. See **Figure 7–9**.

FIGURE 7–9   Fiber-optic cable

Wireless Media

Just like physical media, several wireless options also are available. These include the following:

- *Microwaves*: **Microwave** signals are sent through space in the form of electromagnetic waves. Just like radio signals, they also must be sent in straight lines from one microwave station to another. To avoid interference, most microwave stations are built on mountaintops or placed on the top of large buildings. See **Figure 7–10**.

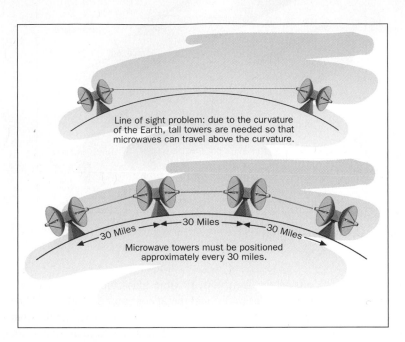

FIGURE 7–10   Microwave tower

- *Satellites*: Communication **satellites** are placed in orbit 22,300 feet above the surface of the Earth. This allows the satellite to maintain a constant position above one point on the Earth's surface by rotating at the same speed as the Earth. The satellite contains equipment that receives the transmission, amplifies it, and sends it back to Earth. See **Figure 7–11**.

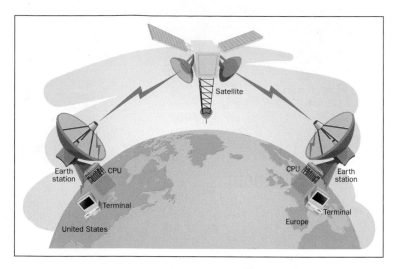

FIGURE 7–11   Satellites

■ *IrDA*: **IrDA** media (also called infrared transmission) send signals using infrared light waves. This type of transmission is used for communication over short distances where the sending and receiving devices are within the line of sight. For example, your television remote control uses infrared to send signals to your TV. Many mobile devices, such as notebook computers, include an infrared port (also called an IrDA port). External devices, such as IrDA keyboards and mice, can be purchased and connected to desktop computers.

■ *Bluetooth*: **Bluetooth** technology uses radio waves to connect mobile devices such as cell phones, PDAs, and notebook computers. See **Figure 7–12**. The radio receivers embedded into these devices are tiny microchips about a half-inch square. Bluetooth supports short-distance transmission—about 30 feet or less between the devices.

▶ **VOCABULARY**

IrDA

Bluetooth

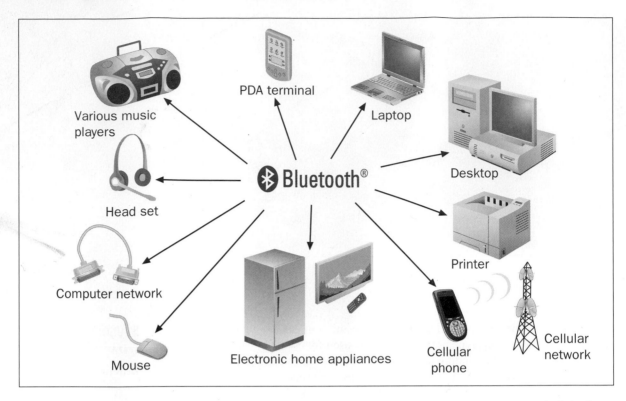

FIGURE 7–12   Short-distance transmission with Bluetooth-enabled devices

▶ **VOCABULARY**
Wi-Fi
WAP

- *Wi-Fi*: **Wi-Fi**, or wireless fidelity, identifies any network based on the 802.11 family of standards governing wireless transmissions. The standards have progressed from supporting transfer rates of 1 or 2 Mbps up to 54 Mbps and higher.

- *WAP*: **WAP** is short for Wireless Application Protocol. This protocol specifies how users access information instantly through mobile devices such as smartphones, pagers, two-way radios, and other wireless media.

The communications media an organization may select to use within a network are determined by several factors: the type of network, the size of the network, and the cost. A network is not limited to one type of media. Many networks include a mix of media types.

The Windows Vista operating system provides several informational screens on networking. You will explore these in Step-by-Step 7.1.

Step-by-Step 7.1

1. Click the **Start** button 🪟 on the Windows taskbar, and then click **Help and Support**. The Help and Support window opens, as shown in **Figure 7–13**. (Your Help and Support window may appear somewhat differently.)

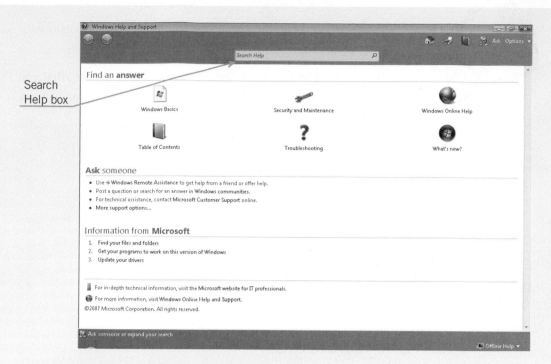

FIGURE 7–13
Windows Help and
Support window

Search
Help box

2.   Type **Networks** in the Search Help box and then press **Enter**.

3.   Point to the **Setting up a home network** link and then click the link. See
     Figure 7–14.

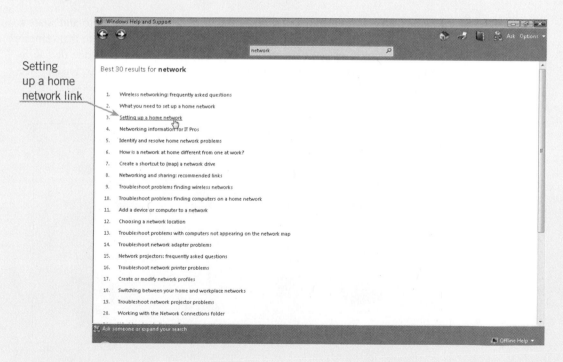

FIGURE 7–14
Search results for
network Help topics

Setting
up a home
network link

4. Read the information in the Help topic. On a sheet of paper or using your word-processing program, write a brief overview of what you learned.

5. Near the top of the Setting up a home network page, click the **What you need to set up a home network** link. Scroll to the bottom of the window and answer the following questions:

   a. What should be the first thing you decide before you begin to set up a home network?

   b. What are the three most common types of network technology?

   c. Assume you are going to set up a wireless network. What hardware would you need?

6. Close the Help and Support window.

Network Topologies

Networks can be designed using a variety of configurations. These configurations are referred to as topologies. A *topology* is simply the geometric arrangement of how a network is set up and connected. The following describes the three basic topologies:

■ *Bus topology*: Within the *bus topology*, all devices are connected to and share a master cable. This master cable is called the bus or backbone. There is no single host computer. Data can be transmitted in both directions, from one device to another. This type of network is relatively easy to install and inexpensive. See **Figure 7–15**.

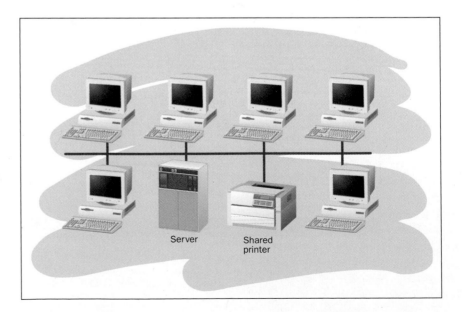

FIGURE 7–15   Bus topology

■ *Ring topology*: A ***ring topology*** is somewhat similar to a bus. However, the devices are connected in a circle instead of a line. Each computer within the circle is connected to adjoining devices on either side. Data travels from device to device around the ring. This type of topology is more difficult to install and manage and is more expensive. However, it does provide for faster transmission speeds and can span large distances. See **Figure 7–16**.

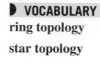

> **VOCABULARY**
> **ring topology**
> **star topology**

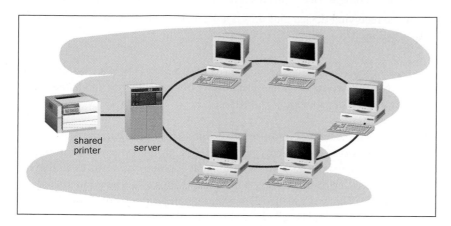

FIGURE 7–16   Ring topology

■ *Star topology*: Within a ***star topology***, all devices are connected to a central hub or computer. All data that transfers from one computer to another must pass through the hub. Star networks are relatively easy to install and manage, but bottlenecks can occur because all data must pass through the hub. This type of network requires more cabling than the other types. See **Figure 7–17**.

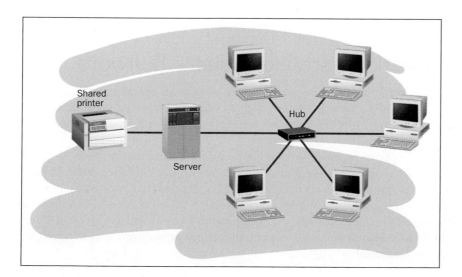

FIGURE 7–17   Star topology

These three topologies also can be mixed or combined to produce hybrid topologies.

Communications Protocols

A protocol is an agreed-upon set of rules and procedures for transmitting data between two or more devices. Some of the features determined by the protocol are as follows:

- How the sending device indicates it has finished sending the message
- How the receiving device indicates it has received the message
- The type of error checking to be used

Many protocols have been developed over the years. However, within networking and LANs, the two most widely used protocols are Ethernet and token ring. On the Internet, the major protocol is TCP/IP.

> **VOCABULARY**
> **Ethernet**
>
> **token ring**

- *Ethernet*: The ***Ethernet*** protocol was the first approved industry standard protocol. It is one of the most popular LAN protocols. Ethernet is based on the bus topology, but can work with the star topology as well. It supports data transfer rates of up to 10 megabits per second (Mbps). Two new Ethernet versions are available. The first is called Fast Ethernet and supports data transfer rates of 100 Mbps. The second is called Gigabit Ethernet and supports data transfer rates of 1000 megabits, or 1 gigabit, per second.
- *Token ring*: The second most widely used LAN protocol is called ***token ring***. Within this type of network, all of the computers are arranged in a circle. A token, which is a special signal, travels around the ring. To send a message, a computer on the ring catches the token, attaches a message to it, and then lets it continue to travel around the network.
- *TCP/IP*: TCP/IP is the acronym for Transmission Control Protocol/Internet Protocol. This protocol is used by both LANs and WANs and has been adopted as a standard to connect hosts on the Internet. Network operating systems, such as Microsoft Server and Novell Netware, support TCP/IP.

Network Operating Systems Software

All computers, including network servers, require an operating system. Network operating systems provide features such as administration, file management, print, communications, security, database, management, and other services to personal computer clients.

Two types of operating systems are necessary in computer networking. The first is the desktop operating system, such as Windows or Mac OS (discussed in Lesson 6). The second is the network operating system (also discussed in Lesson 6). Some desktop operating systems, such as Windows, UNIX, and the Mac OS, have built-in networking functions. These functions work adequately within a very limited environment. To use a network at its highest capacity, however, full-function network operating systems (NOS) software is required.

SUMMARY

In this lesson, you learned:

- Data communication is the transmission of data from one location to another.

- A network is a group of two or more computers linked together.

- The Internet is the biggest network of all.

- Networks have advantages and disadvantages.

- A local area network generally is confined to a limited geographical area.

- A wide area network is made up of several connected local area networks.

- The two popular types of LANs are the client/server network and peer-to-peer network.

- Other types of specialized networks include metropolitan area networks (MANs), personal area networks (PANs), home area networks (HANs), and campus area networks (CANs).

- You can use a network for information sharing, hardware sharing, software sharing, and as a collaborative environment.

- The link through which data is transmitted is the communications channel.

- Transmission media can be either physical or wireless.

- Physical media include twisted-pair cable, coaxial cable, and fiber-optic cable.

- Most networks consist of a network server and computer clients.

- Communications devices facilitate the transmitting and receiving of data, instructions, and information.

- Communications devices include dial-up and cable modems, DSL and ISDN modems, network interface cards, gateways, routers, wireless access points, and hubs.

- Network interface cards enable the sending and receiving of data between the PCs in a network.

- A router directs the Internet or network traffic.

- Wireless media includes microwaves, satellites, IrDA, Bluetooth, and Wi-Fi.

- Network topologies include bus, ring, and star.

- A protocol is an agreed-upon set of rules and procedures for transmitting data between two or more devices.

- The Ethernet protocol is one of the most popular LAN protocols. Token ring is the second most widely used LAN protocol.

- TCP/IP is a protocol used by both LANs and WANs to connect to the Internet.

- All computers on a network require an operating system, and networks require network operating systems.

■ VOCABULARY REVIEW

Define the following terms:

baseband	Ethernet	star topology
broadband	local area network (LAN)	token ring
bus topology	modem	topology
client/server network	peer-to-peer network	transmission media
client	ring topology	wide area network (WAN)
communications channel	router	
data communications	server	

■ REVIEW QUESTIONS

MULTIPLE CHOICE

Select the best response for the following statements.

1. A _____ is confined to a limited geographical area.

    A. wide area network   C. tiny area network

    B. local area network   D. star topology

2. What does the acronym LAN stand for?

   A. limited access network   C. local area network

   B. limited area network   D. local access network

3. A _____ changes analog signals to digital signals and digital signals to analog.

   A. satellite   C. NIC

   B. modem   D. bridge

4. _____ is an example of physical media.

   A. Twisted-pair cable   C. Bluetooth

   B. IrDA   D. Bus topology

5. Which of the following is *not* high bandwidth media?

   A. cable   C. telephone line

   B. fiber   D. DSL

TRUE / FALSE

Circle T if the statement is true or F if the statement is false.

T   F   **1.** A card that allows a computer to connect to a network is called a network interface card (NIC).

T   F   **2.** Information sharing is *not* a network benefit.

T   F   **3.** The 802.11 technology is a family of standards governing wireless transmission.

T   F   **4.** The least expensive type of physical communications media is fiber-optic cable.

T   F   **5.** A router directs network traffic.

FILL IN THE BLANK

Complete the following sentences by writing the correct word or words in the blanks provided.

1. _____ media sends signals using infrared light waves.

2. _____ cable is the primary type of cabling used by the cable television industry and is more expensive than twisted-pair cable.

3. A(n) _____ network covers a large geographical area.

4. In a(n) _____ network, all computers are equal.

5. The least expensive type of cable is _____ cable.

■ PROJECTS

CROSS-CURRICULAR— MATHEMATICS

Assume that you have two computers, a printer, and a scanner that you want to network. Create a report, including a table, listing the hardware and software you would need to purchase, including the cost. How much will your network cost? How will you connect to the Internet, and how much will that cost? List your total cost for the project.

CROSS-CURRICULAR—SCIENCE

Use the Internet and perform a Web search on Bluetooth technology. Find at least one positive and one negative aspect of this technology. Write a one-page report on how this technology is being used. Include your opinion on the future of this technology.

CROSS-CURRICULAR—SOCIAL STUDIES

Assume that you are the system administrator for a local area network. Most networks have a usage policy. Use the Internet and other resources to design a usage policy for your network.

CROSS-CURRICULAR— LANGUAGE ARTS

Select a business that you would like to run from home. Create a report describing your business and how you could market your business using one or more of the following technologies: a network, e-mail, Internet connection, fax modem, and a Web site.

WEB PROJECT

Several popular network operating systems are in use. Visit *www.howstuffworks.com/home-network.htm*. At this site, you will find network specifics on how a home network works. Review the various topics and then prepare a report on the different types of hardware you would select to use in your home network.

 ## TEAMWORK PROJECT

Your supervisor at work is interested in using the company's network to set up a computerized teleconference with several of the other stores throughout the state. However, she would like to get more information on this undertaking. She has asked you and the assistant manager to research this project and to prepare a report.

 # CRITICAL THINKING

You now have three computers, a scanner, a DVD player, a printer, and a copier spread throughout several rooms in your home. You and your family have decided it is time to network the equipment. Your goal is to determine whether to go wired or wireless. After you decide on the technology you will use, write a one-page report listing why you selected this technology and provide an overview of your network plan.

 # EXPLORING GOOGLE

Google's 411 application is a free service that can be accessed directly from any phone by dialing 1-800-GOOG-411. Say the location and business name, and you are connected for free. Access the Google 411 site at *www.google.com/goog411/* and then answer the following questions: (1) Can GOOG-411 send you a text message? (2) Can GOOG-411 send you a map? (3) Is this service available outside of the United States? (4) Which languages are supported? (5) Can you use this service to make emergency calls?

UNIT I REVIEW

Computer Basics

■ REVIEW QUESTIONS

FILL IN THE BLANK

Complete the following sentences by writing the correct word or words in the blanks provided.

1. _____ software often is referred to as productivity software.

2. The transmission of data from one location to another is known as _____.

3. A(n) _____ is a highlighted word or image within a hypertext document that, when clicked, takes you to another place within that document or to another Web site.

4. A(n) _____ is an electronic device that receives data (input), processes data, stores data, and produces a result (output).

5. _____ refers to the tangible, physical computer equipment that can be seen and touched.

6. _____ devices enable you to input data and commands into the computer.

7. The _____ performs arithmetic computations and logical operations.

8. RAM also is referred to as _____.

9. The _____ is a search engine robot that searches the Internet for the keywords.

10. A(n) _____ is a group of two or more computers linked together.

MULTIPLE CHOICE

Select the best response for the following statements.

1. The _____ is the center of all processing.

   A. monitor   C. control unit

   B. motherboard   D. computer system

2. _____ help you perform housekeeping chores.

   A. Utility programs   C. Circuit programs

   B. Control units   D. Controller boards

3. A(n) _____ is an organized collection of data.

    A. Usenet   C. database

    B. index   D. spider

4. A software program that enables the user to search the Internet using keywords is called a(n) _____.

    A. modem   C. search engine

    B. database   D. operating system

5. _____ is an authentication technique using automated methods of recognizing a person based on a physiological or behavioral characteristic.

    A. Biometrics   C. Demonstration

    B. Searching   D. Biostatistics

6. The original name for the Internet was _____.

    A. FTP   C. OSP

    B. ARPANET   D. UNIVAC

7. Which of the following is a network disadvantage?

    A. malicious code   C. software sharing

    B. incompatibility   D. all of the above

8. The _____ is the most commonly used input device for entering numeric and alphabetic data into a computer.

    A. keyboard   C. trackball

    B. mouse   D. joystick

9. On the Internet, the major protocol is _____.

    A. TCP/IP   C. DSL

    B. MAN   D. ISDN

10. In a peer-to-peer network, you do not need a _____.

    A. computer   C. communications channel

    B. server   D. receiving device

TRUE / FALSE

Circle T if the statement is true or F if the statement is false.

T   F   **1.**   ASCII is a coding scheme used to represent data.

T   F   **2.**   A mailing list is a group of Internet providers.

T   F   **3.**   A chat room provides real-time communication between multiple users.

T   F   **4.**   Cold plugging is the ability to add and remove devices to a computer while the computer is running and have the operating system automatically recognize the change.

T   F   **5.**   A host computer stands alone; in other words, it is not part of a network.

T   F   **6.**   The Internet and the World Wide Web are the same.

T   F   **7.**   Bluetooth uses radio waves to connect mobile devices such as cell phones, PDAs, and notebook computers.

T   F   **8.**   The two basic types of software are operating software and system software.

T   F   **9.**   DOS is a command-line interface for microcomputers.

T   F   **10.**   UNIX is a closed-source operating system.

■ PROJECTS

CROSS-CURRICULAR—MATHEMATICS

Use the Internet and other resources to locate information on how computers transmit data—broadband and baseband. Prepare a one-page report listing the difference between these two bandwidths. Provide examples of each.

CROSS-CURRICULAR—SCIENCE

You and your family have four computers in your home and have decided that it is time for a wireless home network. You would like to share files and a printer. Describe the type of equipment you will need to create the network. What type of software and/or other protection will you need?

CROSS-CURRICULAR—SOCIAL STUDIES

Cell phones are becoming more sophisticated almost daily. Can you remember what the early cell phones were like? What were some of their capabilities? Use the Internet and other resources to investigate and prepare a timeline for cell phones showing "new and improved" features. If possible, include pictures of the early cell phones.

CROSS-CURRICULAR—LANGUAGE ARTS

The popularity of e-mail introduced a new form of online communication called "emoticons" or "smileys." These are symbols used to represent a variety of facial expressions to enhance communication. Use the Internet to locate information on this form of communication. Prepare a report to share your findings. Include a list of symbols and an explanation of what each represents.

WEB PROJECT

Online courses have become very popular at colleges, universities, and many high schools. Some schools offer entire degrees online. Students taking online courses do not have to physically attend classes; they use the Internet to complete their course requirements. Use the Internet to research information related to online instruction. Can someone obtain their GED online? Prepare a two- to three-page report that includes a description of how online courses are conducted, their advantages and disadvantages, projections for growth, quality control, and what the future might hold.

TEAMWORK PROJECT

You and a partner have been given an assignment to research information related to safe use of the Internet by young children and teenagers. You have decided to discuss the topic with other students and your local police department in addition to conducting research on the Internet. After you gather information, prepare a document that lists eight to 10 "rules" for safety on the Internet. You may find useful information at the following sites: *www.getnetwise.org, www.fema.gov/kids/on_safety.htm,* and *www.wiredkids.org*.

■ SIMULATION

You and a friend are opening a computer consulting business. You will offer in-home consulting services, providing assistance with application software, minor computer operations, and information research.

JOB 1-1

Your first client has called to ask about input devices for someone who has function in only one hand. She is unable to use the standard keyboard.

   Use the Internet to research alternative input devices that your client could possibly use. Prepare a report that includes the type and description of each device as well as advantages and disadvantages. Include the cost if available. The client also has asked for your recommendation on the best device for her particular situation. Prepare a written response to her request that explains your recommendation.

JOB 1-2

A client wants to purchase a computer that he can use to write papers for an English composition course he is taking. His typing skills are very limited. He has contacted your company for help in determining which computer and software he should purchase. He has a budget of $3000. Use store ads, the Internet, catalogs, and other resources to identify three computers and the type of software that would best meet his needs. Prepare a table that lists information about the hardware and software options. Include items, such as the computer, printer, storage devices, and software. Prepare a written recommendation on the option that you think will work best for your client.

EXPLORING GOOGLE

If you are looking for the meaning of a particular word, then you might want to use Google's definition feature. Google has two options you can use to find the definition of a word. First, you can type a word in the Google search box. If Google has the definition, then the word will appear in the right side of the blue bar that stretches across the top of your search results. If it is a one-word term, "[definition]" appears to the right of the word. Clicking that link will display the word's dictionary definition. If your search contains more than one word, each word will appear underlined. Simply click a word to view its dictionary definition. A second option is to type *define:* into the Google search box followed by the word or phrase for which you are searching. An example: **define: dictionary**.

Now, use Google's definition feature to find the definition of the following terms. Define each term in your own words: **VPN network**, **gateway** (in computer networking), **wireless network**, **extranet**, **CAT 6**, and **satellite Internet**.

VIDEO PROJECT

Visit the Online Companion Web page for this book. Click the link for Unit I Review to watch a video. According to the video, why does the IT industry need to reduce its carbon footprint? What steps can it take to do so? Prepare a report in the form of a written document, electronic presentation, or Web page to describe what you learned. If necessary, search the Web to find recent examples of green technology and explain the environmental problems they solve.

■ PORTFOLIO CHECKLIST

Include the following activities from this unit in your portfolio:

_____	Lesson 1	Science Cross-Curricular Report
_____	Lesson 2	Language Arts Cross-Curricular Report
_____	Lesson 3	Social Studies Cross-Curricular Report
_____	Lesson 4	Mathematics Cross-Curricular Report
_____	Lesson 5	Science Cross-Curricular Report
_____	Lesson 6	Social Studies Cross-Curricular Report
_____	Lesson 7	Language Arts Cross-Curricular Report
_____	Unit I Review	Simulation Job 1-1 Recommendation
_____	Unit I Review	Simulation Job 1-2 Recommendation
_____	Unit I Review	Exploring Google

UNIT II

USING THE COMPUTER

LESSON 8

File Management with Windows Vista

■ OBJECTIVES

Upon completion of this lesson, you should be able to:

- Define file management.
- Identify parts of the Computer window.
- Determine uses of the Computer window.
- Manage folders, subfolders, and files.
- Name and rename folders.
- Name, select, and save files.
- Display views.
- Copy, move, and delete files and folders.
- Get help.
- Search for files.

■ VOCABULARY

Contents pane

destination

Details pane

Explorer windows

file

file management

folder

keyword

Preview pane

source

storage media

...

Files, folders, and storage media—these are your key system resources. Your computer's operating system provides multiple options to help you manage these resources. As discussed in Lesson 6, several operating systems are available for use on personal computers. The Microsoft Windows Vista operating system is one of the more popular. It is available in five editions: Windows Vista Home Basic, Windows Vista Home Premium, Windows Vista Business, Windows Vista Ultimate, and Windows Vista Enterprise. This book uses the Windows Vista Business Edition, so the figures may be somewhat different from what you see on your screen. All editions of Windows Vista provide a number of tools for browsing, accessing, and managing these resources: the Computer window and a variety of file managers called

VOCABULARY

Explorer windows

file management

file

Explorer windows—the Documents Explorer, Pictures Explorer, Music Explorer, Videos Explorer, and Downloads. You can access these tools and folders through the Computer window or by clicking your username at the top of the Start menu's right pane. See **Figure 8–1**.

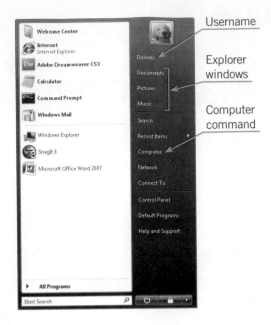

FIGURE 8–1   Windows Vista Start menu

File Management Defined

You most likely will use your computer to create many files and documents. As you create and save files, you must have a logical strategy for file organization. The process of organizing and keeping track of your files is called *file management*. Before you can appreciate and use the Windows Vista file management tools, you should understand the foundation on which they are built: files, folders, and storage media.

Files

Imagine large file drawers for paper documents. If papers simply were stacked in the drawer, not separated or grouped in any way, finding what you wanted would be difficult. If, however, one folder contained reports, another folder contained letters, and a third folder contained memos, then you would be able to find what you wanted much faster with less searching. The same principle applies to storing computer files.

In terms of paper documents, a file may describe a wide range of documents. In computer terms, a file describes a wide range of objects. For example, a *file* can be the instructions the computer needs to operate (called program files or executable files); a file can contain a text document you can read (often referred to as a document); or a file can contain an image, video, or music.

Windows Vista represents files and folders with text names and icons. **Figure 8–2**, for instance, shows icons for a music file, an image, a text document, and a folder.

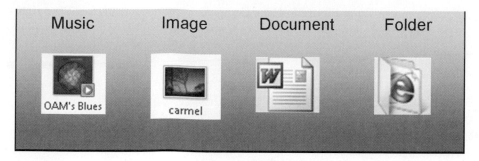

FIGURE 8–2   File and folder icons

Folders

Think of your computer as a virtual file cabinet. The drawers in the cabinet are folders, and the folders in the drawers are subfolders. A *folder* is a container used to store and organize your files. Folders are created and stored on a disk or some other type of storage media. Now, consider your computer's filing system. Your files are stored in a folder or subfolder, which is located on a designated storage device.

For example, you can organize a storage device, such as a hard disk drive or a USB drive, to have a folder that contains only files relating to application programs, another folder for correspondence, another for reports, and so on. Similar to paper folders, media storage folders organize files into manageable groups, and subfolders further separate groups of files within a folder. **Figure 8–3** shows an example of a folder/subfolder structure.

> ▶ **VOCABULARY**
> **folder**
>
> **storage media**

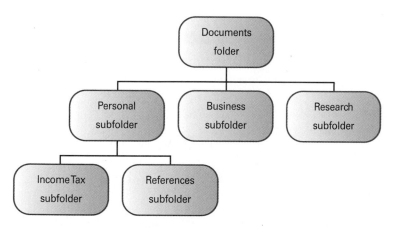

FIGURE 8–3   Folders and subfolders

Storage Media

Storage media can include magnetic disks, optical discs, PC cards, tape, microfilm and microfiche, and mobile storage media such as Flash memory cards, USB flash drives, and smart cards. Lesson 5 contains an overview of these various storage devices.

The Computer Window

As you learned earlier, you can open the Computer window from the Start menu. Most computer systems also display a Computer icon on the desktop from which you can start the program.

As you can see in **Figure 8–4**, the Computer window contains a left and right pane. **Figure 8–4** shows the right pane, or *Contents pane*, of the Computer window in Tiles view. This Contents pane contains a variety of devices, including fixed and removable storage devices.

> **VOCABULARY**
> Contents pane

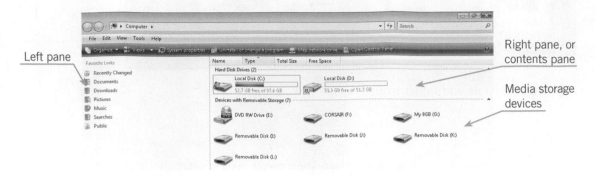

Left pane

Right pane, or contents pane

Media storage devices

FIGURE 8–4   Computer window in Tiles view

In addition to Tiles view, six other views are available: Extra Large Icons, Large Icons, Medium Icons, Small Icons, List, and Details. Clicking the Views button arrow displays a list of the six other View options. See **Figure 8–5**. Clicking the Views button cycles through all seven options. Note that the Views list box has a slider bar that you can use to select other View options.

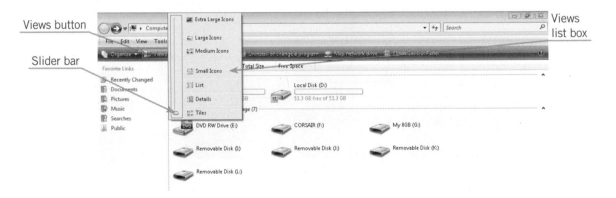

Views button

Slider bar

Views list box

FIGURE 8–5   View options

Identifying the Icons in the Right Pane of the Computer Window

The disk drive icons identify (by letter and type) the storage media devices available on your system. Thus, the icons vary depending on the computer system. Most likely, your system displays icons different from those shown in **Figure 8–4** and **Figure 8–5**. The drives are named by a letter. For most computers:

■   Drives A and B generally are floppy disk drives, though these are becoming obsolete.

■   Drive C typically represents the hard disk. Some computers have more than one hard disk, and some computers have partitioned hard disks.

■ Additional partitioned hard disks and other storage media, such as CDs and DVDs, USB drives, Zip disks, and mobile devices, usually are labeled D, E, F, and so on. Complete Step-by-Step 8.1 to open the Computer window and use the Views button.

Step-by-Step 8.1

1. Click the **Start** button ⊕ on the taskbar, and then point to **Computer**, as shown in **Figure 8–6**.

FIGURE 8–6
Computer selected on the Start menu

2. Click **Computer**. The Computer window opens in Tiles view by default. What storage media are available on your computer? How many hard disk drives are available? How many removable storage devices are available? What letters are used to identify the devices?

3. Click the **Views** button arrow on the command bar, and then drag the slider to access the different views. Which view do you prefer and why?

4. If necessary, return to Tiles view, and then close the Computer window.

Accessing Disk Drives

When the Computer window is displayed, additional information about each storage device also is available. To select a disk, click the appropriate drive icon. When clicked, the disk drive is highlighted as shown in **Figure 8–7** and information on the selected object appears in the **Details pane** in the lower part of the window. In this instance, a hard disk drive named Local Disk (C:) is selected. Note that an additional button (Properties) is available on the command bar. The command bar changes when you click a different object in the Computer window. In this instance, clicking the Properties button opens the Properties dialog box for the selected drive. See **Figure 8–8**.

▶ **VOCABULARY**
Details pane

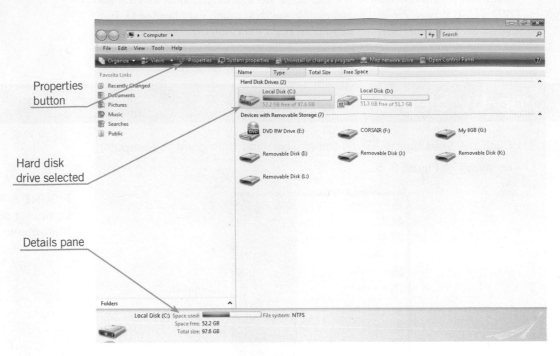

Properties
button

Hard disk
drive selected

Details pane

FIGURE 8–7   Drive selected in Computer window

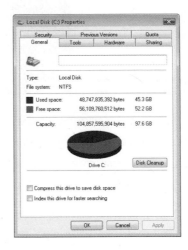

FIGURE 8–8   Local Disk (C:) Properties dialog box

Managing Folders and Files

As you have learned, you use folders to organize files on a disk. Windows Vista has several common Explorer folders to get you started. These folders are the main tool for finding, viewing, and managing information and resources. They help you organize content based on file properties such as filenames, file types, author, or *keywords* (also called tags) that can be associated with files. The following list provides a brief description of these Explorers and suggestions of what documents to store within their folders.

▶ **VOCABULARY**
keyword

- *Documents*: Use this folder for text and word processing files (such as those created with Notepad, WordPad, and Microsoft Office Word), spreadsheets, presentations, and other similar files.

- *Pictures*: Use this folder to store digital pictures, such as photos and graphics.

- *Music*: Use this folder to store digital music.

- *Videos*: Use this folder to store your digital camera or camcorder videos, and downloaded movies or videos.

- *Downloads*: Use this folder to store programs and files that you download from the Web.

To display the five folders listed above, click the Start button and then click Computer or click your name. See **Figure 8–9**, which shows other folders in addition to the five standard Explorer folders.

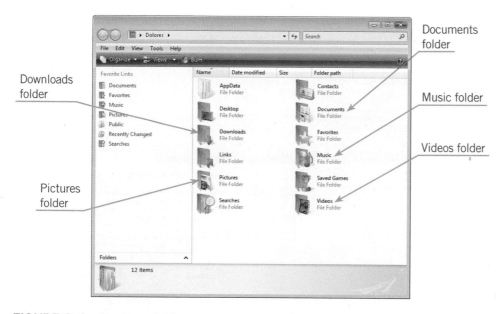

FIGURE 8–9   Explorer folders

When you performed Step-by-Step 8.1, you had an opportunity to review the different views that are available when you select a storage media device. You can use these same views in any of the Explorer folder windows. Additionally, the Documents, Music, and Pictures Explorer *Preview pane* lets you preview the content of documents, pictures, and so on without opening the individual file. In **Figure 8–10**, for instance, the Nature Photos folder in the Pictures folder is selected and Large Icons is the selected view. Clicking one of the images displays the image in the Preview pane. Or, suppose you are searching for a particular PowerPoint presentation. Using the Preview pane, you can view the presentation and determine the contents of the file—without opening the file itself. In **Figure 8–11**, a Microsoft Word document is selected and the contents are displayed in the Preview pane.

▶ **VOCABULARY**
Preview pane

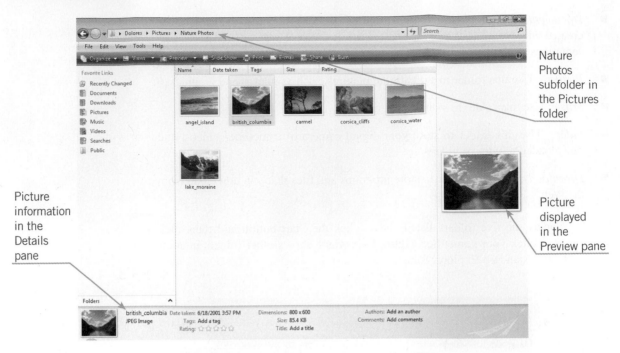

FIGURE 8–10 Photos in a Pictures subfolder

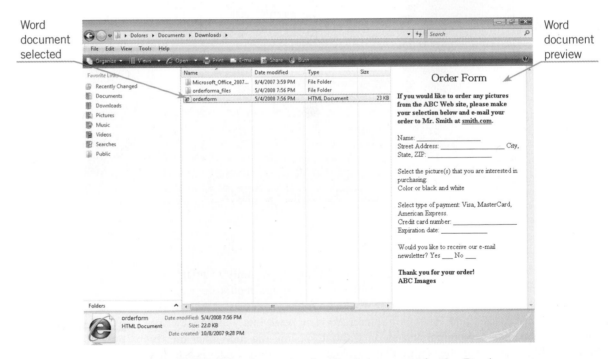

FIGURE 8–11 Contents of a Word document in the Preview pane

Naming Folders and Files

The files and folders that you save on your disk must have names so that you can find them. It is best to make your filenames relevant to the content so that you easily can identify the file when you want to retrieve it.

Filenames can have up to 255 characters. In addition to the name of the file, files also have extensions, which consist of two to four characters. A period separates the filename and the extension. Extensions identify the type of file, such as *docx* for a Microsoft Office Word 2007 document or *xlsx* for a Microsoft Office Excel 2007 workbook. The program in which you are working assigns the default extension. You can change the file type and, therefore, the extension when you save the file using the Save As dialog box.

Creating Folders

In Windows Vista, you can create folders and subfolders in the Computer window, through any of the Explorer folders, and in software programs, such as Microsoft Word and Excel. In Step-by-Step 8.2, you use the Documents Explorer window to create and name folders and subfolders.

Step-by-Step 8.2

1. If necessary, insert your USB drive into an available USB port. (*Note*: If you are saving files and folders to another storage device, you should substitute that device for the USB drive used in this exercise.) Click the **Start** button 🔘 on the taskbar, and then click **Computer**.

2. In the Computer window, double-click the **USB drive** icon (or the icon representing the storage device to which you are saving files and folders).

3. If the menu bar is not displayed in the Computer window, press the **Alt** key. Click **File** on the menu bar, point to **New**, and then point to **Folder**. See **Figure 8–12**. My 8GB (G:) is displayed in the Address bar in Figure 8–12. Most likely, the information displayed in your Address bar will be different.

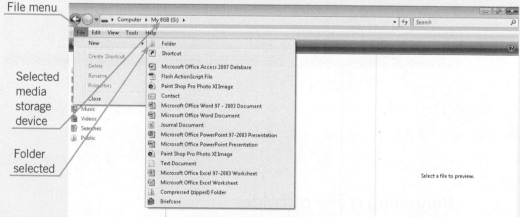

File menu

Selected media storage device

Folder selected

FIGURE 8–12
Creating a folder

4. Click **Folder**. A new folder is created. The default name, New Folder, is assigned and highlighted, as shown in **Figure 8–13**.

FIGURE 8-13
New folder
ready for
renaming

New folder
created

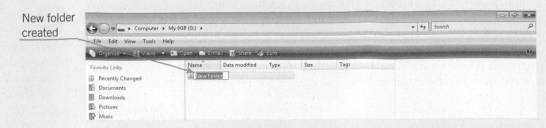

5. Type the folder name **Reports** and then press **Enter**. The folder name is changed from New Folder to Reports, as shown in **Figure 8-14**.

FIGURE 8-14
Renamed folder

New
folder name

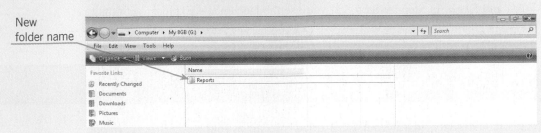

6. Next, create three subfolders in the Reports folder:

    a. Double-click the **Reports** folder to open it.

    b. Press the **Alt** key, if necessary, to display the menu bar. Click **File** on the menu bar, point to **New**, and then click **Folder**. A new folder is created with the default name *New Folder*.

    c. Type **Monthly** for the subfolder name and then press **Enter**.

    d. Click anywhere in the window to deselect the folder.

7. Repeating the instructions in Steps 6b–6d, create two additional subfolders in the Reports folder; name the subfolders **Quarterly** and **Final**. See **Figure 8-15**. Leave this window open for Step-by-Step 8.3.

FIGURE 8-15
Three subfolders in the
Reports folder

Three new
folders
created

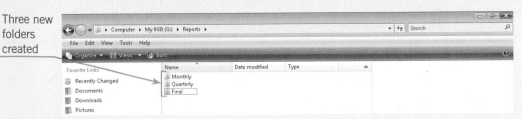

Renaming a File or Folder

Sometimes you might want to change the name of a file or folder, such as to describe its content better or to correct spelling. When renaming a file, you should keep the same filename extension so that you can open it with the correct application.

Renaming a file or folder is a simple process in the Computer window. Three options are available:

■   Click the folder or file to select it, choose Rename on the File menu, and then type the new name in the text box.

■   Click the folder or file to select it, press the F2 key, and then type the new name in the text box.

■   Right-click the folder or file, choose Rename on the shortcut menu, and then type the new name in the text box.

In Step-by-Step 8.3, you rename a folder.

Step-by-Step 8.3

1. Click the **Final** folder.

2. Press the **F2** key.

3. Type the new name **Yearly**, and then press **Enter**. The folder is renamed in the Reports window. See **Figure 8–16**.

Folder is renamed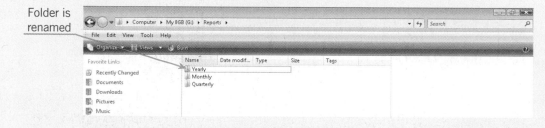

FIGURE 8–16
Renamed folder in the Reports Window

Deleting a File or Folder

Windows provides three options to delete a file or folder:

■   Click the file or folder to select it, and then select Delete on the File menu.

■   Right-click the folder name, and then click Delete on the shortcut menu.

■   Click the file or folder to select it, and then press the Delete key on the keyboard.

Use extreme caution when deleting a folder. When you delete a folder or sub-folder, you also delete all the files in the folder. To verify this is what you really want to do, Windows displays a Delete Folder or Delete File dialog box so you can confirm you want to delete the file or folder. When you delete a file or folder from most media storage devices, it is deleted permanently. When you delete a folder or file from a hard disk, it goes to the Windows Recycle Bin, from which it can be recovered until the Recycle Bin is emptied.

EXTRA FOR EXPERTS

If you unintentionally delete a file, you can restore it from the Recycle Bin. To do so, double-click the Recycle Bin icon on the desktop, and then click the Restore all items button on the command bar to restore all items. If you select one or more items, this button changes to Restore this item or Restore the selected items.

Organizing Files

You also can organize or reorganize your files by moving, copying, and deleting files among folders. The first step in performing any of these functions is to select the files.

To select a single file, click it. To select two or more files that are adjacent to one another, click the first file in the series, press and hold down the Shift key, and then click the last file in the series. See **Figure 8–17**. You also can select all the files in a folder with the Select All command accessed through the Edit menu in the Computer window.

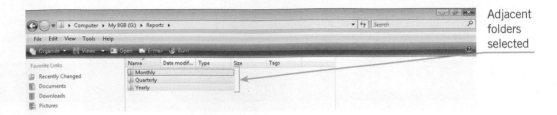

Adjacent folders selected

FIGURE 8–17   Adjacent folders selected in the Reports folder

To select files that are not adjacent, press and hold down the Ctrl key, and then click each of the files. See **Figure 8–18**.

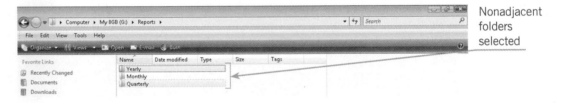

Nonadjacent folders selected

FIGURE 8–18   Nonadjacent folders selected in the Reports folder

You can use the scroll bars to move around the Explorer window when selecting files. Do not worry if the selected object moves out of view. An object will remain selected until you select another object or cancel the selection. When you want to cancel all the selections in a window, click a blank area in the window.

Copying and Moving Files

One of the key advantages of using Windows is the ease with which you can copy, delete, or move files from one location to another. You move or copy files from a source location to a destination. The *source* is the folder or disk containing the file to be copied, and the *destination* is the location (folder or disk) where you are copying or moving the file. Whenever you need to move or copy files, both the source and destination locations should be visible. In this way, you can see what you are moving or copying and where it is going. In the Computer window, you can view the source in the Contents pane and the destination in the left pane. Alternately, you can use the Computer window to make the source and destination windows visible at the same time by changing the Browse folders option in the Folder Options dialog box

▶ VOCABULARY

source

destination

to *Open each folder in its own window*. You open the Folder Options dialog box by clicking Tools on the Computer menu bar or by clicking the Organize button on the command bar and then clicking Folder and Search Options.

Copying Files and Folders

When you copy a file or folder, you place a duplicate of it in a different location and leave the original in place. To copy a file or folder to a new location on a *different* disk, select it, and then drag the file or folder from its source location to its destination location. To copy a file or folder to a new location on the *same* disk, select it and hold down the Ctrl key as you drag to the new location. You can select more than one file to copy using the techniques you learned earlier. You also can select and copy a folder.

Moving Files and Folders

The moving process is similar to the copying process. When you move a file or folder, however, you remove it from its source location and place it in the destination location. To move a file or folder to a new location on a *different* disk, select it and drag it to the destination. To move a file or folder to a new location on the *same* disk, you must hold down the Shift key as you drag it to the destination.

Rather than try to remember when to hold down the Shift or Ctrl key, an alternate method of moving and copying files is to drag the file or folder using the right mouse button. When you drop the file or folder in the destination, a menu appears giving you the options to *Copy Here* or *Move Here*. If you attempt to copy or move a file to a destination containing an identically named file, Windows displays a message box asking you to confirm that you want to replace it. Click Copy and Replace to replace the existing file; click Don't Copy to cancel the copy or move.

Take special care when moving, copying, deleting, and renaming files and folders so that they are not lost. You may inadvertently move a file or folder to a location or rename it and then forget the name or location. Another common error occurs when you rename a file using an application different from the one you used to create the original file, so the file is no longer associated with the original source. You also may find that you can no longer open the renamed file in either the original or the new application. Common problems associated with manipulating and working with files include lost files and file or disk corruption. You can avoid these problems by naming and storing files systematically, backing up data files regularly, and checking compatibility.

Searching for Files

Looking for a file on a computer's hard drive or on other storage media can sometimes be like looking for a needle in a haystack. Windows cannot help you find the needle any faster, but can provide assistance in finding a particular file. In fact, Windows provides three useful search options. The option you select depends on the type of file for which you are searching.

Scenario 1: You are searching for a file located in a common folder such as the Pictures folder. Using the Search box at the top of the folder window almost instantly locates the file for you.

Scenario 2: You are searching for a group of related files, such as all the document files that were modified on a particular date. You can use the Date Modified column heading above the group of files by clicking its list arrow and then selecting the date. In this instance, you are filtering by a single item. See **Figure 8–19**. You also can filter by name, date, and size. Pictures, music, and videos have other headings.

EXTRA FOR EXPERTS

You can also search for programs using the Start Search box on the Start menu. Start typing the first few letters of the program name, and Windows Vista displays all the programs on your computer with names that match your entry.

Scenario 3: You are searching for a group of files by date and size. In this instance, you use the Search folder to select multiple filters. Using this option, you can save your search for future reference.

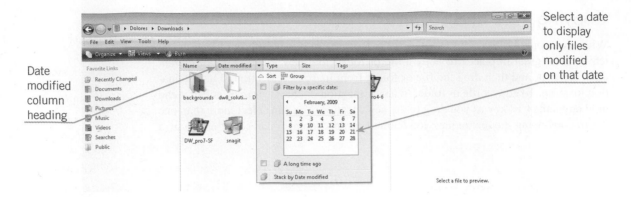

Date modified column heading

Select a date to display only files modified on that date

FIGURE 8–19   Filtering files by date

Getting Help and Support in Windows

Windows provides you with online assistance to most problems you might encounter when working in the Computer window or otherwise working with files. The Help and Support feature can assist you in troubleshooting problems and provide you with an abundance of information on tasks and features. To access this feature, select Help and Support on the Start menu. A window for the Windows Help and Support Center opens, similar to that shown in **Figure 8–20**. In this window, you can click one of the links displayed, use the Browse Help button on the toolbar, or enter a search word in the Search Help text box to locate the Help information you desire.

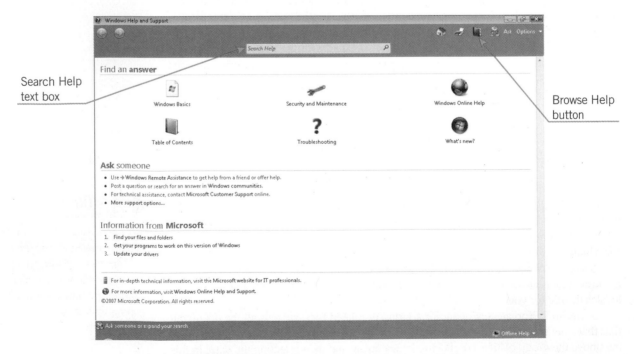

Search Help text box

Browse Help button

FIGURE 8–20   Windows Help and Support window

SUMMARY

In this lesson, you learned:

- The Computer window and Explorer windows are file managers.

- Folders are used to store and organize files on a disk.

- The Views button in the Computer window lets you control how files and folders are displayed in the Contents pane. The viewing options are Extra Large Icons, Large Icons, Medium Icons, Small Icons, List, Details, and Tiles.

- Filenames can have up to 255 characters. They include a two- to four-character extension, which identifies the application in which the file was created.

- You can create folders and subfolders in the Computer window and the Explorer windows.

- Once a file or folder is deleted from a removable media storage device, it is gone forever; however, if you delete a file or folder from a hard disk, it is placed in the Recycle Bin where it can be recovered.

- You can rename a file or folder in the Computer window. You also can move and copy files and folders.

- Several search options are available for locating files.

- The Windows Help and Support Center feature provides assistance and information on Windows features and programs.

■ VOCABULARY REVIEW

Define the following terms:

Contents pane	file	Preview pane
destination	file management	source
Details pane	folder	storage media
Explorer windows	keyword	

■ REVIEW QUESTIONS

MULTIPLE CHOICE

1. A filename can have up to _____ characters.

    A. 255   C. 150

    B. 2800   D. 32

2. The process of organizing and keeping track of your files is called _____.

    A. View plus   C. formatting

    B. file management   D. stacking

3. Files and folders are represented by _____ and _____.

    A. text names, icons   C. icons, thumbnails

    B. thumbnails, details   D. icons, file folders

4. Removing a file from a folder is called _____.

    A. copying   C. renaming

    B. formatting   D. deleting

5. The _____ command allows you to change the name of a file or folder.

    A. Move   C. Rename

    B. Help and Support   D. Delete

TRUE / FALSE

Circle T if the statement is true or F if the statement is false.

T   F   **1.**   The Computer window is a tool for browsing, accessing, and managing files, folders, and storage devices.

T   F   **2.**   You can drag folders to move them to another location.

T   F   **3.**   An optical disc is an example of a storage media device.

T   F   **4.**   Files only can be stored on your computer's hard disk.

T   F   **5.**   The Preview pane can only be used to view images.

FILL IN THE BLANK

Complete the following sentences by writing the correct word or words in the blanks provided.

1. The process of organizing and keeping track of your files is called _____.

2. When you copy a file, you are creating a(n) _____ of the file.

3. Windows provides _____ search options to help you find a file.

4. To copy a file to a location on the same storage media, you must hold down the _____ key while dragging it to the destination.

5. A commonly used letter designation for the local hard disk drive is _____.

■ PROJECTS

CROSS-CURRICULAR— MATHEMATICS

Details view in the Computer window gives you information regarding the storage media devices on your computer. Using Details view, select the various media devices. Create a list indicating the total size, free space, and number of items on each device. To display the number of items, double-click the storage device icon. The number of items is indicated in the Details pane.

CROSS-CURRICULAR—SCIENCE

Some files are very large and use a large amount of space on the disk. This space can be reduced by compressing files. Use the Internet and other resources to investigate compressing files using the Windows Vista operating system, and write a short description on how this process works.

CROSS-CURRICULAR—SOCIAL STUDIES

Use the Internet and other resources to research the history of Microsoft Windows. Prepare a one-page report, giving a brief overview of each version. Include a graphical timeline showing the year when each version of Windows became available. What operating system was used prior to Windows?

CROSS-CURRICULAR— LANGUAGE ARTS

Windows Vista contains a new navigation feature called "breadcrumbs." Research this topic and write a pargraph or two describing this feature. Then answer the following questions: In your opinion, is breadcrumbs a valuable feature? Do you consider this feature a good addition? Why or why not? Would you use it? Why or why not?

WEB PROJECT

Windows Vista includes 11 different accessibility options. Visit the Microsoft Web site at *www.microsoft.com/enable/products/windowsvista*. Select three of the accessibility options. Describe each option and give examples of how someone could use this option.

 ## TEAMWORK PROJECT

Your instructor has given you and your team an assignment to create a hot air balloon service business. As part of the assignment, you will need to store information using your computer. Working with your partner, identify the types of information you will need to store. Design a folder structure to organize your files by creating a main folder with the name of the company, and add folders and subfolders to include at least two levels.

CRITICAL THINKING

Windows version 1.0 was first released by Microsoft in 1985. Since then, many other versions have been released. List three reasons you think new versions are continually being released. If you were going to assist in the creation of the next version, what new features would you add? Explain why you would add these features and how they would be an improvement or beneficial for the user.

 # EXPLORING GOOGLE

If you are searching online for an image, most likely your best bet is to use Google Image Search. It is the largest and most popular image search engine on the Web, with a massive image index. One of the search limitations is that Google displays only up to 1000 results. You can access Google Image Search by going to *google. com* and then clicking the Images link in the upper-left corner. Using the Google Image Search tool, search for Microsoft Windows Vista. How many images were displayed?

1. Open your word-processing program or other text program such as Notepad or WordPad.

2. Select one of the images in the image search results.

3. Right-click the image and then click Copy on the shortcut menu.

4. Access your text program. Right-click anywhere on the page and then click Paste on the shortcut menu.

5. Copy and paste the Web site address into your text document below the image.

6. Select another image and repeat Steps 1 through 5.

LESSON 9

E-mail and Electronic Communication

■ OBJECTIVES

Upon completion of this lesson, you should be able to:

- Understand and use e-mail features in Microsoft Office Outlook 2007.
- Send and receive e-mail.
- Organize and manage e-mail you receive.
- Write effective and professional e-mail messages.
- Manage contacts.
- Explain other types of electronic communication.

Microsoft Office Outlook 2007 is a ***personal information management (PIM)*** program that you can use to organize your schedule, keep track of your contacts, and manage e-mail. E-mail, or electronic mail, one of the most popular services on the Internet, is the focus of this lesson.

You can use e-mail to stay in touch with your family and friends, conduct business, and send attachments such as text and image files. Similar to Microsoft Outlook, ***Windows Mail*** is an Internet e-mail and news reader program included with Windows Vista. Windows Mail does not have the task- and contact-management capabilities of Microsoft Outlook, though the e-mail features of Outlook are very similar to the features of Windows Mail. After you practice using Outlook e-mail in the exercises in this lesson, you will find that you also are able to use Windows Mail. (*Note*: If you currently have Windows Mail set up as your default mail program, some of the commands and buttons might not be available in Outlook.)

■ VOCABULARY

attachments

Contacts

decryption

electronic mail (e-mail)

e-mail address

encrypting

instant messaging

item

packets

personal information management (PIM)

Quick Click Flag Status column

signature

spam

Windows Mail

...

Electronic Mail

Electronic mail (e-mail) is the transmission of files and data using a computer network. It is not that different from regular mail. You have a message, an address, and network protocols that route it from one location to another. You may send e-mail to other people on a network at an organization, or you can use an Internet service provider to send e-mail to any connected computer in the world.

When you send someone an e-mail message, it is broken down into small chunks called *packets*. These packets travel independently from server to server. You might think of each packet as a separate page within a letter. When the packets reach their final destination, they are reassembled automatically into their original format. Unless a technical problem occurs, this process allows e-mail to travel much faster than regular mail (sometimes referred to as "snail mail"). In fact, some messages can travel thousands of miles in less than a minute.

Microsoft Outlook also addresses accessibility issues for a wide range of users, including those who have limited dexterity, low vision, or other disabilities. Keyboard shortcuts, increased text size, and color and sound options are all available. The user can customize toolbars and menus and assign preferred accelerator keys as needed.

E-mail Access

E-mail has become a prevalent way of communicating in our business and personal lives. The ways in which you can access e-mail have multiplied. A number of Web sites and Internet service providers offer e-mail for a monthly fee; some provide the service at no charge. Gmail, America Online, Hotmail, and Yahoo! are examples of companies that provide Web-based e-mail services. After you set up an e-mail account with one of these services, you easily can access your account through the organization's Web page by entering your account name (usually your e-mail address) and a password. Most e-mail programs provide you with the capabilities to read mail, send messages, and manage your electronic communication.

Other programs, such as Microsoft Word and Excel, also have an E-mail option accessed through the Office button. You can click the Office button, point to Send, and then click E-mail to send a message with a file attachment or use an Internet fax service to fax the document.

Wireless communication also has expanded the ways in which e-mail is transmitted and retrieved. Many people have cell phones or handheld computers that they can use to send and receive e-mail.

Microsoft Office Outlook 2007

In addition to sending e-mail, Outlook is a versatile application that can help you organize appointments, keep track of tasks and to-do lists, and maintain addresses. In this lesson, you concentrate on sending, receiving, and managing e-mail with Outlook. You will, however, have the opportunity to experience a short tour of the other program features at the end of this lesson.

Outlook stores information in folders. You can organize different types of information in each Outlook folder. This makes it easy to store many types of personal and business data and then display it at the click of a button. An *item* is a particular piece of information stored in an Outlook folder.

When you start Outlook, a window similar to the one shown in **Figure 9–1** is displayed. Your window may contain different or additional folders. The default opening window is the Mail window, which gives you an option to select any of the other features: Calendar, Contacts, or Tasks. Outlook provides several formats for composing and editing e-mail messages. Composing formats include HTML, Rich Text, and Plain Text. Editing options include using Microsoft Word to edit and read e-mail and Rich Text messages. The figures in this lesson use the default option—HTML—to compose and edit messages.

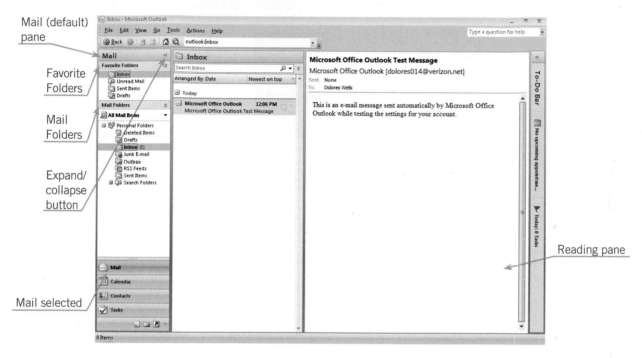

FIGURE 9–1 Outlook default opening window

The default task selected in the Navigation pane is Mail. The name of the selected task (Mail) appears in the task banner at the top of the Navigation pane. The expanded Mail pane contains Favorite Folders and Mail Folders sections. The Favorite Folders section in **Figure 9–1** includes standard folders such as Inbox, Unread Mail, Sent Items, and Drafts. The Mail Folders contains All Mail Items, which includes some of the same folders such as Inbox, Sent Items, and Drafts. Your program might display different folders. The plus and minus signs to the left of a folder indicate that you can expand and collapse the folder. To move a copy of a folder from the All Mail Items Folders into the Favorite Folders list, click the folder and drag it to the Favorite Folders pane.

When you select a folder in the Mail pane, such as the Unread Mail folder, the name of the item is displayed in the Navigation pane, as shown in **Figure 9–2**. Click an item in the message pane to see the full text in the Reading pane. In the other Outlook tasks, such as the calendar, the task window opens directly in the Reading pane.

Name of
selected
folder in
Navigation
pane

The (6)
indicates
six unread
messages

Plus sign

Open
envelope icon

Closed
envelope icon

Reading pane

Inbox

Message
heading of
selected
e-mail

Message
heading
selected

E-mail
message

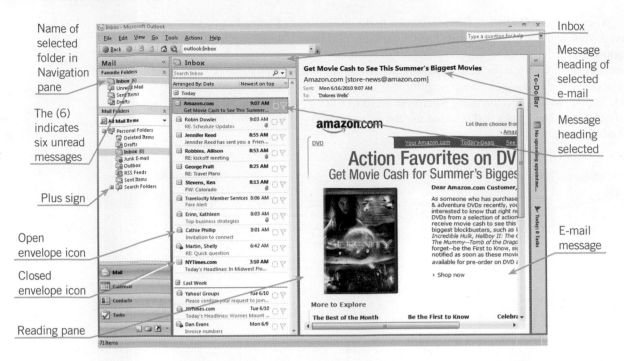

FIGURE 9–2   Navigation pane and Reading pane in the Mail window

Setting Up an E-mail Account

If you do not have an e-mail account, it is suggested that you create one; otherwise, you will not be able to complete the exercises in this lesson. Two Web sites that provide free e-mail accounts are Yahoo! at http://mail.yahoo. com/ and Windows Live Hotmail at http://hotmail.com. Check with your instructor if you are to create an e-mail account using one of these Web sites or if you have access to another option.

After your computer is set up to handle e-mail, you can use the Inbox folder in Outlook to send and receive e-mail messages. An advantage to using Outlook as your e-mail application is that as you create messages, you have easy access to the other Outlook folders. You quickly can address the message to someone in your contacts list, check your calendar to make sure you are available for a meeting, or add a task to your task list when a message requests further action. In addition to sending just a text message, you can include attachments such as pictures or documents.

E-mail Addresses

When you send postal mail to someone, you must know the address. The same thing is true for e-mail. An **e-mail address** consists of three parts:

■   The user name of the account

■   The "@" symbol

■   The user's domain name

For instance, David Edward's e-mail address could be dedwards@msn.com.

▶ **VOCABULARY**
e-mail address

Starting Outlook

When Outlook starts, it sends a request to your mail server. If you have messages, Outlook receives them and stores them in a folder in the Inbox folder in the Mail pane. The number of unread messages is displayed in parentheses. The Inbox displays message headers for any new messages. The message header indicates the sender's name, the subject of the message, and the date and time received. Clicking the header displays the Reading pane and the actual text of the message. See **Figure 9–3**. If you have a number of messages, you can read each one by clicking its message header to display the message text in the Reading pane.

FIGURE 9–3   Message displayed in the Reading pane

As previously indicated, the figures in this lesson use the HTML option to compose and edit. Complete the following Step-by-Step to start Outlook and to change your Mail Format options to HTML if necessary.

Step-by-Step 9.1

1. Click the **Start** button 🪟 on the taskbar, point to **All Programs**, click **Microsoft Office**, and then click **Microsoft Office Outlook 2007**.

2. If necessary, maximize the Outlook window. Click the **Inbox** folder to display message headers for any messages you might have received. (You might not have any messages in your Inbox when you open the Inbox folder in this exercise.)

3. Click **Tools** on the menu bar and then click **Options**. Click the **Mail Format** tab and verify that **HTML** is selected for the *Compose in this message format*. If another option is selected, click the down arrow and select **HTML**. Click **OK** or click **Apply** to close the Options dialog box. Keep Outlook open for Step-by-Step 9.2.

Creating, Receiving, and Sending Messages

Creating and sending an e-mail is as easy as identifying the recipients, providing a Subject, typing your message, and sending it. To display the Untitled Message dialog box, click File on the menu bar, click New, and then click Mail Message. Enter an e-mail address or addresses in the To text box, either by typing the address or by inserting an address from your contacts list (discussed later in this lesson). Separate e-mail addresses of multiple recipients with a semi-colon (;).

You can type additional e-mail addresses in the Cc text box if you are sending copies of the message to other recipients. You also can enter e-mail addresses for recipients who are to be "blind" copied, meaning the primary addressee(s) will not see that others are copied on the message. To do this, you must display the Bcc field. Click the Options tab and then click Show Bcc. If more than one person uses the computer or if you have more than one e-mail address, you also can designate an e-mail address by adding the From field to the message. To add the From field, click the Options tab and then click Show From.

E-mail etiquette requires that you include a subject line for your mail message. The subject should be brief, yet descriptive. Enter this in the Subject text box. **Figure 9–4** shows the Untitled Message window with the fields previously discussed.

▣ EXTRA FOR EXPERTS

The Cc in the e-mail window is the abbreviation for carbon copy. This originated with the old-fashioned typewriter. To send someone a copy of a letter or to create a file copy required that the typist use a sheet of carbon paper between each sheet of paper.

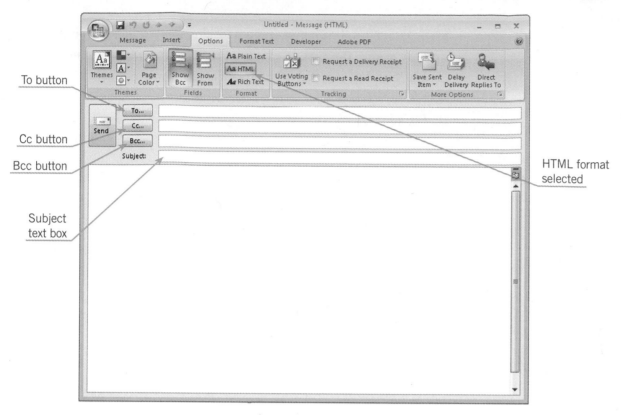

FIGURE 9–4 Message window

After you have completed the fields in the message header, type your message. Then click the Send button to send the e-mail message.

In the following Step-by-Step, you will practice creating an e-mail message that you will send to yourself or to someone else in your class. If necessary, check with your instructor regarding the e-mail address (or addresses) to be used for the exercises in this lesson.

Step-by-Step 9.2

1. Click **File** on the menu bar, point to **New**, and then click **Mail Message**. The Untitled Message window appears.

2. If necessary, click the **To** box. Type your e-mail address (or the e-mail address of the person to whom you are sending the message). If you do not know what e-mail address you should use, check with your instructor.

3. Click the **Subject** box and type **Caribbean cruise**.

4. Click in the message area. The title of the window changes to *Caribbean cruise*.

5. Type the following message: **I am looking forward to going on the cruise next month. Our ports of call are Grand Cayman, Belize, and Cozumel. You can find additional information at www.cruise.com.** Press **Enter** two times and type your name. Your screen should look similar to **Figure 9–5**.

FIGURE 9–5
Completed message

E-mail address

Send button

Subject

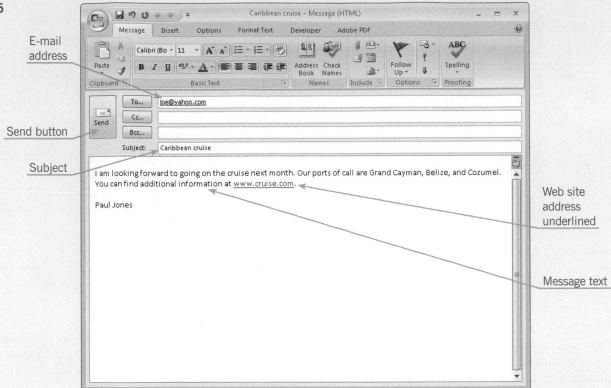

Web site address underlined

Message text

Notice that when you type the Web site address, it is underlined. It also might appear in a different color. Some e-mail programs require you to click, double-click, or hold down the Ctrl key and click to activate the link and open the associated Web page.

6. Click the **Send** button to send the message. Leave Outlook open for Step-by-Step 9.3.

EXTRA FOR EXPERTS

After you send a message, Outlook closes the Message window and temporarily stores the message in the Outbox folder. After the message is sent, Outlook moves the message to the Sent Items folder.

Receiving and Opening E-mail Messages

Now that you have sent a message to yourself (or someone in your class has sent you a message), you should receive it in the Inbox. You use the Tools menu or click the Send/Receive button on the Standard toolbar to check for messages. In the following Step-by-Step, you check for messages and then open the message you sent to yourself or a message you received from another student. In some instances, your instructor might have sent you a message.

Step-by-Step 9.3

1. Click **Tools** on the Standard toolbar, point to **Send/Receive**, and then click **Send/Receive All**. The Inbox receives the message and the message header is displayed, like that shown in **Figure 9–6**.

Message header displayed in Inbox

FIGURE 9–6
Receiving a message

Send/Recieve button

2. Click the message header in the Inbox pane. The message is displayed in the Reading pane, as shown in **Figure 9–7**.

Reply button

Reply to All button

Message header

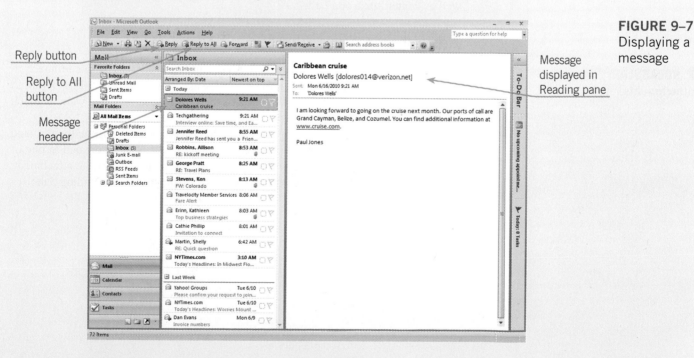

FIGURE 9–7
Displaying a message

Message displayed in Reading pane

3. Close the message. Leave Outlook open for Step-by-Step 9.4.

Saving a Message

When you receive a message, Outlook automatically stores the message in the Inbox or another designated folder until you delete the message. You can save the content of a message, however, as a text file, an HTML document, or a template. To save a message in one of these formats, click File on the menu bar and then select the Save As command. When the Save As dialog box is displayed, type a name in the File name text box, and then select the format by clicking the Save as type text box arrow. Click the Save button to save the file.

Replying to a Message

When replying to a message, first select the message. Then click the Reply or Reply to All button on the Standard toolbar, type your message, and click the Send button. With this format, the original message is included along with your reply message. Suppose, for example, you received an e-mail from a friend and the friend sent a copy of the message to several other people. To reply to the friend, click the Reply button. To reply to the friend and send a copy of the message to the others who were listed in the Cc box, use the Reply to All button. Using the Reply or Reply to All option is appropriate when you are answering a question or responding to specifics in the original message.

When you reply to a message, a Message window is displayed. This window is similar to the one you used to create a new message. When you use this format to reply to an e-mail message, the recipient(s) normally sees the letters "RE" preceding the text in the subject line to indicate that it is a reply message.

Formatting a Message

When you are composing or replying to a message, the Basic Text group on the Message tab contains many of the same features as those in your word-processing program and other similar software. You can change the font type, font size, and text color of an e-mail message. You also can add bold, italics, and underlining to text as well as center it and add bullets.

Attaching a File to an E-mail Message

VOCABULARY
attachments

Attachments are documents, images, figures, and other files that you can attach to your e-mail messages. To attach a file to a message, click the Attach File button in the Include group on the Message tab, locate the file or document you want to attach in the Insert File dialog box, and then click the Insert button.

In the following Step-by-Step, you reply to a message. You change the font and text color, attach a file, and then send the message. Use a file you created in one of the other lessons in this course or as directed by your instructor for the attachment. Outlook should be open and a message should be displayed in the Reading pane.

Step-by-Step 9.4

1. Click the **Inbox**, and then double-click the Caribbean cruise message to open it. Click the **Reply** button in the Respond group on the Message tab. The message window is displayed, similar to that shown in **Figure 9–8**. The e-mail address is displayed automatically in the To box, and the insertion point is blinking in the message area.

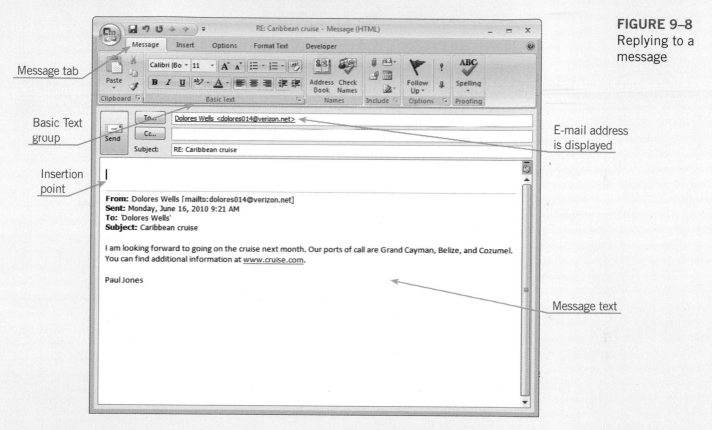

Message tab

Basic Text group

Insertion point

FIGURE 9–8
Replying to a message

E-mail address is displayed

Message text

2. Type the following:

Dolores, (substitute the name of your recipient, and then press **Enter** two times).

Good to hear from you. I am also preparing for the cruise and look forward to seeing you. I have attached some information for you. Press **Enter** two times and type your name.

3. Select the text of your message. Use the buttons in the Basic Text group on the Message tab to change the font to a style of your choice and the font size to **12**. Change the color to one of your choice. Format all of the text in bold.

4. Click the **Insert** tab and then click **Attach File** in the Include group, as shown in **Figure 9–9**. The Insert File dialog box is displayed.

FIGURE 9–9
Attaching a file

Attach File button

Formatted message

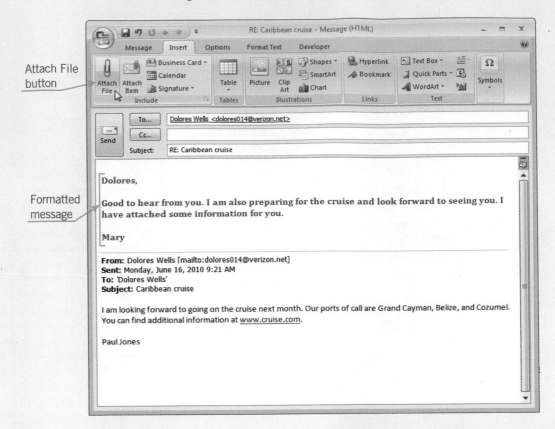

5. Locate and select the file that you want to attach, and then click the **Insert** button. The file is attached, as shown in **Figure 9–10**.

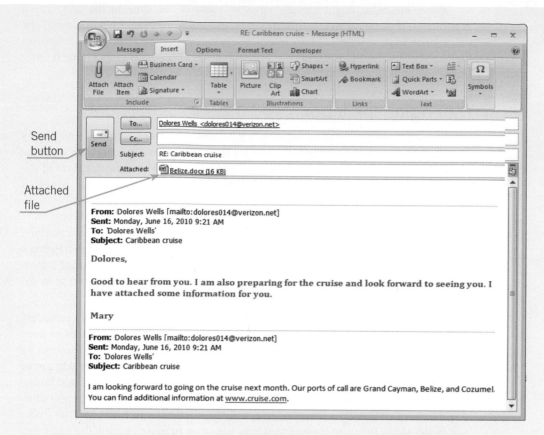

FIGURE 9–10
Message with attached file

6. Click the **Send** button. The message is sent. Leave Outlook open for Step-by-Step 9.5.

E-mail Troubleshooting

Occasionally, when you send an e-mail with an attachment, you receive a return message indicating that the message cannot be sent. This happens because some e-mail service providers limit the size of e-mail attachments. Even if your e-mail provider and program can send a large attachment, you might find that the recipient cannot receive the message or open the attachment.

Other technical problems can prevent messages from being sent or received. This generally means that the recipient's address was entered incorrectly or no longer exists. Other errors, however, might be caused by a problem with the server that handles the mail for your e-mail provider or for that of the recipient.

If you receive a message that says your e-mail could not be delivered or sent, check the address and try to send it again. Sometimes the problems with a server are temporary, and the message can be sent successfully on the second try.

 **EXTRA FOR EXPERTS**

When Outlook is open, you can check your e-mail at any time. Just click the Send/Receive button on the Standard toolbar.

Organizing and Managing E-mail

E-mails require file management skills similar to any other references (electronic or hard copy) you want to keep and manage. Most of the time, you will want to reply to messages you receive, and save important messages for future reference. On the other hand, you probably will want to delete unneeded messages and spam. *Spam* is unsolicited e-mail, essentially electronic junk mail. In many instances, spam is used to advertise products and services. Other spam messages might contain phony offers.

▶ **VOCABULARY**
spam

Some messages might contain viruses—most of the time in the form of an attachment. If you have an antivirus program, generally the program will identify the message as having a virus. Many Internet service providers use firewalls to protect their customers from viruses. Do not open an attachment if you suspect that it has a virus, and immediately delete the message to which it is attached.

Managing the Inbox

When you receive an e-mail message, you have several options. You can send a reply as you did in the previous exercise, forward the message to someone else, save the message to a specified location, delete the message, or select a combination of the aforementioned options. Before you can perform an action on a message, you first must select it by clicking the header in the Inbox pane.

- Forwarding a message: This is similar to replying to a message. Forwarding messages helps cut down on the time you spend retyping a message. It also is a quick way to share information with several people. When you forward a message, the recipient(s) normally sees the letters "FW" preceding the text in the subject line to identify it as a message that is being forwarded.

- Saving a message: You can save an e-mail message in various formats (including text and HTML formats) to disk so that you can open and read it later or keep it for follow-up or reference. You also can save and organize e-mail messages in folders within your e-mail program. In Outlook, for example, you can create folders within your local folders (Inbox, Outbox, Sent Items, and Deleted Items) to organize your messages further. To move a message into a folder, right-click the message header, select the Move to Folder option, and then select the folder in the Move Items dialog box to which you want to move or copy the message.

- Deleting a message: You can delete an e-mail message by selecting it and then pressing the Delete key or clicking the Delete button on the e-mail program's toolbar. In some e-mail programs, such as Outlook, this moves the message into a deleted mail folder. To delete it permanently, you must delete it from this location.

Message Icons

Icons in the message headers listed in the Navigation pane offer clues about each message. For example, an icon that looks like the back of a sealed envelope indicates a message that has been received but not read; an exclamation point icon means the sender considers it an urgent or high-priority message; a paper clip icon indicates that the message has an attached file. You also can manually mark a message as read or unread, or add a flag icon as a reminder to follow up on the message.

In the following Step-by-Step, you create a folder, move a message from one folder to another, forward a message, and print a message. Outlook should be open and the Inbox displayed.

Step-by-Step 9.5

1. Click **File** on the menu bar, point to **New**, and then click **Folder** to display the Create New Folder dialog box. Type **Cruise** in the Name text box. Click **Personal Folders** in the *Select where to place the folder* box. If necessary, click the plus sign to the left of Personal Folders to display the subfolders. The dialog box should look similar to that shown in **Figure 9–11**.

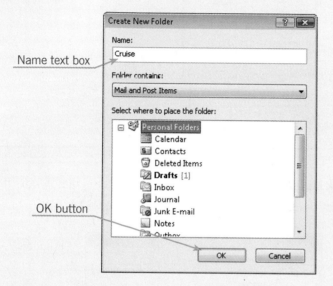

Name text box

OK button

FIGURE 9–11
Create New Folder dialog box

2. Click the **OK** button. The folder is displayed as a subfolder in the Personal Folders folder, as shown in **Figure 9–12**.

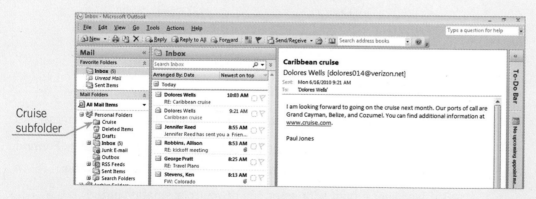

Cruise subfolder

FIGURE 9–12
New folder created

3. You should have two messages in your Inbox regarding the cruise. Click the first Caribbean cruise message; hold down the **Ctrl** key and click the second Caribbean cruise message. Both messages are selected. (If you are creating other messages or do not have two cruise messages, select any other two messages.)

4. Right-click the selected messages to display the shortcut menu. Point to **Move to Folder**, as shown in **Figure 9–13**.

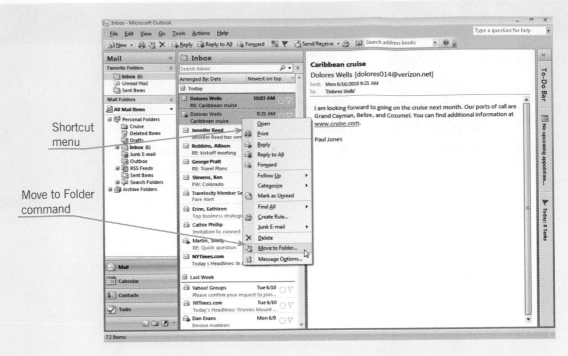

Shortcut
menu

Move to Folder
command

5. Click **Move to Folder** to display the Move Items dialog box. If necessary, select the **Cruise** folder, as shown in **Figure 9–14**.

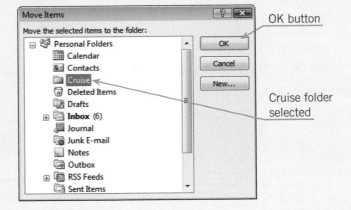

OK button

Cruise folder
selected

6. Click the **OK** button. Click the **Cruise** folder to display the two messages.

7. Right-click the first message to display the shortcut menu. Click **Forward**. The message is displayed with *FW:* indicated in the Subject box.

8. Type your e-mail address or one of your classmates' in the To box. Type your instructor's e-mail address (or an e-mail address to another classmate) in the Cc box. See **Figure 9–15**.

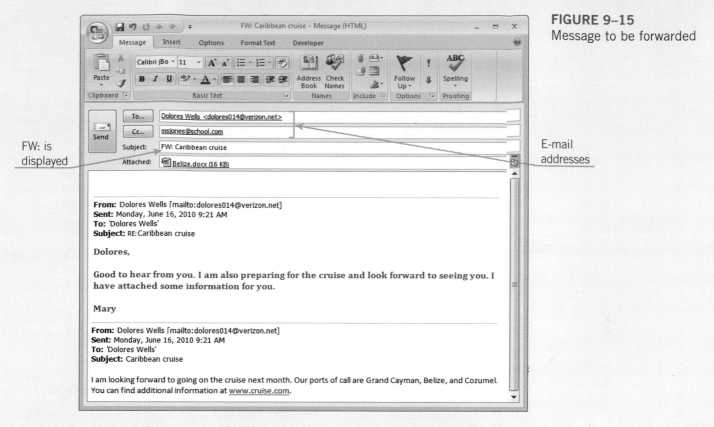

FW: is displayed

E-mail addresses

FIGURE 9–15
Message to be forwarded

9. Click the **Send** button.

10. Right-click the first Caribbean cruise message to display the shortcut menu. Click **Print** to print a copy of the message. Leave Outlook open for Step-by-Step 9.6.

Special E-mail Features

Most e-mail programs come with a variety of features and options that make it easy to send a copy to multiple recipients, generate an automatic reply, block messages from specific senders, and customize the look and feel of your messages.

Copying to Multiple Recipients

As previously indicated, you can insert more than one address in the To, Cc, and Bcc boxes. The message will go to all the addressees at the same time. If you are sending or copying an e-mail to more than one person, each e-mail address should be separated by a semicolon.

Automatic Message Responses

It is possible to configure e-mail programs such as Outlook to deal automatically with e-mail messages you receive. The automatic controls you can set in Outlook include the following:

- Automatic "out of the office" *response*: Automatically replies to all received e-mail messages when you are unable to reply to messages yourself. This feature requires special e-mail servers and might not be available on your system.

■   Forwarding command: Automatically redirects your mail to another e-mail address; this feature is accessed through the Rules and Alerts command on the Tools menu.

■   Redirect messages to your mobile phone: Automatically redirects your mail to your mobile telephone; this feature is accessed through the Options command on the Tools menu. Click Preferences to display the option.

■   Blocked Senders List: Prevents messages from designated addresses from being placed in your Inbox; this is particularly useful to block unwanted advertisements that often are sent repeatedly to the same e-mail address.

■   Safe Senders/Safe Recipients List: Similar to the Blocked Senders list, selecting this option indicates to Outlook to accept all e-mails from the sender names contained in the list. A similar feature is the Safe Senders Domain List, which contains a list of all safe domains (@msn.com, for example) that you want to accept.

The Blocked Senders and Safe Senders lists are accessed through the Actions menu Junk E-mail command. Click Junk E-mail Options and click the Safe Senders, Safe Recipients, or Blocked Senders tab. Click the Add button, type the e-mail address, and then click the OK button.

Use the Outlook Help feature to find out more about how to block, forward, or automatically respond to messages. Use the key term junk e-mail to generate a list of topics in Help.

Adding a Signature and Stationery to a Message

Earlier in this lesson, you formatted your message text by changing font style and font color. Outlook also includes other options that add visual interest. You can change backgrounds by adding stationery and special signatures for new messages and for replies and forwarded messages.

A *signature* consists of text or pictures that you create and Outlook automatically adds to the end of any outgoing messages. You can create unique signatures for different addresses. For instance, you might want a signature for friends and family and another signature for business purposes.

In the following Step-by-Step, you create a special signature for your personal e-mail messages and then add a background image.

▶ **VOCABULARY**
signature

Step-by-Step 9.6

1.   Outlook should be open. Click **Tools** on the menu bar, click **Options**, and then click the **Mail Format** tab on the Options dialog box, as shown in **Figure 9–16.**

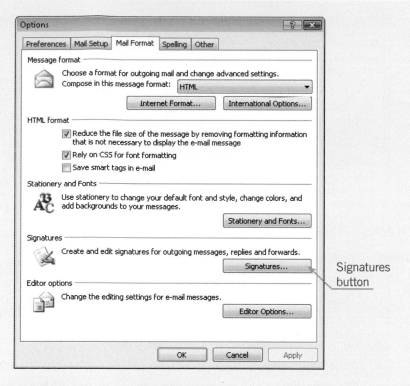

FIGURE 9–16
Options dialog box

2. Click the **Signatures** button to display the Signatures and Stationery dialog box, shown in **Figure 9–17**.

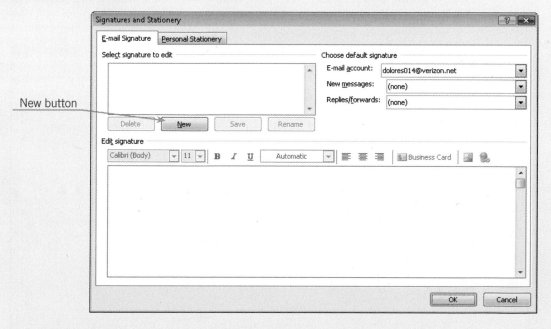

FIGURE 9–17
Signatures and
Stationery dialog box

3. Click the **New** button to display the New Signature dialog box. Type your name. See **Figure 9–18**. Click the **OK** button.

FIGURE 9–18
Creating a signature

FIGURE 9–18
Creating a signature

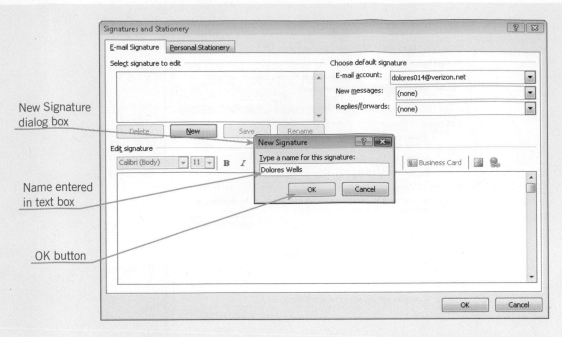

New Signature
dialog box

Name entered
in text box

OK button

4. Click the **Edit signature** text box and type your signature. Click the **Font** arrow to display a list of fonts and select a font type of your choice. Click the **Font Color** arrow and change to a color of your choice. Click the **Bold** **B** button. Change the font size to a size of your choice. See **Figure 9–19**. Most likely your choices will be different from those in **Figure 9–19**.

FIGURE 9–19
Formatting a signature

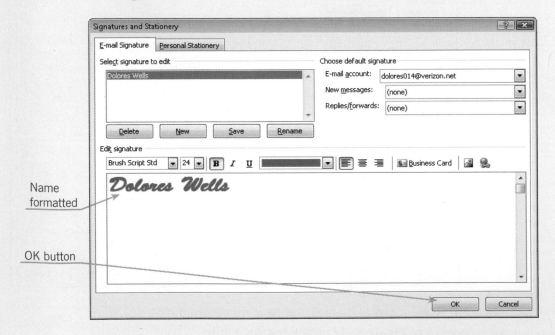

Name
formatted

OK button

5. Type a title or other information that you might want to include. Then, click the **OK** button to redisplay the Options dialog box.

6. In the Options dialog box, click the **Stationery and Fonts** button. If necessary, click the **Personal Stationery** tab and then click the **Theme** button. Scroll through the list of Stationery options and select one of your choice. Some choices might not be displayed. This is determined by the Microsoft Office installation on your computer. In **Figure 9–20**, the Expedition theme is selected.

Expedition theme selected

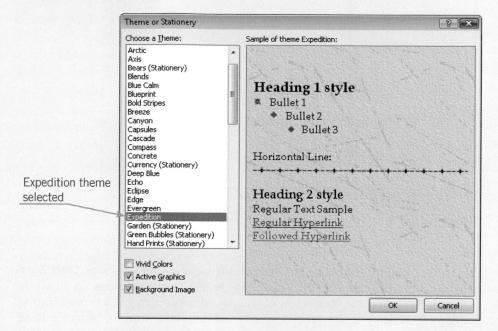

FIGURE 9–20
Theme or Stationery dialog box

7. Click the **OK** button to return to the Signatures and Stationery dialog box. The stationery name you selected is shown in the Theme section. Verify that this is correct, and then click the **OK** button to return to the Options dialog box. Click the **OK** button in the Options dialog box to return to Outlook. Leave Outlook open for Step-by-Step 9.7.

Flagging and Sorting

Located to the right of the message heading in the Inbox is the *Quick Click Flag Status column*. In this instance, the column contains flags that can be assigned one of six different colors. You can use the flags as reminder notices or other indicators that are needed for your personal or business use. For instance, in **Figure 9–21**, a red category flag is displayed to the right of a message as a reminder.

VOCABULARY
Quick Click Flag Status column

EXTRA FOR EXPERTS

The Junk E-mail filter in Outlook is turned on by default. This filter automatically evaluates whether unread messages should be saved in the Junk E-mail folder. You can change the default settings to your own personal settings through the Options command on the Tools menu.

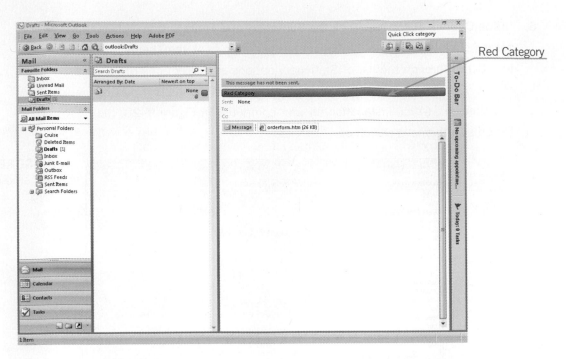

FIGURE 9–21   Flagging a message

After flagging messages, you can sort the messages by flag color. Click View on the menu bar, and point to Arrange By to display the submenu, as shown in **Figure 9–22**. You can then select Categories to select a flag color. Note also in **Figure 9–22** that you can sort messages in numerous other formats, including Date, Size, Subject, Type, and so on.

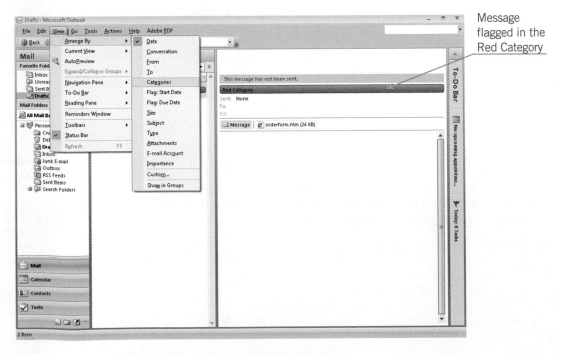

FIGURE 9–22   Arrange By commands

ETHICS IN TECHNOLOGY

E-mail/E-aches

Although e-mail is one of the more popular services of the Internet, its widespread use has created several problems. One of the more time-consuming problems it causes is the overflow of e-mail messages many users find in their Inboxes. Similar to your telephone number, marketers and news groups can locate your e-mail address, enabling them to send you many unwanted e-mails.

E-mail communications also can lead to confusion and misinterpretation. Receivers often are guilty of not thoroughly reading an e-mail message before they reply, or they might not use the Reply All option correctly. It is important to pay close attention to whom you are sending your messages and replies. You do not want to reply automatically to all addressees if the content of the message is not relevant to everyone.

Encoding or Encrypting E-mail

The process of *encrypting* information in a message is accomplished by "scrambling" it so that it cannot be read. When the intended recipient opens the message, he or she uses a key for *decryption* that unscrambles the information and returns it to the original text. To use this feature requires that certificates for digital signing and encryption from a certificate authority be obtained.

▶ **VOCABULARY**
encrypting
decryption
Contacts

Managing an Address Book

The *Contacts* feature in Outlook allows you to create an address book to store information about friends, family, work associates, and other individuals with whom you communicate on a regular basis. As you insert information about a contact, Outlook creates an address card for that person or business. Outlook arranges the address cards in alphabetical order so you easily can locate each one by scrolling through the list, or you can use the numeric/alphabetical list finder at the right side of the window.

Adding and Deleting Contacts

To add a new contact, click the Contacts tab located in the Navigation pane. Outlook displays the Contacts folder. Click Actions on the menu bar and then click New Contact to display a new Contact form. See **Figure 9–23**. You can add as much or as little information as you choose. At a minimum, you should include the full name and e-mail address of the contact. After you fill in the contact information in the dialog box, Outlook adds a new address card to the Contacts folder.

In the following Step-by-Step, you will add a contact and create an e-mail message to the contact. A fictitious name and e-mail address is used in the Step-by-Step instructions. Use the name of one of your contacts or check with your instructor as to what name you should use.

Step-by-Step 9.7

1. Click **Contacts** in the Navigation pane.

2. Click **Actions** on the menu bar, and then click **New Contact** to open the Contact window.

3. Click in the **Full Name** box and type **Tracy Coady** (or the name of one of your own contacts).

4. Press **Tab** to move the insertion point to the next box. Notice that the *File as* box automatically fills in *Coady, Tracy*. Click the **Job title** box and type **Office Manager**.

5. Click the **E-mail** box, type **tcoady@mail.com**, and then press **Tab**.

6. In the Addresses section, click the box arrow, and then click **Home**. Click the **This is the mailing address** check box. Type the following in the Address box (or substitute this with the address of your own contact):

   444 East Street

   Tampa, FL 33630

   See **Figure 9–23**.

FIGURE 9–23
Adding a new contact

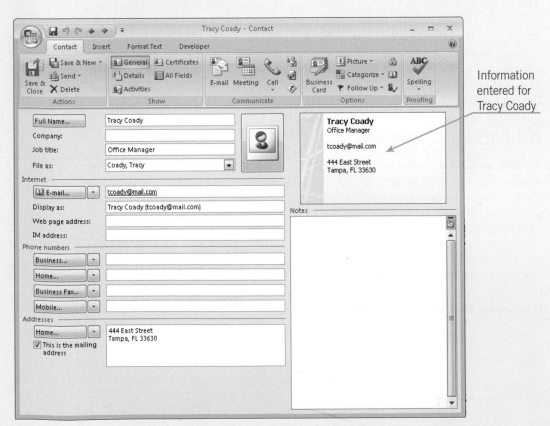

Information entered for Tracy Coady

7. When you have finished entering the information, click the **Save & Close** button in the Actions group on the Contact tab. The form closes and the contact information appears in the Contacts window Reading pane. See **Figure 9–24**.

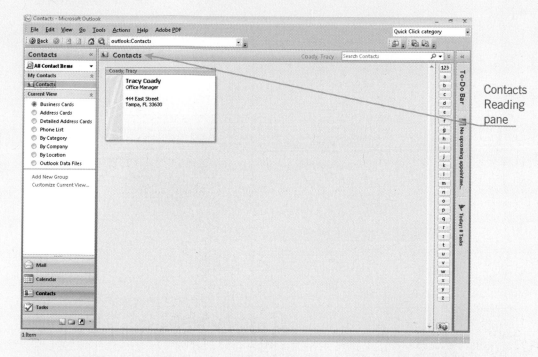

FIGURE 9–24
Contacts window

Contacts Reading pane

8. Repeat Steps 2 through 7 and add two more contacts. Check with your instructor as to what names you should use. After adding the contacts, your Contacts window should look similar to that shown in **Figure 9–25**. Most likely, however, the names of your contacts will be different.

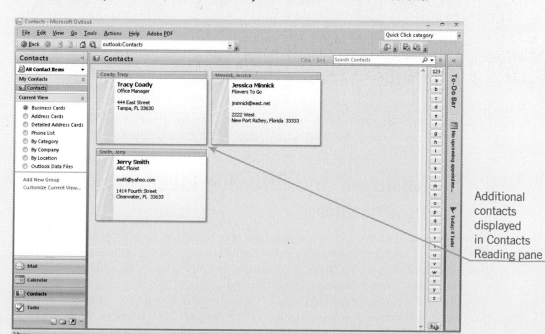

FIGURE 9–25
Contacts window with additional names

Additional contacts displayed in Contacts Reading pane

To send a message to a contact stored in the Contacts folder, click Mail. Click Actions on the menu bar, and then click New Mail Message. When the message window is displayed, click the To button. The Select Names: Contacts dialog box opens to allow you to select a contact name, as shown in **Figure 9–26**.

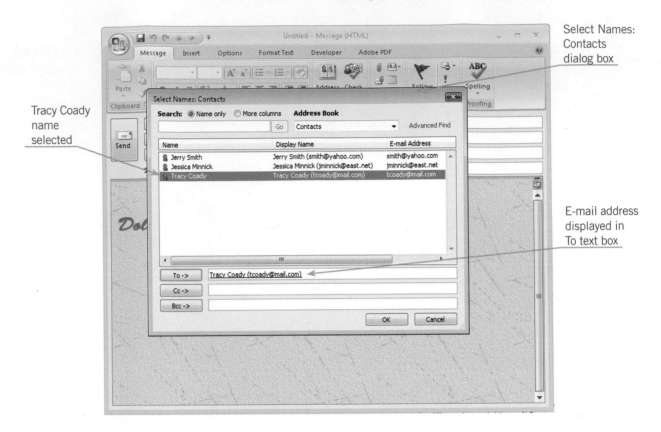

FIGURE 9–26   Select Names: Contacts dialog box

You stored the e-mail address for that contact in the Contacts folder, so you do not have to retype the address. The contact's name appears in the To text box, and the message will be sent automatically to the e-mail address you previously stored.

If you want to send a copy of the message to another person, click the Cc button to open the dialog box with contact names again. If an e-mail address is not in your address book, you can also type it in the Cc box.

You easily can remove an address card from the contacts list. Right-click the name to be removed and then select Delete on the shortcut menu.

Professional and Effective Electronic Communication

E-mail has become a common form of communication for both personal and business users. While it can be informal in nature—much like a telephone conversation—e-mail communication should be courteous and professional, especially among business users. E-mail messages can be printed and saved, so they can serve as written proof of what has transpired, much like a signed letter or other official document. Keep in mind the following elements of professional and effective electronic communication when you compose your e-mail messages:

- Proofread your messages before sending them. Most e-mail programs have spell checkers that can help identify spelling and grammatical mistakes.

- Limit your use of emoticons (keyboard symbols used to show emotion, such as :-o to show surprise), humor, and jokes in your messages. They easily can be misunderstood and misinterpreted.

- Keep your messages short and to the point. If you are soliciting a response from the receiver of the message, you will find that a brief message with a pointed list of questions is most effective in getting that response.

- Try to limit each message to a single subject. For work-related communications, your message might become part of someone's file on the subject, and it is easier to track the information if it is subject specific.

- Double-check the addresses in the To, Cc, and Bcc text boxes before sending a message to avoid sending inappropriate or irrelevant messages. If you use the Reply All feature, you might accidentally embarrass yourself by sending a message to the wrong person or inconvenience the recipient with unwanted and unneeded communications.

- Remember that e-mail sent through company networks or Internet e-mail sites is not private.

- Use the appropriate mail format to send your messages. Sometimes excessive formatting in a specific word-processing format or in HTML format can prevent the receiver from reading a message if they do not have the appropriate application to view it.

Other Features Tour

As indicated earlier, this lesson focuses on using the Outlook mail feature. However, in Step-by-Step 9.8, you take a short tour of Outlook by opening two other Outlook folders. You can customize most Outlook folders to display the information in a folder in several different ways. When you open a folder, you will see the view that was used the last time that folder was opened.

Step-by-Step 9.8

1. If necessary, start Outlook.

2. Click **Calendar** in the Navigation pane. This feature is used to set up appointments and meetings. If no one has entered any meetings in Outlook yet, this folder will be empty.

3. Click **Tasks** in the Navigation pane. A grid used to organize information about tasks you want to accomplish is displayed in the Reading pane. If no one has entered any tasks in Outlook yet, this folder will be empty.

4. Close Outlook.

If you have the opportunity, use the Help feature to find out more about how you can use the application to organize many aspects of your work and personal tasks effectively.

Other Forms of Electronic Communications

▶ **VOCABULARY**
instant messaging

As mentioned previously, it is now possible to send e-mail using a cell phone, a personal digital assistant, or handheld computer. Other forms of text messaging are available besides e-mail, and these methods are available on many kinds of electronic devices. *Instant messaging* is a popular medium for correspondence in business as well as social settings. The Instant Messaging feature in Outlook, for example, enables you to send messages in real time. In other words, you can send and receive messages while you and the contact are both logged on to the Internet. Each contact must have an instant messaging account available.

Instant messaging is set up through the Options command on the Tools menu. In the Options dialog box, select the Other tab. Click the check boxes to Display online status next to a person's name and Display online status in the To and Cc fields when the mouse pointer rests on a person's name.

SUMMARY

In this lesson, you learned:

■ Microsoft Outlook includes features to manage appointments, tasks, and e-mail. The Navigation pane displays shortcuts that give you quick access to each of the Outlook folders.

■ Electronic mail is similar to regular mail because it requires an address, a message, and a carrier to get it from the sender to the receiver.

■ E-mail messages are broken into smaller portions of electronic data called packets, which are sent independently and then reorganized into the original message.

■ You can access e-mail on a computer using a program like Microsoft Outlook, or you can send and receive e-mail messages using a Web site with a built-in e-mail program, such as America Online or Hotmail.

■ Wireless communication makes it possible to send and receive e-mail using a handheld computer or cell phone with e-mail capabilities.

■ E-mail addresses consist of three parts: the user name, the "@" symbol, and the domain name.

■ An e-mail message header includes the address of the recipient, the subject of the message, and information about to whom the message is sent as a copy.

■ You can use the Inbox folder in Outlook to send and receive e-mail messages.

■ An attachment is a file that is sent with an e-mail message and can be opened by the recipient.

■ You can reply to an e-mail message, forward a message to a new recipient, delete a message, or save a message.

■ Spam, or junk e-mail, consists of unsolicited messages that take up space in your Inbox unnecessarily.

■ E-mail messages are organized in folders of incoming messages, sent messages, deleted messages, and junk e-mail. You also can create additional folders to organize your own e-mail.

■ Special e-mail features let you add an automatic signature to messages, block messages from certain addresses, create personalized stationery for your messages, and set up an automatic response or forward your messages to another address.

■ Professional electronic communication requires courtesy and brevity. Always check that the spelling and grammar is correct, and that the message is being sent to the intended recipient(s).

■ The Contacts folder is designed to store information about business and personal contacts with whom you often communicate.

■ You can create address cards that hold information such as name, address, phone number, e-mail address, and so on. Address cards are listed in alphabetical order in the Contacts folder.

■ Other forms of electronic communication are available such as instant messaging, which allows you to send messages in real time.

VOCABULARY REVIEW

Define the following terms:

attachments   encrypting   Quick Click Flag Status column
Contacts   instant messaging   signature
decryption   item   spam
electronic mail (e-mail)   packets   Windows Mail
e-mail address   personal information management (PIM)

 REVIEW QUESTIONS

MULTIPLE CHOICE

Select the best response for the following statements.

1. A file sent with an e-mail message is called a(n) _____.

   A. attachment   C. packet

   B. program   D. interface

2. Junk e-mail marketing a product or service is called _____.

   A. trash   C. packet

   B. program   D. spam

3. A(n) _____ is a keyboard symbol used to convey a tone or feeling in an electronic communication.

   A. plus   C. minus

   B. emoticon   D. @ symbol

4. A small chunk into which an e-mail message is broken as it is sent to the recipient is called a(n) _____.

   A. attachment   C. user name

   B. packet   D. domain name

FILL IN THE BLANK

Complete the following sentences by writing the correct word or words in the blanks provided.

1. An e-mail address consists of three parts: the _____, the @ symbol, and the user's domain name.

2. The inbox displays a message _____ for any new message.

3. You can save a message in _____ different formats.

4. _____ _____ enables you to send messages in real time.

5. _____ is unsolicited messages.

TRUE / FALSE

Circle T if the statement is true or F if the statement is false.

T   F   **1.**   Each Outlook folder organizes a different type of information.

T   F   **2.**   The default task selected in the Navigation pane is Mail.

T   F   **3.**   You can type only one e-mail address in the Cc text box.

T   F   **4.**   Click the Receive button to send a message.

T   F   **5.**   Long messages are appropriate for e-mail if you cover several topics in one message.

PROJECTS

CROSS-CURRICULAR— MATHEMATICS

Access the following link and review the top ten benefits of Microsoft Office Outlook 2007: http://office.microsoft.com/en-us/outlook. Click "Top 10 Reasons to Try" in the left pane of the Web page. After you review the topics, write a one- to two-page report explaining which three benefits you feel are most important and why you selected those benefits.

CROSS-CURRICULAR—SCIENCE

Microsoft has several informational links that are accessible at http://office.microsoft.com/en-us/outlook. Click "Outlook Home" in the left pane of the Web page, if necessary, and then scroll down to the What's new, Learn the basics, and Stay connected headings. Select one of these three topics and click the link to review the topic. When you are finished with the topic, use your word-processing program to write a report listing what you learned and how you can apply it.

CROSS-CURRICULAR—SOCIAL STUDIES

Access the Web site http://websearch.about.com/od/whatistheinternet/a/usewww.htm to read an article on "How The World Wide Web Has Changed Society." After you read the article, write a report expressing your opinion about the article. Do you agree or disagree with the author's statements? Explain why you agree or disagree.

CROSS-CURRICULAR—LANGUAGE ARTS

Access the Microsoft Web site at http://office.microsoft.com/clipart/ where you can download clip art and other media files. Select at least three clip art images to download. Send an e-mail to your instructor with one of the clip art images attached. Include a message that you downloaded the file from the Microsoft Web site.

WEB PROJECT

In addition to Microsoft Office Outlook, there are many other e-mail programs. Do an online search and locate at least two other e-mail client programs. Then compare the features contained in these programs with the features in Microsoft Outlook. After comparing the features, write a report indicating which program you consider the best and explain why. A good place to start your research is at http://en.wikipedia.org/wiki/Comparison_of_e-mail_clients.

TEAMWORK PROJECT

Individuals who use e-mail for frequent communication often are annoyed by unsolicited e-mail called spam. Spam can be obnoxious, offensive, and a waste of your time. Some countries have laws against spam. Your Internet service provider might try to block spam before it reaches your mailbox. However, you still might be inconvenienced by junk e-mail. Working with a partner, research spam to learn more about what it is used for, how marketers get addresses, how effective spam is, and ways that you can stop spam. Prepare a report on your findings. Include information on both good and bad instances of spam, if it is a nuisance or problem, and how you can stop it before it reaches your e-mail Inbox. At the end of your report, answer the following questions: Is spam ever useful? Should there be laws to restrict spam? Do you think you can block all spam from reaching your Inbox?

CRITICAL THINKING

A number of Web sites provide free access to e-mail. If you do not have a computer, public libraries, schools, and even some "Internet cafes" offer free or inexpensive computer access to the World Wide Web that you can use to check incoming messages and send your own e-mail. What kind of features would you like to have for a personal e-mail account? You might want to investigate some Web sites, such as *www.hotmail.com*, *www.usa.net*, or www.yahoo.com, to find out about the options available and then list the ones you think are most important. Why do you believe you would need these features for your e-mail account?

EXPLORING GOOGLE

Google also has an e-mail program called Gmail. This was introduced in an earlier chapter, and you already may have a Gmail account. Review the features of Google's Gmail program and compare them with those contained in Microsoft Office Outlook. Then create a short review explaining which program you prefer. List at least three reasons why you prefer the program you selected.

LESSON 10

Word Processing

■ OBJECTIVES

Upon completion of this lesson, you should be able to:

- Identify the components of the word-processor window.
- Save, open, and print a document.
- Select commands using the Ribbon, menus, and toolbars.
- Create and edit a document.
- Apply character, paragraph, and document formatting.
- Insert and modify pictures and drawn objects.
- Create, edit, and format a table.
- Use the Word Help system.
- Correct spelling and grammar in a document.
- Select synonyms from the Thesaurus.

Microsoft Office

The Microsoft Office 2007 suite consists of several programs, the four most popular being Word, Excel, PowerPoint, and Access. As you work through this lesson and Lessons 11-13, you will have an opportunity to explore these four programs. This lesson introduces you to Microsoft Office Word 2007, Microsoft's powerful, full-featured word-processing program. Word contains many features—some more commonly used than others. In this lesson, you will learn how to create and edit documents, how to apply and use some of the more popular Office features, and how to use Help when you need additional information. Designed as a component of the *Office Fluent* user interface that groups tools by task, you will find that much of what you learn in this lesson also can be applied to the other Office applications.

■ VOCABULARY

border

editing

font

font style

Format Painter

formatting

hard copy

insertion point

margins

Office Fluent

points

printout

sans serif

section

section break

selecting

serif

sizing handles

table

watermark

word wrap

...

Exploring the Word Window

You start all Office programs in the same way: Click the Start button on the Windows taskbar, point to All Programs, click Microsoft Office, and then click the program name to start the program and display the main window. **Figure 10–1** shows the main Word window, open to a blank document.

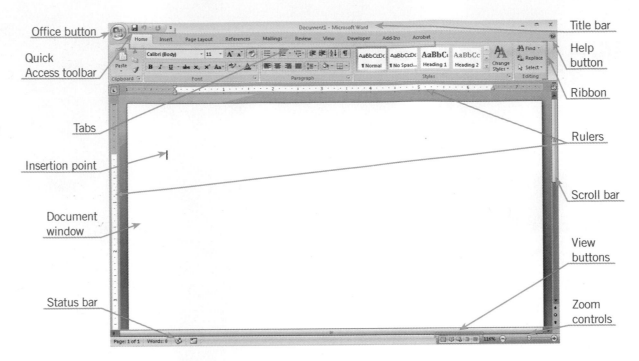

FIGURE 10–1   Opening Word window

EXTRA FOR EXPERTS

If your desktop contains a Word icon or an icon for another Office program, you can double-click the icon to start the program.

The following list describes most of the features displayed in this figure.

- *Document window*: Area where you type and work with a document
- *Help button*: Opens a new window with a Search text box
- *Office button*: Located in the upper-left corner of the Word window, this button replaces the File menu
- *Quick Access toolbar*: Located in the title bar and contains a repository of the most-used functions; fully customizable
- *Ribbon and groups*: Panels that contain command buttons and icons
- *Rulers*: Show the positioning of text, tabs, margins, insertion point, and any other elements on the page
- *Scroll bars*: Used to scroll vertically and horizontally through a document that is too large to fit in the document window
- *Status bar*: Displays the number of the current page and the total number of pages in the document; also indicates the on/off status of Word features such as spelling and grammar checking
- *Tabs*: Part of the Ribbon, tabs are organized around specific scenarios or objects; the controls on each tab are organized into several groups
- *Title bar*: Displays the name of the software program and the name of the document on which you are working; the default name of a document is DocumentX, where X is a number

- *View buttons*: Allow you to switch among Print Layout view, Full Screen Reading view, Web Layout view, Outline view, and Draft view
- *Zoom controls*: Allow you to zoom in for a close-up view of your file or zoom out to see more of the page at a reduced size

Entering Text

After you start Word, you are ready to begin creating a new document. When you type in the document window, the ***insertion point*** moves across the screen indicating where the next character will be placed, as shown in **Figure 10–2**.

▶ **VOCABULARY**
insertion point
word wrap

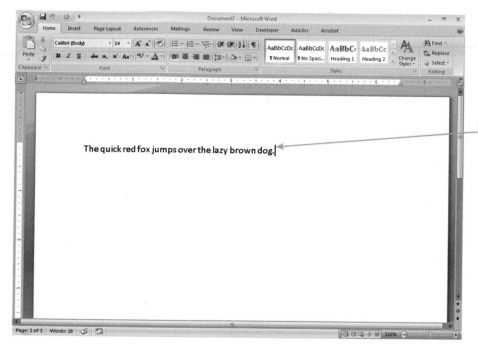

Insertion point

FIGURE 10–2   The insertion point shows your location in the document

Most word-processing programs, including Word, come with a ***word wrap*** feature. When the text reaches the end of a line, the insertion point automatically moves, or wraps, to the next line. To start a new line of text manually, you press the Enter key.

⎯⊙⎯ **WARNING**

As you work in a document, it is a good idea to save it regularly so you don't lose your work.

Saving a File

To retain a copy of a document permanently, you need to save it. You can do so by clicking the Save button on the Quick Access toolbar. The first time you save a document, the Save As dialog box opens, as shown in **Figure 10–3**. In this dialog box, first indicate the storage media device and location where you want to save the file. Then click the File name text box, if necessary, type the document name, and then click the Save button. After you've saved a document, you can open the Save As dialog box by clicking the Office button and then clicking Save As.

▦ **EXTRA FOR EXPERTS**

You can also save a document by pressing Ctrl+S or clicking the Office button and then clicking the Save command.

Save As
dialog box

Storage media
device and
location

Filename

Save button

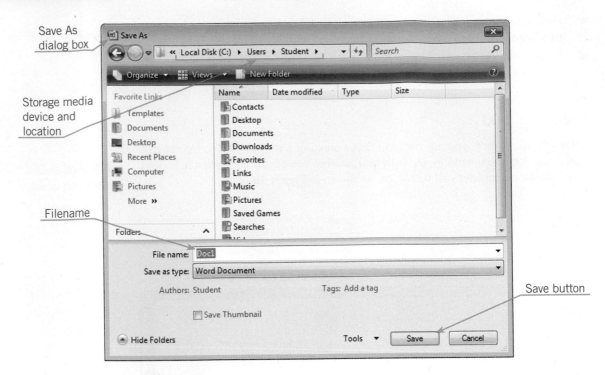

FIGURE 10–3   Save As dialog box

Printing a File

Often, you will want to print a copy of a document. A printed copy of a document is called *hard copy* or a *printout*. Before you print a document, you should view it in the Print Preview window. This gives you an image of how the document will look when it prints. To access the Print Preview window, click the Office button to display the Office button menu, point to Print, and then click Print Preview on the Print submenu.

You can print an entire document, a single page, or selected pages. Click the Office button, point to Print, and then click Quick Print to use the default print settings (for example, printer, specific pages, and number of copies). To change the default settings, click the Office button, point to Print, and then click Print on the Print submenu. This option displays the Print dialog box where you can view and change print settings. In **Figure 10–4**, Current page is selected and Number of copies is increased to 6. Most likely your printer name will be different from that in **Figure 10–4**.

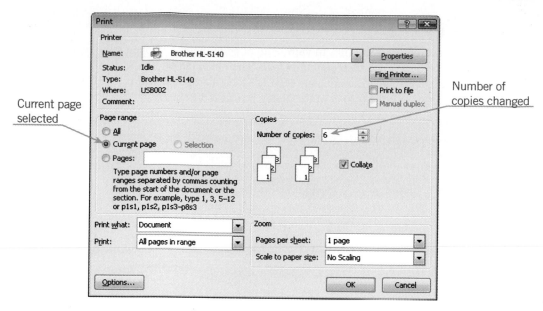

FIGURE 10–4 Print dialog box

Closing a File and Word

When you are finished working on a file and your changes are saved, you should close the document. Click the Office button and then click Close. You can also click the Close button on the title bar. If any changes you made have not been saved, a Microsoft Office Word dialog box is displayed. You have an opportunity to save or not save your changes or to cancel the Close command.

When you are finished working with a program, you should close it. To close Word, click the Office button and then click Exit Word. See **Figure 10–5**. You close other Microsoft Office 2007 programs in the same way.

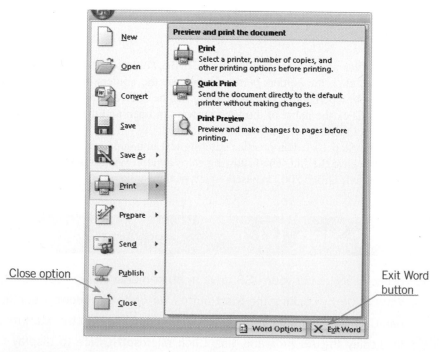

FIGURE 10–5 Closing a file and exiting Word

Opening an Existing File

You can open saved files to view, edit, or print them. You open a file by clicking the Office button and then clicking Open. The Open dialog box is displayed, as shown in **Figure 10–6**. (The contents of your Open dialog box will differ. If you are using Windows XP, the format of the dialog box also differs.)

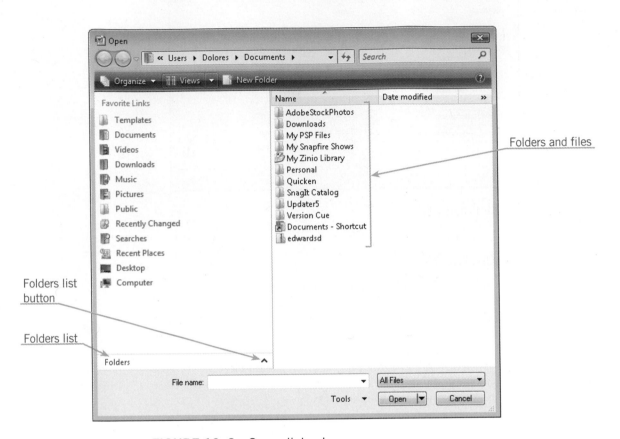

FIGURE 10–6   Open dialog box

A list of files and folders are displayed. If the Folders list appears below the Folders button, click the Folders button to collapse the Folders list. The filenames displayed in your Open dialog box most likely will be different from those shown in **Figure 10–6**. Click the name of the file you want to open and then click the Open button. The document appears in the Word window.

In Step-by-Step 10.1, you practice entering text in a document by composing a letter. You then save the file. The following steps assume Windows Vista is running and that Microsoft Office 2007 is based on a typical installation.

Step-by-Step 10.1

1. If necessary, insert your USB drive or other media storage device. Start Word 2007 by clicking the **Start** button 🔵 on the Windows Vista taskbar. Click **All Programs** at the bottom of the left pane on the Start menu to display the All Programs list. Click **Microsoft Office** to display the Microsoft Office list, and then click **Microsoft Office Word 2007**. A new blank document is displayed. If necessary, maximize the Word window.

2. Press **Enter** three times. This places the insertion point four lines from the top of the page.

3. Type the current date and then press **Enter** two times.

4. Type the following lines, pressing **Enter** once after each line except the third line. Press **Enter** two times after the third line.

   Mr. John Jernigan
   2250 East Bay Street
   Tampa, FL 34697

5. Type the salutation, **Dear Mr. Jernigan,** and then press **Enter** two times.

6. Type the following text. As you type, note how the text automatically wraps to the next line.

   Our records show that you have been a preferred customer of Books&More since our grand opening last year. We would like to thank you for your business by inviting you to our preferred customer Summer Extravaganza this Saturday.

7. Press **Enter**, and then type the following paragraph:

   This event is by invitation only. All of our books and other stock will be marked down by 20–30 percent. Complimentary refreshments will be served. We look forward to seeing you on June 21.

8. Press **Enter**, and then type **Sincerely** followed by a comma. Press **Enter** two times.

9. Type **Your Name** and press **Enter**.

10. Type **Manager**.

11. Click the **Save** button 🖫 on the Quick Access toolbar to display the Save As dialog box. Select the location to which you are saving files. Type **Books** in the File name text box. Click **Save**. Leave the document open for Step-by-Step 10.2.

Selecting Text

If you want to modify text in a document, you first have to identify the text. You do this by *selecting* the text. To select several words or paragraphs, click at the beginning of the text you want to modify, hold down the mouse button and drag to the end of the text you want to change. You can double-click a word to select it. Or, you can triple-click to select an entire paragraph. Once the text is selected, you can edit it or format it. Editing and for matting are covered later in this lesson. To deselect a block of text, click anywhere outside the selection or press any arrow key.

    You also can copy or cut selected text and then paste it to another location. You do this by using the Cut, Copy, and Paste buttons in the Clipboard group on the Home tab. When you cut or copy text, it is placed on the Clipboard, which is a temporary storage area. Click the location where you want to paste the cut or copied text, and then click the Paste button.

▶ **VOCABULARY**
selecting

Editing Text

After creating a document, you can make changes to it without having to retype the document. Making changes to an existing document is called *editing*. Once you select the text, you can edit it by deleting it, replacing it, moving it, copying it, and so on. You can move the insertion point to any position in a document to make corrections or to insert text. You move it either with the arrow keys or by clicking the mouse.

The following list includes some easy-to-use methods for quickly correcting text:

- Use the *Backspace* key to delete text to the left of the insertion point. Each time you press Backspace, a character of text or blank space is deleted. For example, if your insertion point is to the right of the "r" in *computer* and you press Backspace, the "r" is deleted.

- Use the *Delete* key to delete text to the right of the insertion point. Each time you press Delete, a character or space in front of the insertion point is deleted. For example, if the insertion point is to the left of the "p" in *computer* and you press Delete, the "p" is deleted.

- Most word-processing programs function in *Insert mode* by default. This means that wherever you place the insertion point, the text that you type at that point and the text to the right of the insertion point moves to the right.

- *AutoCorrect* is another feature found in Microsoft Word and in many other word-processing programs. The program automatically corrects errors, such as commonly misspelled words. For example, if you accidentally type "teh", the software changes it to "the". You can customize this feature to include words that you often misspell.

EXTRA FOR EXPERTS

If you delete text by mistake, immediately click the Undo button on the Quick Access toolbar to restore the deleted text.

Using Spell Check

In addition to the AutoCorrect feature, Word comes with a spell check tool. You can check the spelling of one word at a time, a group of words, or the entire document.

The spell check tool does not check for correct word usage, so using the spell check feature does not eliminate the need to carefully proofread a document. For example, if you type cite in a document when you should have used site, spell check would not detect the error. To use the spell checker, press F7 or on the Review tab, in the Proofing group, click Spelling & Grammar. The Spelling and Grammar dialog box opens, as shown in **Figure 10–7**.

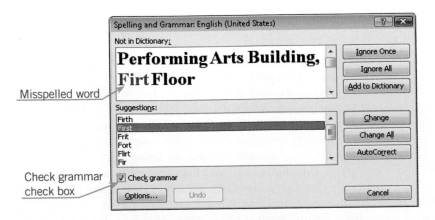

FIGURE 10–7 Spelling and Grammar dialog box

The "Firt" spelling error is identified in the top box, and suggestions for replacing it are provided in the box below. If the correct word is in the list of suggestions, click it to select it. Note that several buttons are located on the right side of the dialog box. Click the Change or Change All button to accept the highlighted word in the Suggestions box. If the word is spelled correctly, click the Ignore Once or Ignore All button. After you click one of these buttons, Word continues to check the document.

In addition to proofreading your document for misspelled words, you also can check grammar. When you use the grammar checking tool, the content is checked to verify that you have used correct punctuation and capitalization, complete sentences, the right tense, and so on. This process is similar to correcting spelling errors. To activate the Grammar feature, click the Check grammar check box in the Spelling and Grammar dialog box as shown in **Figure 10–7**.

Using the Thesaurus

The Thesaurus feature allows you to look up synonyms for words. To use the Thesaurus, select the word that you want to change. Click the Review tab and then click Thesaurus in the Proofing group. The Research task pane opens. As shown in **Figure 10–8**, the word for which you want to find a synonym is displayed in the Search for text box. Synonyms for the selected word are listed in the box below. Point to a synonym and a down arrow is displayed to the right of the selected word. Click the down arrow, and then click Insert to replace the existing word in your document. Click the Close button on the task pane to remove it from the Word window.

> **EXTRA FOR EXPERTS**
>
> Words that are not recognized by the dictionary are identified with a wavy red underline. Grammatical errors are identified with a wavy green underline.

> **EXTRA FOR EXPERTS**
>
> You also can find a synonym by right-clicking a word. On the shortcut menu, point to Synonyms and then select a synonym on the submenu.

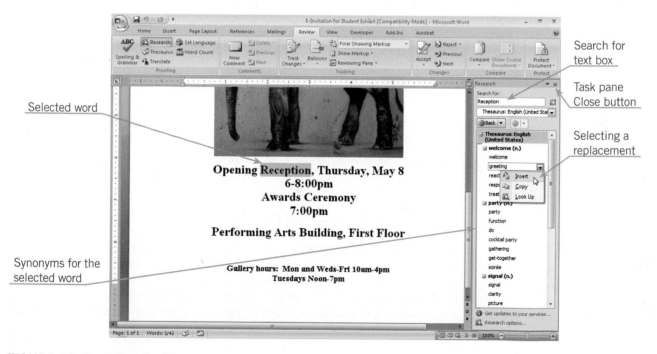

FIGURE 10–8   Using the Thesaurus

In Step-by-Step 10.2, you edit the document you created in Step-by-Step 10.1.

Step-by-Step 10.2

1. If necessary, open the **Books** document. In the first paragraph, change Saturday to **Sunday**.

2. In the next paragraph, select **20-30** and change it to **25-35**, and then change the date to **June 28**.

3. In the first paragraph, double-click the word **preferred** to select it. Click the **Review** tab, and then click **Thesaurus** in the Proofing group.

4. In the Research task pane, point to a synonym of your choice, click its **down arrow**, and then click **Insert**. Close the Research task pane.

5. Click the **Close** button ✕ on the title bar to close the *Books* document. When the message box opens asking if you want to save your changes, click **Yes**.

Formatting Text

You can enhance the appearance of a document by using Word formatting features. *Formatting* refers to the appearance and layout of text. Using different fonts, font sizes, colors, and styles in a document can make it look more professional. You can format characters, paragraphs, or the entire document.

- Character formats include font size and font color and attributes such as bold, italics, and underlining. These are applied to selected characters.
- Paragraph formats include line spacing and indents. These are applied to an entire paragraph; they cannot be applied to a portion of a paragraph.
- Document formats apply to an entire document. These include margins and paper size.

Fonts and Character Formatting

The Font group is located on the Home tab. Using different fonts, font sizes, and font styles is a quick way to enhance the appearance of a document. A *font* is the design of a typeface. Different *font styles* will have different results on various documents. Adding color, italics, underlining, and other available effects allows you to create impressive documents. Some of the more commonly used fonts are Times New Roman, Arial, and Courier.

> This is Times New Roman.
> This is Arial.
> This is Courier.

Fonts are either *serif* or *sans serif*. Serif fonts have extra strokes at the ends of the letters. Sans serif fonts do not have these extra strokes. Generally, you use serif fonts for the body of text because they are easier to read in large blocks of text. Times New Roman is a serif font. Sans serif fonts often are used for headings. Arial is a sans serif font.

The size of fonts is measured in *points*—72 points equal one inch. Sizes vary from one font to the next; 10 point in one font might look bigger than 12 point of another font. The most common font size for text is a 12-point font. Sizes over 18 points are good for headlines and banners.

▶ **VOCABULARY**
points

This is 10-point font size.

This is 12-point font size.

This is 14-point font size.

This is 18-point font size.

This is 36-point font size.

You also can add attributes such as bold, underline, italics, and color to characters. These attributes can be applied as you type the text or after you have finished typing.

You can bold your text.
You can underline your text.
You can double underline your text.
You can type your text in italics.
You can add ***more than one attribute to your text.***
You can add color to your text.
~~You can strike through your text.~~

You can apply these and other options through the Font group located on the Home tab. See **Figure 10–9**.

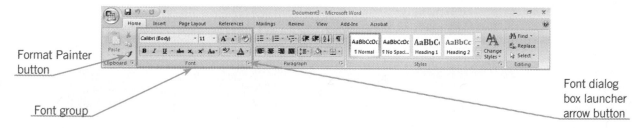

Format Painter button

Font group

Font dialog box launcher arrow button

FIGURE 10–9   Font options on the Home tab

Clicking the Font dialog box launcher arrow button opens the Font dialog box shown in **Figure 10–10**. Using this dialog box, you can apply several formats at one time such as the font size, style, color, and so on.

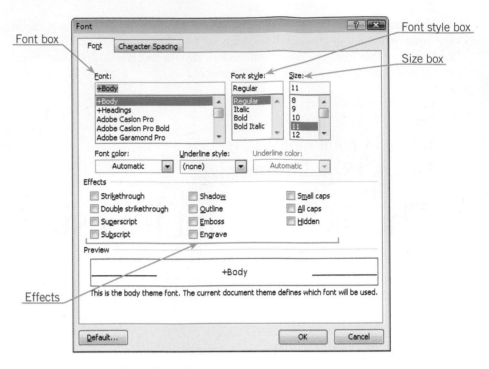

FIGURE 10–10   Font dialog box

To apply the same formatting to different text within a document, such as making all headings 18-point Arial bold, you can use the ***Format Painter***. This tool, located on the Home tab with the Cut, Copy, and Paste buttons, provides a time-saving way to apply formats consistently throughout a document. Select the text that contains the formatting you want to copy, click the Format Painter button, and then select the text to which you want to apply the formatting. Double-click the Format Painter button to apply formatting to more than one item.

In Step-by-Step 10.3, you format a document using the buttons and features in the Font group. This group, shown in **Figure 10–11**, is part of the Home tab.

Step-by-Step 10.3

1. If necessary, open Word. Click the **Office** button 🔲, click **New**, and then click **Create** in the New Document window.

2. Type your birth month and press **Enter** two times.

3. Select the name of your birth month. Click the **Bold** button **B** in the Font group. See **Figure 10–11**.

FIGURE 10–11
Font group on the Home tab

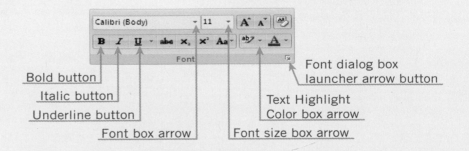

4. Click below your birth month. Click the **Underline** button U in the Font group. Type the name of your zodiac sign. It will be underlined as you type.

5. Click the **Underline** button U to turn off underlining. Press **Enter** two times.

6. Click the **Italic** button *I* in the Font group. Type the name of the city and state in which you live.

7. Select your birth month. Click the **Font** box arrow `Calibri (Body) ▼` in the Font group. Select **Arial**. Click the **Font Size** box arrow `11 ▼`, and then click **24**.

8. Select the name of your zodiac sign. Click the **Text Highlight Color** box arrow `ab▾` and then select a **color** of your choice.

9. Place the insertion point at the end of the text on the page and click the **Italic** button *I* to turn off italics, if necessary. Press **Enter** two times. Type the following paragraph:

   I can use word-processing software to create documents such as letters, reports, flyers, and envelopes. I also can use word-processing software to enter text in a document and later make changes to the text. This is called editing.

10. Double-click the word *editing* to select it and then click the **Bold** button **B** in the Font group.

11. The word *editing* should still be highlighted. Click the **Format Painter** button ✔ in the Clipboard group. The pointer changes to a paintbrush icon ▲I.

12. Select the first occurrence of the term **word-processing**. Release the mouse button. The text *word-processing* should now be bold. Use the same process to apply bold to the next occurrence of *word-processing*.

13. Save the document as **Personal**. If instructed to do so, print and then close the document.

Paragraph Formatting

Paragraph formatting is the process of changing the appearance of an entire paragraph. The Paragraph group is located on the Home tab and provides a variety of options for formatting a paragraph. The following list describes the features in the Paragraph group. See **Figure 10–12**.

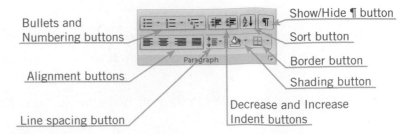

FIGURE 10–12   Paragraph group on the Home tab

- *Bullets*: Used to emphasize and organize a list in a document; available in a variety of styles
- *Numbering and Multilevel List*: Used to add numbers to a list; the Multilevel List button contains a number of styles for listing items in more than one level, as in an outline
- *Decrease Indent/Increase Indent*: Decreases or increases the indent level of a paragraph
- *Sort*: Sorts numerical data or alphabetizes selected text
- *Show/Hide ¶*: Displays or hides paragraph symbols and other hidden formatting symbols
- *Align Text*: Four align text options: left, right, center, and justify
- *Line spacing*: Changes the spacing between lines of text
- *Shading*: Applies color to the background behind the selected text or paragraph
- *Border*: Applies a variety of border options to selected text or paragraph; includes horizontal line and table options

In Step-by-Step 10.4, you adjust spacing, alignment, and indents in a document. You use the various buttons in the Paragraph Group to apply the formatting.

EXTRA FOR EXPERTS

You also can use keyboard shortcuts to align text: Ctrl+L for left alignment, Ctrl+E for center alignment, Ctrl+R for right alignment, and Ctrl+J for justified alignment.

Step-by-Step 10.4

1. If necessary, open Word. Click the **Office** button, and then click **Open**.

2. In the Open dialog box, navigate to and open **Step10-4** from the Lesson10 folder in the data files supplied for this course.

3. Click the **Office** button, and then click **Save As**. Use the Save As dialog box to save the document as **Paragraph**. If a dialog box opens advising you about using a new file format, click the **OK** button.

4. Click the **Show/Hide ¶** button ¶ in the Paragraph group to show paragraph marks and other formatting symbols, if necessary.

5. Select the title of the document and then click the **Center** button ≡ in the Paragraph group.

6. Indent the first line of each paragraph by clicking in front of the first character and pressing the **Tab** key. Do *not* indent the four-item list in the middle of the document.

7. Select the first two paragraphs of text after the title. Click the **Line spacing** button ▼ in the Paragraph group and click **1.5**.

8. Select the list of four items below the second paragraph. Click the **Bullets** button arrow ▼ in the Paragraph group and select the **check mark bullet**.

9. Select the remaining two paragraphs of text and change the line spacing to **1.0** (single spacing).

10. Save the document. If instructed, print a copy and then close the file. Leave Word open for Step-by-Step 10.5.

Page Setup

Page setup is the process of changing the appearance of a page by modifying the document size, adding columns, inserting line numbers, and so on. The Page Setup group is located on the Page Layout tab and provides a variety of options for formatting a page. The following list describes the features in the Page Setup group. See **Figure 10–13**. (Your Page Layout tab might differ depending on the width of your Word window.)

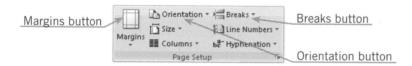

Margins button   Orientation ▼   Breaks ▼   Breaks button
                        Size ▼   Line Numbers ▼
                Margins
                        Columns ▼   Hyphenation ▼
                        Page Setup   Orientation button

FIGURE 10–13   Page Setup group on the Page Layout tab

- *Margins* lets you select the margin sizes for the entire document or current selection.
- *Orientation* switches the pages between portrait and landscape mode.
- *Size* lets you select a specific paper size.
- *Columns* is used to split the text into two or more columns.
- *Breaks* is used to insert page and section breaks.
- *Line Numbers* can be added in the margin alongside of each line.
- *Hyphenation* lets you turn hyphenation on, which is used to break lines between the syllables of words.

Margins are the white space around the edges of the page that frame the document. By default, the top and bottom and left and right margins are set at 1 inch.

Often, you will create multipage documents. Word automatically moves text to the next page, based on the margins. You manually can determine where text breaks occur by inserting a page or section break. A *section* is a portion of a document that is separated from the rest of the document. You can format a section differently from the rest of the pages in the document. To insert a *section break*, position the insertion point where you want the break, and then click the Breaks button arrow. The Page Breaks and Section Breaks options are displayed in the Breaks gallery, as shown in **Figure 10–14**. Click the break you want to insert into the document; a section break is indicated by a double dotted line, and a page break is indicated by a single dotted line.

▶ **VOCABULARY**

margins

section

section break

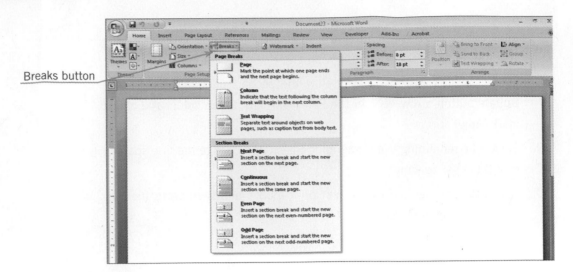

Breaks button

FIGURE 10–14   Breaks gallery

You also can set the orientation of the document through the Page Setup group. You can print a page in Portrait orientation, where the top of the page is oriented to the shorter side of the paper. Or, you can print in Landscape orientation, where the top of the page is oriented to the longer side of the paper.

Borders and Color

The Page Background group, also located on the Page Layout tab, provides options to add color and interest to the background of the page. See **Figure 10–15**.

FIGURE 10–15   Page Background group on the Page Layout tab

- *Watermark* is text or a picture that is displayed behind document text.
- *Page Color* primarily is used for a Web page to create an interesting background for online viewing.
- *Page Borders* can be used to add interest and emphasis to various parts of the document.

Clicking each of these buttons opens a related gallery or dialog box. Borders and coloring can add emphasis to a document and call out important information. You can apply a border and shading to a portion of the document or to the entire document. Select the text to which you want to add the border or shading, and then click Page Borders in the Page Background group. The Borders and Shading dialog box opens, as shown in **Figure 10–16**. You can select from a variety of border styles and widths. You also can apply color to a border. Click the Apply to arrow to select what part of the document to apply the border: Whole document, This section, This section – First page only, or This section – All except first page. Click the Shading tab in the dialog box to select a fill color for the selected text. When you apply shading, choose a shade that is light enough so that the text can be read easily.

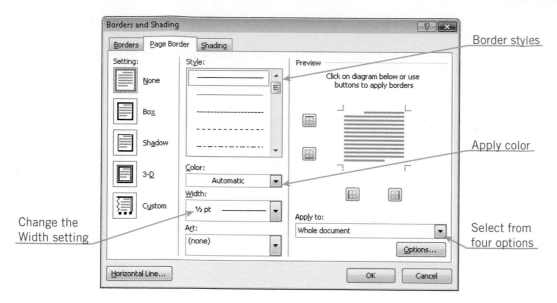

FIGURE 10–16   Borders and Shading dialog box

A *watermark* inserts ghosted text behind the page content and often is used to indicate that a document is confidential, should not be copied, and so on. Clicking the Watermark button displays the Watermark gallery where you can select from the default options or create a custom watermark using the Printed Watermark dialog box.

Clicking the Page Color button opens a gallery of colors. In addition to the Theme Colors and Standard Colors, you can select More Colors and Fill Effects.

▶ **VOCABULARY**
watermark

Headers and Footers

The header and footer feature allows you to insert information on every page, either at the top or bottom of the page.

- *Header*: Information at the top of the page
- *Footer*: Information at the bottom of the page
- *Page Number*: Page numbers, which are associated with headers and footers, can be added to the top, the bottom, or the margins of a document

You can type any information in the header or footer, such as the title of the document, date it was written, author, page number, and so forth. The Header & Footer group is located on the Insert tab.

To insert a header and/or footer, click the Insert tab and then click the Header or the Footer button to display a gallery. Select an option—such as Blank, Blank (Three Columns), Alphabet, or Annual—and type the header text; to add a footer, click the Footer button, select a Footer option, and type the footer text. Click the Close Header and Footer button in the Close group on the Ribbon to return to the body of the document.

You also can add page numbers to a document by using the Page Number command. Clicking the Page Number button in the Header & Footer group on the Insert tab displays a list of the following options: Top of Page, Bottom of Page, Page Margins, and Current Position. Click the option you want to select it.

Illustrations

Also located on the Insert tab is the Illustrations group. Adding graphics and other images to a document can provide visual appeal and help to communicate a message.

- *Picture*: Used to insert a picture from a file
- *Clip Art*: A collection of graphic images that is part of Microsoft Word
- *Shapes*: Sets of ready-made shapes, such as arrows, squares, rectangles, and so on
- *SmartArt*: A graphic or diagram used to visually communicate information
- *Chart*: Used to illustrate and compare data

Clip art, shapes, and SmartArt are parts of a collection of graphic images that comes with the Word program and which you can insert into a document. You also can add photos, symbols, and drawings to a document. After you insert a picture into a document, you can move it, resize it, and make other modifications.

To insert clip art, click the Clip Art button. The Clip Art task pane opens. See **Figure 10–17**. In the Search for text box, type a word or two that describes the type of clip art you want to insert and then click the Go button. Word will search in the default *All collections* for the specified art. The matches are displayed as thumbnail images in the results box. Click a picture to insert it into the document.

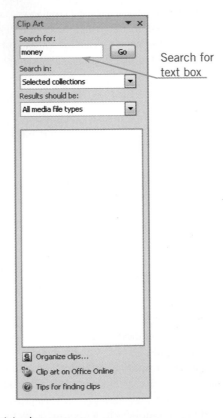

FIGURE 10–17 Clip Art task pane

After placing the image in the document, you can select the image to move it or resize it. When the image is selected, the Picture Tools Format tab opens. See **Figure 10–18**. This tab contains buttons for making additional changes to the image. *Sizing handles* also surround the image. Drag a handle to resize the picture.

EXTRA FOR EXPERTS

Some Web sites offer free clip art that you can download.

EXTRA FOR EXPERTS

If you create a text box and then insert the clip art in the text box, it will be easier to move the graphic around in the document.

▶ VOCABULARY

sizing handles

FIGURE 10–18   Picture Tools Format tab

Also located on the Insert tab is the Symbols group. These are special characters, such as mathematical symbols or currency symbols, which can be inserted in documents. To insert a symbol, click the Symbol button. The Symbol gallery opens, similar to that shown in **Figure 10–19**. Select the symbol you want. The symbol is inserted at the position of the insertion point. If the symbol you want is not displayed in the Symbol gallery, click More Symbols to open the Symbol dialog box.

FIGURE 10–19   Symbol gallery

In addition to clip art and symbols, a variety of ready-made shapes is available. Clicking the Shapes button will display a gallery of tools that include lines, arrows, circles, rectangles, and more. Additionally, you can draw your own shape by clicking New Drawing Canvas located at the bottom of the gallery. See **Figure 10–20**.

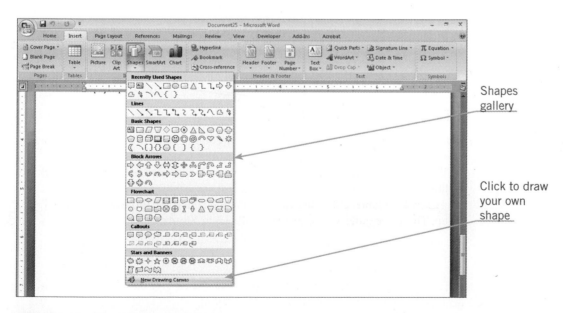

FIGURE 10–20   Shapes gallery

Complete Step-by-Step 10.5 to insert a graphic into a document.

Step-by-Step 10.5

1. If necessary, start Word and open a new blank document. Save the document as **Board Meeting.**

2. Type **BOARD MEETING** as the document title. Select the title and change the font size to **20**, apply bold formatting, and center it. Click after the text to deselect it, and then press **Enter** three times.

3. Click the **Insert** tab and then click **Clip Art** in the Illustrations group.

4. Type **meeting** in the Clip Art task pane Search for text box and then click the **Go** button.

5. Scroll through the displayed images and click to select one of your choice. The graphic appears in your document at the insertion point.

6. Click to select the image. Close the Clip Art task pane.

7. Drag the image sizing handles so it is approximately 3 inches wide, and then make sure it is centered on the page.

8. Click anywhere to the right of the image and press **Enter** three times. Set the font size to **14** and type the following:

   Tuesday, January 14
   1:30 pm
   Room 423
   Discussion of School Board issues

9. Select the text you just typed and then center it, if necessary.

10. Save the document.

11. If instructed, print the document and then close it.

Creating a Simple Table

A *table* is an arrangement of information in columns and rows. In tables, *rows* go across while *columns* go down. A *cell* is the intersection of a column and row, and the lines that divide the columns and rows are called *borders*. A table is a useful way to illustrate information in a concise format.

To create a table, click the Insert tab and then click the Table button in the Tables group. The Table gallery is displayed as shown in **Figure 10–21.**

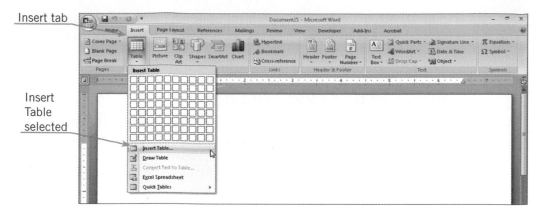

FIGURE 10–21   Table gallery

Click Insert Table to display the Insert Table dialog box. See **Figure 10–22**.

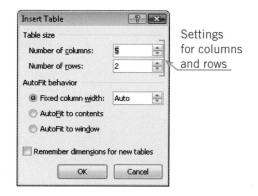

FIGURE 10–22   Insert Table dialog box

Click the up and down arrows in the Number of columns and Number of rows boxes to select the size of your table. You also can type the number of columns and rows. Then click the OK button. The empty table structure is inserted into the document. The insertion point is in the upper-left cell of the table. When the insertion point is in the table, the Table Tools Design tab becomes the active tab. See **Figure 10–23**. A number of options are available through this tab, including a variety of Table Styles and options to add shading and borders to your table.

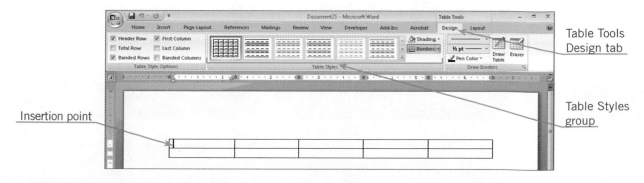

FIGURE 10–23   Table Tools Design tab

To add data to a cell, click in a cell and begin typing. Use the Tab key to move to the next cell and the keyboard up and down arrow keys to move from one row to another.

Formatting and Modifying a Table

In addition to using the Table Styles, you can modify the structure of a table and format the text in the cells in other ways. Selecting a cell or a number of adjacent cells and then right-clicking the selection displays a menu of options and the mini toolbar. See **Figure 10–24**. The mini toolbar contains formatting buttons and appears when you make selections in a document so you can quickly format the selection.

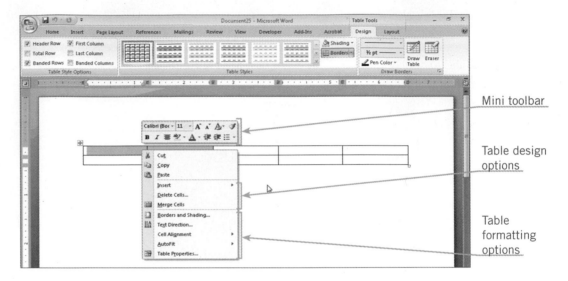

FIGURE 10–24   Table shortcut menu

The following list describes the table formatting and design options:

- *Insert rows and columns*: Inserting a row or rows above or below and a column or columns to the left or right of the selected cell or cells.
- *Delete rows and columns*: Deleting the selected rows or columns
- *Merge cells*: Merging the contents of the selected cells into one
- *Increase column width and row height*: Adjusting the width and height of the selected cells by dragging the column or row borders
- *Borders and shading*: Applying a border or shading to the selected cells

In Step-by-Step 10.6, you create a table in a document.

Step-by-Step 10.6

1. If necessary, open Word and start a new, blank document. Save the document as **Mileage**.

2. Type **MILEAGE FOR JOHN JERNIGAN** as the title. Select the title and change the point size to **18**, apply bold formatting, and center it. Click to the right of the title to deselect it.

3. Press **Enter** two times. Change the font size to **12**, click the **Bold** button **B** in the Font group to deselect it, and then click the **Align Text Left** button ≡ in the Paragraph group.

4. Click the **Insert** tab and then click the **Table** button in the Tables group. Create a table with four rows and five columns.

5. Next, you enter data in the table, as shown in **Figure 10–25**. Notice that you will need one more row. Right-click any cell in the first row of the table, point to **Insert**, and then click **Insert Rows Above**.

6. Continue to enter the data as shown in **Figure 10–25**. Press **Tab** to move from cell to cell.

7. Select the first row by pointing to the first cell and dragging to the last cell. Click the **Bold** button **B** in the Font group on the Home tab.

8. Select the last row and click the **Bold** button **B** on the mini toolbar. Click the **Font Color** button arrow **A** in the Font group and click **Red** in the Standard Colors row.

9. Select all the cells containing numeric data (this should include all cells except those in the first column and first row). Click the **Align Text Right** button ≡ in the Paragraph group on the Home tab.

10. Select the first row. Click the **Center** button ≡.

11. Save the document, which should look like that shown in **Figure 10–25**.

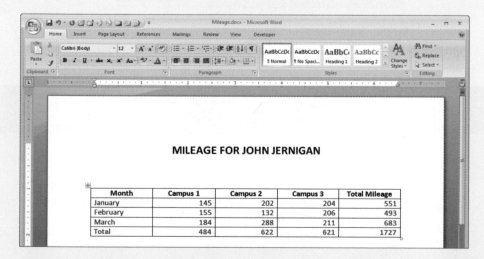

FIGURE 10–25
Inserted table in a Word document

12. If instructed, print the document. Close it and exit Word.

Getting Help

Word comes with a Help feature that provides quick access to information on Word features and step-by-step instructions on how to use the features. To use the Help system, click the Microsoft Office Word Help button located in the upper-right corner of the Word window. This opens the Word Help window, as shown in **Figure 10–26**. Click a topic in the Browse Word Help section or type a word or two describing the feature for which you need help. Click the Search button to start the search. Click a result to view the Help information.

FIGURE 10–26   Word Help window

SUMMARY

In this lesson, you learned:

■ Word-processing software is used to create documents such as letters, reports, memos, brochures, and Web pages.

■ Commands for using the features of a word-processing program are selected from tabs and groups. You also can use keyboard shortcuts to execute some commands.

■ Word-processing programs come with powerful editing tools. You can make changes quickly and easily to text, cut or copy text, and delete it.

■ The spell checker checks documents for possible misspelled words. Word also has a grammar-checking tool that identifies grammatical mistakes, and a Thesaurus, which displays synonyms for a selected word.

- You can apply formatting to characters, paragraphs, or an entire document. Word comes with a variety of formatting tools that enable you to enhance the appearance of documents.
- Clip art can be added to documents to enhance their visual appearance.
- Tables are used to present information in an organized manner.
- Word's Help system offers a variety of resources for getting help and information on features and tools.

VOCABULARY REVIEW

Define the following terms:

border	insertion point	section break
editing	margins	selecting
font	Office Fluent	serif
font style	points	sizing handles
Format Painter	printout	table
formatting	sans serif	watermark
hard copy	section	word wrap

REVIEW QUESTIONS

MULTIPLE CHOICE

Select the best response for the following statements.

1. The Office Fluent user interface groups tools by _____.

   A. tasks
   B. titles
   C. numbers
   D. alphabetical order

2. Which Word feature corrects errors as you type?

   A. AutoCorrect
   B. Spelling and Grammar
   C. Thesaurus
   D. Undo and Redo

3. Times New Roman, Arial, and Courier are types of _____.

   A. templates
   B. fonts
   C. commands
   D. formatting

4. To place the name of a document at the top of every page in the document, create a _____.

   A. margin
   B. justification
   C. header
   D. footer

5. You can tell that a graphic is selected by small squares on its border. These squares are called _____.

   A. symbols
   B. borders
   C. sizing handles
   D. clip art

TRUE/FALSE

Circle T if the statement is true or F if the statement is false.

T   F   **1.** In a table, rows go across and columns go down.

T   F   **2.** Editing documents means making changes to existing text.

T   F   **3.** It is possible to apply more than one formatting attribute to the same text.

T   F   **4.**   A group is the design of a typeface.

T   F   **5.**   Paragraph formatting is the process of changing the appearance of a paragraph.

FILL IN THE BLANK

Complete the following sentences by writing the correct word or words in the blanks provided.

1. The _____ are the white spaces around the edges of a document.

2. The _____ feature automatically moves text to the next line when you reach the end of the current line.

3. A table is composed of rows and _____.

4. To retain a copy of a document permanently, you need to _____.

5. A printed copy of a document is called a(n) _____ or _____.

■ PROJECTS

CROSS-CURRICULAR— MATHEMATICS

Use the Internet and other resources to research five to ten roller coaster rides at amusement parks in the United States. Gather information to include the name of the ride, a brief description, the name and location of the amusement park, and the height, length, and speed of the roller coaster. Present your data in a Word table. Format your table using Word's formatting features.

CROSS-CURRICULAR—SCIENCE

Use the Internet and other resources to identify five women who have received the Nobel Prize for Science. Use your word-processing program to prepare a written report. The report should be a minimum of two typewritten pages. Include the name of the scientist, her birth country, her contribution to science, and the year in which she received the award. Try to find a picture of the women and insert the pictures into the report. If you cannot locate a picture, insert an appropriate clip art image. Divide the report into five sections, using the Continuous Section Break option.

CROSS-CURRICULAR—SOCIAL STUDIES

Add a title to your page. Then create a table with a minimum of three columns and 11 rows. Merge the three columns in the first row and add a title. Create a dictionary of a minimum of 10 new terms you have learned up through Lesson 10. Type the term name in the first column, the definition in the second column, and add a clip art image representing the term in the third column. Bold the term and add a color. Select a unique font of your choosing. The list of terms should be in alphabetical order.

CROSS-CURRICULAR—LANGUAGE ARTS

Most word-processing programs have features that are especially useful to writers, such as styles, formatting, and comments. Use the Internet, Help tools, and any other resources to identify these and other features that are useful to writers. Prepare a report that includes the name of each feature and why it is useful.

WEB PROJECT

Computer crimes have increased rapidly over the last few years. These crimes involve illegal use of or the unauthorized entry into a computer system or computer data to tamper, interfere with, damage, or manipulate the system or data. Use the Internet and other resources to research and prepare a report on various security devices to guard against computer crime. The report should be a minimum of two pages. Set a top margin of two inches and side margins of one inch. Include at least two graphics in your report.

 ## TEAMWORK PROJECT

Do you like trying to solve mysteries? Work with a partner to investigate the mystery of the Bermuda Triangle. Many planes and boats have mysteriously disappeared there! Along with a partner, use the Internet and any other resources to find information on the Bermuda Triangle. You might want to include some background information such as its location, documented disappearances, and unexplained events; thoughts of other researchers; and your conclusion. Prepare a report with your findings. Be sure to format it attractively.

CRITICAL THINKING

Many instructors require students to use a style guide when preparing a report. One of the more popular guides is the MLA Handbook for Writers of Research Papers. It includes information on writing and formatting research papers. You probably have used this tool in some of your report assignments. Use the Internet and any other resources to research the MLA guidelines for formatting a research paper. Use those guidelines and Word features to prepare a one- to two-page report on your findings.

 # EXPLORING GOOGLE

In an earlier lesson, you learned how to search for images. Google, however, indexes millions of images; and your search results can result in hundreds or even thousands of images. Most likely, many of these images do not match your search topic. To limit the number of images to your particular quest, you can use the Advanced Image Search link. Starting on the main page of the Google Image Search, click the Advanced Image Search link located to the right of the Search Images button. Clicking this link takes you to the Advanced Image Search page. On this page, you can use text boxes to limit your search, relate it to an exact phrase, or relate it (or not relate it) to any specific words. You also can specify content type, size, coloration, file type, domain, and safe search with filtering options.

Using Google, search for Academy Award winners. Select three of the winners for whom you would like additional information and do an advanced search on these three people. Use Word to write a paragraph about each of the three winners that you selected. Next, use Google's image search tool and find at least two images that relate to each winner. Insert the images into your document within the paragraphs that relate to each winner. Use section breaks between the paragraphs and add a title to the page.

LESSON 11

Presentation Graphics

■ OBJECTIVES

Upon completion of this lesson, you should be able to:

■ Describe presentation software.

■ Explain the advantage of using visuals.

■ Describe the guidelines for effective presentations.

■ Create a presentation.

■ Work in different views.

■ Insert new slides.

■ Select appropriate slide layouts.

■ Apply a theme.

■ Add charts and clip art.

■ Add transitions and animations.

■ Print a presentation and handouts.

■ VOCABULARY

animation

charts

multimedia

Normal view

Notes pane

Outline tab

placeholder

presentation software

slide layout

Slide Show view

Slide Sorter view

Slides tab

theme

transitions

...

Presentation Software Defined

Presentation software is used to organize and present information, normally in the form of a slide show. Through the use of sequential slides, enhanced with a variety of special effects and features, a presentation is an effective and professional way to communicate topics and ideas. In addition, presentation software provides options for generating notes for the presenter and handouts for the audience. Equipment requirements for the presentation include a projector and computer.

Presentation software is a form of multimedia software because it enables you to combine multiple types of media, such as text, graphics, animation, and video clips, in a single slide show, and even in a single slide! In general, *multimedia* is defined as the use of text, graphics, audio, and video in some combination to create

> **VOCABULARY**

presentation software

multimedia

an effective means of communication and interaction. Multimedia technology is a very effective tool in applications such as Microsoft Office PowerPoint, as well as in Web-based communications. Presentations also can be saved in Web page format or as hyperlinks.

As indicated, presentation programs are excellent for creating on-screen shows, but that is not the only output option. Other options include the following:

- *Self-running presentation*: Job fairs, demonstrations, and conventions are a few examples of where you might see a self-running presentation. When the presentation is completed, it automatically restarts.

- *Online meetings*: Using programs such as PowerPoint with Windows Meeting Space makes it easy to set up a meeting and share documents, programs, or your desktop with up to ten people. The participants can be located in different buildings, cities, states, or even countries.

- *Presentation broadcasting*: You can use the Web to broadcast your presentation to locations all over the world.

- *Web presentation*: You can save a presentation as a Web page and upload it to your organization's Web site or to your personal Web site.

- *Overhead transparencies*: If you do not have access to a computer and projector for your presentation, you can create and print either black-and-white or color transparencies. This requires using plastic transparency sheets in your printer.

- *35mm slides*: Each screen can be saved as a separate slide and then converted to a 35mm slide.

- *Audience handouts*: Printed handouts support your presentation. Smaller versions of your slides can be printed two, three, four, six, or nine to a page.

- *PDF document*: Portable Document Format (PDF) is a common format for sharing documents online and through other channels.

Several software companies produce presentation graphics programs. Some of the more popular of these include Microsoft PowerPoint—both Macintosh and Windows versions—Corel Presentations, and OpenOffice.org Impress.

Effective Presentation Guidelines

You can use presentation tools to make any presentation more effective and interesting. However, be cautious! Presentation programs contain many features and options, so it sometimes is difficult to avoid getting carried away. Often, the first-time user is tempted to add distracting sounds, animations, and excessive clip art to each slide. Before you create a presentation, therefore, you need to plan and outline the message that you want to communicate. As you develop the outline for your presentation, consider your audience and determine the presentation's purpose, the location in which it will be given, and the equipment you will need.

Follow these guidelines to create an effective presentation:

- Keep the text simple—use the "6 by 6 rule," which is six lines of text, six words per line.
- Use no more than 50 words per slide, including titles and subtitles.
- Do not clutter your slide with large paragraphs displayed in a small font size. Use one-sentence comments and fill in the details orally.
- Use bullets, not numbers, unless providing specific step-by-step instructions. Bullets indicate no significant order, while numbers indicate rank or sequence.
- Cover one topic per slide.

- Use readable typefaces and fonts. Use serif fonts for body text and sans serif fonts for titles.

- Choose color carefully.

- Use simple tables to present numbers.

- Add clip art sparingly and only where appropriate.

- Don't try to dazzle your audience with graphics, sound, transitions, and other available effects.

Creating a Presentation

As mentioned earlier, several presentation programs are on the market. This lesson uses Microsoft Office PowerPoint 2007. You start all Office 2007 programs in the same way: Click the Start button on the Windows Vista taskbar, point to All Programs, click Microsoft Office, and then click the program name to display an opening screen—in this instance, Microsoft Office PowerPoint 2007. The opening PowerPoint screen looks like that shown in **Figure 11–1**. The basic unit of a PowerPoint presentation is a *slide*. By default, PowerPoint opens in *Normal view*. The Ribbon and task panes are similar to those used in Microsoft Word.

View buttons are located at the bottom of the window and include Normal, Slide Sorter, and Slide Show. The Quick Access toolbar is located at the top of the window, and the Slides and Outline tabs are displayed on the left side of the window. The *Slides tab* displays thumbnail images of each slide in the presentation. Select a slide to display it in the Slide pane. The *Outline tab* displays slide text in an outline format. You easily can center and edit text on this tab.

The *Notes pane*, located at the bottom of the window, is used to enter notes and other slide details to which the presenter can refer as the presentation is being delivered.

Placeholders are boxes with dotted borders that reside within a slide layout and are displayed when you create a new slide. All slide layouts contain content placeholders except the Blank slide layout. The slide in **Figure 11–1** contains two placeholders.

▶ **VOCABULARY**
Normal view
Slides tab
Outline tab
Notes pane
placeholders

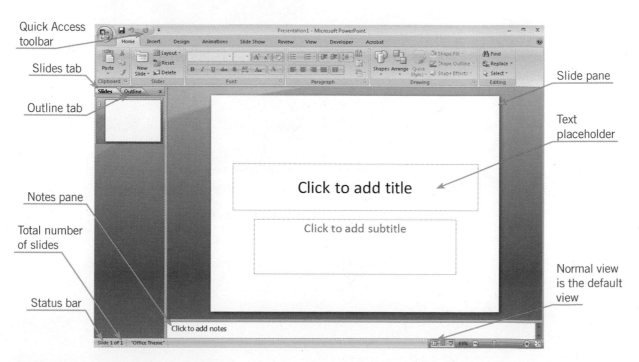

FIGURE 11–1 PowerPoint window

The options for creating a new presentation are described below:

- *Blank presentation*: Add slides one at a time to the presentation, selecting from various layouts for the text and other content.
- *From Themes*: Use a set of formatting choices that include a set of theme colors, a set of theme fonts (including heading and body text fonts), and a set of theme effects (including lines and fill effects).
- *From an existing presentation*: Create a presentation that is based on an existing presentation.
- *From templates*: Apply a predesigned set of slide layouts.

Applying a Document Theme

VOCABULARY

theme

A *theme* is a predesigned set of fonts, colors, lines, fill effects, and other formatting that can be applied to a presentation to maintain consistency and to give the presentation a professional, finished look. Themes save you the time involved in setting up the layout of each slide and then formatting it. PowerPoint comes with many themes; you also can access additional themes online. In most cases, you should use only one theme throughout a presentation. You can modify and customize a theme if you choose to do so.

To view the themes, click the Design tab. You will see many themes from which to choose. See **Figure 11–2**. Point to a theme to view the design on the slide. Clicking the up or down arrow button to the right of the themes displays additional themes. Clicking the More button displays available themes.

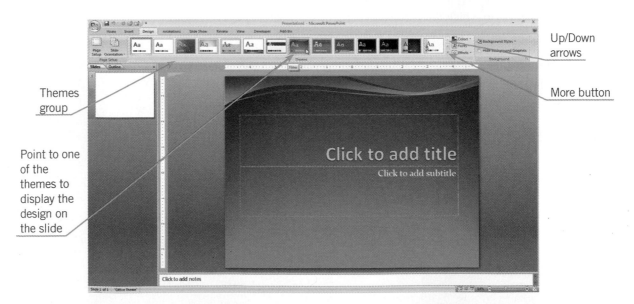

FIGURE 11–2 Previewing a presentation theme

In Step-by-Step 11.1, you create a new presentation using a theme.

Step-by-Step 11.1

1. If necessary, insert your USB drive or other media storage device. Start PowerPoint 2007 by clicking the **Start** button 🔵 on the Windows Vista taskbar. Click **All Programs** on the Start menu to display the All Programs list. Click **Microsoft Office** to display the Microsoft Office list, and then click **Microsoft Office PowerPoint 2007**. A new blank presentation is displayed. If necessary, maximize the PowerPoint window.

2. Click the **Design** tab. The Themes group is displayed, including a number of themes from which to choose.

3. Click the **More** button ⬇ to display all available themes. Point to the themes to display their names, and then click the **Trek** theme to apply the theme to the presentation. See **Figure 11–3**.

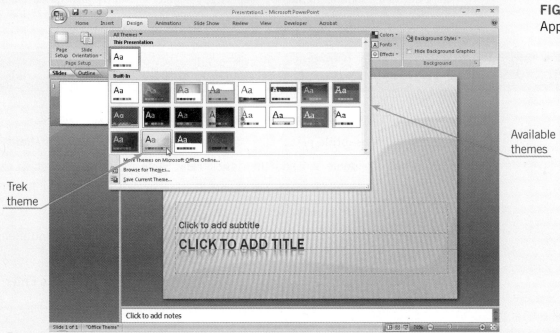

FIGURE 11–3
Applying the Trek theme

Available themes

Trek theme

4. Click the **Office** button 🔵 and then click **Save**.

5. In the Save As dialog box, select the location to which you are saving files, type **PowerPoint Tips** in the File name box, and click **Save**. Leave the presentation open for Step-by-Step 11.2.

Working in Different Views

As was discussed earlier, you can look at a presentation in three different views—Normal, Slide Sorter, and Slide Show. You already are familiar with Normal view. In *Slide Sorter view*, the slides are displayed as thumbnails. In this view, you

▶ **VOCABULARY**
Slide Sorter view

▶ **VOCABULARY**
Slide Show view

slide layout

easily can change the order of slides in the presentation. *Slide Show view* shows the presentation as an electronic slide show where each slide fills the screen.

Inserting New Slides

To add slides to your presentation, click the New Slide button on the Home tab. The theme you selected for the presentation is automatically applied to the new slide.

Entering Text on Slides

You can enter text on a slide by typing in the Outline pane, or you can enter text directly on the slide. In most instances, you should select a slide theme for the slide before you enter text or any other content. The *slide layout* refers to the way that text and other objects are arranged on the slide. These layouts include placeholders for text, titles, and/or other content, such as pictures, tables, and charts. In most cases, the first slide of every presentation is the title slide. In Step-by-Step 11.1, the Title Slide layout was applied to the slide by default. Notice that there are placeholders for a title and a subtitle. In Step-by-Step 11.2, you enter text in the placeholders and practice changing views.

Step-by-Step 11.2

1. Click the **title placeholder** and type **Basic PowerPoint Guidelines**.

2. Click the **subtitle placeholder** and type **Tips for Effective Presentations**.

3. Click the **Home** tab and then click **New Slide** in the Slides group to insert a new slide.

4. Click the **title placeholder** and type **Text**.

5. Click in the text placeholder, type **Six by Six Rule**, press **Enter**, and then press **Tab**.

6. The next bullet is indented. Type **Six lines of text** and then press **Enter**. Type **Six words per line** and then press **Enter**.

7. Type **Avoid large paragraphs with small fonts**.

8. Change to Slide Sorter view by clicking the **Slide Sorter** button ⊞ in the lower-right corner of the status bar.

9. Click the **Normal** button ▣ on the status bar to return to Normal view. See **Figure 11–4**.

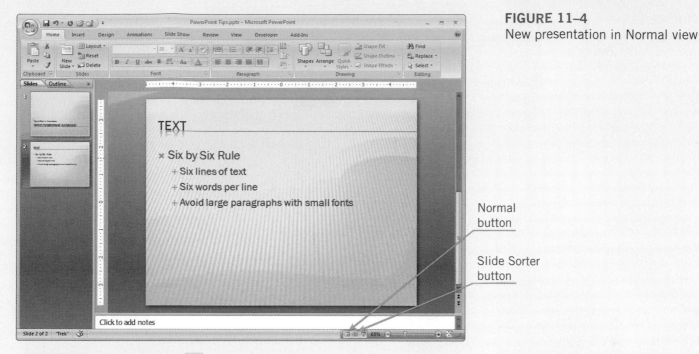

FIGURE 11–4
New presentation in Normal view

10. Click the **Save** button on the Quick Access toolbar and leave the presentation open for Step-by-Step 11.3.

Adding clip art to your presentation enhances its visual appeal and makes your presentation look professional. Microsoft Office contains a Clip Organizer, which is a collection of clip art and other media files, including photographs, movies, and sound clips. You can add these professionally designed media objects to your presentation. You also can obtain clip art from other sources such as the Internet.

Adding Clip Art to a Presentation

After an object is placed on a slide, you can manipulate and edit it. First, you click to select it. When selected, eight small squares, called sizing handles, are displayed on the border of the object. You can use the handles to resize the object. You also can cut, copy, paste, delete, or move the object. In Step-by-Step 11.3, you insert clip art on a slide.

> **EXTRA FOR EXPERTS**
>
> Use photos, clip art, and graphics instead of words for a more powerful presentation.

Step-by-Step 11.3

1. Click the **New Slide** button arrow in the Slides group on the Home tab and then click the **Two Content** layout. See **Figure 11–5**.

FIGURE 11–5
Adding a new
slide with the Two
Content layout

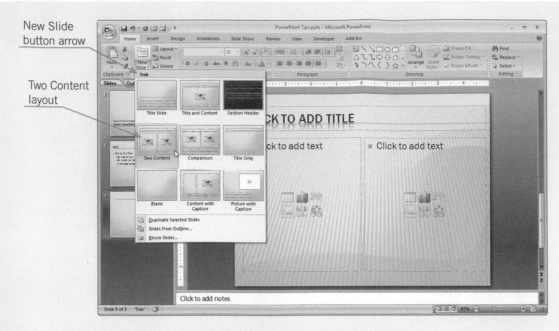

2. Click in the title placeholder and type **Graphics**.

3. In the content placeholder, click the **Clip Art** button. The Clip Art
   task pane opens, as shown in **Figure 11–6**.

FIGURE 11–6
Preparing to insert
clip art

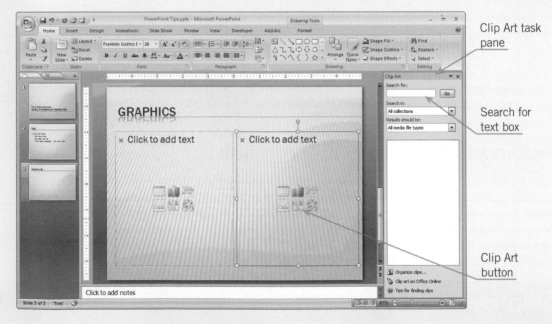

4. Click the **Search for** text box, type **alphabet**, and then click **Go**.
   PowerPoint will search the Clip Organizer for all pictures related to this
   word and display them in the Clip Art task pane.

5. Scroll through the results to find clip art of the letter "G". Click the
   image. The clip art is inserted on the slide, as shown in **Figure 11–7**.
   (The image you selected might be different from the one shown in the
   figure.)

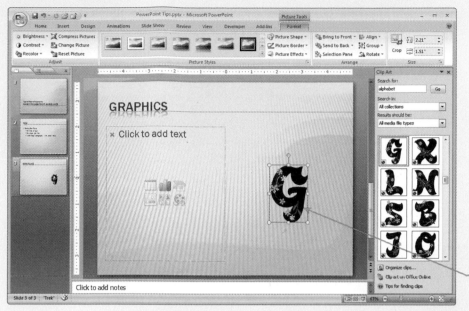

FIGURE 11–7
Inserting clip art

Graphic
inserted
on slide

6. Click the **text placeholder** and type **Use clip art sparingly and where appropriate**. (Do not type a period at the end of the line.) Press **Enter**.

7. Type **Do not try to dazzle with art and images**.

8. You can reposition the clip art to balance it with the text. Click the **graphic** to select it. Point to the center of the image. The pointer changes to a four-headed arrow ⊕. Drag the image up to position it on the page.

9. Close the Clip Art task pane. Click the **Save** button 💾 on the Quick Access toolbar to save your changes and leave the presentation open for Step-by-Step 11.4.

Adding a Chart to Your Presentation

Presentations often include statistical and financial data that is best presented in a chart. *Charts* can help an audience analyze and assess numerical information and simplify complex data.

In the following Step-by-Step, you add a chart to a presentation.

▶ **VOCABULARY**
charts

Step-by-Step 11.4

1. Click the **New Slide** button arrow in the Slides group to insert a new slide.

2. Select the **Title Only** layout.

3. Click the **title placeholder** and type **Presentation Software Sales**. The slide layout looks like that shown in **Figure 11–8**.

FIGURE 11–8
Entering a title

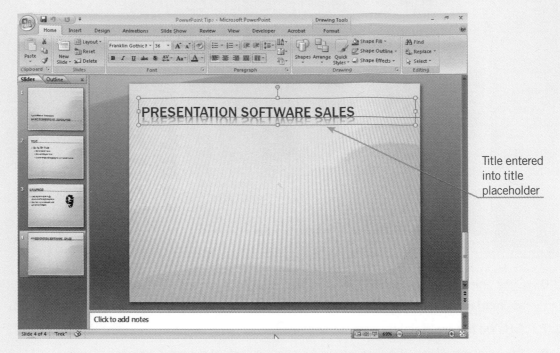

Title entered
into title
placeholder

4. Click the **Insert** tab and then click **Chart** in the Illustrations group. The Insert Chart dialog box is displayed. See **Figure 11–9**.

FIGURE 11–9
Insert Chart dialog box

First chart in
Column row
selected

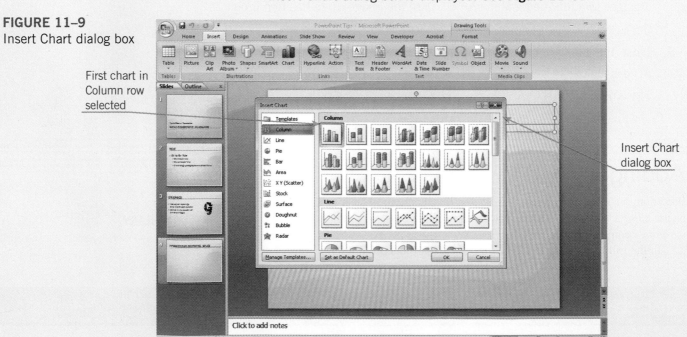

Insert Chart
dialog box

5. If necessary, click the **first chart** in the Column row and then click the **OK** button. A sample chart and an Excel worksheet are displayed as shown in **Figure 11–10**.

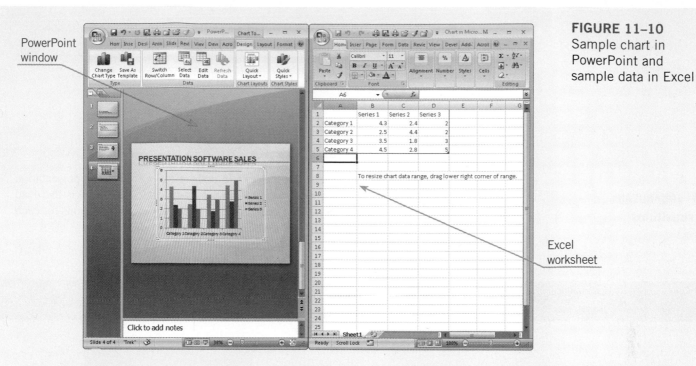

PowerPoint
window

PRESENTATION SOFTWARE SALES

Click to add notes

Excel
worksheet

FIGURE 11–10
Sample chart in
PowerPoint and
sample data in Excel

6. In the worksheet, click cell **A2** (the cell that contains "Category 1"),
   type **Store 1**, and then press **Enter**. Notice that the change is reflected
   in the chart.

7. Type **Store 2**. Press **Enter** and type **Store 3**. Press **Enter** and type **Store 4**.

8. Enter the rest of the data, as shown in **Figure 11–11**. You can use the
   arrow keys to move from cell to cell or click the cell in which you want
   to type.

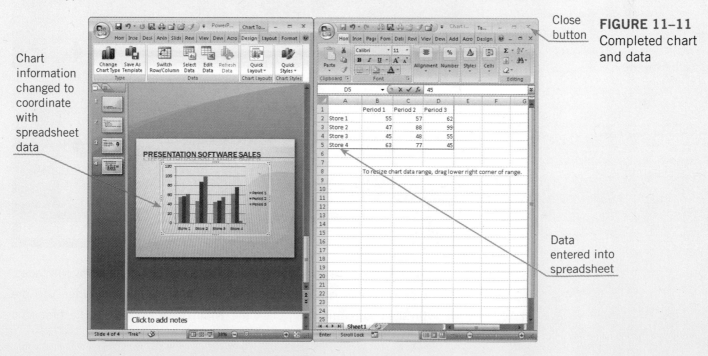

Chart
information
changed to
coordinate
with
spreadsheet
data

PRESENTATION SOFTWARE SALES

Click to add notes

Close
button

Data
entered into
spreadsheet

FIGURE 11–11
Completed chart
and data

9. When you are done, click the **Close** button 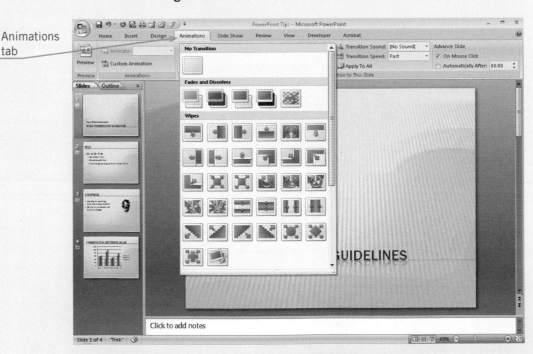X in the Excel window.

10. Click the **Save** button 💾 on the Quick Access toolbar to save your changes, and leave the presentation open for Step-by-Step 11.5.

Adding Transitions to Slides

▶ **VOCABULARY**
transitions

You can determine how each slide moves in and out of view in your presentation by assigning transitions. *Transitions* are special visual and sound effects that lead the audience from one slide to the next. You can assign different transitions for each slide or the same transition to all the slides in the presentation.

In Step-by-Step 11.5, you add transitions to slides.

Step-by-Step 11.5

1. On the Slides tab, click **slide 1**.

2. Click the **Animations** tab, and then click the **More** button ▼ in the Transition to this Slide group. The Transitions gallery is displayed, as shown in **Figure 11–12**.

FIGURE 11–12
Transitions gallery

Animations tab

3. Move the mouse pointer over the icons and observe the various fades, dissolves, and wipes to see how they affect the slide. When you are finished experimenting, click the **Wipe Down** transition, the first icon located in the first Wipes row.

4. In the Transition to This Slide group, you can change the speed of the transition and add sound to the slide as it comes into view during the

presentation. Click the arrow on the **Transition Speed** box and then click **Medium**. Do not change the Sound setting.

5. In the Advance Slide section, you determine how the slides will advance. You can have the slide advance on the click of the mouse or automatically at intervals of time that you specify. If necessary, select the **On Mouse Click** check box to insert a check mark.

6. Click the **Apply to All** button in the Transition to This Slide group.

7. If necessary, select **slide 1** in the Slides tab. Click the **Slide Show** tab and then click the **From Beginning** button in the Start Slide Show group. Recall that you must click the mouse to advance to the next slide.

8. When you reach the end of the show, click to exit the slide show and return to Normal view.

9. Save the presentation and leave it open for Step-by-Step 11.6.

Adding Animation to Slides

You can animate objects on a slide to help make a presentation more engaging. PowerPoint comes with a variety of *animation* effects that add movement to the object selected. The object can be text, titles, or graphics. You can also attach sounds to animations. You can apply an animation scheme to one slide or to all slides, or you can apply it to only a certain object on a slide.

In Step-by-Step 11.6, you add animation to slides.

> **VOCABULARY**
> animation

> **⊟ EXTRA FOR EXPERTS**
>
> In Slide Show view, click the right mouse button and then click Previous to return to the previous slide.

Step-by-Step 11.6

1. If necessary, click **slide 2** in the Slides tab to select it.

2. Click the **Animations** tab and then click **Custom Animation** in the Animations group. The Custom Animation task pane is displayed, as shown in **Figure 11–13**. Verify that the AutoPreview check box at the bottom of the task pane is checked.

FIGURE 11–13
Preparing to add
an animation

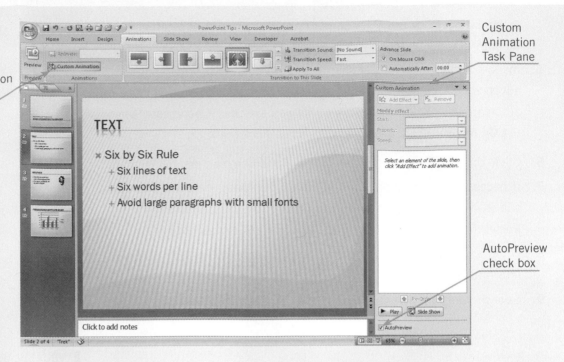

3. Select **slide 4** in the Slides tab and then click the **chart** in the slide to select it.

4. Click the **Add Effect** button in the Custom Animation pane, point to **Entrance**, and then click **Diamond**. (If Diamond does not appear in the list, click a different effect.) In the Modify section, click the arrow on the **Speed** box and click **Medium**, if necessary. Do not change the Start and Direction options.

5. Click **slide 1** in the Slides tab and then click the **Slide Show** button 🖵 on the status bar to view the presentation. Because the "start" of the animations is set to occur on the mouse click, you must click to activate the animations as well as to advance to the next slide.

6. At the end of the show, click to exit and return to Normal view. Close the Custom Animation task pane.

7. Save the presentation and leave it open for Step-by-Step 11.7.

Checking Spelling in the Presentation

As you continue to add information to your presentation, you need to review and proofread your slides for errors. You can use the Spelling tool to perform these tasks. Remember, you still must proofread for punctuation and word usage because this feature recognizes only misspelled words, not misused words.

In Step-by-Step 11.7, you check the spelling in the presentation.

Step-by-Step 11.7

1. Click the **Slide Sorter** button 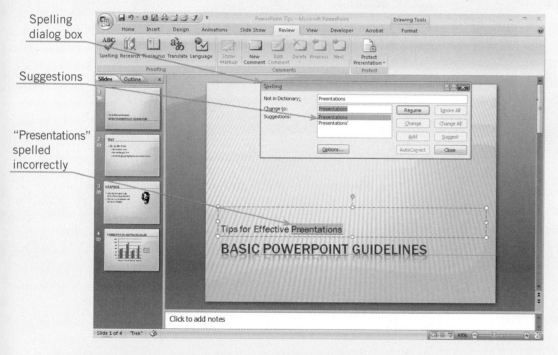 on the status bar, and then click **slide 1** if necessary.

2. Click the **Review** tab, then click **Spelling** in the Proofing group.

3. If your presentation contains a misspelled word, the Spelling dialog box opens, as shown in **Figure 11–14**. The misspelled word appears in the Not in Dictionary box. Suggestions for correct spellings are listed in the Suggestions box, with the best choice listed in the Change to box. If you want to use the highlighted word, click **Change**. If the word is spelled correctly, click **Ignore**. Once all spell checking is complete, click **OK**. (If your presentation does not contain any misspelled words, a message box appears indicating that the spelling check is complete.)

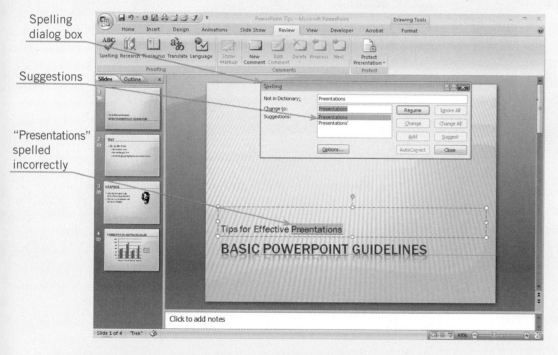

FIGURE 11–14
Spelling dialog box

4. Save the presentation and leave it open for Step-by-Step 11.8.

Printing the Presentation

PowerPoint provides several options for printing a presentation. For example, you can print your entire presentation—the slides, outlines, and notes—in color, gray-scale, or black and white. You also can print specific slides, notes pages, or outline pages. The presentation also can be printed in the form of handouts. You can select to have one, two, three, four, six, or nine slides on a page. These can be used by your audience for reference or to follow along as you give your presentation.

In Step-by-Step 11.8, you print handouts of the slides with three slides to a page.

Step-by-Step 11.8

1. Click the **Office** button and then click **Print**. The Print dialog box opens, as shown in **Figure 11–15**. Most likely your printer will be different from that shown in **Figure 11–15**.

FIGURE 11–15
Print dialog box

Handouts selected

3 slides per page selected

OK button

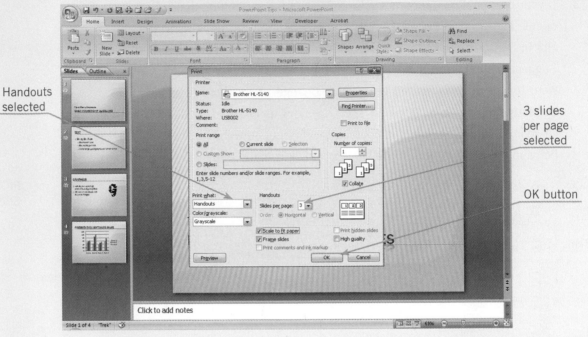

2. Click the **Print What** arrow in the Page Setup group, and then click **Handouts**.

3. In the Handouts section, click the **Slides per page** arrow, and then click **3**.

4. Click **OK** to print the handouts.

5. Save and close the presentation. Exit PowerPoint.

Viewing the Presentation

After you have created the slides, you can view your presentation. Your slides will be displayed with the transitions and animations that you applied.

To view a presentation:

1. With PowerPoint running, click the Slide Show tab.

2. In the Start Slide Show group, select From Beginning.

3. Click to advance the slides one by one.

You can return to a previous slide, go to a specific slide, end the show, and so on by right-clicking to display a shortcut menu. PowerPoint also has a feature on this shortcut menu that allows you to "write" on slides while the show is playing. Right-click the slide to display the Pointer Options. See **Figure 11–16**. Select an option on the submenu. Depending on your choice, a dot or block will appear on the slide. Move the mouse to write or highlight text. You can erase text with the Eraser option, located on the shortcut menu by pointing to Pointer Options. You can choose whether to save the pen annotations or discard them when you close the presentation preview.

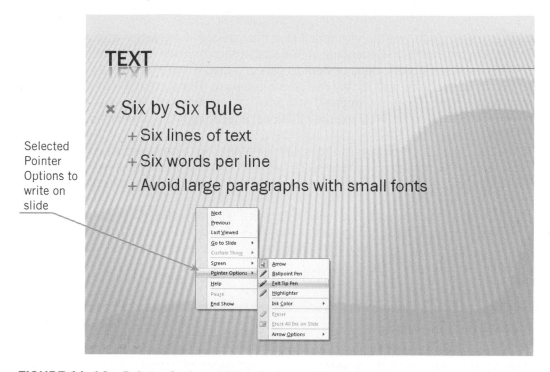

FIGURE 11–16 Pointer Options when playing a slide show

Delivering the Presentation

Many people fear public speaking. Most of us, however, will, at one time or another, find ourselves in a position where we must talk to a group or give an oral presentation. Several professional organizations train people in presentation skills. Even with training, most people will not become professional speakers overnight. There are, however, some special techniques you can use. If you practice and use some of the following suggestions, you might find that you actually enjoy public speaking:

■ *Plan*: Know the purpose of your presentation, plan your content, and know your audience.

■ *Prepare*: Have an attention-getting opener, be positive, and develop a memorable closing.

■ *Outline your main points*: Outlining helps you stay focused, but do not be afraid to skip some points or move ahead if that is what your audience wants.

■ *Talk*: Do not talk too slow or too fast; watch your audience and take your cue from them.

■ *Present*: Make eye contact, be natural and sincere; involve your audience.

■ *Take questions*: Be sure to leave time at the end of your presentation to answer questions.

TECHNOLOGY CAREERS

Presentation Expert

Presentations are an organization's most direct communication effort. Many times, a presentation can make or break a sale or prevent a company from landing that big contract. As more and more employees are using computers and presentation graphics programs, companies are beginning to realize the importance of this media.

A growing trend in large companies is to hire a presentation expert to oversee the creation and delivery of presentations within the organization. Depending on the size of the company and the number of presentations required, this person might work alone or work as part of a media department. The media department generally functions as a service bureau for the rest of the company. The presentation manager might also be responsible for design. They must stay updated and aware of technological advances in the areas of multimedia. This position will most likely require additional education such as workshops, conferences, and classes.

Many large companies have a standard set of master slides and templates. All employees are expected to use these standards. The presentation manager might be responsible for creating these masters and templates and might even be responsible for teaching physical presentation delivery skills or coaching frequent speakers.

Because there are no certifications or degrees for presentation managers, many people employed in this field have graphics design and/or Web design backgrounds. They may or may not have a four-year degree. It is not unusual to find someone with a community college two-year degree in design or someone with design certifications employed in this type of job.

Salaries are varied and can range from as little as $20,000 to as much as $80,000 or more.

SUMMARY

In this lesson, you learned:

- You use presentation software to illustrate a sequence of ideas in a slide show format.

- Use presentation software for on-screen shows, self-running presentations, online meetings, presentation broadcasting, Web presentation, overhead transparencies, 35mm slides, audience handouts, and PDF documents.

- Some of the more popular presentation programs are Microsoft PowerPoint, Corel Presentations, and OpenOffice.org Impress.

- Some general presentation rules to consider are: keep each slide's content simple; use words or phrases; don't clutter; and use art and images appropriately.

- Most presentation programs come with a collection of professionally designed templates.

- The addition of clip art, transitions, and animations can make your presentation more entertaining.

- Techniques to help you give a better presentation include planning, preparing, outlining, talking at a moderate rate, following cues from the audience, and leaving time for questions.

VOCABULARY REVIEW

Define the following terms:

animation

charts

multimedia

Normal view

Notes pane

Outline tab

placeholder

presentation software

slide layout

Slide Show view

Slide Sorter view

Slides tab

themes

transitions

REVIEW QUESTIONS

MULTIPLE CHOICE

Select the best response for the following statements.

1. With a presentation program, you can _____ .

   A. create slides

   B. create handouts

   C. create overhead transparencies

   D. all of the above

2. Presentation software generally is used to organize and present information in the form of a(n) _____.

   A. slide show

   B. animated graphic

   C. spreadsheet

   D. chart

3. The maximum number of words that should be included on a single slide is _____.

   A. 25

   B. 50

   C. 75

   D. 100

4. The basic unit of a presentation is a(n) _____.

   A. transition

   B. graphic

   C. slide

   D. animation

5. The _____ tab displays slide text in an outline format.

   A. Animation

   B. Insert

   C. Slides

   D. Outline

TRUE/FALSE

Circle T if the statement is true or F if the statement is false.

T   F   **1.**   Each slide in your presentation should contain a lot of detail.

T   F   **2.**   You should rarely use visuals in your presentation.

T   F   **3.**   A theme is a predesigned set of fonts, colors, lines, and other formatting that can be applied to a slide.

T   F   **4.**   Normal view is the only view available for viewing a presentation.

T   F   **5.**   You can add slides to a presentation by clicking the Add Effect button in the Animation task pane.

FILL IN THE BLANK

Complete the following sentences by writing the correct word or words in the blanks provided.

1. In _____ view, thumbnails of each slide are displayed.

2. _____ can be used to analyze and assess numerical data.

3. To present an on-screen presentation, you need the software, a computer, and a(n) _____ .

4. A(n) _____ presentation is one that automatically restarts when it reaches the end.

5. When adding text to your presentation, use the _____ rule.

 PROJECTS

CROSS-CURRICULAR— MATHEMATICS

Many women have made great contributions in the field of mathematics. Use the Internet and other resources to research the life and contributions of a woman mathematician. Prepare a presentation with four or five slides on your findings. Include various layouts, graphics, transitions, and animations in your presentation.

CROSS-CURRICULAR—SCIENCE

DNA has become a very sought-after tool to determine the fate of those accused of crimes. Conduct research on this "alphabet of life" and prepare a five- to six-slide presentation that covers what it is, how it works, how it is used, and other pertinent information. Include animation, sound, graphics, and other objects that will make the presentation interesting to other students. Print handouts to be distributed to the class.

CROSS-CURRICULAR—SOCIAL STUDIES

Use the *wikipedia.org* Web site and research the history of the Declaration of Independence. Create a five- to seven-slide presentation that includes the history and background, and an overview of the document. Include a chart with applicable dates. Locate a picture or two online and include these as part of your presentation. Print handouts to be distributed to the class.

CROSS-CURRICULAR—LANGUAGE ARTS

Select a poem of your choice. Using the selected poem, turn it into a dancing, singing work of art as a PowerPoint slide show. Images, colors, transitions, and sounds should be added to each slide. Print a set of speaker's notes that you will use as you discuss each line of the poem when giving your presentation. Print audience handouts for the class to use.

WEB PROJECT

You have just returned from a year abroad as an exchange student. You have been asked to prepare a slide presentation of your experience. Prepare an eight- to ten-slide presentation. Include information regarding the country and its culture, the school you attended, the family with whom you lived, and any other interesting information. Research a country on the Web for information to use in your presentation. Use various slide layouts, animations, and graphics.

TEAMWORK PROJECT

Work with a teammate to research "Juneteenth." Use the Internet and other resources. This is a holiday that has been around for more than 125 years, but is not widely celebrated. Together, prepare an eight- to ten-slide presentation that will include the history, purpose, festivities, the decline and resurgence, and any other interesting information regarding this holiday. Include as many features as necessary to make this an interesting presentation.

 CRITICAL THINKING

The presentation you worked on in this lesson covered some of the basic tools and features you can use to prepare an effective presentation. Following is an outline that provides more comprehensive information. Use the outline to create a new presentation. You also can use the Internet to gather more information on how to design an effective presentation and integrate this information into your presentation. Use a theme of your choice, and add graphics, transitions, and animations as desired. Be sure to spell check your presentation. Save it as **Presentation Basics.**

TITLE: Basic PowerPoint Guidelines

SUBTITLE: Tips for Effective Presentations

    I.   Text

          - 6 by 6 Rule: 6 lines of text; 6 words per line

          - No more than 50 words per slide, including titles and subtitles

          - Avoid large paragraphs with small fonts

    II.   Fonts

          - Use at least 16-point size font

          - Limit to no more than three fonts

          - Use serif for body text

          - Use sans serif for titles

    III.   Graphics

          - Support point of current slide

          - Use only high-quality photographs or graphics

         - Use one graphic element per slide   - Avoid reading your slides

         - Use appropriate size graphic elements   - Identify additional materials

IV.   Presentation Tips

         - Show one slide per minute

■ EXPLORING GOOGLE

Personal medical records are important and should be kept in a location where they are readily available. Google Health provides a service that organizes your health information in one location and stores the information securely and privately.

    To learn more about Google Health, go to *https://www.google.com/health/html/tour/index.html* and then complete the Google Health tour. After you complete the tour, write a review of what you learned. Include the following information: Would you elect to use this program? Why or why not? Would you recommend it to friends? What advantages and disadvantages do you see in a program such as this? What is the most positive aspect of this program? The most negative?

LESSON 12

Spreadsheets

■ OBJECTIVES

Upon completion of this lesson, you should be able to:

- Understand the purpose and function of a spreadsheet.
- Identify the parts of a spreadsheet window.
- Enter labels, values, formulas, and functions in a spreadsheet.
- Use the AutoSum feature to enter the SUM function.
- Understand relative and absolute cell references.
- Change column width and row height.
- Format data in a spreadsheet.
- Insert and delete cells, rows, and columns.
- Save and print a spreadsheet.
- Add headers and footers in a spreadsheet.
- Sort data in a spreadsheet.
- In sert clip art in a spreadsheet.
- Create a chart from spreadsheet data.

■ VOCABULARY

absolute cell reference

active cell

cell

cell reference

chart

footer

formula

formula prefix

function

header

label

order of evaluation

range

relative cell reference

spreadsheet

theme

value

workbook

worksheet

...

Spreadsheet Software Defined

A **spreadsheet** is a row and column arrangement of data. Electronic spreadsheet software such as Microsoft Office Excel 2007 is used to evaluate, calculate, manipulate, analyze, and present numeric data. Calculations are updated automatically, which makes this type of software very effective for numerous applications, such as preparing budgets, financial statements, payrolls, sales reports, and managing inventory. Spreadsheet software also is used to make forecasts and identify trends.

The Anatomy of a Spreadsheet

▶ VOCABULARY

spreadsheet

worksheet

cell

cell reference

active cell

workbook

range

A spreadsheet looks much like a page from a financial journal. It is a grid with columns and rows. This grid in Excel is referred to as a **worksheet**. The terms **spreadsheet** and **worksheet** are used interchangeably. The Excel worksheet window is shown in **Figure 12–1**. The columns are identified by letters of the alphabet, and the rows are identified by numbers. The point at which a column and a row intersect or meet is called a *cell*. Each cell has a name, called the **cell reference** (or cell address), which is represented by the column letter and the row number. For example, the first cell in a worksheet is cell A1. It is located in column A and in row 1. The **active cell** is the cell in which you are working currently and is surrounded by a thick border. Note that cell A1 is the active cell in **Figure 12–1** (as indicated in the Name box) and that 26 rows and columns A through O are displayed. The worksheet, however, contains 16,384 columns and 1,048,576 rows; therefore only a small portion of the worksheet is displayed in **Figure 12–1**. Individual worksheets are stored within a **workbook**. By default, a workbook contains three worksheets named Sheet1, Sheet2, and Sheet3, as shown on the sheet tabs at the bottom of the window. (Sheet is another word for worksheet.)

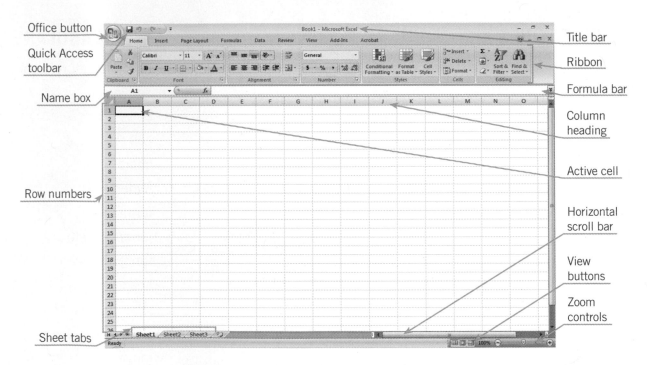

FIGURE 12–1   The Excel window

Selecting Cells

To enter data in a spreadsheet, you first select the cell, using either the mouse or the keyboard. To select a cell with the keyboard, use a keyboard shortcut listed in **Table 12–1**. To select a cell with the mouse, point to the cell and click. You can select a group of cells by clicking the first cell and dragging the mouse to the last cell of the group. When you select a group of cells, the group is called a **range**. It is identified by the address of the cell in the upper-left corner, followed by a colon, and then the cell in the lower-right corner; for example, A1:D5 identifies all the cells from cell A1 through cell D5. When you select a range, all cells but the first cell in the range are shaded. You can select an entire column by clicking the column letter at the top of the spreadsheet or an entire row by clicking the row number.

If you want to select a cell that is not visible on the screen, you can use the vertical and horizontal scroll bars or scroll boxes to display the area of the spreadsheet that contains the cell(s) you want to select. You also can use keyboard shortcuts to move around the spreadsheet and select cells. **Table 12–1** lists some shortcuts for moving around the spreadsheet and selecting a cell.

TABLE 12–1 Keyboard shortcuts

PRESS THIS KEY	TO MOVE
Arrow keys	Up, down, left, or right one cell
Page Up	The active cell up one full screen
Page Down	The active cell down one full screen
Home	The active cell to column A of the current row
F5 (function key)	To any cell (pressing F5 opens the Go To dialog box, in which you enter the cell address of the cell you want to make active)
Tab	To the next cell
Ctrl+right arrow	To the last cell with data in a row
Ctrl+left arrow	To the first cell in a row
Ctrl+End	To the last cell with data in the document
Ctrl+Home	To the beginning of the spreadsheet, or cell A1

Entering Data in a Spreadsheet

The data that is entered in a spreadsheet will be one of four types—a label, a value, a formula, or a function. A **label** is alphabetical text and aligns at the left side of the cell. It also can contain numerical data not used in calculations, such as zip codes, telephone numbers, dates, and so on. A **value** is a number and aligns at the right side of the cell. A **formula** is an equation that performs a calculation. A **function** is a built-in formula that is a shortcut for common calculations, such as totaling numbers or finding the average. Each type of data has a particular use and is handled in a unique way.

When you press Enter, the next cell down in the column becomes the active cell. You also can press the Tab key to enter the data and move to the next cell in the row. Or, you can press one of the arrow keys to enter the data and move to the next cell in the direction of the arrow.

You can edit data in a cell by selecting the cell and then typing the new data. You also can double-click the cell and then move the insertion point to where you want to edit the data. Use the Delete or Backspace keys or retype the data as desired.

In Step-by-Step 12.1, you open a new workbook and enter values and labels in the worksheet.

▶ **VOCABULARY**
label
value
formula
function

EXTRA FOR EXPERTS

You can use the Undo command (Ctrl+Z) to undo your most recent actions. You can use the Redo command (Ctrl+Y) to reverse the Undo command.

Step-by-Step 12.1

1. Start Excel by clicking the **Start** button on the Windows Vista taskbar, point to **All Programs**, click **Microsoft Office**, and then click **Microsoft Office Excel 2007**.

2. If necessary, click cell **A1** and then type **Trade Today**. Press **Enter** to move to cell A2. (Do not be concerned if data extends into the nearby cells.)

3. Type **Part-time Employees**. Press **Enter** to move to cell A3.

4. Type **Weekly Payroll**. Press **Enter** to move to cell A4.

5. Type **Week Ending July 1, 2009** (replace "2009" with the current year, if necessary). Press **Enter**.

6. Click **cell A6**. Type **Employee**. Press the **right arrow** key to move to cell B6.

7. Type **MON**. Press the **right arrow** key.

8. Enter the rest of the data as shown in **Figure 12–2**. In the figure, the column width has been adjusted to display all of the data. As mentioned previously, some of your cell data will extend into the next column or be cut off and your spreadsheet most likely will not fully resemble those in the figures. You will learn how to adjust column width later in this lesson. In the meantime, correct any errors by selecting the cell and entering the correct data, or by double-clicking the cell and using the Backspace or Delete keys, or retyping the data as necessary.

FIGURE 12–2
Part-time payroll
worksheet

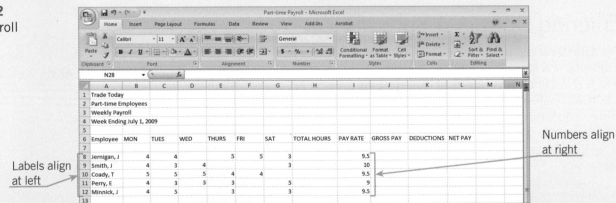

Labels align at left

Numbers align at right

9. Click the **Office** button and then click **Save As**. In the Save As dialog box, select the location to which you are saving files from the Save in box. Enter **Part-time Payroll** in the File name text box, and then click **Save**. Leave the workbook open for Step-by-Step 12.2.

Entering Formulas and Functions

A formula performs calculations, such as adding, subtracting, averaging, and multiplying. You can type a formula directly in a cell or in the formula bar. To enter a formula in a cell, you first type an equal sign (=). This symbol, called the **formula prefix**, identifies the data as a formula and not a label. For the formula, you can enter cell references, arithmetic operators, and/or functions. The arithmetic operators indicate the desired arithmetic operations. These include addition (+), subtraction (−), multiplication (*), and division (/). These keys are on the numeric keypad as well as the keyboard.

Formulas that contain more than one operator are called complex formulas. When there is more than one operator, the **order of evaluation** determines the sequence of calculation. Formulas are evaluated as follows:

- Multiplication and division are performed before addition and subtraction.
- Calculations are performed from the left side of the formula to the right side.
- You can change the order of evaluation by using parentheses. Calculations enclosed in parentheses are performed first.

Figure 12–3 provides examples to illustrate the order of evaluation.

VOCABULARY

formula prefix

order of evaluation

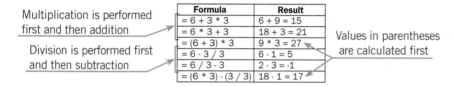

Formula	Result
= 6 + 3 * 3	6 + 9 = 15
= 6 * 3 + 3	18 + 3 = 21
= (6 + 3) * 3	9 * 3 = 27
= 6 - 3 / 3	6 - 1 = 5
= 6 / 3 - 3	2 - 3 = -1
= (6 * 3) - (3 / 3)	18 - 1 = 17

Multiplication is performed first and then addition

Division is performed first and then subtraction

Values in parentheses are calculated first

FIGURE 12–3   Examples of order of evaluation

For even more complex calculations, you can use Excel functions. A function is a prewritten formula that automatically calculates a value based on data you insert. Excel comes with a variety of functions that range from simple, such as the SUM function that calculates a total, to complex, like the PMT function, which calculates the payment for a loan based on constant payments and a constant interest rate. **Table 12–2** shows a list of commonly used functions.

TABLE 12–2   Common functions

FUNCTION NAME	DESCRIPTION
AVERAGE	Gives the average of specified values
COUNT	Counts the number of cells in a range
IF	Specifies a logical test to perform, then performs one action if test result is true and another if it is not true
MAX	Identifies the maximum value in a range of cells
MEDIAN	Gives the middle value in a range of cells
MIN	Identifies the minimum value in a range of cells
ROUND	Rounds the value to the nearest value in one of two ways—with the specified number of decimal places or to the nearest whole number
SUM	Totals a range of cells

To enter a function, you type the equal sign (=), the name of the function (such as SUM, AVERAGE, and so on), an opening parenthesis, the value(s), cell, or range of cells to be calculated in the function (referred to as the *argument*), and then the closing parenthesis. The argument for a range of cells consists of the cell address of the first cell in the range, followed by a colon (:), and then the address of the last cell in the range. For example, to use the SUM function to total the values in cells B9 through G9, you would type *=SUM(B9:G9)*. You also can insert a function by clicking the Formulas tab and then selecting Insert Function in the Function Library group.

As you type a formula or a function, it is displayed in the formula bar. After you press Enter, the formula is displayed in the formula bar and the result of the formula is displayed in the active cell.

You can use the AutoSum feature as a shortcut for entering the SUM function. Click the cell where the result is to appear, and then click the AutoSum button in the Editing group on the Home tab or in the Function Library group on the Formulas tab. Excel will display an outline around the group of cells in the column above the highlighted cell or row of cells adjacent to the highlighted cell. If the highlighted cells are not the ones that you want, click the first cell of the group you want and drag to the last cell in the range you want to add. Press Enter or click the AutoSum button again to complete the formula.

Be cautious when entering formulas. Typing the incorrect cell reference, using a semicolon instead of a colon to identify a range, or even misspelling a function could cause your result to be incorrect. However, if you enter a formula incorrectly, you can make the correction in the formula bar. Just click the cell in which the formula appears, click in the formula bar where you want to make the change, and make the correction.

In Step-by-Step 12.2, you enter formulas in a worksheet.

Step-by-Step 12.2

1. If necessary, open the Part-time Payroll file. Click cell **H8**, type **=B8+C8+D8+E8+F8+G8** and then press **Enter** to calculate the total hours worked by Jernigan, J., and move to cell H9.

2. Type **=B9+C9+D9+E9+F9+G9** to calculate the total hours worked by Smith, J. Press **Enter** to move to cell H10.

3. Type **=**, click cell **B10**, type **+**, click cell **C10**, type **+**, click cell **D10**, type **+**, click cell **E10**, type **+**, click cell **F10**, type **+**, and then click cell **G10** to calculate the total hours worked by Coady, T. Press **Enter** to move to cell H11.

4. Type **=SUM(B11:G11)** to calculate the total hours worked by Perry, E. Press **Enter**.

5. Type **=SUM(B12:G12)** to calculate the total hours worked by Minnick, J.

6. Click cell **B14**. Type **=SUM(B8:B12)** and press **Enter** to calculate the total hours worked on Monday by all employees.

7. Click cell **C8** and drag to cell **C14**. Click the **AutoSum** button in the Editing group. This automatically calculates the total hours worked on Tuesday by each employee. Click elsewhere in the worksheet to deselect the cells.

8. Your worksheet should resemble the one shown in **Figure 12–4**. Click the **Save** button on the Quick Access toolbar to save the workbook. Leave the workbook open for Step-by-Step 12.3.

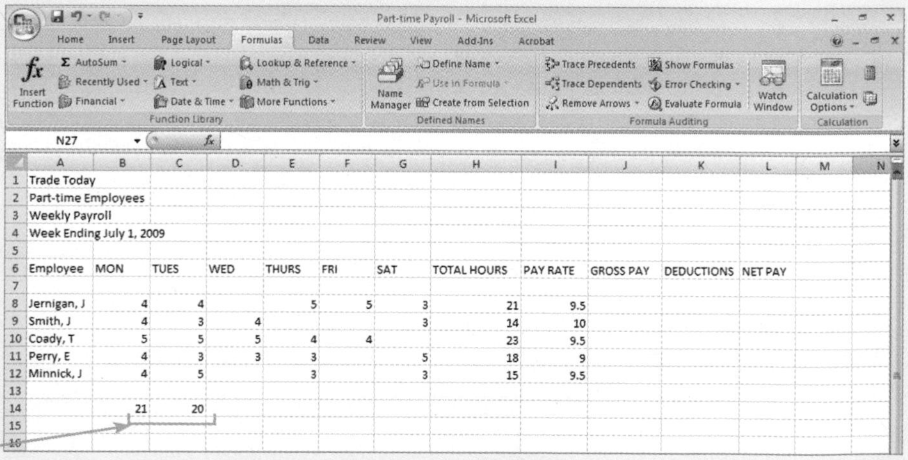

Total hours worked on Monday and Tuesday by all employees

FIGURE 12–4
Formulas entered

Copying Data

In Step-by-Step 12.2, you entered a fairly lengthy formula to calculate the total hours worked for the week by employees Jernigan, Smith, and Coady. Instead of entering that formula for each employee, you can copy the formula. Excel provides several ways to copy data. You can use the Copy and Paste commands, the drag-and-drop method, or the fill handle.

To use the Copy and Paste commands:

1. Click the cell to be copied.

2. On the Home tab, click the Copy button in the Clipboard group.

3. Click the cell into which you want to paste the data. You also may select a range of cells in which to paste the data.

4. Click the Paste button in the Clipboard group.

To use the drag-and-drop method:

1. Select the cell or range of cells you want to copy.

2. Hold down the Ctrl key and point to the border of the selection.

3. When the pointer becomes a copy pointer, drag the cell or cells to the location to which you want to copy the data.

4. Release the mouse button.

To use the fill handle:

1. Click the cell to be copied. The active cell has a black square at its lower-right corner. This black square is called a fill handle. See **Figure 12–5**.

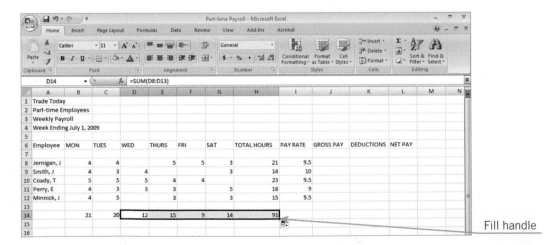

FIGURE 12–5   Fill handle on a selected cell

2. Move the mouse pointer over the fill handle. When the pointer changes shape to the move pointer, drag the fill handle, highlighting the cells into which you want to copy the data.

3. Release the mouse button. Note that filling works only when you want to copy to adjacent cells.

Relative and Absolute Cell References

When you copy cells that contain formulas, the cell references change to accommodate the new location. This is called a **relative cell reference**. If you want the value of a cell referenced in a formula to remain constant when copied, then you need to make it an **absolute cell reference**. This means that the content of the cell will not change when copied to another cell.

    To create an absolute cell reference, type a $ before the column letter and a $ before the row number in the cell reference you want to remain the same. For example, A4 is an absolute cell reference for cell A4.

    In Step-by-Step 12.3, you use various methods to copy data.

▶ **VOCABULARY**
relative cell reference

absolute cell reference

Step-by-Step 12.3

1. If necessary, open the Part-time Payroll workbook. Click cell **C14**. Notice that the formula bar contains the formula =SUM(C8:C13).

2. If necessary, click the **Home** tab and then click the **Copy** button 📋 in the Clipboard group.

3. Click cell **D14** and click the **Paste** button in the Clipboard group. Notice in the formula bar how the cell references changed in reference to the new location of the copied formula.

4. Cell D14 should still be selected. Drag its fill handle to cell **H14**, as shown in **Figure 12–5**.

5. Click cell **J8**. Type **=H8*I8** and press **Enter** to determine gross pay for Jernigan, J.

6. Use either the Copy and Paste buttons or the fill handle to copy the formula in J8 to **J9:J12**.

7. Click cell **K8**. Type **=J8*.27** and press **Enter** to determine the amount of deductions taken from Jernigan's pay. (The amount of deductions is 27% of gross pay.)

8. Copy the formula in cell K8 to **K9:K12** to determine deductions for the other four employees.

9. Click cell **L8**. Type **=J8-K8** and press **Enter** to determine net pay for Jernigan, J.

10. Copy the formula in L8 to **L9:L12** to determine net pay for the other four employees.

11. Click cell **J14**. Type **=SUM(J8:J13)** to total the gross pay for all employees.

12. Copy the formula in cell J14 to cell **K14** and cell **L14**. Your worksheet should resemble the one shown in **Figure 12–6**.

FIGURE 12–6
Payroll with copied data

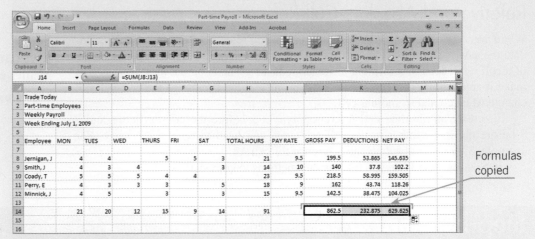

Formulas copied

13. Save the workbook and leave it open for Step-by-Step 12.4.

Formatting a Spreadsheet

The appearance of the spreadsheet is almost as important as the accuracy of the data that it contains. You can use formatting to emphasize specific entries, enhance the appearance of the spreadsheet, and make the information easier to read and understand. In **Figure 12–7**, you see how formatting can affect the appearance of the data.

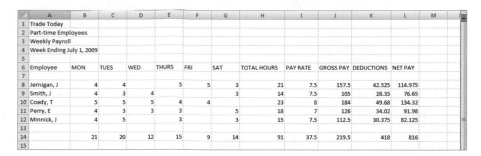

a.

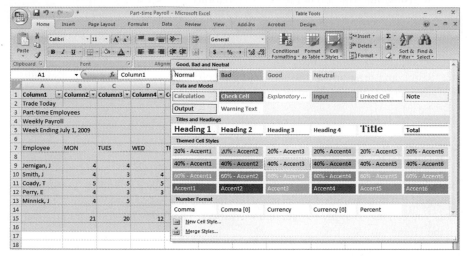

b.

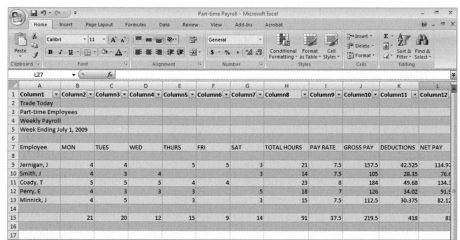

c.

FIGURE 12–7   (a) Unformatted data (b) Cell styles applied (c) Theme applied

Changing Column Width and Row Height

When you enter data in a cell that is too long for the width or height of the cell, one of the following will happen: a series of # characters appears in the cell, the text spills over into the next cell, or some of the characters are cut off.

To adjust the column width:

1. Position the pointer on the vertical line between the column letters at the top of the worksheet. The pointer changes shape to a double-headed black arrow.

2. Click and drag to the right to widen the column. Drag to the left to decrease the column width. You can also double-click to adjust the column width to its best fit.

Adjusting the row height improves readability. To adjust row height:

1. Position the pointer on the line between the row numbers at the left of the worksheet. The pointer changes shape to a double-headed arrow.

2. Click and drag upward to increase the height of the row and drag downward to decrease the height of the row. Double-click to adjust the row height to its best fit.

EXTRA FOR EXPERTS

You can press F1 to access the Excel Help window quickly.

Formatting Data

As noted earlier, the appearance of the data in a spreadsheet can have an impact on how well the information is understood. Following is a list of some of the formatting tools you can use to apply to data in a worksheet. The following tools are all located on the Home tab.

■   *Alignment*: By default, text is aligned to the left in a cell and numeric data is aligned to the right. You can change alignment using the Align Left, Center, Align Right, and Merge & Center buttons in the Alignment group. The Merge & Center format is ideal for worksheet titles and subtitles.

■   *Orientation and wrapping*: Data in cells can be rotated or wrapped to make it fit better within the cell. The Orientation button and the Wrap Text button are located in the Alignment group on the Home tab. To rotate text, click the Orientation button and select an option from the gallery. To wrap text within the cell margins, click the Wrap Text button.

■   *Font*: You can change the font, font size, font style, and font color of data just as you would in a word-processing document. Use buttons located in the Font group.

■   *Format Painter*: The Format Painter provides a time-saving way to apply formats consistently throughout a worksheet. To use this tool, located in the Clipboard group on the Home tab, select the text that contains the formatting you want to copy, click the Format Painter button, and then select the text to which you want to apply the formatting. Double-click the Format Painter button to apply the formatting to multiple items.

Inserting and Deleting Cells, Rows, and Columns

As you work on a worksheet, you might find it necessary to insert a cell or range of cells, or even an entire row or column to accommodate new data.

To insert a cell, rows, or columns, click Insert in the Cells group on the Home tab. The Insert gallery is displayed with options to Insert Cells, Insert Sheet Rows, Insert Sheet Columns, and Insert Sheet.

You can delete cells, rows, and columns by selecting them and then using Delete in the Cells group or by pressing the Delete key.

Formatting Numbers

Much of the data you enter in a worksheet is numeric. This data is more meaningful if it is presented in a formatted display. For example, monetary values should be formatted as currency and dates should be formatted in a recognized date format. You can format numbers to have a set number of decimal places, to have a comma (signifying the thousands separator), or to be displayed as a percentage. Some of the more commonly used formats can be applied using buttons in the Number group on the Home tab. Other options can be selected by clicking the Number Dialog Box Launcher (the small arrow button in the lower-right corner of the Number group). See **Figure 12–8**. **Table 12–3** contains a list of number formats and descriptions.

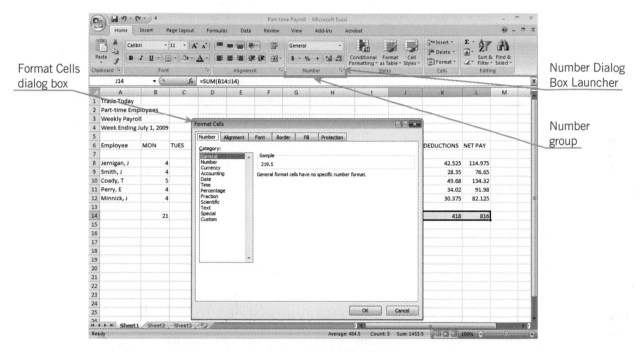

FIGURE 12–8   Formatting numbers

ETHICS IN TECHNOLOGY

Physical Security

Spreadsheets often contain information valuable to people and organizations, such as sales figures, payroll data, and profit forecasts. Users should take steps to protect this information, including securing computer hardware and other equipment. It generally is fairly easy for an unauthorized person to access systems by removing them from a valid user's desk.

Machines and consoles should be kept in a secure place. Only a limited number of persons should have access. A list of authorized users should be kept up to date. Some organizations have security guards to monitor computer rooms and control entry.

Remember that limited access means less opportunity for computer equipment and/or data to be stolen. Alternative methods for getting into a computer room should not be available. This includes hidden spare keys in an unsecured place.

Some organizations have taken computer safety an extra step by securing equipment physically to desks and tables. This might seem like overkill, but you should protect your investment and your data by whatever means necessary.

TABLE 12–3   Number formats and descriptions

FORMAT	DESCRIPTION
General	Default number format; displayed the way the numbers are typed
Number	General display of numbers; can include decimals and negative numbers
Currency	Displays general monetary values with default currency symbol
Accounting	Aligns currency symbols and decimal points
Date	Displays date and time serial numbers as date values
Time	Displays date and time serial numbers as time values
Percentage	Multiplies the cell value by 100 and displays results with a percent sign
Fraction	Displays a number as a fraction
Scientific	Displays a number in exponential notation
Text	Displays content exactly as it is typed
Special	Displays a number as zip code, phone number, or Social Security number
Custom	Used to create a custom number format

Creating and Applying Styles to a Cell

Excel cell styles allow you to quickly apply professional-looking formatting to a cell or a group of cells. On the Home tab, in the Styles group, click the Cell Styles button to select a *style*, which is a collection of formatting selections, such as cell color, font, and font size. Using the same format on a group of related cells gives your worksheet a consistent look.

Applying Themes to a Worksheet

To give your worksheet a more professional look, you can apply a theme. A **theme** is a predefined set of attributes, including fonts, colors, chart styles, cell styles, and fill effects. The document theme named Office is applied by default to every new document created in Microsoft Word, Excel, and PowerPoint. This default theme, however, can be modified by using one of the specially designed theme options within Microsoft Office. To apply a theme, select the rows and columns in the worksheet, click the Themes button in the Themes group on the Page Layout tab, and then select the theme from the Themes gallery.

Printing a Spreadsheet

Most likely you will want to print a copy of your spreadsheet. You can preview the spreadsheet to see how it will look before you print it. Click the Office button, point to Print, and then click Print Preview. The Print Preview tab is displayed along with an image of the spreadsheet as it will appear when printed. Clicking Page Setup in

VOCABULARY

theme

the Print group will display the Page Setup dialog box, where you can adjust print settings. For example, you might want to include the row and column headings on the printout. Or, you might want the gridlines to print to make it easier to read the data. You specify these settings on the Sheet tab of the Page Setup dialog box, as shown in **Figure 12–9**.

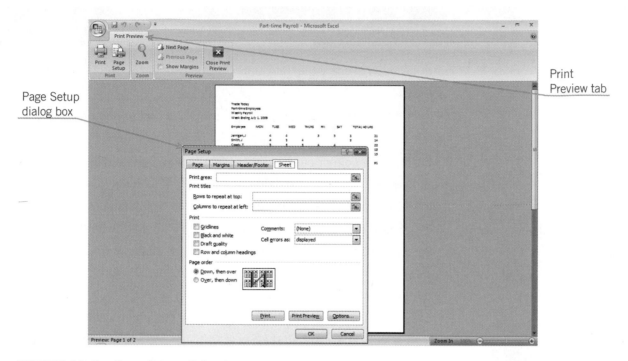

FIGURE 12–9 Page Setup dialog box

You also can determine the orientation in which the spreadsheet prints. In portrait orientation, the page is oriented toward the short side of the paper. In landscape orientation, the page is oriented toward the long side of the paper. You can set orientation on the Page tab of the Page Setup dialog box (or using the Orientation button in the Page Setup group on the Page Layout tab of the Ribbon).

In some instances, you might want to print only a portion of the spreadsheet. You can define the part you want to print by selecting it first. On the Page Layout tab, in the Page Setup group, click Print Area, and then click Set Print Area. See **Figure 12–10**.

EXTRA FOR EXPERTS

A useful feature of spreadsheet software is a macro, a recorded series of keystrokes that can be replayed as needed. For example, all of the keystrokes necessary to print a spreadsheet to a certain printer can be recorded as a macro.

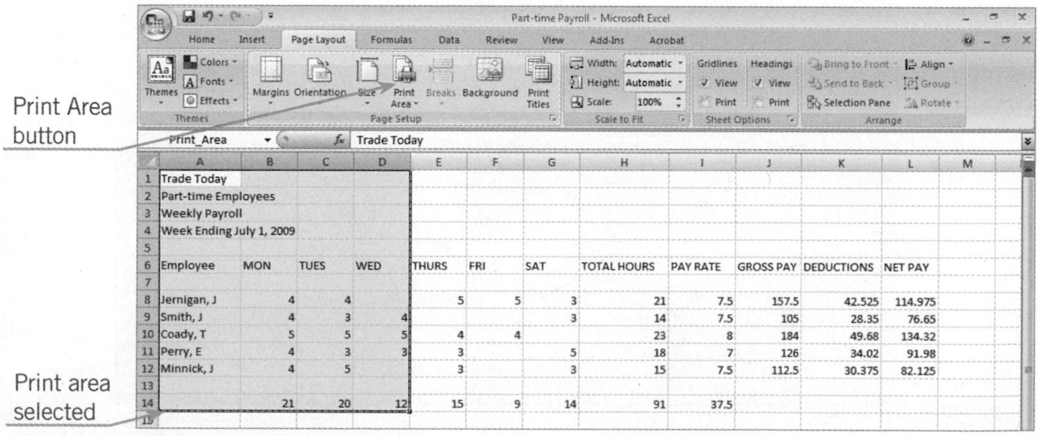

FIGURE 12–10 Selecting a print area

UNIT II   Using the Computer

To print the entire spreadsheet as is, click the Office button, point to Print, and then click Quick Print. To clear the selected Print area, click the Print Area button and then click Clear Print Area.

In Step-by-Step 12.4, you add formatting to the worksheet and print it.

Step-by-Step 12.4

1. If necessary, open the Part-time Payroll workbook. Select the range **A1:L1**.

2. Click the **Merge & Center** button in the Alignment group on the Home tab. Do the same for the ranges **A2:L2**, **A3:L3**, and **A4:L4**.

3. Position the pointer on the vertical line between column A and column B. Drag the pointer to the right until column A is wide enough to display the complete names in the cells. Do the same to adjust columns H, J, and K so they are wide enough to display their contents on one line.

4. Select **J8:L14**. In the Number group, click the **Dialog Box Launcher**, select **Currency** on the Number tab, and then click **OK**. Click anywhere in the worksheet to deselect J8:L14.

5. Click the **Page Layout** tab. In the Page Setup group, click **Orientation** and then select **Landscape**. In the Sheet Options group, click the **Dialog Box Launcher** to display the Page Setup dialog box. If necessary, click the **Sheet** tab and then click the **Gridlines** check box. Click **OK** to close the Page Setup dialog box.

6. If instructed to do so, click the **Office** button, point to **Print**, and then click **Quick Print**.

7. Select the range **A1:L14**. On the Home tab, in the Styles group, click **Cell Styles** to display the Cell Styles gallery. Under Themed Cell Styles, click **20% - Accent 1**. Your worksheet should resemble that shown in **Figure 12–11**.

FIGURE 12–11
Formatted worksheet

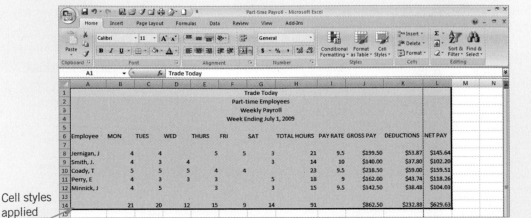

Cell styles applied

8. Save the workbook. If instructed to do so, click the **Office** button 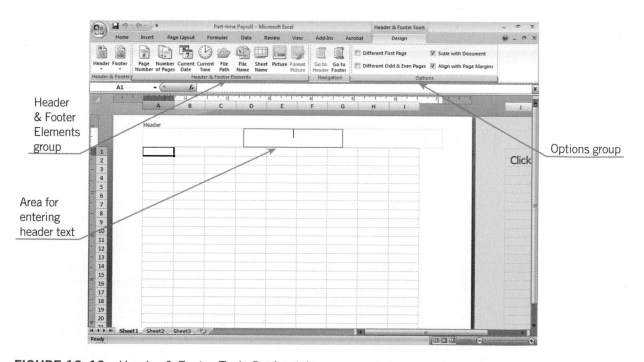, point to **Print**, and then click **Quick Print**. Leave the workbook open for Step-by-Step 12.5.

Working with Other Spreadsheet Tools

You can make spreadsheets more useful and attractive by inserting headers, footers, and other objects such as clip art. You can sort the data in a spreadsheet according to a specified column or columns. You also can hide data that might be sensitive or classified. These features are discussed in the next sections.

Headers and Footers

Use **headers** and **footers** to place information at the top or bottom of the spreadsheet. If your spreadsheet is more than one page long, the header and footer information will appear on every page. For example, a footer might include the date the spreadsheet was prepared and the name of the person who prepared it. Excel comes with several standard header and footer elements from which you can choose. To select one, click the Insert tab and then click Header & Footer in the Text group. The Design tab opens with Header & Footer Tools displayed. A variety of elements are available in the Header & Footer Elements group. See **Figure 12–12**.

> **VOCABULARY**
> **header**
> **footer**

Header
& Footer
Elements
group

Area for
entering
header text

Options group

Click

FIGURE 12–12   Header & Footer Tools Design tab

You also can create your own custom headers and footers. Clicking the Header or Footer button in the Header & Footer group displays a gallery of suggested options. See **Figure 12–13**.

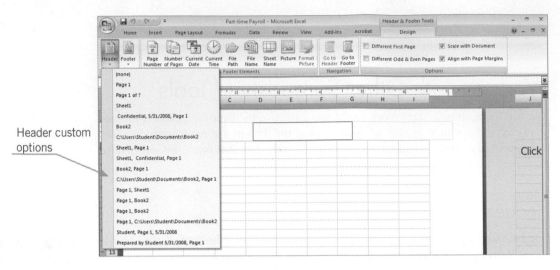

Header custom options

FIGURE 12–13   Customizing a header

Sorting Spreadsheet Data

Sorting is organizing or rearranging data in either ascending or descending order. When you sort data in ascending order, the alphabetic information is arranged in A to Z order and numeric information sorts from the lowest to the highest number. When you sort data in descending order, alphabetic information is sorted from Z to A and numbers from highest to lowest. You can sort data in a worksheet according to the data in one column or more than one column.

To sort data, select the range to be sorted, click the Sort & Filter button located in the Editing group on the Home tab, and then click Sort A to Z or Sort Z to A. This sorts the data by the first column in the range. You can sort by a specific column or columns by using the Sort dialog box. To open the Sort dialog box, click the Sort & Filter button and then click Custom Sort.

Hiding Data

Often, spreadsheets contain sensitive information or data that you do not want others to see. In this case, you can hide the data. Select the column you want to hide. Click the Format button in the Cells group on the Home tab to display the Format gallery. Under Visibility, point to Hide & Unhide, and then click Hide Rows or Hide Columns. You can also hide a column by right-clicking it and then selecting Hide on the shortcut menu. To redisplay a hidden column, first select the columns to the left and right of the hidden column. Right-click the selection and then click Unhide on the shortcut menu, or click Format in the Cells group, point to Hide & Unhide, and then click Unhide Columns.

Adding Objects to a Spreadsheet

You can add clip art, photos, and other objects to a spreadsheet to enhance its appearance. You can use tools in the Illustrations group on the Insert tab to add objects, such as Pictures, Clip Art, Shapes, and SmartArt graphics. (SmartArt is a collection of professionally created diagrams.)

To insert clip art:

1. Click the Insert tab and then click Clip Art in the Illustrations group. The Clip Art task pane opens.

2. Enter the type or category of clip art that you want in the Search for box and then click Go. The results are displayed, as shown in **Figure 12–14**.

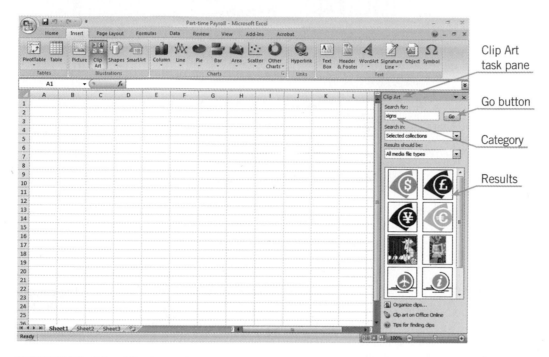

FIGURE 12–14   Clip Art task pane

3. Scroll through the displayed images using the vertical scroll bar at the right of the task pane. Once you locate the clip art you want, click it to display it in the spreadsheet.

To insert a shape:

1. Click the Insert tab and then click Shapes in the Illustrations group. The Shapes gallery is displayed. See **Figure 12–15**.

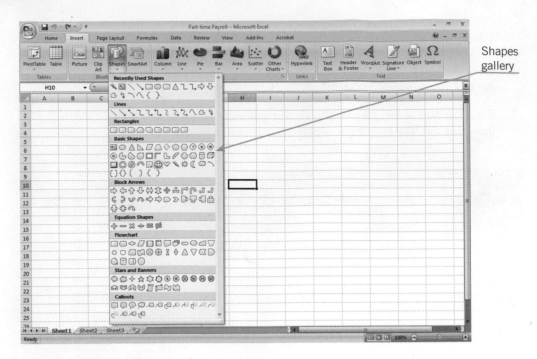

FIGURE 12–15   Shapes gallery

2. Click the shape representing the object you want to insert.

3. Click the cell in the worksheet where you want to insert the shape. The embedded shape is selected and the Format tab appears on the Ribbon with a label identifying it as Drawing Tools. The Drawing Tools Format tab appears when you select a shape. You can resize the shape, align and group shapes, fill and outline shapes, or apply a variety of Shape Effects.

To insert a picture:

1. Click the Insert tab on the Ribbon and then click Picture in the Illustrations group. The Insert Picture dialog box is displayed. Generally, this defaults to the Pictures folder.

2. Scroll through the displayed images using the vertical scroll bar at the right.

3. Once you locate the picture you want, click it to select it and then click Insert. You can use the handles surrounding the picture to resize it or move the mouse pointer on the selected image and drag it to a different location.

To insert a SmartArt graphic:

1. Click the Insert tab on the Ribbon and then click SmartArt in the Illustrations group.

2. Select an option from the Choose a SmartArt Graphic dialog box and then click the OK button to insert SmartArt in the worksheet.

3. Resize using the handles surrounding the graphic or move the mouse pointer to a border on the selected graphic and drag it to a different location.

4. To delete any of these objects, select the object and press the Delete key.

In Step-by-Step 12.5, you use additional spreadsheet tools to enhance the worksheet.

Step-by-Step 12.5

1. Select the range **A8:L14** and then click the **Sort & Filter** button in the Editing group on the Home tab. Click **Sort A to Z** in the Sort & Filter gallery.

2. Right-click the column letter **I**, which shows the employees' pay rates. Click **Hide** on the shortcut menu. The column no longer is displayed.

3. Drag across the column headings **H** and **J**, right-click the selected columns, and then click **Unhide** on the shortcut menu to redisplay the pay rate data in column J.

4. Create a header with your name, page number, and date of completion:

   a. Select the **Insert** tab on the Ribbon and then click **Header and Footer** in the Text group. The Design tab is displayed with the Header & Footer Tools title.

   b. If necessary, click in the centered section panel in the header and then type your first and last name.

   c. Press **Tab** to move to the right section panel and click the **Page Number** button in the Header & Footer Elements group.

   d. Press **Tab** to move to the far left section panel and click the **Current Date** button.

   e. Click anywhere on the spreadsheet to close the header.

5. Insert a clip art picture related to money:

   a. If necessary, click the **Insert** tab on the Ribbon and then click **Clip Art** in the Illustrations group.

   b. In the Clip Art task pane, type **money** in the Search for box and click **Go**.

   c. Scroll through the pictures and click one of your choice.

   d. If necessary, click one of the handles on the clip art to resize it so it is about 1 inch by 1 inch in size. Close the Clip Art task pane.

   e. Position the clip art in the upper-left corner of the worksheet. Click elsewhere in the worksheet to deselect the clip art.

6.   Click the **View** tab on the Ribbon. In the Workbook Views group, click **Normal**. Your worksheet should look similar to that shown in **Figure 12–16**. Click the **Office** button 🔘, point to **Print**, and then click the **Print Preview** button.

FIGURE 12–16
Clip art added to worksheet

Clip art added

Formatted worksheet

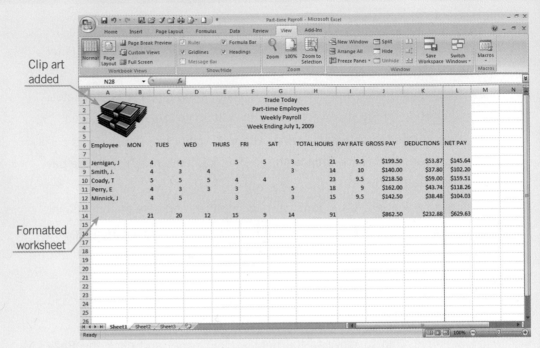

7.   Click the **Close Print Preview** button to return to Normal view. Make any changes you think are necessary.

8.   Save the workbook and then print the worksheet if instructed to do so. Leave the workbook open for Step-by-Step 12.6.

TECHNOLOGY CAREERS

Data Warehouse Developer

The data warehouse developer is responsible for translating business requirements into computer solutions. This is accomplished by understanding the users' needs and assisting in the design of physical databases to address those needs. The data warehouse developer also provides secondary technical support. This position requires teamwork skills. The qualifications include a bachelor's degree in Computer Technology, Computer Science, or Engineering. Excellent oral and written communication skills are also required. Salary range varies depending on location, responsibilities, and qualifications.

Creating Charts

A **chart** is a visual representation of spreadsheet data. Charts can help make the data more interesting and easier to understand. Before creating a chart, you need to plan how you want your chart to look and what information to include. The chart type that you select will depend on the data you want to represent. **Table 12–4** lists the Excel chart types and a description of the types of data best illustrated with each chart.

▶ VOCABULARY
chart

TABLE 12–4   Chart types

CHART TYPE	DESCRIPTION
Area	Effective for emphasizing trends because it illustrates the magnitude of change over time
Bar	Helpful when you want to make comparisons among individual items
Bubble	Compares sets of three values
Column	Useful in showing changes over a period of time, or for making comparisons among individual items
Doughnut	Shows comparisons between the whole and the parts, but enables you to show more than one set of data
Line	Illustrates trends in data at equal intervals
Pie	Compares the sizes of portions as they relate to the whole unit and illustrates that the parts total 100%; effective when there is only one set of data
Radar	Compares the aggregate values of a number of data series
Scatter	Illustrates scientific data, specifically showing even intervals—or clusters—of data
Stock	Illustrates the fluctuation of stock prices or other data that changes over time
Surface	Displays optimum combinations between two sets of data

To insert a chart:

1. Select the data range that you want to chart.

2. Click the Insert tab on the Ribbon.

3. Select the chart type from the Charts group.

4. Click the chart subtype in the Chart gallery.

In Step-by-Step 12.6, you create a chart in the payroll worksheet that displays the net pay of employees.

Step-by-Step 12.6

1. Select the range **A8:A12**. Hold down the **Ctrl** key and then select the range **L8:L12**. (Both ranges of data will appear on the chart.)

2. Click the **Insert** tab.

3. Click **Column** in the Charts group, and then select the first chart sub-type in the second row (**3-D Clustered Column**).

4. The chart is inserted into the center of the worksheet and three contextual Chart Tools tabs open on the Ribbon: Design, Layout, and Format.

5. Click the **Chart Tools Layout** tab, click the **Chart Title** button in the Labels group, and then click **Above Chart** in the gallery.

6. Double-click in the **Chart Title** text box to select the text and type **Net Pay for Employees**. Press **Enter**.

7. Click anywhere in the chart to deselect the title.

8. If necessary, scroll down. Position the mouse pointer over a blank area of the chart, and then drag the chart below the worksheet so the upper-left corner of the chart is in cell D17.

9. Click a blank cell to deselect the chart.

10. Click the **View** tab and then click the **Zoom** button in the Zoom group to display the Zoom dialog box. Click the **Custom** text box, type **80**, and then click the **OK** button. The worksheet size within the screen is reduced. See **Figure 12–17**.

FIGURE 12–17
Chart added to worksheet

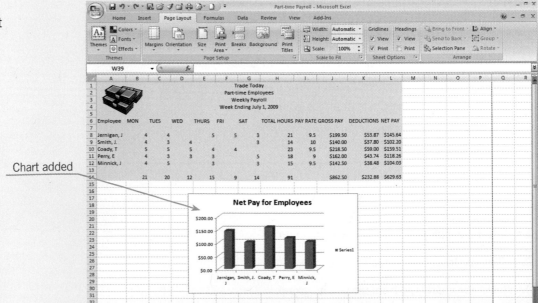

Chart added

11. Save the workbook and print a copy of the worksheet if instructed to do so. Exit Excel by clicking the **Office** button and then clicking **Exit Excel**.

SUMMARY

In this lesson, you learned:

- The primary use of Excel spreadsheets is to enter, calculate, manipulate, and analyze numbers.

- Columns in spreadsheets are identified by letters, and rows are identified by numbers.

- The point at which a row and a column intersect is a cell.

- A cell that has been selected (highlighted or outlined with a black border) is referred to as the active cell.

- A range of cells is a group of closely situated cells.

- Alphabetic text information in cells is referred to as labels; numeric information in cells that can be calculated is referred to as values.

- A formula is a type of data that performs a calculation. To enter a formula in a cell, you must first type an equal sign.

- A function is a built-in formula that performs calculations ranging from simple to complex.

- You can copy data by using the Copy and Paste commands or the fill handle.

- A relative cell reference refers to cells that change when they are copied into other locations. An absolute cell reference refers to cells that do not change when they are copied into other locations.

- The AutoSum feature enables you to quickly add a range of cells.

- You can change the appearance of data by using a variety of formatting tools and options or by applying one of the Excel cell styles.

- Selected data in a spreadsheet can be hidden so it will not be displayed or printed.

- The contents of a spreadsheet can be displayed in chart format. A chart displays the spreadsheet data visually so that data can be understood more easily.

■ VOCABULARY REVIEW

Define the following terms:

absolute cell reference	formula prefix	spreadsheet
active cell	function	theme
cell	header	value
cell reference	label	workbook
chart	order of evaluation	worksheet
footer	range	
formula	relative cell reference	

■ REVIEW QUESTIONS

MULTIPLE CHOICE

Select the best response for the following statements.

1. A collection of related worksheets is called a(n) _____.

   A. volume   C. AutoFormat

   B. spreadsheet   D. workbook

2. Each cell has a name, called the _____.

   A. cell reference   C. cell spreadsheet

   B. cell address   D. Answer A or B

3. A formula in a selected cell is displayed in the _____.

   A. formula bar   C. status bar

   B. Cell task pane   D. View group on the Formulas tab

4. Pie, bar, column, and line are examples of types of _____.

   A. spreadsheets   C. charts

   B. worksheets   D. cells

5. A _____ is alphabetical text in a worksheet.

   A. label   C. function

   B. chart   D. heading

TRUE/FALSE

Circle T if the statement is true or F if the statement is false.

T   F   **1.**   A worksheet is the same as a spreadsheet.

T   F   **2.**   By default, a workbook contains five worksheets.

T   F   **3.**   A formula is an equation that performs a calculation.

T   F   **4.**   Charts can be embedded in a spreadsheet.

T   F   **5.**   In a formula, multiplication and division are performed before addition and subtraction.

FILL IN THE BLANK

Complete the following sentences by writing the correct word or words in the blanks provided.

1. A cell address consists of a(n) _____ letter and a(n) _____ number.

2. To enter data in a spreadsheet, you first select the _____.

3. To identify a cell reference as absolute, type a(n) _____ before the letter and number in the cell address.

4. By default, text is aligned to the _____ in a cell.

5. A(n) _____ is a collection of formatting selections.

■ PROJECTS

CROSS-CURRICULAR—MATHEMATICS

You have volunteered to research the cost of three possible two-week vacation locations for your family. Prepare a worksheet that will show the cost of each trip, including line items for transportation, hotel, car rental, meals, activities, and any miscellaneous costs. Apply a cell style to the data. Chart the information for each vacation location.

CROSS-CURRICULAR—SCIENCE

Prepare a spreadsheet that displays your weight on different planets. Use the Internet and other resources to find information on how to determine relative gravity. The spreadsheet might have columns labeled "Planet," "Relative Gravity," "Current Weight," and "Planet Weight." Include clip art in the spreadsheet and format it as desired.

CROSS-CURRICULAR—SOCIAL STUDIES

Use the Internet and other resources to research national parks within your state. Prepare a spreadsheet that shows the name, location, distance from where you live to each park, the features of each park, and whether camping is available. Format the spreadsheet using appropriate cell styles. Sort the spreadsheet to show the distance and location. Print the spreadsheet after each sort.

CROSS-CURRICULAR—LANGUAGE ARTS

You have been asked to prepare a report on teen drug abuse. Use the Internet and other sources for your research. Include statistical data as part of the written report. Present the statistical data in a spreadsheet. It should include the top five drugs used by teenagers, the amount of money spent on drugs yearly, the number of deaths yearly, and any other statistics that would support your report. Include a footer containing the name of the report, the page number, and the date. Include clip art, and format the spreadsheet as desired.

WEB PROJECT

Locate a Web site that includes information about the periodic table of elements and create a worksheet listing a minimum of 10 elements and their properties. The following should be included for each element: abbreviations, boiling point, element symbols, melting point, number of protons, and number of neutrons. Create a chart that compares the physical properties of each of the elements.

 ## TEAMWORK PROJECT

You and a classmate are to gather information regarding the top 10 careers for the next decade. You should collect data on projected need, current salary, expected salary, training needed, and cost of training. Enter this information in a spreadsheet. Sort the data according to the projected need. Format the spreadsheet as desired.

CRITICAL THINKING

You have been given the responsibility of maintaining scores for your bowling team. Enter the following information in a spreadsheet. Enter your own data in the missing cells.

TEAM MEMBER	WEEK 1	WEEK 2	WEEK 3	WEEK 4
David Edwards		175	150	250
Laura Smith	90		125	105
John Brown	200	220		185
Paul Fugate	110	100	135	
George Jones	120		132	170

Add your name and your scores below the last row. In a column to the right of the Week 4 column, enter a formula to determine the monthly average for each player. Enter weekly averages for the team on the row below the last team player. Include appropriate column and row headings for the data. Add a title to the spreadsheet. Format the data as desired and insert clip art or a drawing that you create using the Shapes tools. Create a chart that illustrates the monthly average information.

EXPLORING GOOGLE

In many instances, converting units of measurement from one format to another can become a time-consuming chore. Google's calculator not only evaluates mathematical expressions, but also converts many other units of measurement. For instance, using Google's search box, you quickly can convert U.S. currency to Euros, years into minutes, or a decimal number into binary. You can find information and examples at *www.google.com/help/calculator.html*. At the end of the page, you can find a number of expressions with which you can experiment. Additional information and examples also can be found at *www.googleguide.com/calculator.html*.

After you complete your experimenting, try some conversions of your own. Create an Excel worksheet that contains your name and two columns. The first column should contain the information to be converted and the second column should contain the results of the conversion. The worksheet should contain at least ten different types of conversions. Add a header with your name and date. Print a copy if instructed to do so.

LESSON 13

Databases

■ OBJECTIVES

Upon completion of this lesson, you should be able to:

- Define the purpose and function of database software.
- Identify uses of databases.
- Identify and define the components of a database.
- Plan a database.
- Create a table using a wizard.
- Enter records in a table.
- Add a form using a wizard.
- Create a query using a wizard.
- Create a report using a wizard.

Effective information management is the core of a successful business or organization and is important in one's personal life. **Data** is unorganized text, graphics, sound, or video. **Information** is data that has been organized and processed so that it is meaningful and useful. Every organization and most individuals need a method to store data and convert it into accurate, relevant, and timely information when needed.

■ VOCABULARY

data

database

database management system (DBMS)

datasheet

Datasheet view

data type

Design view

fields

forms

information

object

primary key

query

records

report

table

views

...

Database Software Defined

A *database* is a collection of related information organized in a manner that provides for rapid search and retrieval. A *database management system* (*DBMS*) is a software program that is used to create, maintain, and provide controlled access to data. A database and spreadsheet are somewhat similar. Like spreadsheets, database tables are composed of rows and columns. Both programs enable you to organize, sort, and calculate the data. A database, however, provides additional comprehensive functions for manipulating the data. This lesson introduces you to some of the basic features for entering, organizing, and reporting data in Microsoft Access 2007, a powerful program that offers many features. As you continue to learn and use Microsoft Access, you will have the building blocks you need for using this software for more advanced applications.

Before you begin to design and develop a database, you should do some planning. Consider what data you will include and what information you want to create. After you have made these decisions, you are ready to create your database.

Database Structure

To use Access effectively, you first need to understand some basic terminology. In Access, a database can consist of one table or a collection of tables. A *table* is composed of columns and rows, referred to as fields and records in Access. **Figure 13–1** shows a sample database table for customers of the Flower Store. The Flower Store provides wholesale products to florists, so its customers are small flower shops.

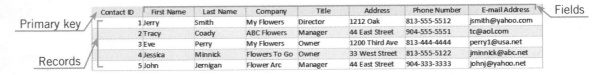

	Contact ID	First Name	Last Name	Company	Title	Address	Phone Number	E-mail Address	
	1	Jerry	Smith	My Flowers	Director	1212 Oak	813-555-5512	jsmith@yahoo.com	Fields
	2	Tracy	Coady	ABC Flowers	Manager	44 East Street	904-555-5551	tc@aol.com	
	3	Eve	Perry	My Flowers	Owner	1200 Third Ave	813-444-4444	perry1@usa.net	
	4	Jessica	Minnick	Flowers To Go	Owner	33 West Street	813-555-5122	jminnick@abc.net	
	5	John	Jernigan	Flower Arc	Manager	44 East Street	904-333-3333	johnj@yahoo.net	

Primary key — / Records

FIGURE 13–1   Table in a sample database

Following is a description of the three table components identified in **Figure 13–1**:

The rows in the table are called *records*. Each record is a group of related fields, such as all of the information regarding each member in a membership database or each customer in a customer table.

The columns in the table are called *fields*. Each field contains a specific piece of information within a record. In the table in **Figure 13–1**, for example, the Phone Number field contains the customer's phone number.

The *primary key*, which is assigned to a field, uniquely identifies each record in a table. It tells the database program how your records will be sorted, and it prevents duplicate entries. In **Figure 13–1**, the primary key is the Contact ID field.

When you start Access, the window you see is similar to other Microsoft Office 2007 applications in several ways—it displays a title bar, the Ribbon, and a status bar. Unlike Word, Excel, and PowerPoint, however, Access does not have a standard document view. The Access window changes based on the *object* you are using as you work with the database. Furthermore, many of the Ribbon buttons are unique to Access.

Using the data stored in the table, you can use Access to create the following objects: queries, forms, and reports. A *query* asks a question about the data stored in the table. The database program searches for and retrieves information from a table or tables to answer the question. You use *forms* to enter data into a table, and a *report* to print selected data. All of these objects—tables, forms, queries, and reports—are stored in a single file, which is the database.

When creating a database, you can use an Access *template*, a sample database that is contained within the Access program, or you can create a database from scratch. In Step-by-Step 13.1, you start Access and create a database file.

▶ **VOCABULARY**

query

forms

report

template

Step-by-Step 13.1

1. Start Access by clicking the **Start** button 🌐, pointing to **All Programs**, clicking **Microsoft Office**, and then clicking **Microsoft Office Access 2007**. The Access window opens, as shown in **Figure 13–2**. Your opening window may look somewhat different than that shown in the figure.

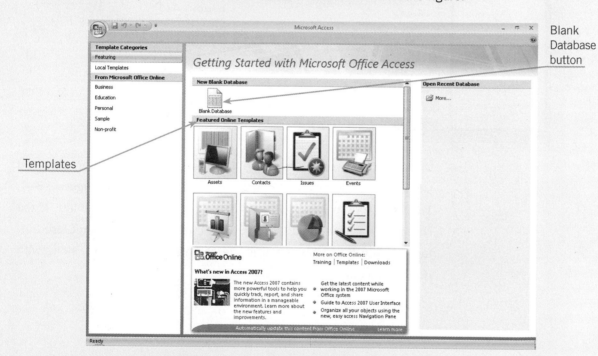

Blank Database button

Templates

FIGURE 13–2
Getting Started with Microsoft Office Access window

2. Click the **Blank Database** button. The Blank Database task pane opens, and a default file name is displayed in the File Name text box. Double-click the default file name and then type **Flower Shop** in the File Name text box.

3. Click the **folder** icon 📁 to the right of the File Name text box, locate the drive and folder where you will store your file, and then click **OK** to confirm the selection. In **Figure 13–3**, the F:\ drive is displayed as the file location. Most likely your drive and location will be different.

FIGURE 13–3
Creating a database

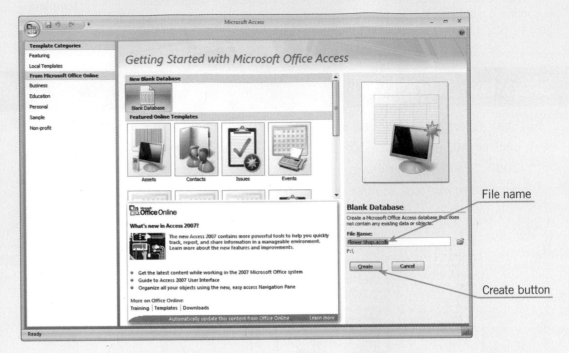

4. Click the **Create** button to create the database. The database is created and a new table opens in Datasheet view, as shown in **Figure 13–4**. The Navigation pane showing All Tables is displayed on the left. If the Navigation pane is not displayed, click the **Shutter Bar Open/Close** button ». The Navigation pane is the command center for working with Access objects.

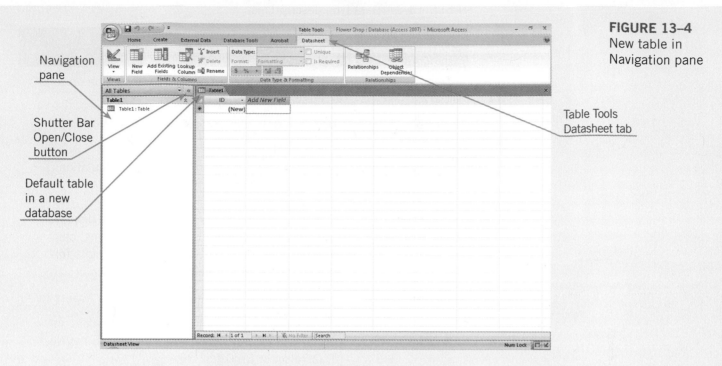

FIGURE 13–4
New table in
Navigation pane

Navigation pane

Shutter Bar Open/Close button

Default table in a new database

Table Tools Datasheet tab

5. Leave Access and the database open for Step-by-Step 13.2.

When you create a database from scratch, Access supplies the first table for you and opens it in Datasheet view by default. A *view* is a format used to display and work with various objects. You will learn more about views shortly.

▶ **VOCABULARY**
view
data type

Tables

After you create and save a new database, the next step is to add fields and then add data to the table. Tables are the primary objects in a database because they contain the data. Most databases contain multiple tables.

Creating a Table

Access provides several ways to create a table, including the following:

- Create a table by creating a new database.
- Add a table to an existing database using the Tables group on the Create tab.
- Create a table based on a table template using the Tables group on the Create tab, selecting Table Templates, and then selecting an available template.

A default table was added automatically to the database you created in Step-by-Step 13.1. The table is named Table1 and contains one field—the ID field, also called the primary key, which uniquely identifies each record.

Each field that you add to a table has a unique name and a designated data type. The *data type* indicates the type of data that can be entered into a field. For instance, to store a name or other alphanumeric data, you use a text field; to store numbers, you use a numeric field, and so on. **Table 13–1** lists the available data types and describes the type of data.

TABLE 13–1   Data type descriptions

DATA TYPE	DESCRIPTION
Text	Can contain any characters; entries can be up to 255 characters in length
Memo	Used for alphanumeric data with more than 255 characters
Number	Numeric data used in mathematical calculations
Date/Time	Used to hold dates and times
Currency	Contains only monetary data—values are displayed with currency symbols, such as dollar signs, commas, and decimal points, and with two digits following the decimal point
AutoNumber	A unique sequential number assigned by Access for each record entered
Yes/No	Stores one of two values—the choices are Yes/No, True/False, or On/Off
OLE object	Used for more advanced features, such as storing or linking objects in a table
Hyperlink	Stores a hyperlink to an URL, other document, or other object
Attachment	In Access 2007 databases, stores a link to a file
Lookup Wizard	Creates a field that can be used to choose a value from another table or query

After you have assigned a data type, you also can set properties for the field. Field properties are specifications that allow you to customize the data type settings. The field properties available depend on the data type selected. One of the most common field properties is the field size. The default size for text fields is 255 characters, but you can change that as necessary. Another common field property is format. The format specifies how you want Access to display numbers, dates, times, and text.

Adding Fields to a Table

As indicated previously, you store information items in a field. Access provides three options to add fields in Datasheet view:

- Add fields to a table directly in the datasheet.
- Add fields using the Field Templates pane; you display this pane by clicking the New Field button in the Fields & Columns group on the Datasheet tab.
- Add a field from an existing table using the Field List pane.

The next step is to name the primary key and use the Datasheet view option to add other fields to the table, increase the width of two fields, and then save and name the table. It is assumed that all customers live in the same city, so in this instance, city and state are not included as part of the address.

Step-by-Step 13.2

1. If necessary, start Access and open the **Flower Shop** database. If a Security Warning is displayed, click **Options** and then click the **Enable this content** option button in the Microsoft Office Security Options dialog box. Click the **OK** button. In the Navigation pane, double-click **Table1** to open it. The Table Tools Datasheet tab should be selected.

2. Click **row 1**, **column 1** and then click **Rename** in the Fields & Columns group on the Datasheet tab. Type **Contact ID** for the column heading and then press **Enter**.

3. Click the **Add New Field** column. Click **Rename** in the Fields & Columns group. Type **First Name** and then press the **Tab** key. Type **Last Name** and press the **Tab** key. Continue adding the following fields: **Company**, **Title**, **Address**, **Phone Number**, and **E-mail Address**.

4. Move the mouse pointer to the column separator line between Phone Number and E-mail address. The pointer changes to a ✛ shape. See **Figure 13–5**.

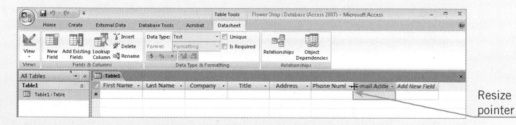

FIGURE 13–5
Preparing to resize a column

5. Drag to the right to display the Phone Number field name.

6. Repeat this process to increase the column width for the E-mail Address.

7. Click the **Office** button and then click **Save** to display the Save As dialog box.

8. Type **Customers** in the Table Name text box and then click the **OK** button to save the new Customers table. See **Figure 13–6**.

FIGURE 13–6
Fields added to a table

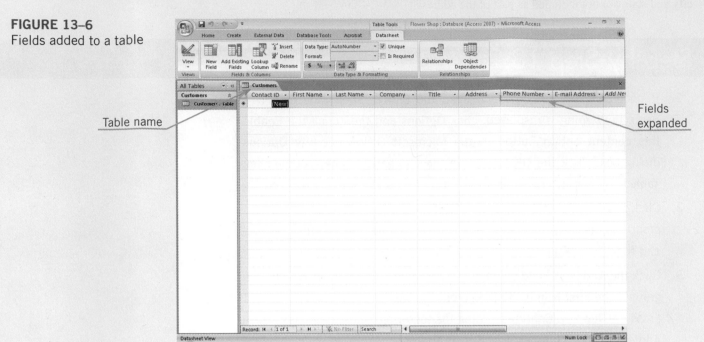

Table name

Fields expanded

VOCABULARY
Design view
Datasheet view
datasheet

Adding Records to a Table

Creating a table is the first step in a three-step process, and adding fields is the second step. The third step is to populate or add records to the table. When editing or adding records to a table, you can create and use a form or use Datasheet view. Recall that views are formats used to display and work with the various objects. Access contains two basic views for working with tables:

- *Design view*: You use *Design view* to create a table, form, query, and report
- *Datasheet view*: In *Datasheet view*, Access displays a row-and-column view of the data in tables, forms, and queries; the table is called a *datasheet* and resembles an Excel worksheet

You can switch between views by selecting the Home tab or the Datasheet tab and then selecting the View button in the Views group.

When data is entered in a cell, it is called an entry. To move from one cell to another, you can use the mouse to click in a cell or you can use the keyboard to navigate in a table. **Table 13–2** contains a list of keyboard navigations.

TABLE 13–2   Keys for navigating in Datasheet view

KEY	DESCRIPTION
Enter, Tab, or right arrow	Moves the insertion point to the next field
Left arrow or Shift+Tab	Moves the insertion point to the previous field
Home	Moves the insertion point to the first field in the current record
End	Moves the insertion point to the last field in the current record
Up arrow	Moves the insertion point up one record and stays in the same field
Down arrow	Moves the insertion point down one record and stays in the same field
Page Up	Moves the insertion point up one screen
Page Down	Moves the insertion point down one screen

You learn how to create and use a form to add records later in this lesson. In Step-by-Step 13.3, you use Datasheet view to enter records in the table.

Step-by-Step 13.3

1. If necessary, click the **Shutter Bar Open/Close** button « to close the Navigation pane. Click the first empty cell (the *First Name* field), and type **Jerry**. Notice that as you enter the text, Access automatically assigns the primary key *1* in the Contact ID field.

2. Press **Tab** to move from field to field, and complete each entry by typing the following information in the respective fields. Resize the field when necessary to accommodate the data. When you are done, the table should look like that shown in **Figure 13–7**.

   Last Name: **Smith**
   Company: **My Flowers**
   Title: **Director**
   Address: **1212 Oak**

Phone Number: **813-555-5512**

E-mail Address: **jsmith@yahoo.com**

FIGURE 13–7
Adding a record

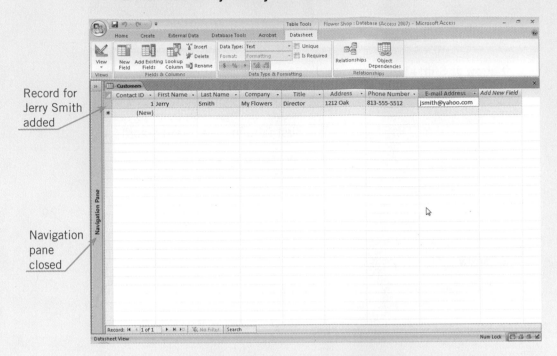

Record for Jerry Smith added

Navigation pane closed

3. Press **Tab** two times to move to the First Name field in the next row. Refer to **Table 13–3** and enter the data for records 2 through 5. Adjust column width if necessary.

TABLE 13–3   Records to add to the Customers table

CONTACT ID	FIRST NAME	LAST NAME	COMPANY	TITLE	ADDRESS	PHONE NUMBER	E-MAIL ADDRESS
2	Tracy	Coady	ABC Flowers	Manager	44 East Street	904-555-5551	tc@aol.com
3	Eve	Perry	My Flowers	Owner	1200 Third Ave	813-444-4444	perry1@usa.net
4	Jessica	Minnick	Flowers To Go	Owner	33 West Street	813-555-5122	jminnick@abc.net
5	John	Jernigan	Flower Arc	Manager	100 First Ave	904-333-3333	johnj@yahoo.net

4. Press the **Tab** key after the last entry. Your screen should resemble **Figure 13–8**. Click the **Save** button 💾 on the Quick Access toolbar to save the changes. Leave the database open for Step-by-Step 13.4.

Additional records added to Customers table

FIGURE 13–8
Records added to Customer table

Printing a Table

You can print a table from Datasheet view. To print the table in landscape mode (in which the lines of text are parallel to the long dimension of the page), click the Office button, point to Print, and then click Print Preview. The Print Preview tab is displayed. Click the Landscape button in the Page Layout group to display the print preview as shown in **Figure 13–9**. Click the Print button in the Print group. The Print dialog box is displayed. You have a choice of printing all records or selected records. Click the OK button and then click the Close Print Preview button in the Close Preview group.

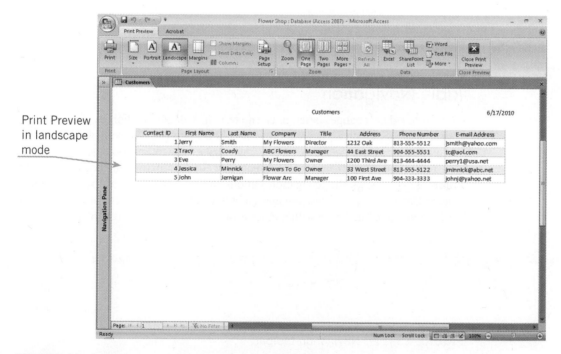

Print Preview in landscape mode

FIGURE 13–9 Preview of the Customers datasheet

Sorting a Table

The data in a table can be sorted in ascending or descending order. In ascending order, the records are sorted from A to Z, or smallest to largest. In descending order, the records are sorted from Z to A, or largest to smallest. In Datasheet view, click the field name that you want sorted; the column is highlighted. Click the arrow to the right of the column name to display the shortcut menu. Select Sort A to Z or Sort Z to A. In **Figure 13–10**, the Last Name field is highlighted so the data will be sorted according to that field. Click the check box to the left of a name to deselect or select any of the names.

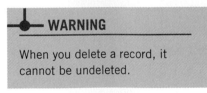

▶ **VOCABULARY**

text filter

Note also in **Figure 13–10** that you can use a *text filter*. A filter provides options to change the data that a form or report displays without altering the form or report design. For example, you can select to view the records of only those customers whose telephone prefix is 904.

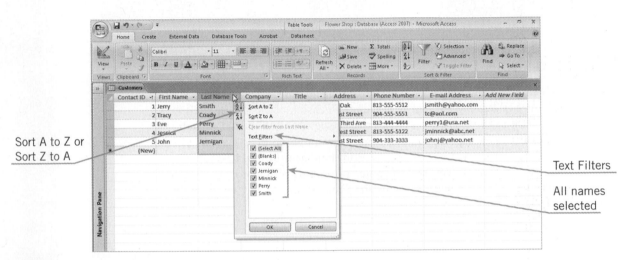

Sort A to Z or
Sort Z to A

Text Filters

All names
selected

FIGURE 13–10   Sorting records

┼── **WARNING**

When you delete a record, it cannot be undeleted.

Table Navigation

Quite often data changes after it is entered in a database. For example, one of your customers changes their address or phone number. Or, you want to add a new customer to the database. Access provides a navigation toolbar that makes it easy for you to move from record to record or locate a particular record in a table. **Figure 13–11** shows the navigation buttons that are displayed at the bottom of a table in Datasheet view. These navigation buttons are especially useful when you are working in a large database with hundreds or even thousands of records.

Current
record

Next record

Last record

New (blank)
record

FIGURE 13–11   Navigation toolbar

Modifying a Table Structure

After you have created a table, you can modify it by adding and deleting columns (fields) and rows (records) in Datasheet view. When you delete a column or a row from the table, all the data contained in the column or row is deleted from the database. Delete columns or rows from a table when they are no longer needed to store data. Click the header for the column or row to select it and then right-click to display the shortcut menu. See **Figure 13–12**.

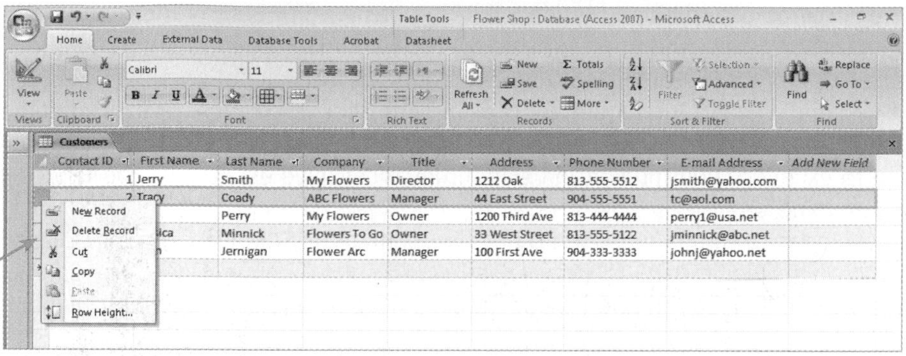

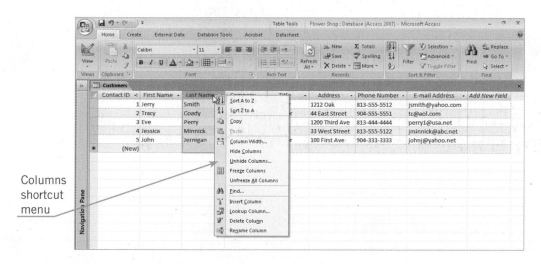

Shortcut menu

FIGURE 13–12   Adding or deleting a record with a shortcut menu

Selecting a column and then right-clicking the header row to display the shortcut menu provides additional options. For example, you can apply the following to a column: sort, hide, delete, freeze, copy, and so on.

To insert a column, right-click the field name that is to the right of the new field, and then click Insert Column on the shortcut menu. To delete a column, right-click the field name, and then click Delete Column. See **Figure 13–13**.

Columns shortcut menu

FIGURE 13–13   Options for working with columns

To add a record, right-click the selected row, and then click New Record. You also can add a record by clicking in the last field of the last record and then pressing Tab or Enter. To delete a row (or record), select the row. Right-click the selected row, and then click Delete Record on the shortcut menu.

TECHNOLOGY CAREERS

Database Developer

A database developer creates and modifies databases. Data in a database can be reorganized, dispersed, and accessed in several ways. Databases are important to companies and organizations because they contain records or files, such as sales transactions, product catalogs and inventories, and customer profiles.

Database developers create management systems to provide effective and efficient access to information stored in databases. They provide expertise and guidance in the design, implementation, and maintenance of database management systems. An important part of this work involves implementing and controlling security procedures to protect the database from accidental or intentional damage or loss.

These individuals must be good at communicating not only in computer languages, but with people as well. They write descriptions about programs, prepare manuals, create help screens, and explain new systems to users. In addition to excellent communication skills, they must have extensive experience with hardware, software, and systems and processes.

To become a database developer, an individual should have a Bachelor of Science degree in Computer Science, as well as specific computer certifications. Prior experience also is recommended. The salary for this position will vary depending on the location and size of the organization and an individual's experience.

Forms

In addition to adding and viewing records in Datasheet view, you also can create and use a data-entry form. A form provides a convenient way to enter and view records in a table. When you create a form, you are adding a new object to the database. You can create the form manually or use the Form Wizard. The wizard asks you questions and formats the form according to your preferences. Use the Form Wizard to create a form in Step-by-Step 13.4.

Step-by-Step 13.4

1. Close the Customers table by clicking the **'Close Customers'** button ☒.
   See Figure 13–14. If you have resized any columns, you are asked if you want to save changes to the layout of the table. Click **Yes**.

FIGURE 13–14
Closing an object

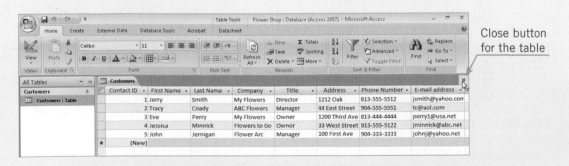

Close button
for the table

2. Click the **Create** tab and then click the **More Forms** button in the Forms group to display the Form Wizard option. See **Figure 13–15**.

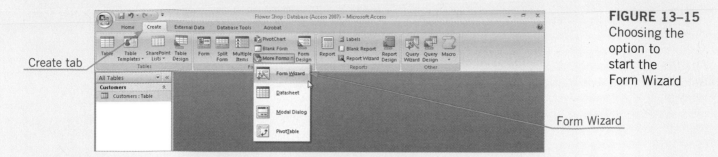

FIGURE 13–15
Choosing the
option to
start the
Form Wizard

3. Click **Form Wizard** to display the Form Wizard dialog box. The Form Wizard dialog box is displayed. Note that the list of Available Fields shows the same fields you added when you created the table.

4. Click the **Select All** `>>` button. All of the fields are copied to the Selected Fields box, as shown in **Figure 13–16**.

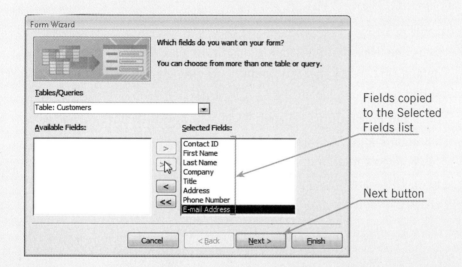

FIGURE 13–16
Selecting fields in the Form Wizard

5. Click the **Next** button. In the Form Wizard dialog box, you select the layout for the form. If necessary, click the **Columnar** option and then click **Next**.

6. In the next Form Wizard dialog box, you select the style for the form. Click the **Civic** style, as shown in **Figure 13–17**.

FIGURE 13–17
Selecting a form style in the Form Wizard

FIGURE 13–17
Selecting a form style in the Form Wizard

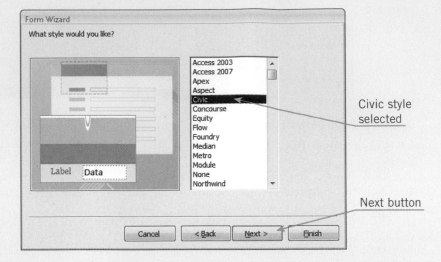

Civic style selected

Next button

7. Click the **Next** button. The Form Wizard displays Customers as the default title. Verify that the **Open the form to view or enter information** option button is selected.

8. Click the **Finish** button. A form is displayed in the Access window, as shown in **Figure 13–18**. This form contains the Jerry Smith data, which you entered earlier in this lesson. Note the controls at the bottom of the form. These are the same controls located in the table's Datasheet view. Leave the form open for Step-by-Step 13.5.

FIGURE 13–18
New form created with the Form Wizard

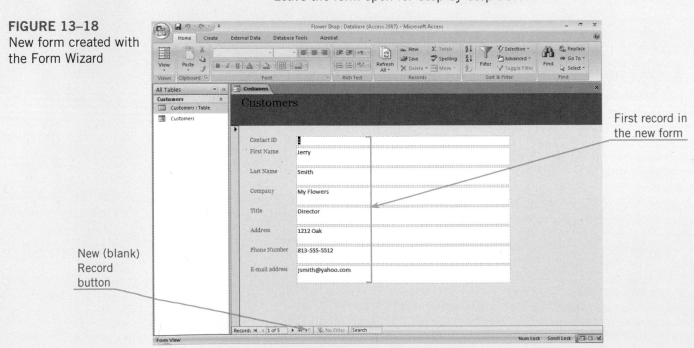

First record in the new form

New (blank) Record button

Entering and Editing Data in a Form

Entering data in a form is similar to entering data in a table in Datasheet view. You use the same keys to move the insertion point among the fields. Furthermore, the same navigation buttons are available at the bottom of the form. To add a new record, click the New (blank) record button. To edit an existing record, use the navigation keys to display the record and make the changes in the fields on the form. Complete Step-by-Step 13.5 to add a new record to the database.

> **EXTRA FOR EXPERTS**
>
> Using the Form tool, you can create a form from a table formatted as a datasheet.

Step-by-Step 13.5

1. Click the **New (blank) record** button ▶ to display a blank form, as shown in **Figure 13–19**.

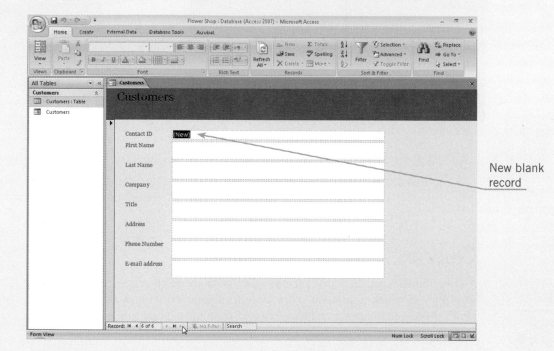

FIGURE 13–19
New record in a form

New blank record

2. Click the **First Name** box and type **Laura**. Press **Tab** to move to the Last Name box.

3. Type **Smith** and press **Tab**. Use the following information to complete the rest of the fields for this record:

   Company: **XYZ Flowers**
   Title: **Director**
   Address: **601 Walnut**
   Phone Number: **813-222-2222**

E-mail address: **lsmith@abc.net**

The form should look like that shown in **Figure 13–20**.

FIGURE 13–20
Adding a record
using a form

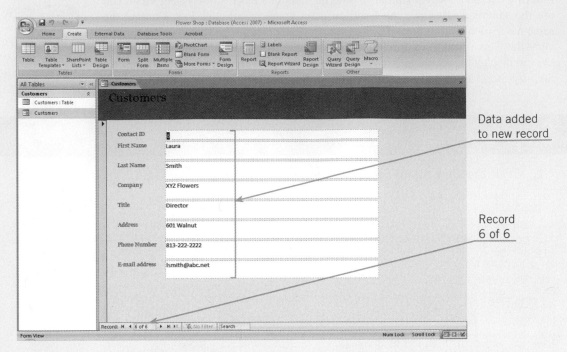

Data added
to new record

Record
6 of 6

4. Click the **Save** button 🖫 on the Quick Access toolbar and then click the
    form's **Close** button ✕. Keep the database open for Step-by-Step 13.6.

Queries

A query enables you to locate records that match specified criteria by providing a
way for you to ask a question about the information stored in a database table or
tables. Access searches for and retrieves data from the table(s) to answer your question. Access provides four Query options:

- *Simple Query Wizard*: creates a select query from the selected fields
- *Crosstab Query Wizard*: displays data in a spreadsheet format
- *Find Duplicates Query Wizard*: locates records with duplicate field values
- *Find Unmatched Query Wizard*: locates records in one table that have no related
  records in another table

Suppose, for example, that you want a list of all customers within a specified zip
code. When you create a query, you determine what fields you want displayed in the
query results. Often, you only need to see certain fields in the query results instead
of all the fields in the table. In the preceding example, for instance, you might want
only the customer's last name and the zip code displayed. The order in which you
select the fields will determine the order in which the information is displayed in the
query results.

In Step-by-Step 13.6, you create a query to display specified fields.

Step-by-Step 13.6

1. Click the **Shutter Bar Open/Close** button ≫ to open the Navigation pane, click the **Customers** table in the Navigation pane, if necessary, and then click the **Create** tab.

2. Select **Query Wizard** in the Other group to display the New Query dialog box, as shown in **Figure 13–21**. If necessary, click **Simple Query Wizard** in the New Query dialog box.

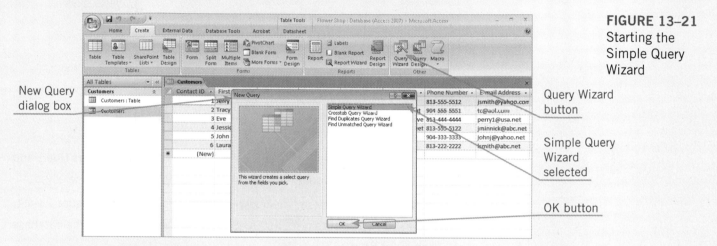

New Query dialog box

FIGURE 13–21
Starting the Simple Query Wizard

Query Wizard button

Simple Query Wizard selected

OK button

3. Click **OK** to start the Simple Query Wizard. Click **Last Name** and then click the **Add Field** > button. See **Figure 13–22**.

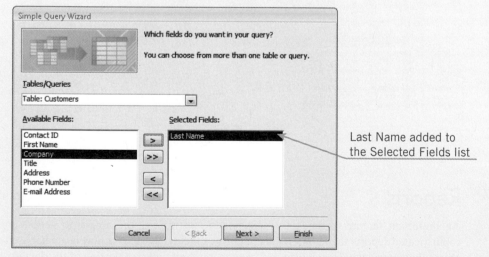

FIGURE 13–22
Selecting the Last Name field in the Simple Query Wizard

Last Name added to the Selected Fields list

4. Click the **Phone Number** field and then click the **Add Field** > button.

5. Click **E-mail Address** and then click the **Add Field** [>] button. See **Figure 13–23**.

FIGURE 13–23
Selecting other fields in the Simple Query Wizard

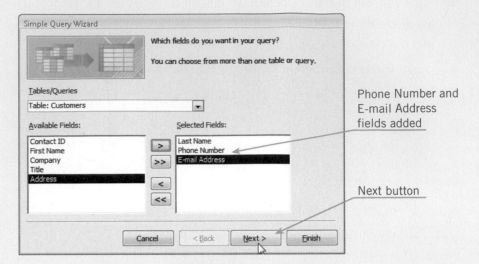

Phone Number and E-mail Address fields added

Next button

6. Click the **Next** button, and then verify that the title is **Customers Query** and that the **Open the query to view information** option button is selected.

7. Click the **Finish** button. The query is displayed, as shown in **Figure 13–24**. Click the **Close** button ✕ in the query results window. Leave the database open for Step-by-Step 13.7.

FIGURE 13–24
Results of
Customers Query

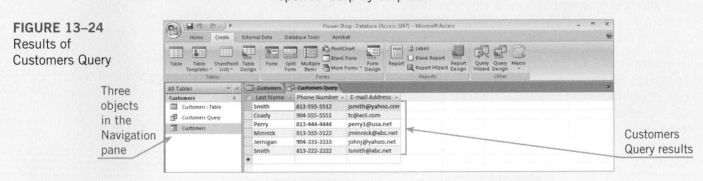

Three objects in the Navigation pane

Customers Query results

Reports

An important feature of database management software is the ability to generate sophisticated reports that contain the contents of the database. A report is a database object that allows you to organize, summarize, and print all or a portion of the data in a database. You can create a report based on a table or a query. You can decide what formatting you want to use, such as headings, spacing, and graphics. After the report is generated, you can decide which records you want included in the report, you can sort the report, and you can insert a picture in the report.

Although you can produce a report manually, the Report Wizard, similar to the Query Wizard, provides an easy and fast way to design and create one. The wizard asks questions about which data you want to include in the report and how you want to format the data.

In Step-by-Step 13.7, you use the Report Wizard to create a report.

Step-by-Step 13.7

1. In the Access window, click the **Create** tab, if necessary, and then click **Report Wizard** in the Reports group. See **Figure 13–25**.

Report Wizard dialog box

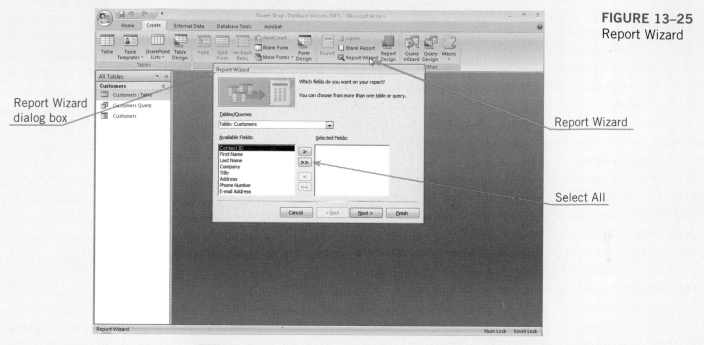

FIGURE 13–25
Report Wizard

Report Wizard

Select All

2. Click the **Select All** button >> to move all of the Available Fields to the Selected Fields box, as shown in **Figure 13–26**.

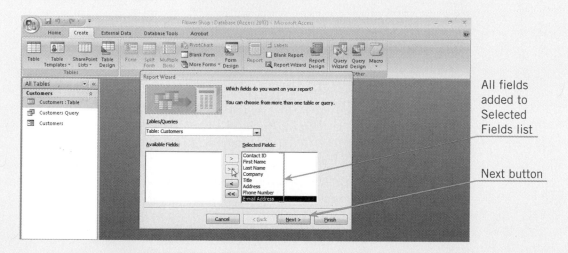

FIGURE 13–26
Selecting all fields in the Report Wizard

All fields added to Selected Fields list

Next button

3. Click the **Next** button. A Report Wizard dialog box is displayed and has options for grouping a report by fields. No grouping is applied to this report. Click the **Next** button.

4. The Report Wizard dialog box opens with options for the sort order of the records. Click the down arrow on the first box and then click **Last Name**, as shown in **Figure 13–27**. If necessary, click the button to the right of the Last Name selection so it displays "Ascending."

FIGURE 13–27
Selecting a sort field and order

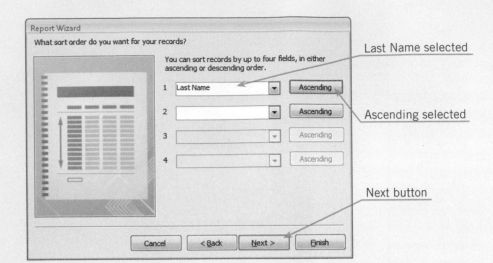

5. Click the **Next** button. The Report Wizard dialog box displays options for the layout and orientation for the report. Click the **Justified** option under Layout and click the **Landscape** option under Orientation. Verify that the **Adjust the field width so all fields fit on a page** check box is selected. See **Figure 13–28**.

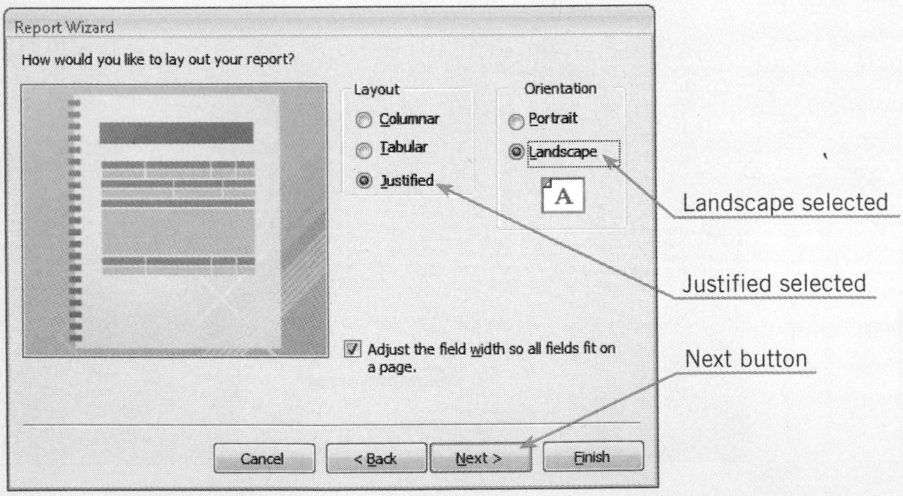

FIGURE 13–28
Layout options for the report

6. Click the **Next** button to display the Report Wizard dialog box with options for report styles. Click **Module**, as shown in **Figure 13–29**.

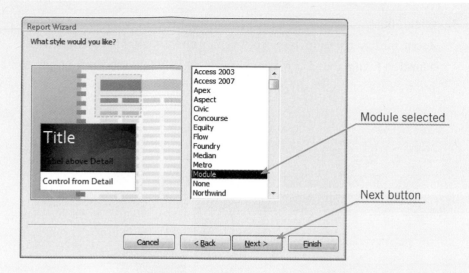

FIGURE 13–29
Style options for the report

Module selected

Next button

7. Click the **Next** button to display the Report Wizard dialog box in which you enter a title for the report. Type **Flower Shop Customers**. Verify that the **Preview the report** option button is selected as shown in **Figure 13–30**.

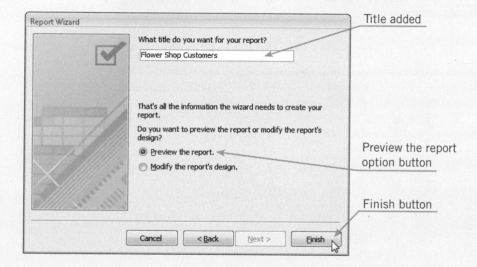

Title added

Preview the report option button

Finish button

FIGURE 13–30
Completing the Report Wizard

8. Click **Finish** to display the report. On the Print Preview tab, click the **Zoom** button arrow in the Zoom group and select **Fit to Window**, as shown in **Figure 13–31**. If instructed to do so, click the **Print** button to print a copy of the report.

FIGURE 13–31
Completed report in Print Preview

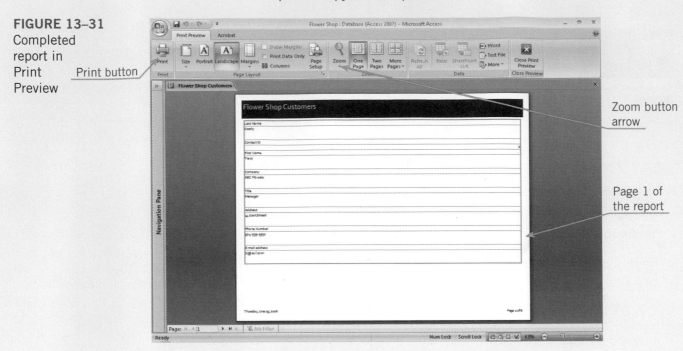

Print button

Zoom button arrow

Page 1 of the report

9. Close Access by clicking the **Close** button ⊠ in the title bar.

SUMMARY

In this lesson, you learned:

- Databases allow for organizing, storing, maintaining, retrieving, and sorting data.

- The components of a database are objects. These include tables, queries, forms, and reports.

- You should plan the database structure first and then create it.

- After the table structure is created, you add records to the table.

- Records can be sorted in ascending or descending order.

- You can create a form or use the Form Wizard to enter records in a table. Forms are designed to simplify data entry.

- You can design a query or use the Query Wizard to find records that meet specified criteria.

- A report is a formatted display of table records. In a report, you can organize, summarize, and print all or a portion of the data.

VOCABULARY REVIEW

Define the following terms:

data

database

database management system
   (DBMS)

datasheet

Datasheet view

data type

Design view

field

forms

information

object

primary key

query

records

report

table

views

REVIEW QUESTIONS

MULTIPLE CHOICE

Select the best response for the following statements.

1. The rows in a table are called _____.

   A. records

   B. fields

   C. columns

   D. primary

2. A(n) _____ is a single piece of information in a database.

   A. field

   B. record

   C. entry

   D. table

3. In Datasheet view, clicking the Home key moves the insertion point to _____.

   A. the last field in the current record

   B. the first field in the current record

   C. the previous field

   D. the next record

4. A table can be sorted in _____ order.

   A. ascending

   B. descending

   C. right-to-left

   D. both A and B

5. The _____ uniquely identifies each record in a table.

   A. field name

   B. memo field

   C. primary key

   D. file

TRUE/FALSE

Circle T if the statement is true or F if the statement is false.

T   F   **1.**   You can add records to a table at any time.

T   F   **2.**   After a table is created, the structure cannot be modified.

T   F   **3.**   Data in a table may be sorted in ascending or descending order.

T   F   **4.**   It is unnecessary to plan your database structure.

T   F   **5.**   The only way to create a form is to use the Form Wizard.

FILL IN THE BLANK

Complete the following statements by writing the correct word or words in the blanks provided.

1. Tables are the primary _____ in a database.

2. _____ is a data type that can contain any characters and entries can be up to 255 characters in length.

3. A(n) _____ is a question you ask about the data stored in a database.

4. Access provides a total of _____ different options to add fields to a database.

5. The _____ data type contains only monetary data.

■ PROJECTS

CROSS-CURRICULAR— MATHEMATICS

Use the Internet and other resources to locate statistical information on five NBA teams. Create a database named NBA and a table named Stats. The table will consist of statistical information from the previous season for at least five teams. Determine the fields in the table. These might include Team Name, Games Played, or Games Won, for example. Enter the data in the table. Next, gather information for two additional teams and use a form to add them to the table. Prepare a report using the data in the table. Create a query that shows the teams that won fewer than five games during the season. Print your table and report if instructed to do so.

CROSS-CURRICULAR—SCIENCE

Create a database named Nutrition. Include a minimum of five fields in the table. Name the table Good Nutrition. Add a minimum of 10 records to the table that relate to good nutrition. Use the Internet and other resources to gather your data. Create a query and a report using the data in the table. Print a copy of the report if instructed to do so.

CROSS-CURRICULAR—SOCIAL STUDIES

Create a database named Brown's Cab Company. Create a table based on the Customer Service table template in the Business category (display the Tables group on the Create tab, select Table Templates, and then select Customer Service from the Business sample tables). Include a minimum of seven of the Sample Fields in the table. Name the table Customer Service. Add a minimum of 10 records to the table. Sort the table on two fields. Create a query, specifying criteria that apply to the sample fields you chose. Create a report using all the data in the table. Print a copy of the query results and a copy of the report if instructed to do so.

CROSS-CURRICULAR—LANGUAGE ARTS

Create a database named Authors. Create a table named Shakespeare with the following fields: Title, Type, Date, and Subject. Include records for at least 15 of Shakespeare's works. Use the Internet and other resources to gather your data. Print a query that shows one type of his work. Print the table sorted by Date.

WEB PROJECT

You are investigating various schools, colleges, and universities. You have decided what you want to study and now need to find the best school for that field of study. However, you need to consider other features, such as tuition, distance from home, required SAT score, student population, and so on. Create a database with a table to record college features. The table should have at least five fields. Research at least six schools. Create a report and three printouts showing different sorts, such as all colleges with tuition under a certain amount or schools in a certain state.

TEAMWORK PROJECT

You are the chairman of a nonprofit service organization. You and your co-chair are busy signing up other groups in your community to participate in the Go Green project. You have decided to use a database to organize and manage the information for this project. Create a database named Go Green. Create a table named Save Green. Consider the following and any additional fields you think will be useful: Organization, Contact, Telephone, Climate Change, and Go Green products. Create a form to enter at least eight records. Create a report sorted by Organization. Prepare and print a report grouped by task if instructed to do so.

CRITICAL THINKING

Decide how using database software could assist you in school, work, or other activities. Examples would be to organize your CD collection or create a family directory. Prepare a database to address a selected need. Use the various capabilities of the software to perform a query, prepare a report, and print at least two sorted lists if instructed to do so.

 EXPLORING GOOGLE

Google Product Search is a price comparison service. Located at www.google.com/products, the interface provides an HTML form similar to that created with Access. After clicking the Advanced Product Search link, you can type a topic into the form text box, and then select results with all of the words, with the exact phrase, with at least one of the words, or without the words. Results requested can be as few as 10 or as many as 100. You can elect to sort by relevance, by price, by product rating, and by seller rating.

Access the Google Product Search page and complete a search for a computer-related or technology products such as iPods, cell phones, digital cameras, PDAs, DVD players, and so on. Create a report outlining your results and list which product you would purchase and why. Then write a short paragraph comparing your search to how a database program relates to this activity. Print your report if instructed to do so.

LESSON 14

Software Integration

■ OBJECTIVES

Upon completion of this lesson, you should be able to:

- Describe software integration.
- Integrate data between Microsoft Office 2007 applications.
- Describe the Paste and Paste Link commands.
- Describe linked objects.
- Describe embedded objects.

■ VOCABULARY

container application

destination program

embedded object

linked object

object

object linking and embedding
(OLE)

source program

...

Software Integration

As you have discovered, you can use individual applications, such as those in Microsoft Office, to perform common tasks in the workplace, in education, and for personal use. In addition to producing individual documents with Microsoft Office applications, you also can integrate data from one program into the other programs. An *object* is the data or information that you want to share between the programs. Microsoft Office provides three methods for inserting objects from one Office document into another Office document: copying and pasting, embedding, and linking. Each method has advantages and disadvantages. Understanding each of these methods helps you select the best option for a particular task.

Copying and Pasting

Copying and pasting data between programs or documents is similar to copying and pasting text or other objects within a single document. Assume that you have a chart or worksheet in Excel and you want to add a copy of it to a Word document. In the Excel document you select and copy the content. Next, you open a Word document, click the location where you want to paste the copied data, and then click the Paste button. In this instance, the worksheet becomes a table in Word and can be modified. A chart pasted into a Word document can be modified in Word by double-clicking it. Changes made to these objects in Word are not reflected in Excel, and changes made in Excel are not reflected in Word.

To copy and paste an Excel object into a Word document:

1. Open the Excel document and then select the content you want to copy.

2. Select the Copy button located on the Home tab in the Clipboard group or press Ctrl+C.

3. If necessary, open the Word document. Click the location where you want to paste the copied data, and then click the Paste button on the Home tab in the Clipboard group.

In Step-by-Step 14.1, you copy and paste an Excel worksheet into a Word document.

Step-by-Step 14.1

1. If necessary, insert your USB drive or other media storage device in the appropriate drive on your computer. Start Microsoft Office Word 2007.

2. Open the Word **banquet_letter** data file and save it as **banquet_letter01**. Insert the current date and your name where noted in the document.

3. Start Microsoft Office Excel 2007. Open the **banquet_tasks** data file and save it as **banquet_tasks01**.

4. In Excel, select the range **A1:D8** to select the Banquet Expenses table.

5. On the Home tab in the Clipboard group, click **Copy**, or press **Ctrl+C**.

6. On the taskbar, click the **Microsoft Word** program button.

7. Click the blank line between the first and second paragraphs in the letter body.

8. On the Home tab in the Clipboard group, click **Paste**, or press **Ctrl+V**. The Excel data is pasted into the Word document.

9. In the Description column of the Banquet Expenses table, add **/Drinks** following Food. Select the Banquet Expenses table and then center it. See **Figure 14–1**.

10. Save the **banquet_letter01** document. Print a copy if instructed to do so and then close the file.

11. Review the banquet_tasks01 workbook and note that the data you changed in the Word document was not changed in the workbook.

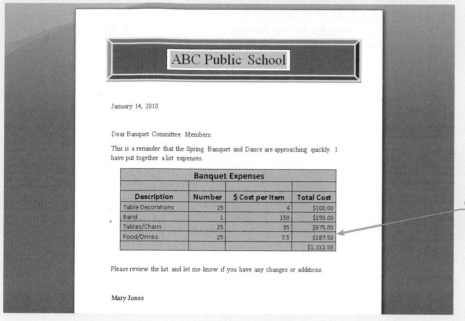

FIGURE 14–1
Excel data integrated in Word document

Excel data is pasted into Word document

The spreadsheet data you pasted into your word-processing document becomes part of the Word document and can be edited in the Word document as necessary. Any changes in the copied data do not affect the Excel source document, and any changes in the Excel source document do not affect the spreadsheet data pasted into the Word document.

The primary advantage of the copy and paste method is that it is easy. Disadvantages include that this method increases file size, the object is not updated when the source document is updated, and occasionally the object cannot be edited.

Object Linking and Embedding

Object Linking and Embedding (OLE) is a technology developed by Microsoft that lets you create a document or object in one program and then link or embed the data into another program. You can embed or link all or part of an existing file. For example, you can create a form letter using Microsoft Word, link it to an Access database file that contains a list of names and addresses, and then merge the form letter with the names and addresses.

As indicated earlier in this lesson, an object is the data or information that you want to share between the programs. In the form letter/addresses example, the list of names and addresses would be the object. An object also can be a table, an image, a video, a chart, and so on. The program used to create the object is called the *source program*, and the program that will contain the linked or embedded object is called the *destination program* or *container application*. The main differences between linked objects and embedded objects are where the data is stored and how you can update the data after you place it in the destination program.

Embedding an Object

> **VOCABULARY**
> embedded object

In Lesson 10, you inserted an image into a Word document from the Microsoft Clip Art collection. When you added that image, you added an embedded object. An *embedded object* is static. If changes are made to the object in the source program, those changes are not reflected in the object in the destination program. The object, however, can be modified in the destination program. When you double-click the object within your Word document, the Picture Tools tab is displayed on the Ribbon. You can use these tools to resize the clip art object, recolor it, and so on. The clip art object is modified within your Word document, but the original clip art object is not changed. Likewise, if you embed a Word document in an Excel workbook, you can modify the Word document using the Word program menus. The Word document is updated in the Excel workbook, but the original Word file (source document) is not changed. In Step-by-Step 14.2, you embed a Word into an Excel spreadsheet.

Step-by-Step 14.2

1. In Excel, make sure the **banquet_tasks01** workbook is open.

2. Click **cell B10**. See **Figure 14–2**.

FIGURE 14–2
Cell B10 selected in the Excel workbook

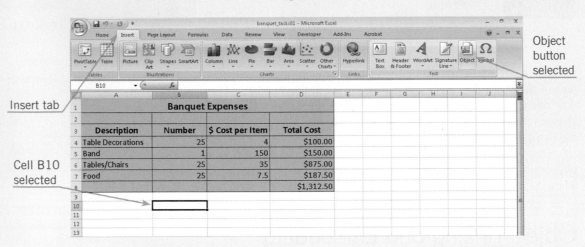

3. Click the **Insert** tab and then click the **Object** button in the Text group. The Object dialog box is displayed. Click the **Create from File** tab. See **Figure 14–3**.

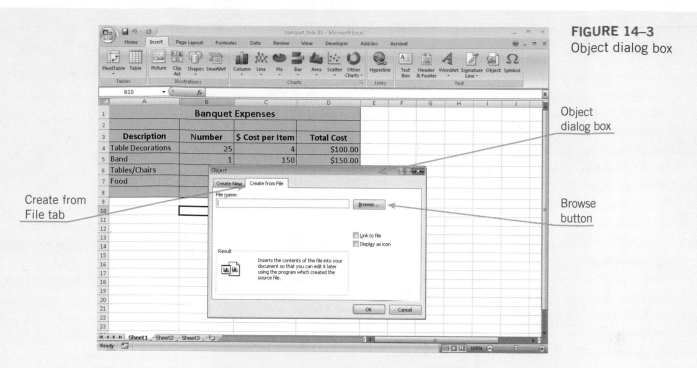

FIGURE 14–3
Object dialog box

Object
dialog box

Create from
File tab

Browse
button

4. Click the **Browse** button, navigate to the location of your data files, and then click the **tasks** file. Click the **Insert** button, and then click **OK**. The Word tasks document is embedded into the Excel worksheet. See **Figure 14–4**.

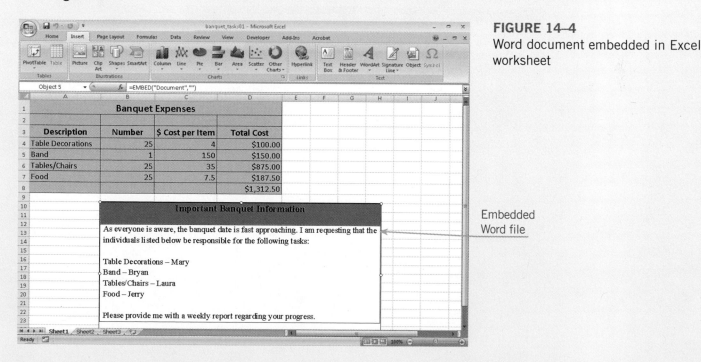

FIGURE 14–4
Word document embedded in Excel worksheet

Embedded
Word file

5. Double-click the box containing the Word tasks document.

The title bar displays the Excel filename. However, as shown in **Figure 14–5**, the Word Ribbon and its tools are displayed within the Excel window. You can use the Word tools to edit the object because the object is embedded in the Excel worksheet.

FIGURE 14–5 Word tools displayed in the Excel window

Microsoft Excel window

Word Ribbon displayed

Word document

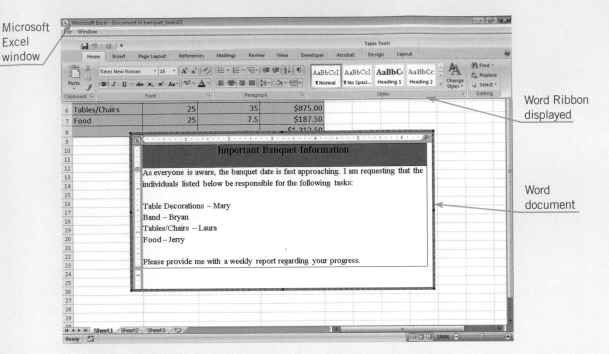

6. Double-click **Mary** and change the name to **Jessica**.

7. Click to the right of Food and add **/Drinks**.

8. Select the list in the middle of the embedded Word document. Bold the text and change the text color to **Dark Blue, Text 2**. See **Figure 14–6**.

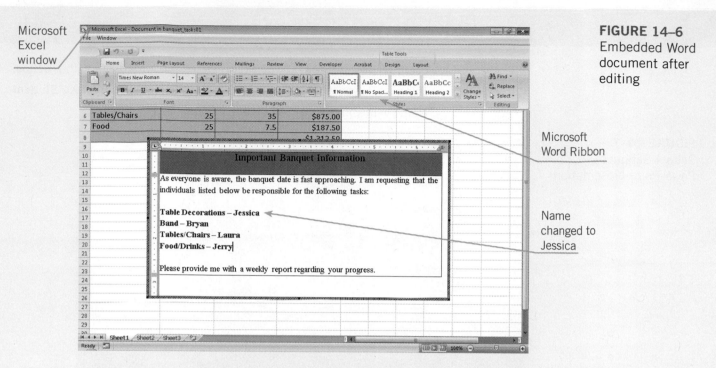

Microsoft Excel window

Microsoft Word Ribbon

Name changed to Jessica

FIGURE 14–6
Embedded Word document after editing

9. Click anywhere outside the embedded Word object to return to Excel. Save the file as **banquet_tasks02** and then close the workbook.

The main advantage of embedding is that you have an independent copy of the data. You do not need access to the original file to make changes because the object can be edited by the source application. Disadvantages include the following: embedding requires more random access memory when updating the source object, the embedded object is not updated if the source is updated, and embedding increases file size. Another issue relates to security. Regardless of what part of the source document you selected to embed, the entire source document is embedded in the target document. If the source document contains confidential or private data, this data could be exposed.

Linking an Object

Keeping embedded data current can be a problem if the information changes often. A *linked object*, on the other hand, retains a connection to the original file; the source document displays a representation of the linked data. Any changes made to the source file are reflected in the linked object. Assume that you inserted a linked spreadsheet object into a PowerPoint document. If the spreadsheet data in the Excel program is modified, then the linked spreadsheet object in the PowerPoint document also is modified.

Linking is useful when information is maintained independently. You also can link an entire file to another program. For example, suppose employee records are maintained by the Personnel Department. Other departments within the company use this data for sending mailings, creating interoffice documents, and so on. A link to the employee records would verify that the information was current.

In Step-by-Step 14.3, you link the banquet_tasks02 Banquet Expenses spreadsheet to a PowerPoint file.

▶ **VOCABULARY**
linked object

EXTRA FOR EXPERTS

In addition to embedding and linking Microsoft Office files, you also can link a variety of other files, including Adobe and Paint Shop Pro files, video clips, wave sounds, media clips, and others.

Step-by-Step 14.3

1. Start Microsoft Office PowerPoint 2007, and then open the **School Banquet** PowerPoint presentation file. On the first slide, replace **Student Name** with your name. See **Figure 14–7**.

FIGURE 14–7
School Banquet
PowerPoint presentation

Student
name added
to title slide

Next Slide
arrow

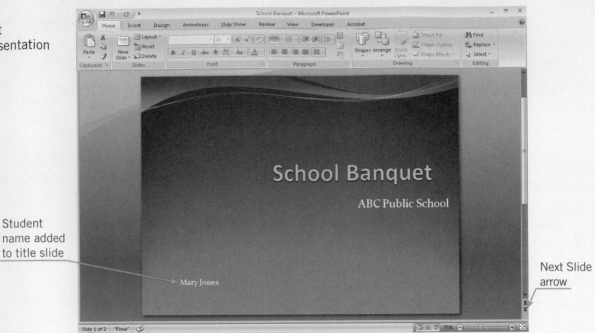

2. Click the **Next Slide** arrow to move to slide 2.

3. Click the **Insert** tab and then click **Object** in the Text group. The Insert Object dialog box is displayed. See **Figure 14–8**.

FIGURE 14–8
Insert Object dialog
box in PowerPoint
presentation

Insert Object
dialog box

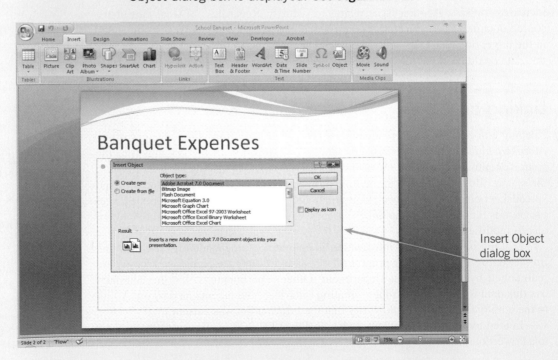

4. Click the **Create from file** option button. Click the **Browse** button and navigate to the location of the banquet_tasks02 Excel file. Click the **banquet_tasks02** file, click the **OK** button, and then click the **Link** check box in the Insert Object dialog box. See **Figure 14–9**.

Create from
file selected

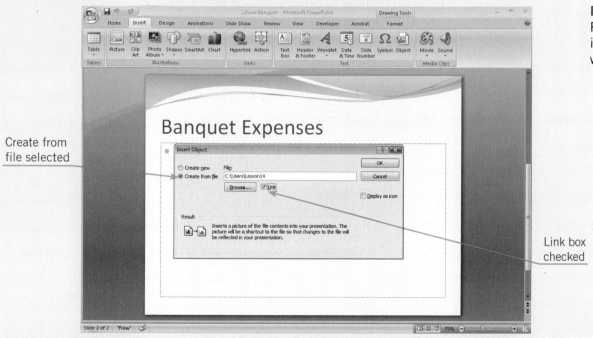

Link box
checked

FIGURE 14–9
Preparing to
insert an Excel
worksheet

5. Click the **OK** button. The data from the banquet_tasks02 Excel spreadsheet is displayed in the PowerPoint slide. See **Figure 14–10**.

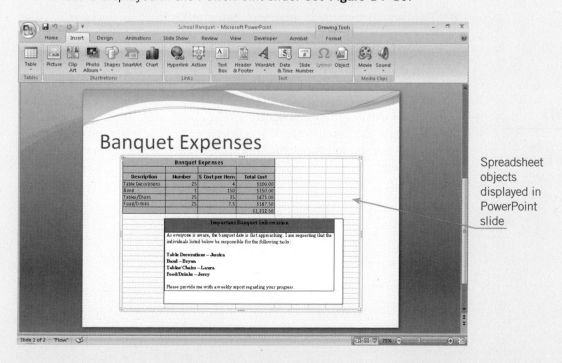

Spreadsheet
objects
displayed in
PowerPoint
slide

FIGURE 14–10
Excel and Word data
linked to PowerPoint
slide

6. Open your **banquet_tasks02** Excel file. In the $ Cost per Item column, change the **4** to a **5**. Save **banquet_tasks02**, and then close Excel.

7. In PowerPoint, double-click the **linked data** (the Banquet Expenses table and Important Banquet Information box). Note that the table automatically updates to coordinate with the changes in the Excel spreadsheet. See **Figure 14–11**.

FIGURE 14–11
Linked data updated in the PowerPoint slide

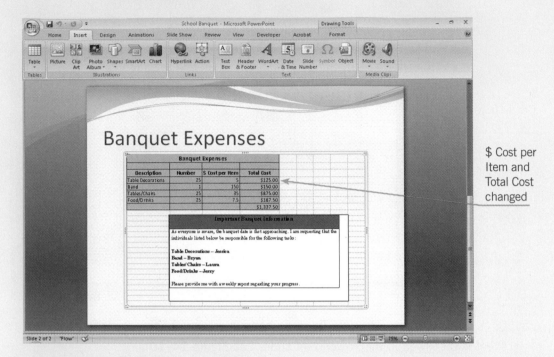

$ Cost per Item and Total Cost changed

8. Save your presentation as **school_banquet02**. Print a copy of your slides if instructed to do so, and then close all open windows.

Two advantages of linking are that your files stay small and you maintain data in one place for easy editing and updating. The disadvantage is that the link really is only a pointer to a specific file. If you delete, rename, or move the original file, you can't edit it in the destination file. You also need access to the source program to make any changes.

SUMMARY

In this lesson, you learned:

- Three methods are available to integrate Microsoft software applications and other software programs.
- Copy and paste is copying data or an object from one program and pasting it into a program.

- Object linking and embedding technology was developed by Microsoft.
- An embedded object is static.
- A linked object is modified in the container application when it is changed in the source document.

VOCABULARY REVIEW

Define the following terms:

container application	linked object	object linking and embedding (OLE)
destination program	object	source program
embedded object		

REVIEW QUESTIONS

MULTIPLE CHOICE

Select the best response for the following statements.

1. Copying and pasting from one document to another is _____.

    A. difficult

    B. similar to copying and pasting within a single document

    C. the same as hunting and pecking

    D. all of the above

2. To copy and paste an object, you first must _____.

    A. select it

    B. double-click it

    C. edit it

    D. bold the text

3. A(n) _____ is static.

    A. embedded object

    B. linked object

    C. single object

    D. all of the above

4. OLE is an abbreviation for _____.

    A. on left edge

    B. off left edge

    C. object linking and embedding

    D. open link and embed

5. Changes made to a source file are reflected in a(n) _____ object.

    A. static

    B. linked

    C. pasted

    D. embedded

TRUE/FALSE

Circle T if the statement is true or F if the statement is false.

T   F   **1.**   An embedded object can be edited by the source application.

T   F   **2.**   You can link an Excel worksheet to an e-mail message.

T   F   **3.**   Only Microsoft Office application files can be linked.

T   F   **4.**   With an embedded object, you have an independent copy of the data.

T   F   **5.**   A linked object is static.

FILL IN THE BLANK

Complete the following statements by writing the correct word or words in the blanks provided.

1. A(n) _____ is the data or information that you want to share between programs.

2. The program containing the linked or embedded object is called the _____ program.

3. When you embed a Word document into an Excel worksheet, you use tools in the _____ program to edit the object.

4. The primary advantage of the copy and paste method is that it is _____.

5. OLE was developed by _____.

■ PROJECTS

CROSS-CURRICULAR— MATHEMATICS

Use the Internet and other resources to conduct some comparison shopping for a new car. Obtain prices for the car from three different sources. Create a spreadsheet to display your data. Include information that determines the monthly payments, the total amount of loan interest, and the total price for the car. Include a 10 percent down payment. After completing the spreadsheet, write a letter to your parents or a friend to show them you have conducted a search for the perfect car. Copy and paste your spreadsheet into the letter.

CROSS-CURRICULAR—SCIENCE

Plants generally are characterized as annuals, perennials, and biennials. Use PowerPoint to create a slide presentation about plants, describing each of the three types. Include an image of each type, care instructions, and any other information that makes your presentation informative. Use Word to create an introduction and overview of your presentation. Embed the presentation into the Word document.

CROSS-CURRICULAR—SOCIAL STUDIES

Use PowerPoint to create a slide show with six slides. The slide show should cover an American history event. The first slide should be a title slide and the last slide should be a bibliography slide. Next, use Word to create an introduction to and an overview of your presentation. Link the presentation to your Word document.

CROSS-CURRICULAR—LANGUAGE ARTS

Use your word-processing program to prepare a one-page family newsletter. Include information regarding family member accomplishments. Create a spreadsheet that includes the names of at least five family members. Other data that should be included is address, telephone number, and relationship to you. Link the spreadsheet to the newsletter.

WEB PROJECT

You are going to remodel your kitchen. Assume that the size of the kitchen is 12 feet by 12 feet. Use the Internet to locate resources that you want to include in your remodeling project. Create a spreadsheet listing required appliances and other items that you want to include. Each item should be priced individually. Also calculate a total for similar multiple items and a grand total for everything. Use the Internet to locate the names and addresses of three companies in your area that do remodeling. Write a letter to the three companies explaining your plans and ask for a quote. Embed the spreadsheet in the letter.

TEAMWORK PROJECT

Working with two other members of your class, create a PowerPoint presentation that includes an introduction slide and a minimum of six additional slides. Use the Internet and/or other sources to locate information on five of your favorite video games. Create a slide for each of the games and an ending slide with the names of the team members. Use your word-processing program to create a letter with a short overview of your project. Link the PowerPoint presentation to your letter.

CRITICAL THINKING

This lesson discusses the advantages and disadvantages of copying and pasting, linking, and embedding. Write a short paragraph describing each of the three methods. Give an example of when and why you could use each method, and then list two reasons why you would select that particular method.

EXPLORING GOOGLE

Google Talk is Google's program that lets you talk, or "chat," with other online individuals. To use Google Talk, you must have a Gmail account. You can use Google Talk online or you can download Google Talk. Online features include instant messaging, group chat, and media previews. Once you download Google Talk, you have access to other programs, including Gmail notifications, PC-to-PC voice calls, and file transfers. Google Talk also is available for the iPhone. You can add the Google Talk gadget to your Google home page and/or copy and paste Google Talk code into your own personal Web page.

To use Google Talk online: If necessary, log on to your e-mail account. Along with a group of your classmates, access Google Talk at *google.com/talk* and then click the Launch Google Talk Gadget link. Search, add, or invite other members of your class to your Google Talk screen. Print a copy of your conversation(s) if instructed to do so.

UNIT II REVIEW

Using the Computer

■ REVIEW QUESTIONS

MULTIPLE CHOICE

Select the best response for the following statements.

1. The Office Fluent user interface groups tools by _____.

    A. tasks   C. numbers

    B. titles   D. alphabetical order

2. Filenames can have up to _____ characters.

    A. 25   C. 200

    B. 255   D. 150

3. Times New Roman, Arial, and Courier are types of _____.

    A. templates   C. commands

    B. fonts   D. formatting

4. To place the name of a document at the top of every page in the document, create a _____.

    A. margin   C. header

    B. justification   D. footer

5. You can tell that a graphic is selected by small squares on its border. These squares are called _____.

    A. symbols   C. sizing handles

    B. borders   D. Clip art

TRUE / FALSE

Circle T if the statement is true or F if the statement is false.

T F **1.** In a table, rows go across and columns go down.

T F **2.** Editing documents means making changes to existing text.

T F **3.** It is possible to apply more than one formatting attribute to the same text.

T F **4.** An animation is a special visual and sound effect that leads the audience from one slide in a presentation to another.

T F **5.** File management is the process of organizing and keeping track of your files.

FILL IN THE BLANK

Complete the following sentences by writing the correct word or words in the blanks provided.

1. The _____ are the white spaces around the edges of a document.

2. The _____ _____ feature automatically moves text to the next line when you reach the end of the current line.

3. A(n) _____ is composed of rows and columns.

4. To retain a copy of a document permanently, you need to _____ it.

5. A printed copy of a document is called a(n) _____ or _____.

■ PROJECTS

CROSS-CURRICULAR—MATHEMATICS

Use the Internet and other resources to research five to ten roller coaster rides at amusement parks in the United States. Gather information to include the name of the ride, a brief description, the name and location of the amusement park, and the height, length, and speed of the roller coaster. Present your data in an Excel workbook. Format your table using Excel's formatting features.

CROSS-CURRICULAR—SCIENCE

Use the Internet and other resources to identify five women who have received the Nobel Prize. Use your word-processing program to prepare a written report. The report should be a minimum of two pages. Include the name of the woman, her birth country, her contribution that won the prize, and the year in which she received the award. Locate a picture of each of the women and/or pictures related to her contribution. Insert the pictures into the report. If you cannot locate pictures, insert an appropriate clip art image. Spell check the report and then save it. Submit it in the format indicated by your instructor.

CROSS-CURRICULAR—SOCIAL STUDIES

Create a presentation using the design theme of your choice. Add a title slide to your presentation. On another slide, create a table with a minimum of 3 columns and 11 rows. Merge the three columns in the first row and add a title. Create a dictionary of a minimum of 10 new terms you have learned in Lessons 8–14. Type the term name in the first column, the definition in the second column, and add a clip art image representing the term in the third column. Bold the term and add a color. Select a unique font of your choosing. The list of terms should be in alphabetical order.

CROSS-CURRICULAR—LANGUAGE ARTS

Most word-processing programs have features that are especially useful to writers, such as styles, formatting, and comments. Use the Internet, online Help, and any other resources to identify these and other features that are useful to writers. Prepare a report that includes the name of each feature and why it is useful.

WEB PROJECT

Computer crimes have increased rapidly over the last few years. These crimes involve illegal use of or the unauthorized entry into a computer system or computer data to tamper, interfere with, damage, or manipulate the system or data. Use the Internet and other resources to research and prepare a report on various security devices to guard against computer crime. Use the Office application of your choice to prepare the report, which should contain a minimum of two pages or six slides. Include at least two graphics in your report.

TEAMWORK PROJECT

Do you like trying to solve mysteries? Work with a partner to investigate the mystery of the Bermuda Triangle. Many planes and boats have mysteriously disappeared there! Along with a partner, use the Internet and any other resources to find information on the Bermuda Triangle. Include some background information such as its location, documented disappearances, and unexplained events; thoughts of other researchers; and your conclusion. Prepare a slide presentation with your findings.

CRITICAL THINKING

Many instructors require students to use a style guide when preparing a report. One of the more popular guides is the *MLA Handbook for Writers of Research Papers*. It includes information on writing and formatting research papers. You probably have used this tool in some of your report assignments. Use the Internet and any other resources to research the MLA guidelines for formatting a research paper. Use those guidelines and Word features to prepare a one- to two-page report on your findings.

EXPLORING GOOGLE

In an earlier lesson, you learned how to search for images. Google, however, indexes millions of images; and your search results can result in hundreds or even thousands of images. Most likely, many of these images do not match your search topic. To limit the number of images to your particular search, you can use the Advanced Image Search link. Starting on the main page of the Google Image Search, click the Advanced Image Search link located to the right of the Search Images button. Clicking this link takes you to the Advanced Image Search page. This page has text boxes where you can limit your search, relate it to an exact phrase, or relate it or not relate it to any specific words. You also can specify content type, size, coloration, file type, domain, and safe search with filtering options.

Using the traditional Search tool, search for actors, actresses, or directors who have won Academy Awards. Select three of the winners for whom you would like additional information, and do an advanced search on these three people. Also conduct an advanced image search to find images related to the film. Use Word to write a paragraph about each of the three winners that you selected. Use section breaks between the paragraphs and add a title to the page.

VIDEO PROJECT

Visit the Online Companion Web page for this book, and then click the link for the Unit 2 Review to watch a video. According to the video, how are Microsoft Windows Vista, Microsoft Office, and Windows Live connected? What is meant by the statement: "Windows Vista is not about searching. It is about finding."? Describe shadow copying. If necessary, search the Web to find additional information regarding shadow copying and how it is applied. Prepare a report in the form of a written document, electronic presentation, or Web page to describe what you learned.

SIMULATION

JOB 2–1

Create a database. Use the following list of six customers and then add four names and addresses of your own choosing. Determine the fields from the list. Name the database **Computer Help OnCall**. Create a table and name the table **Customers**. After you have created the table and entered the records, create a report to alphabetize the records by customer last name. Submit the report to your instructor.

Jessica Minnick	**Tracy Coady**
1967 Jamesville Road	**909 Harbor View Way**
Lutz, FL 23510	**Tampa, FL 23456**
555-1234	**555-4567**

Bryan Richard	**Micah Waterbury**
104 Winding Creek	5157 Central Street
Tampa, FL 23502	New Port Richey, FL 23702
555-5678	555-3456
Laura Smith	**Jerry Smith**
3821 Windsor Lake Drive	777 Commerce Road
Tampa, FL 23513	Tampa, FL 23323
555-2978	555-1180

JOB 2-2

Your company, Computers For You, offers the following services: computer setup, network support, virus detection and removal, software installation, laptop computer repair, printer services, data backup and restore, and wireless network setup. Use your word-processing software to prepare a flyer announcing these services. Use fictitious information for the address, telephone number, and other information. Use clip art, a variety of fonts, and color to make the flyer attractive.

JOB 2-3

Prepare your USB drive or disc with the folder structure for files that you will be using for Computers For You. Begin with the following folders: Customers, Services, Budget, and Miscellaneous. Move your current files into the appropriate folder. Save future files in the appropriate folder.

■ PORTFOLIO CHECKLIST

Include the following activities from this unit in your portfolio:

_____	Lesson 8	Teamwork Project
_____	Lesson 9	Web Project
_____	Lesson 10	Science Activity
_____	Lesson 11	Google Activity
_____	Lesson 12	Language Arts Report
_____	Lesson 13	Teamwork Project
_____	Lesson 14	Mathematics Project
_____	Unit 2 Review	Mathematics Cross-Curricular Spreadsheet
_____	Unit 2 Review	Teamwork Report/Slide Presentation
_____	Unit 2 Review	Job 2-2 Flyer

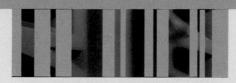

UNIT III

COMPUTERS AND SOCIETY

LESSON 15

Evaluating Electronic Information

■ OBJECTIVES

Upon completion of this lesson, you should be able to:

- Identify reasons for evaluating Internet resources.
- Identify criteria for evaluating electronic information.
- Describe software piracy.
- Identify Internet resources.
- Understand the rules of copyright.
- Identify false information, including hoaxes and urban legends.
- Cite Internet resources appropriately.
- Explore other legal and ethical issues concerning information you obtain from the Internet.

■ VOCABULARY

copyright

currency

hoax

identity theft

navigation

patent

plagiarism

public domain

shareware

software license

software piracy

sponsored site

trademark

urban legends

...

Information is only as good as the source. Anyone, anywhere, can put anything on the Internet. The information might be true; it might not be true. How can you determine if the information is legitimate? Developing the ability to evaluate information critically on the Internet is important today because so many people depend on electronic resources in so many areas of their lives. For example, you might have used information you found on the Internet to research a paper for a science class, and of course you want to ensure that the data you use is accurate. But consider some other types of information you might depend on, such as consumer information on the safety of a certain make of automobile, unbiased news about candidates running for office in your city or state, guidelines for training your pet, or information about your health. You do not want to be steered wrong in any of these areas, and you must carefully assess the wealth of information available.

Criteria for Evaluating Electronic Resources

The Internet provides opportunities for students, teachers, scholars, and anyone needing information to find it from all over the world. It is fairly easy to locate information and to publish it electronically. However, because anyone can put information on the Internet, it is not always accurate or reliable. Anyone using information obtained from the Internet needs to develop skills to evaluate what they find.

Pages on the Web have many different looks. Some pages are filled with pictures, sounds, animations, links, and information. Some are very exciting; others are plain. Sometimes the appearance of the page alone might draw you to a site and, after reading it, you realize it is not the site you need.

Following are some questions you might want to ask when you view a Web page:

- Did the page take a long time to load?
- Are the graphics on the page related to the site?
- Are the sections on the page labeled?
- Who wrote the information on this page?
- Can you communicate with the author?
- When was the page last updated?
- Does it contain appropriate links to other Web pages?
- Is it easy to follow the links?
- Can you tell what the page is about from its title?
- Is the information useful to you?
- How old is the information?
- Does any of the information contradict information you found somewhere else?
- Did the author use words such as *always*, *never*, *best*, or *worst*?
- Do you think the author knows the information he or she is sharing?

These questions represent just the beginning of the process involved in evaluating electronic information.

Determining Authorship

A well-developed resource identifies its author and/or producer. You should be given enough information to determine whether the originator is a reliable source. What expertise or authority does the author have that qualifies him or her to distribute this information? Be sure to look for a name and e-mail address of the person who created or maintains the information. See **Figure 15–1**. This person generally is the Web site developer.

EXTRA FOR EXPERTS

The Internet epitomizes the concept of *caveat lector*—reader beware.

EXTRA FOR EXPERTS

Links that are no longer active are called "dead links."

FIGURE 15-1 Determining a Web site author

If you cannot find information at the site regarding the author or originator, you should use a search engine to search for the author's name. This also could lead to other information by the same author. If an e-mail address is visible, use it to request information regarding the author's credentials and expertise.

The domain portion of the Web site address also gives you information concerning the appropriateness of the site for your area of study. Examples are:

- .edu for educational or research information
- .gov for government resources
- .com for commercial products or commercially sponsored sites
- .org for nonprofit organizations
- .mil for military branches

Relevance and Reliability

Do not accept any information presented on the Internet at face value. Is the purpose of the Web site stated? Is the information accurate? Does the information provide enough content? Has the information been reviewed? The source of the information should be clearly stated—whether it is original or borrowed from somewhere else. Make sure you understand the agenda of the site's owner. Is the site trying to sell a product or service? Is it trying to influence public opinion? As you read through the information, pay close attention to determine if the content covers a specific time period or an aspect of a topic, or if it is broader. Check other resources, such as books or journals at the local school or public library, which contain similar information.

▶ **VOCABULARY**
currency

navigation

Timely Content

A very important consideration of an effective site is its **currency**, which refers to the age of the information, how long it has been posted, and how often it is updated. Some sites need to be updated more often than others to reflect changes in the type of information they provide. Medical or technological information, for instance, needs to be updated more often than historical information. Out-of-date information might not give you the results you need. Does the site contain links that are no longer active? If so, this could be a clue that the information on the Web site might not be up to date.

Validity and Bias

The style of writing and the language used can reveal information about the quality of the site. If the style is objective, the chances are the information is worthy of your attention. However, if it is opinionated and subjective, you might want to give second thought to using it. Ideas and opinions supported by references are additional signs of the value of the site. Determine the validity of the site by checking other resources that contain similar information.

The overall layout of the page also is important. The page should be free of spelling and grammatical errors. Even if the page appears to contain valuable information, misspelled words and incorrect grammar usage tend to bias a reader regarding the validity of the information.

Site Navigation

Navigation is the ability to use links to move through a site. Being able to move quickly around a Web site is an important element. Having the information laid out in a logical design so you can locate what you need adds to the efficiency of the site. The consistency of the layout from page to page usually means you can navigate easily. The first page, or home page, of a Web site indicates how the site is organized and what options are available. Some sites also contain a site map that gives you a good idea of the overall organization of the site.

You move through a site by clicking links on the page. Some pages consist of many links; others might only contain a few. Regardless, the links should be:

- Easy to identify
- Grouped logically
- Pertinent to the subject of the original page

Each page should contain a link that takes you back to the home page and a link that allows you to e-mail the author. **Figure 15–2** shows an example of multiple types of links. On the Web page in **Figure 15–2**, the footer contains a Feedback link so viewers can contact the site designers.

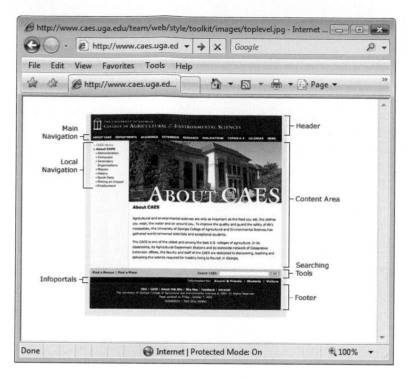

FIGURE 15–2   Web site navigation

ETHICS IN TECHNOLOGY

Restricting Internet Access

In various situations, people might want to block access to specific Internet sites or to sites that contain certain content. For instance, parents often want to prevent their children from visiting sites with adult-oriented material. Or companies might want to deny their employees access to online shopping and entertainment sites that are not business-related.

Several tools are available for restricting site access. A low-tech solution is simply to have someone oversee computer users and what is on their monitors. At the other end of the spectrum, software programs can be installed on a computer or network that automatically block access to user-specified sites or to sites with specified content.

Types of Internet Resources

The types of electronic resources available on the Internet include the following:

- Journals and journal articles
- Magazines and magazine articles
- Newspapers and newspaper articles
- E-mail
- Mailing lists
- Commercial sites
- Organizational sites

- Subject-based sites
- Blogs
- Videos, such as those on YouTube

Some of these are presented in complete form; others are only portions of the electronic resource. Regardless of the type, the site should give information concerning:

- Identity of the publisher
- Reviewers of the article
- Special hardware requirements to use the site
- Availability of older copies of the article, newspaper, or journal
- Currency of the site

Search Engines

Search engines, discussed in detail in Lesson 3, are programs written to query and retrieve information stored in a database. They differ from database to database and depend on the information stored in the database itself. Examples of search engines are Google, AltaVista, Excite, and Yahoo. If you used one of the many search engines available to locate information on the Internet, you need to know:

- How the search engine decides the order in which it returns information requested. In most instances, the search engine companies generally sell the top spaces (the first sites listed) to advertisers. Therefore, the first sites listed are not always the best sites or the most accurate and reliable.
- How the search engine searches for information and how often the information is updated.

You might be surprised to find that even the most academic subjects result in sponsored sites in your search results. A **sponsored site** is a site that has paid the search engine a fee in exchange for being listed in the "Sponsored Sites" section on many of their pages. Sponsored sites are unlikely to provide balanced and impartial information, and you should consider the intent of the sites when judging the reliability of the information provided. Additionally, if information in a search result appears to be out of date or irrelevant, consider trying the search again with a different search engine and compare the results when assessing the information. See **Figure 15–3** for an example of a list of sponsored sites.

▶ **VOCABULARY**
sponsored site

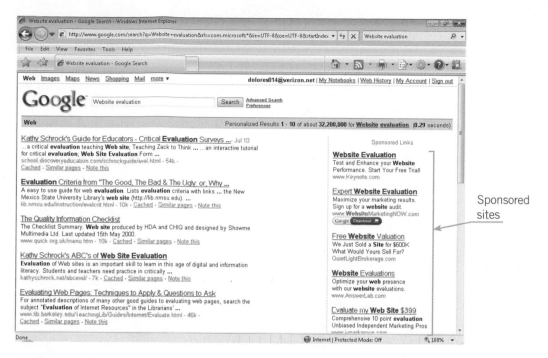

FIGURE 15-3   Sponsored sites in a Google search for Web site evaluation

Web Sites and Copyright Rules

For the most part, information displayed on an Internet site is easy to copy. Often you can select the text or graphics that you want to copy, use the Copy command, and then paste the content into another document. Or you can print an entire page that is displayed on the monitor. However, the fact that users can copy information easily does not mean that users have a legal right to do so. Internet publications can claim the same legal protection as books, newspapers, CDs, movies, and other forms that are protected by copyright rules.

Most sites have copyright information. **Copyright** is the exclusive right, granted by law for a certain number of years, to make and dispose of literary, musical, or artistic work. Even if the copyright notice is not displayed prominently on the page, someone is responsible for the creation of whatever appears on a page. This means that you should not use the information as your own. You must give credit to the person who created the work.

If Internet content, such as a music file, is copyrighted, it cannot be copied without the copyright holder's permission. To do so is a violation of copyright laws. Copying content can lead to criminal charges for theft as well as civil lawsuits for monetary damages.

A company's logo or other graphic information on a Web site may be protected as a **trademark**, which means much the same thing as copyright but relates specifically to visual or commercial images rather than text or intellectual property. In addition, processes and business methods may be protected by **patents**, which guarantee the inventor exclusive copyright to the process or method for a certain time period.

Copyright law does provide certain exceptions to the general prohibition against copying. If copyright protection has lapsed on certain material, then it is deemed to be in the **public domain** and is available for anyone to copy. Also, the law allows for the fair use of properly identified copyrighted material that is merely a small part of a larger research project, for instance, or cited as part of a critique or review. For

▶ **VOCABULARY**
copyright
trademark
patents
public domain

example, many government Web sites, such as the National Park Service (*www.nps. gov/*), U.S. Fish and Wildlife Service (*www.fws.gov/pictures/*), NASA (*www.nasa. gov*), and the National Oceanic and Atmospheric Administration (*www.photolib. noaa.gov*), provide images that can be downloaded and used in Web pages and other documents. The Gateway to Astronaut Photography of Earth Web site (*http://eol.jsc. nasa.gov*) is shown in **Figure 15–4**. This site includes a page detailing the conditions for using the photos it provides.

FIGURE 15–4   The Gateway to Astronaut Photography of Earth Web site

Software Piracy

Software piracy is the unauthorized copying of software. When you purchase a software program, you are not purchasing the software—you are purchasing a **software license** to use the program. Most commercially marketed software is copyrighted. Copyrighted software cannot be duplicated legally for distribution to others. Many companies, government organizations, and educational institutions purchase volume licenses. This gives these organizations the right to install a program on a specific number of computers.

Originally, many software companies attempted to stop the piracy by copy-protecting their software. They soon discovered, however, that this strategy was not foolproof and that software piracy is almost impossible to stop. Many software companies now require some sort of registration. This strategy works better than copy protection, but is not infallible and does not stop software piracy. **Shareware** is an alternative used by some companies. This software—usually downloadable from the Internet—is distributed on an honor system. Most shareware is free for an evaluation period but requires payment if you continue to use it beyond the evaluation period.

TECHNOLOGY CAREERS

Internet Web Designer/Webmaster

Every page on the Internet was designed and created by someone. Today, that someone is called a Web designer. The way a page looks on the Internet is the responsibility of the Web designer. The overall goal of the Web designer is to design and create a page that is efficient and appealing.

Each page on the Internet has to be maintained and kept up to date. The Webmaster is responsible for this task. A typical Webmaster manages a Web site. That usually includes creating content, adapting existing content in a user-friendly format, creating and maintaining a logical structure, and running the Web server software.

Not so long ago, both the design and maintenance functions were the responsibility of the Webmaster. However, with today's growing technology in hardware and software, these tasks are becoming more specialized and therefore performed by more than one person. Webmasters and Web designers can work in any organization that has a Web site. Typical organizations include educational institutions, museums, libraries, government agencies, and of course, businesses.

A person working in either of these two capacities needs to have skills in graphic design, HTML, Web design software programs, general programming, Javascript, SQL, and the ability to adapt to new Web technology as it evolves. An associate or bachelor's degree in computer science or graphic design usually is required. However, many employers accept persons with extensive experience in graphic design combined with good computer skills. The starting salary for a Webmaster or Web designer varies depending on location and experience. The average salary is around $60,000.

Citing Internet Resources

Internet resources used in reports must be cited. In other words, you must give proper credit to any information you include in a report that is not your original thought. This also provides the reader of the document with choices for additional research. In addition, it allows the information to be retrieved again. You can find general guidelines for citing electronic sources in the *MLA Handbook for Writers of Research Papers*, published by the Modern Language Association. *The Chicago Manual of Style* is another source for this information.

Here are some samples of citing Internet resources as suggested in the *MLA Handbook for Writers of Research Papers*:

- *Online journal article*: Author's last name, first initial. (date of publication or "NO DATE" if unavailable). Title of article or section used [Number of paragraphs]. Title of complete work. [Form, such as HTTP, CD-ROM, E-MAIL]. Available: complete URL [date of access].

- *Online magazine article*: Author's last name, first initial. (date of publication). Title of article. [Number of paragraphs]. Title of work. [Form, such as HTTP, CD-ROM, E-MAIL]. Available: complete URL [date of access].

- *Web site*: Name of site [date]. Title of document. [Form, such as HTTP, CD-ROM, E-MAIL]. Available: complete URL [date of access].

- *E-mail*: Author's last name, first name (author's e-mail address) (date). Subject. Receiver of e-mail (receiver's e-mail address).

Remember, anyone can put information on the Internet. Carefully evaluate any resources that you choose to use to ensure you have a high-quality resource that could really be of value to you.

Hoaxes, Urban Legends, and other False Information

A **hoax** is an attempt to deceive an audience into believing that something false is real. Sometimes this is perpetrated as a practical joke with a humorous intent; other times, it is an attempt to defraud and mislead.

Perhaps one of the most well-known media hoaxes—one that many consider the single greatest of all time—occurred on Halloween eve in 1938. Orson Welles shocked the nation with his Mercury Theater radio broadcast titled "The War of the Worlds." Despite repeated announcements before and during the program, many listeners believed that invaders from Mars were attacking the world.

In the twenty-first century, hoaxes, along with urban legends, myths, and chain letters, grow and flourish through the Internet. **Urban legends** are stories that at one time could have been partially true, but have grown from constant retelling into a mythical yarn. Much of this false information is harmless; however, some of these, such as chain letters, can have viruses attached to the message. It is not always easy to spot an e-mail or chain letter containing a virus, but looking for some of the following will help detect possible harmful files. Lesson 17 discusses viruses in detail.

- The e-mail is a warning message about a virus.
- The message might be very wordy, be in all capital letters, or include dozens of exclamation marks.
- The message urges you to share this information with everyone you know.
- The message appears credible because it describes the virus in technical terms.
- The message comes with an attachment, and you do not know who it is from.

If you identify any of the above, it is wise to delete the e-mail immediately. Also, use antivirus software and keep it updated.

One of the more popular Web sites displaying information about myths and hoaxes is the Vmyths Web site. You will visit this site in Step-by-Step 15.1. (Internet access is required for this exercise.)

▶ VOCABULARY

hoax

urban legends

Step-by-Step 15.1

1. Start your browser and then type **www.vmyths.com** in the Address text box. Click the **Go** button or press **Enter** to display the Vmyths.com Web site, similar to that shown in **Figure 15–5**.

FIGURE 15–5
Vmyths Web site

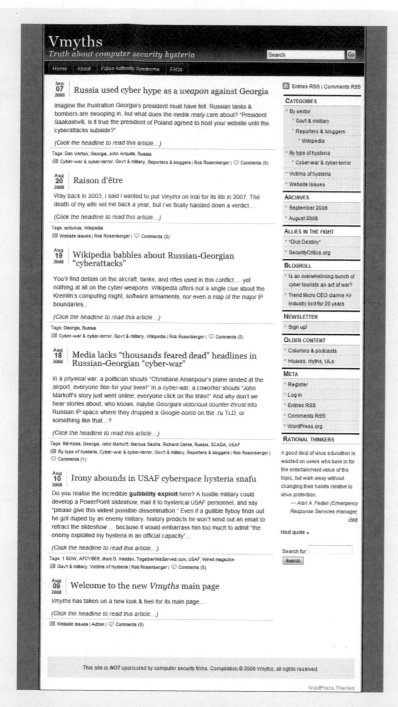

2. Click one of the featured articles or one of the links in the right column.

   Click the **Archives** link.

3. Scroll down as necessary and click the **Hoaxes, myths, ULs** link.

FIGURE 15–6
Hoaxes, myths, urban
legends page

4. Select one of the myths or legends. Follow your instructor's directions to either print a copy or write a paragraph summarizing what you read.

5. Keep your browser open for Step-by-Step 15.2.

Other Legal and Ethical Issues

The ease of obtaining information from the Internet and of publishing information on it can contribute to other legal problems as well. Just because information is obtained from an Internet site does not mean that someone can copy it and claim it as his or her own, even noncopyrighted information. That's **plagiarism**. The Internet does not relieve an author of responsibility for acknowledging and identifying the source of borrowed material.

Likewise, the Internet does not relieve anyone of the burden of ensuring that information they publish is true. If someone publishes information about another person or organization and it is not true, they can be sued for libel and forced to pay compensation for any damage they caused. The Internet makes widespread publication of information easy. It also creates the potential for huge damages if the information turns out to be false.

▶ **VOCABULARY**
plagiarism

The free flow of information via the Internet also creates opportunities for criminals to gather personal information, acquire credit, and conduct transactions using false identities. **Identity theft**, as it is called, is a growing problem that can cause big headaches for unsuspecting victims. Other criminal problems that the Internet has been fueling include sexual advances made to minors, anonymous threats, and rumors to manipulate stock prices. All are made easier by the Internet, but they are just as illegal and just as wrong.

Not all improper activities that make use of the Internet are necessarily illegal. Pranks, hoaxes, and making unfair use of free-trial "shareware" software may not be against the law, but they can still cause harm to innocent people—often more harm than their perpetrators might realize. The Internet is a powerful tool, for good and ill, and needs to be handled with care.

▶ **VOCABULARY**
identity theft

Evaluation Survey

You can use the information discussed in this lesson to construct a survey to evaluate electronic resources. **Figure 15–7** shows a sample survey. In Step-by-Step 15.2, you use this survey form to evaluate a Web site.

CRITERIA FOR EVALUATING ELECTRONIC RESOURCES

1. Can you identify the author of the page?   Yes ☐   No ☐

2. Is an e-mail address listed?   Yes ☐   No ☐

3. Can you access the site in a reasonable time?   Yes ☐   No ☐

4. Is the text on the screen legible?   Yes ☐   No ☐

5. Are the commands and directions easy to follow?   Yes ☐   No ☐

6. Is the information current?   Yes ☐   No ☐

7. When you perform a search, do you get what you expect?   Yes ☐   No ☐

8. Are instructions clearly visible?   Yes ☐   No ☐

9. Is the information updated regularly?   Yes ☐   No ☐

10. Make any comment you would like concerning the site.

FIGURE 15–7 Survey form

Step-by-Step 15.2

1. Use your word-processing program and open Step15-2 from the data files supplied for this course. This file contains the survey form presented in **Figure 15–7.**

2. Identify a site on the Internet and use the survey to evaluate the site. You may select a site containing a magazine article of interest to you, or any topic on which you might want to gather information.

3. Find a site that contains noncopyrighted images. Copy one or two of the images and paste them into your criteria evaluation page. Save the survey file using your first and last name.

4. Close your browser and your word-processing program. Submit your survey to your instructor.

SUMMARY

In this lesson, you learned:

- The criteria for evaluating Internet resources include authorship, content, copyright information, navigation, and quality.

- The Internet contains various types of resources, including electronic journals, magazines, newspapers, Web sites, and e-mail messages.

- Internet publications and Web site content can claim the same legal protection as books, newspapers, CDs, movies, and other forms that are protected by copyright law.

- You must cite any information that you use from the Internet. The MLA style is widely used for citing electronic resources.

- Internet hoaxes, urban legends, and false information continue to increase because of the Internet.

- Using the Internet introduces legal and ethical issues such as plagiarism, which is copying information from another source and claiming it is your own, even if the information is not copyrighted. Another growing problem is identity theft, which occurs when criminals gather personal information, acquire credit, and conduct transactions using false identities.

▪ VOCABULARY REVIEW

Define the following terms:

copyright	patent	software piracy
currency	plagiarism	sponsored site
hoax	public domain	trademark
identity theft	shareware	urban legends
navigation	software license	

■ REVIEW QUESTIONS

MULTIPLE CHOICE

Select the best response for the following statements.

1. _____ is the illegal copying or use of software.

   A. Piracy
   B. Webmastering
   C. Counterfeiting
   D. Surfing

2. _____ is only as good as the source.

   A. A link
   B. Information
   C. Currency
   D. A dead link

3. A company's logo or other graphic information might be protected as a _____.

   A. trademark
   B. patent
   C. public domain
   D. copyright

4. _____ are stories that at one time could have been partially true.

   A. Links
   B. Hoaxes
   C. Urban legends
   D. Resources

5. _____ is the ability to move through a Web site.

   A. Linking
   B. Grouping
   C. Citing
   D. Navigation

TRUE/FALSE

Circle T if the statement is true or F if the statement is false.

T   F   **1.** You can assume that all information found on the Internet is accurate.

T   F   **2.** It is acceptable to copy information from the Internet and present it as your own.

T   F   **3.** Items contained in public domain are considered to be copyrighted.

T   F   **4.** Software piracy is the unauthorized copying of software.

T   F   **5.** Chain letters sent through the Internet possibly could contain a virus.

FILL IN THE BLANK

Complete the following sentences by writing the correct word or words in the blanks provided.

1. A(n) _____ is an attempt to deceive an audience into believing that something false is real.

2. A Web site ending in _____ indicates this is an educational site.

3. When purchasing software, you are purchasing a software _____.

4. _____ refers to the age of the information.

5. A(n) _____ is responsible for managing and maintaining a Web site.

PROJECTS

CROSS-CURRICULAR— MATHEMATICS

Search the Internet for Web sites containing information on Grammy Award winners. In the results list, pick at least two sites that you think might contain information relating to the number of awards won. Using the survey form shown in Figure 15–7, evaluate each site. Write a 100-word report on your evaluation of the sites. Be sure to include the Web site address of the site and elaborate on what you found in your answer to each of the survey questions.

CROSS-CURRICULAR—SCIENCE

Access the Web site *www.howstuffworks.com*. Select one of the topics of your choice or a topic assigned by your instructor. Use your word-processing program to prepare a 100-word report that explains the site's system for navigating. Be sure to mention any problems you had in getting around the site.

CROSS-CURRICULAR—SOCIAL STUDIES

Use Google or another search engine and search for urban legends. Find one or two urban legends of particular interest, and write a report on why you think so many people believed the story to be true. Include the Web site addresses of sites that you accessed for this information.

CROSS-CURRICULAR— LANGUAGE ARTS

One infamous question that most of us have heard is "Why did the chicken cross the road?" Use a search engine of your choice to find the answer to the question. How many links did you find? Prepare a report on your findings and present it to your class. Explain how you evaluated at least three of the sites.

WEB PROJECT

Start your browser. Do an online search for Web site evaluation. Select and evaluate at least three different sites that discuss Web site evaluation. Use your word-processing program to prepare a report on your findings, including an overview of at least three things you learned about Web site evaluation. The report should be a minimum of two pages.

 TEAMWORK PROJECT

The Web site located at *urbanlegendsonline.com* contains information regarding a number of urban legends and superstitions. Use your browser to access this site. Each team member selects one or more of the legends or superstitions and then uses a word-processing program to create a summary or overview of the legend or superstition. The team then consolidates the summaries to create a two- to three-page report and adds clip art and/or other images to illustrate their findings.

 CRITICAL THINKING

WYSIWYG is a Web site project located at *www.saskschools.ca/~ischool/tisdale/integrated/wysiwyg/students.htm*. Access this Web site and complete the activities to create a set of reliability rules. Share your set of rules with the other students or submit a written report to your instructor.

 EXPLORING GOOGLE

Similar to most other Internet mapping Web sites, Google's free mapping service application provides the user with step-by-step driving directions from one location to another. Google's map service, however, contains several additional features that are not found on some of the other Internet mapping services. Google maps are interactive. Use the slider to zoom in and out. Use the navigation arrows to move from left to right or up and down. Hold down the left mouse button and move the map left, right, up, or down.

Access Google's map service at *http://maps.google.com*. Enter an address such as your home address or your school address, and then click the Search Maps button. Click the Get Directions link and

type in a location different from your home address and/or school address. Click the Get Directions button. Print a copy of the directions if instructed to do so.

If necessary, redisplay the map with the address you used previously. Click each of the buttons at the top of the map (Street View, Traffic, Map, Satellite, and Terrain). Use your word-processing program and write a sentence or two describing the screen that is displayed when each button is selected.

LESSON 16

Creating a Web Page

■ OBJECTIVES

Upon completion of this lesson, you should be able to:

- Understand how a Web page works.
- Create a planning document.
- Understand and describe basic HTML syntax.
- Insert headings.
- Apply bold and italics.
- Insert and work with lists.
- Add links.
- Add graphics.
- Publish a Web page.

Web page authoring programs, such as Adobe Dreamweaver and Microsoft Expression Web, are used to create Web pages and to develop Web sites. A *Web site* is a group of related Web pages. These Web page authoring programs create the underlying code for the Web page. However, the process of creating a Web page independently of these programs is not difficult. To comprehend and fully understand Web page creation and to better use an authoring program, you should understand the hypertext markup language (HTML) that makes up much of the code. The basic HTML tags are covered in this lesson.

■ VOCABULARY

absolute link

attribute

background

body

Cascading Style Sheets

character entities

e-mail link

headings

home page

images

lists

mobile browser

relative link

style sheet

title

Web site

...

How a Web Page Works

Have you ever wondered how a Web page works? When you consider the billions of Web pages on the Internet, you might assume that creating a Web page is easier said than done. In fact, not only is it incredibly easy to create a Web page, it also is a lot of fun.

Before beginning to create a Web page, you need an understanding of some basic terminology:

- *Web page*: This is a plain text document on a server connected to the World Wide Web. Every Web page is identified by a uniform resource locator (URL), or unique Web address.

- *HTML*: This is the basic language of the Web. HTML is a series of tags that are integrated into a text document. These tags describe how the text should be formatted when a Web browser displays it on the screen.

- *Web browser*: A Web browser is an application program that interprets the HTML tags within the page and then displays the text on the computer screen. Some of the most popular Web browsers are Microsoft Internet Explorer, FireFox, and Mozilla. A **mobile browser** is a browser designed for use with mobile devices.

- *Web server*: A Web server displays Web pages and renders them into final form so they can be viewed by anyone with an Internet connection and a Web browser. Every Web server has a unique Web address or URL.

You might infer from these basic terminology definitions that you need a Web server before you can create your Web page. This is not true. The only tools you need are your Web browser and a text-editing program such as WordPad or Notepad. A Web browser easily can display your Web page from a personal computer. Once you create a Web page and have it in final format, most likely you will want to publish it to a Web server. Publishing a Web page is covered later in the lesson.

Planning a Document

Many times when people start a project, they have a tendency to jump right in without any planning. Sometimes this works, but more often than not, they find themselves having to back up and redo some of the work. Planning might take some extra time in the beginning, but it will save considerable time in the long run. Before you start creating your personal Web page, consider some of the elements you might want to include. **Figure 16–1** shows a suggested list of items.

▶ **VOCABULARY**
Web site
mobile browser

📟 **EXTRA FOR EXPERTS**
_____

You can view the HTML code for most Web pages on the Web. Access the Internet with your browser and find a Web page that you like. On your browser's menu bar, click View and then click Source to display the HTML code.

📟 **EXTRA FOR EXPERTS**
_____

Some browsers, such as the recent versions of Internet Explorer and Firefox, allow multiple tabs to be opened, each showing different pages.

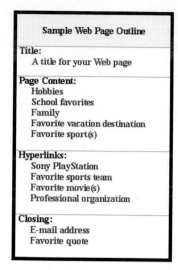

FIGURE 16–1   Sample Web page outline

■ *Title*: The ***title*** can be anything you choose, but should be relevant to the content of the page. An example title is "Bryan Richard's Personal Web Page." (You would substitute your name for Bryan Richard.) When someone accesses your Web page on the Internet, the title is displayed on the browser's title bar; it is not displayed in the Web page content. Your Web page always should have a title.

■ *Page content*: Determine what you want to include in your Web page. Do you want to share information about your family, your hobbies, your school, or sports? Make a list of what features you would like to include. Limit the content to one topic per Web page.

■ *Links*: A link is a graphic, line of text, or both that connects one Web page to another page on the same Web site or to one on a Web server located anywhere in the world. To what other Web pages would you like to link? Make a note of these. You will need the URL, or Web site address, for each link.

■ *Closing comments*: Do you want to include any closing comments? Perhaps you want to add your e-mail address so that someone accessing your Web page can contact you. Do not include any personal information such as your home address and/or home telephone number.

▶ VOCABULARY
title

home page

A Basic Page

An HTML page has two components—page content and HTML tags. The page content is that part of the document that is displayed in the browser. This could be, for example, a list of your hobbies or other information about yourself, your place of employment, and so on. The main page or index page of most Web sites is referred to as the ***home page***.

HTML tags are easily identifiable because they are enclosed in brackets: <html>. The tags are not displayed in the browser. The HTML tags define the structure and layout of the Web page.

■   Most tags come in pairs with a start tag and an end tag. For instance, <title> is a start tag and </title> is an end tag. You identify an end tag by including the slash (</>) character before the name of the tag. The start and end tag identify the content between them as being HTML formatted. These sometimes are called container tags.

■   Some tags can be a single entity—that is, they do not have to have an end tag. An example is the <br> tag, which indicates a line break. However, adding an end tag will not affect how the content is displayed and generally is considered good format.

■   Tags are not case sensitive, but it is best to select a format and stay with it. In this lesson, lowercase letters are used for all HTML tags.

▶ **VOCABULARY**
attributes

■   Some tags can contain *attributes*, which are identifiers for the tag. For example, the <body> tag is required for all HTML documents. But if you wanted the background color of your Web page to be blue, you can add an attribute so your <body> tag would look like this: <body bgcolor = "Blue">.

Each new page you create requires a standard set of tags structured in a particular sequence. This sequence is shown in **Figure 16–2**. When creating this structure, you can type the tags on individual lines, like that shown in **Figure 16–2**. The lines can be single-spaced or double-spaced. Or, you can type the tags on one continuous line, such as the following: <html><head><title></title></head><body></body></html>. Generally, for readability purposes, it is better to use separate lines for tags.

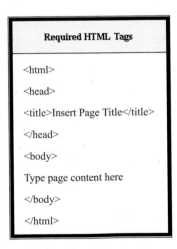

FIGURE 16–2   Required HTML tags

In addition, inserting spaces or tabs between the tags in a line does not affect how the content appears in the browser. In other words, it does not make any difference if you press the Spacebar 20 times or press the Tab key 50 times! The only content that appears is that which is contained between the two <title> tags and that contained between the two <body> tags.

Following is an explanation of the tags.

■   *html*: As shown in **Figure 16–2**, the first line in the document is <html>, which is a start tag; the last line is </html>, which is an end tag. All other tags and page content are contained within these two tags.

- *head*: The head tag can contain information about the document. This information does not appear as part of the Web page content when displayed in a browser. The <title> tag is one of the more commonly used tags that is contained within the start and end <head> tags. Keywords also often are contained within the head tag. Keywords describe the Web page document and are used by some search engines.

- *title*: The title tag defines the page's official title. The content entered between the start and end title tags is displayed on the browser's title bar.

- *body*: All Web page content, or the *body* of the page, is contained between the start and end <body> tags.

▶ **VOCABULARY**
body

In the examples in this book, Windows Notepad is used as the text editor to create the HTML documents and Internet Explorer is used as the browser to display the Web page. As mentioned previously, however, you can use any browser to display your Web page and any text-editing program to create a Web page. You can use a word-processing program for text editing, for instance, but you must save your document in text format with an .htm extension.

In Step-by-Step 16.1, you create a template containing the tags shown in **Figure 16–2**.

Step-by-Step 16.1

1. Start your text-editing program. If you are using Notepad, click **Start** ⊕, point to **All Programs**, click **Accessories**, and then click **Notepad**.

2. Type the following tags. Press the **Spacebar** five times between the <title> tags to create the space and press the **Enter** key four times between the <body> tags.

   <html>

   <head>

   <title>   </title>

   </head>

   <body>

   </body>

   </html>

3. Compare your screen to **Figure 16–3a**. Each tag should be on its own line. Do not worry if the spacing between tags differs from that shown in the figure.

4. Click **File** on the menu bar and then click **Save**. In the Save As dialog box, enter **template.htm** in the File name box. Click the **Save as type** button arrow, and then click **All Files** as shown in **Figure 16–3b**. Then click **Save**.

FIGURE 16–3
(a) HTML template
(b) Notepad Save As
dialog box

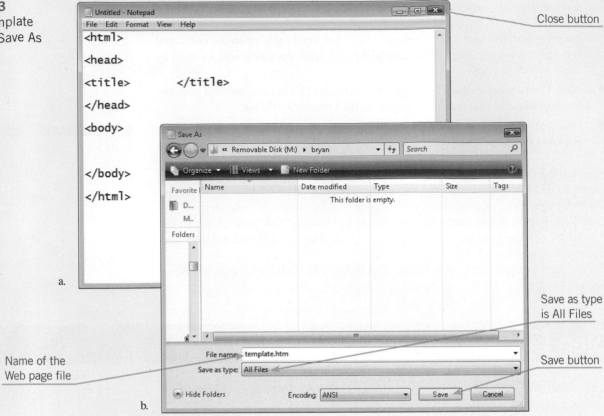

Close button

Save as type
is All Files

Save button

Name of the
Web page file

a.

b.

5. Close your text-editing program.

When you create HTML documents in the future, you can open this template file, save it with a different filename, and add your page content. Your next task, in Step-by-Step 16.2, is to open the template, add a Web page title and a line of page content, and then view your Web page in your browser. Note that most programs save with a particular file type or extension. To display this document name and to open the document, most likely you will have to change the Files of type option to All Files to view the list of documents.

Step-by-Step 16.2

1. If necessary, start Notepad or another text-editing program. Click **File** on the menu bar, click **Open**, and then navigate to the location where you saved template.htm. If you do not see the template file, click the **Files of type** button arrow, click **All Files**, and then click **template**, as shown in **Figure 16–4**. Next, click **Open**.

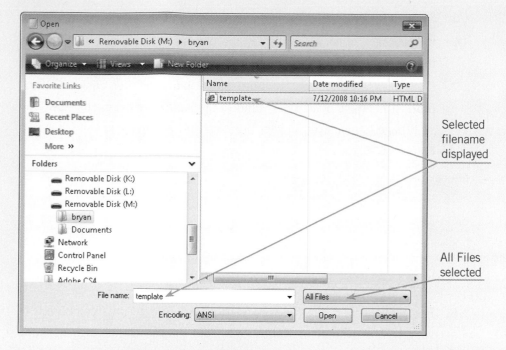

FIGURE 16–4
Notepad Open dialog box

Selected
filename
displayed

All Files
selected

2. Click between the start and end <title> tags, and type **[Your first and last name]'s Web page**. (In other words, enter your name as part of the title, as in Bryan Richard's Web page.) When the browser displays the page, any extra spaces between the two title tags will be ignored. Therefore, it is acceptable, but not necessary, to delete the spaces.

3. Between the two <body> tags, type **Welcome to my Web page!**

4. Click **File** on the menu bar and then click **Save As**. Save the document using your first and last name and the .htm extension. Use an underscore (_) between your first and last name (example: *Bryan_Richard.htm*). Change the Save as type to **All Files**. Click **Save**. Your Web page will look similar to that shown in **Figure 16–5**.

Filename

Web page
content

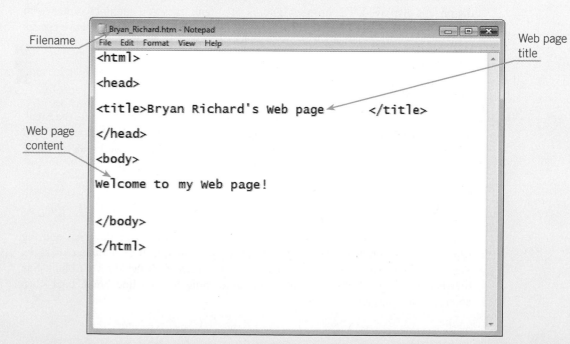

Web page
title

FIGURE 16–5
HTML source page

5. Start your browser.

6. If necessary, press **Alt** to display the browser's menu bar. Click **File** on the menu bar and then click **Open** to display the Open dialog box.

7. Click **Browse**, locate your .htm file, click **Open**, and then click **OK**. If the browser needs to open a new window to display the page, click **OK**. The Web page is displayed in your browser, and is similar to that shown in **Figure 16–6**.

FIGURE 16–6
Web page displayed in Internet Explorer

Web page title

Web page content

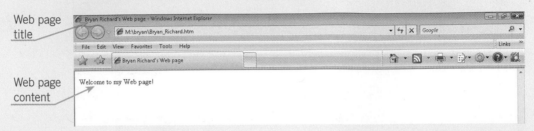

8. Review your Web page as it appears in the browser and compare it to your HTML document. Notice that none of the HTML tags appears. Close all open browser windows. Keep your Welcome to my Web page! document open for Step-by-Step 16.3.

The text you typed between the start and end <title> tags in your HTML document is displayed in the browser's title bar. This text is not displayed as part of the document itself. The only text that is displayed as part of the document content is the text you typed between the start and end <body> tags: *Welcome to my Web page!*

Page Formatting

One of the first things you will discover when creating a Web page is that pressing the keyboard's Enter key has no effect on how a Web page appears in a browser. You can press the Enter key a dozen times or more, but it will not make a difference when the page is displayed. The browser ignores any blank lines you attempt to enter from the keyboard. Instead, you use HTML tags to start a new line and/or to leave spaces between lines.

Line Breaks

If you want to start a new line but not leave a space between lines, you use the break tag: <br>. The break tag is a single entity. That is, you do not need a start and end tag. You can use the break tag to start a new line or you can use two break tags, one after the other, to insert a blank line.

Paragraph Breaks

A second way to insert a blank line is with the paragraph tag: <p>. An end tag </p> is not required, but most Web programmers include it as a matter of style. When the Web page is displayed in a browser, a paragraph tag shows a blank line between two paragraphs—basically the same thing as two line break tags <br> entered consecutively.

In Step-by-Step 16.3, you add content to your Web page, using break and paragraph tags to format the page.

Step-by-Step 16.3

1. If necessary, open your Welcome to my Web page! document. At the end of the *Welcome to my Web page!* line, type **
**.

2. Press **Enter**. (Remember that pressing Enter does not affect the way the Web page is displayed in a browser. You press Enter for readability purposes within your Web page text document. Starting a new line or adding blank lines when creating your Web page makes it easier to read and edit your document.)

3. Type **I enjoy watching Spiderman movies**. Press **Enter** two times.

4. Type **<p>** and press **Enter**. Type **My favorite subject is science.</p>**. Press **Enter**.

5. Type **<p>** and press Enter. Type **Skateboarding is my favorite sport.</p>**.

6. Click **File** on the menu bar and then click **Save**. The document should look similar to that shown in **Figure 16–7**. (Do not worry if the line spacing between tags on your page is different from that shown in the figure.)

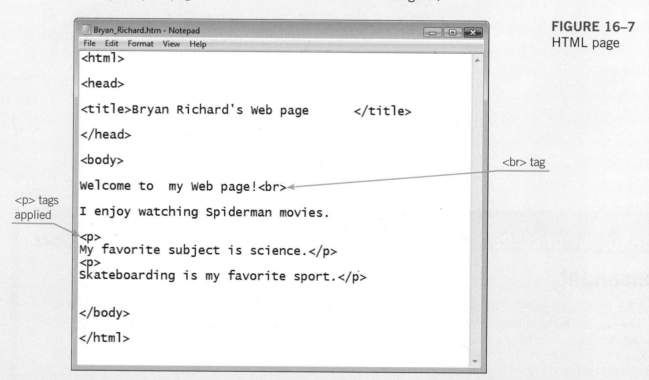

<p> tags applied

 tag

FIGURE 16–7
HTML page

7. Start your browser.

8. If necessary, press **Alt** to display the browser's menu bar. Click **File** on the menu bar and then click **Open**.

9. Click **Browse**, locate your .htm Web page file, click **Open**, and then click **OK**. (If the browser needs to open a new window to display the page, click OK.) Your page opens in the browser, as shown in **Figure 16–8**.

FIGURE 16–8
Web page displayed in the browser

Space between lines

No space between lines

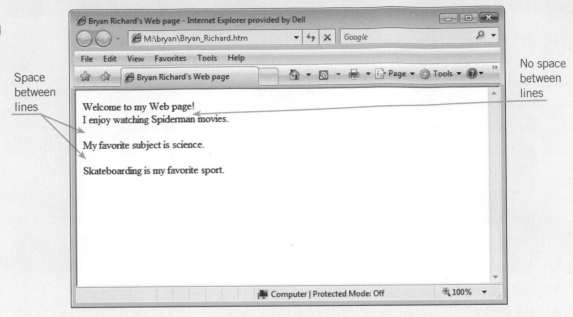

10. Compare your Web page to your HTML document. Note there is no blank line between the first two lines where you typed the <br> tag, and there are blank lines between the two sentences where you typed the <p> tags.

11. Close your browser but keep Notepad open for the next Step-by-Step exercise.

TECHNOLOGY CAREERS

Consultant

Consultants provide professional advice or services. They have specialized knowledge that they can sell to their clients. Many consultants work on short-term projects for companies that might not have employees with the required skills for a particular job. Many consultants telecommute, or work from home.

You can find successful consultants in just about every field imaginable. For instance, garage-sale consultants help you organize your garage and other consultants help you arrange your closets. However, the information technology field has created an entire new field of consultants. Some examples are programming consultants, database consultants, and even Web designer and Web development consultants. If you enjoy working with computers and, in particular, developing Web pages, consulting might be a job field that you would want to investigate.

Lists

Organizing content on your Web page makes it more attractive and easier to read. Statistics indicate that people rarely read Web pages word by word; instead, they scan the page, picking out individual words and sentences. *Lists* are a popular way to arrange and organize text on a Web page, and suit the way people read Web pages. Within HTML, three types of lists are available:

▶ **VOCABULARY**
lists

- *Ordered list*: This generally is a numbered list and requires a start <ol> and an end </ol> tag. Each item in the list begins with <li>.

- *Unordered list*: This generally is a bulleted list and requires a start <ul> and an end </ul> tag. Each item in the list begins with <li>.

- *Definition list*: This is a list of terms with indented definitions, generally used for glossary items or other definitions. This list requires a start tag <dl> and an end tag </dl>. In addition, the tag <dt> is required for the term and <dd> is required for the definition.

In Step-by-Step 16.4, you create the three types of lists.

Step-by-Step 16.4

1. If you are using Notepad, click **File** on the menu bar and then click **Open**. In the Open dialog box, click the Files of type button arrow and then click **All Files**. Select the **template.htm** file and then click **Open**.

2. Click **File** on the menu bar and then click **Save As**. Click the **Save as type** button arrow, and then click **All Files**. Click in the File name box, type **HTML_examples.htm**, and then click **Save**.

3. Type **HTML_examples** between the two title tags.

4. Click below the <body> tag and type **Ordered List**. Press **Enter**.

5. Type **<ol>** to begin your ordered list. Press **Enter**.

6. Type **<li>** to begin the first item in the list.

7. Type **roses**. Press **Enter**. Type **<li>** and then type **gardenias**. Press **Enter**. Type **<li>** and then type orchids. Press **Enter**. Type **</ol>**. Press **Enter**.

8. Type **<p></p>**. Press **Enter**. Type **<p></p>**. Press **Enter** two times.

9. Type **Unordered List**. Press **Enter**.

10. Type the following. Press **Enter** after each line.

    <ul>

    <li>red

    <li>blue

    <li>green

    </ul>

    <p></p>

    <p></p>

11. Press **Enter** two times. Type the following. Press **Enter** after each line.

    Definition List

    <dl>

    <dt>Apple

    <dd>a fruit

    <dt>Tomato

    <dd>a fruit

    <dt>Corn

    <dd>a vegetable

    </dl>

    <p></p>

    <p></p>

12. Compare your document to **Figure 16–9**, make corrections if necessary, and then save your file. Note that the entire HTML document is not displayed in **Figure 16–9**—just the text and HTML tags you entered in this exercise.

FIGURE 16–9
HTML tags for list types

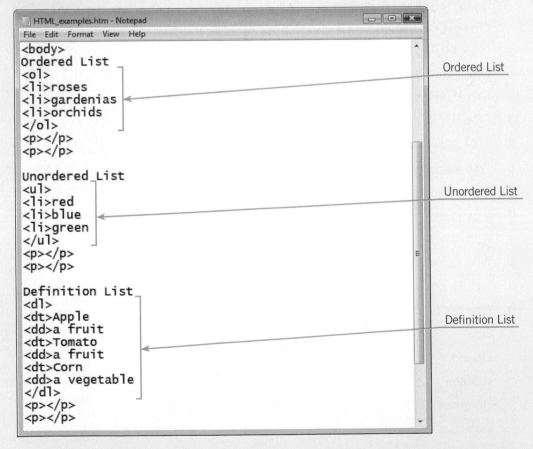

13. Display the file in your browser. It should look like the page shown in **Figure 16–10**. Close the browser, and then close your file.

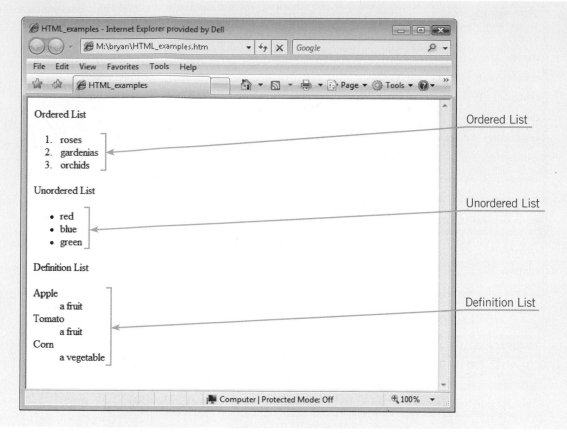

FIGURE 16–10
List types displayed in
the browser

Text Formatting

Now that you have learned some ways you can control the placement of text in the browser, it is time to learn how to format the text. Just like formatting text within a word-processing program, you also can apply formatting to text that is displayed in a Web browser. Some of the text formatting tags you can apply are as follows:

■ *Bold*: To bold text requires start <b> and end </b> tags. Text that is surrounded by these tags appears as bold in your browser.

■ *Italics*: To display italicized text, use the start <i> and end </i> tags.

■ *Underline*: To underline text, use the start <u> and end </u> tags.

You can apply one tag such as bold to a word, sentence, or paragraph, or you can apply two or all three tags at one time to the same text.

Center

Another way to organize text on the page is to use the <center> tag. This tag requires both a start and end tag. Simply enclose the text between the start tag and the end tag and the text will be centered when displayed in a browser. You can center a single word, a sentence, a paragraph, a series of paragraphs, a table, or even an image.

Figure 16–11 shows how to enter the HTML formatting and centering tags and illustrates what they look like in a browser.

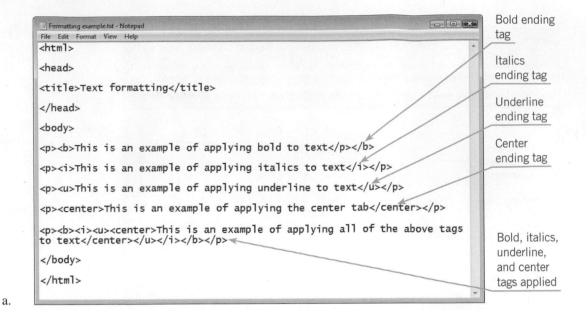

Bold ending tag

Italics ending tag

Underline ending tag

Center ending tag

Bold, italics, underline, and center tags applied

a.

b.

FIGURE 16–11   (a) HTML for bold, italics, underline, and center (b) Text formatting displayed in a browser

Headings

A style is a set of formatting characteristics that you can apply to text in your document to change its appearance quickly. HTML does support styles, but only through style sheets. **Style sheets**, also known as **Cascading Style Sheets (CSS)**, are a collection of formatting rules that control the appearance of content in a Web page. Style sheets are an advanced topic and are not covered in this book. The HTML heading tags, however, do provide some formatting options. The characteristics of **headings** include the typeface, size, and the extra space above or below the heading. The browser you use, however, determines the final appearance.

▶ **VOCABULARY**
style sheet
Cascading Style Sheets (CSS)
headings

Six levels of HTML headings are available. The start tag for the first level is <h1> and the end tag is </h1>. For the other five levels, just substitute the desired number within the start and end tags. Level 1 is the largest and level 6 is the smallest. In **Figure 16–12a**, notice that no break <br> or paragraph <p> tags are added following each line because they are not needed. In **Figure 16–12b**, in which the Web page is displayed in the browser, space appears between each of the headings. This is a characteristic of the heading tag.

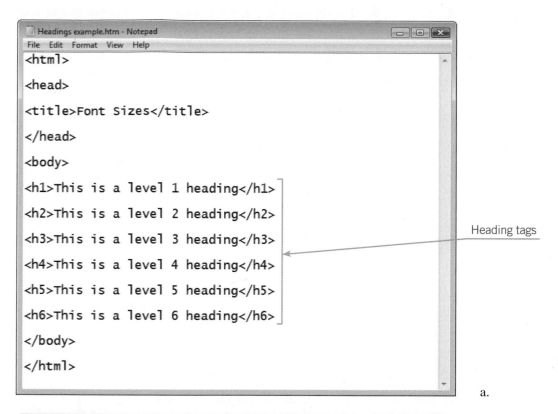

a.

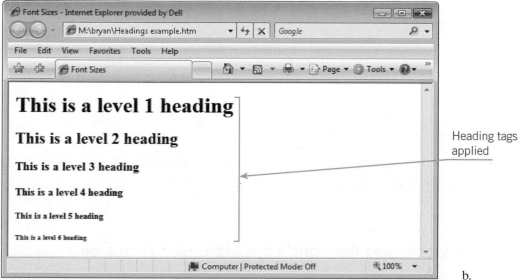

b.

FIGURE 16–12   (a) HTML for heading tags (b) Formatted headings displayed in the browser

In Step-by-Step 16.5, you add and center a heading.

Step-by-Step 16.5

1. If necessary, open your text editing program. Open your **template.htm** document and then save it as **home_page.htm**. Type **[Your name]'s Web page** between the start and end <title> tags.

2. Click below the **<body> tag**. Type **<h1> Welcome to the Web page of [your name]! </h1>**. This applies the h1 heading format to the line of text and centers it on the page. Type **
** at the end of the line.

3. Press **Enter** two times.

4. Type **My three favorite subjects are:** Use the **<b>** text formatting tag to apply bold to the text you just typed.

5. Create an unordered list (using <ul>) listing your three favorite school subjects. Use the <i> text formatting tag to apply italics to each item in the list only. (Be sure to add an end </i> tag after the list.)

6. Save your file and then display it in your browser. Your Web page should look similar to that shown in **Figure 16–13**, but your data will be different.

FIGURE 16–13
Web page displayed in the browser (your data will differ)

7. Close your browser. Keep your home_page.htm file open for Step-by-Step 16.6.

Changing the Font, Font Size, and Font Color

When you browse the Internet, your browser displays the text based on a default font size, type, and color. Recall that a font is a design of type. The font, font size, and font color, however, can be changed. This is done through the start <font> and end </font> tags.

You probably know from experience that changing the font or text size in a word-processing program is easy; you can quickly make the text very small or very large. Your options within HTML are not as flexible as they are within a word-processing program. Most browsers support and display seven different font or text sizes. The sizes range from 1, which is the smallest, to 7, which is the largest. The default font size is 3. Recall that an attribute is an identifier for the tag. To change the font size, you add the size attribute to the font tag, for example: <font size = 5>. **Figure 16–14a** shows the HTML tags used to change font sizes, and **Figure 16–14b** shows how the various font sizes look in a browser.

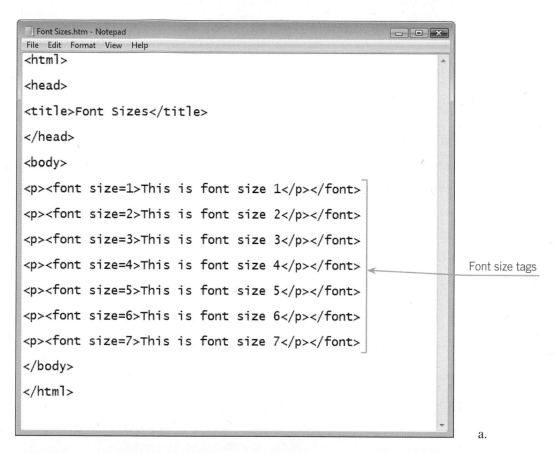

a.

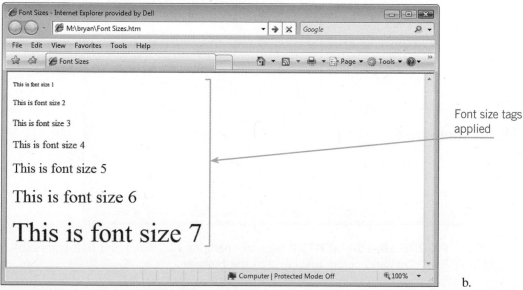

b.

FIGURE 16–14   (a) HTML tags for changing font sizes (b) Font sizes displayed in the browser

Changing the font color is just as easy as changing the font size. This is accomplished by using the color attribute, for example: <font color = red>. Another option is to combine the font size and font color within one tag, as in <font size = 1 color = red>. **Figure 16–15a** shows the HTML tags used to change font color and size, and **Figure 16–15b** illustrates how the font color and size appear in a browser.

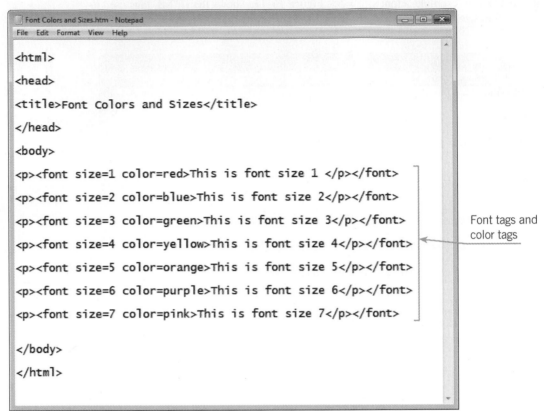

a.

```
<html>
<head>
<title>Font Colors and Sizes</title>
</head>
<body>
<p><font size=1 color=red>This is font size 1 </p></font>
<p><font size=2 color=blue>This is font size 2</p></font>
<p><font size=3 color=green>This is font size 3</p></font>
<p><font size=4 color=yellow>This is font size 4</p></font>
<p><font size=5 color=orange>This is font size 5</p></font>
<p><font size=6 color=purple>This is font size 6</p></font>
<p><font size=7 color=pink>This is font size 7</p></font>

</body>
</html>
```

Font tags and color tags

b.

This is font size 1
This is font size 2
This is font size 3
This is font size 4
This is font size 5
This is font size 6
This is font size 7

Font and color tags applied

FIGURE 16–15   (a) HTML tags for changing font sizes and font colors (b) Font sizes and colors displayed in the browser

You also can change the font type. This is accomplished by using the face attribute; for example: <font face = arial>. If desired, you can specify font color, size, and face all within one start and end tag. **Figure 16–16** shows examples of applying and displaying the face, color, and size attributes.

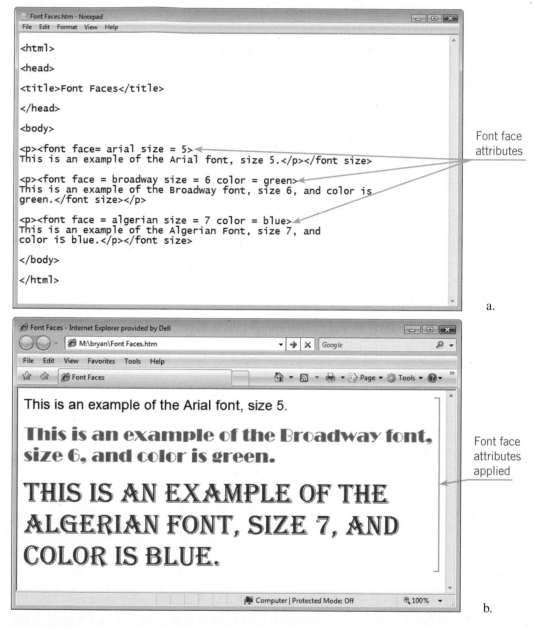

a.

b.

FIGURE 16–16   (a) Font tags specifying face, color, and size (b) Font face, color, and size displayed in the browser

In Step-by-Step 16.6, you apply the <font> tag and the face, size, and color attributes.

Step-by-Step 16.6

1. If necessary, open your **home_page.htm** document, and then save it as **home_page2.htm**. Click below the last unordered list </ul> tag, and then press **Enter** two times.

2. Type **My favorite author is Shakespeare**.

3. Apply the <font> tag and the following attributes to the sentence you typed in Step 2: **<font face = times new roman size = 6 color = red>**. Do not forget to add the ending **</font>** tag.

4. Save your file and display the Web page in your browser. It should look similar to that shown in **Figure 16–17**.

5. Close your browser. Keep your home_page2.htm file open for Step-by-Step 16.7.

FIGURE 16–17
Web page displayed in the browser

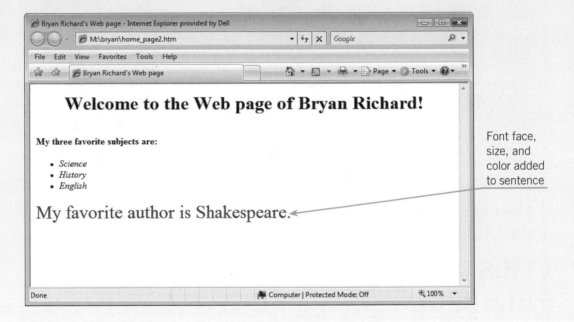

Font face, size, and color added to sentence

Links

A defining feature of any Web page is its links or hyperlinks, which are active references to other parts of the same document or to other documents. The other documents can be on the same computer in another folder or disk, on a local network server (intranet), or stored on a computer in another city, state, or country. When you click a link, the Web page associated with the link is displayed on the screen. Links within a document generally are absolute links, relative links, and e-mail links.

Absolute Links

Providing links between documents gives the user easy access to related information. Recall from Lesson 2 that every Web page on the Internet has its own unique address. If you know the address or URL of the document and the address of the computer on which it resides, you can link to it. *Absolute links* (also called external links) are links that give the full address to a Web page on the Internet. These links use a fixed file location or Web address. The fixed location identifies the destination by its full address. An example of an absolute link is *<a href = http://www.rockclimbing.com> Rock Climbing </a>*. The <a> within this tag represents *anchor* and the href represents *hyperlink reference*. **Figure 16–18a** shows how to create absolute links in an HTML document; **Figure 16–18b** shows how they appear in a browser.

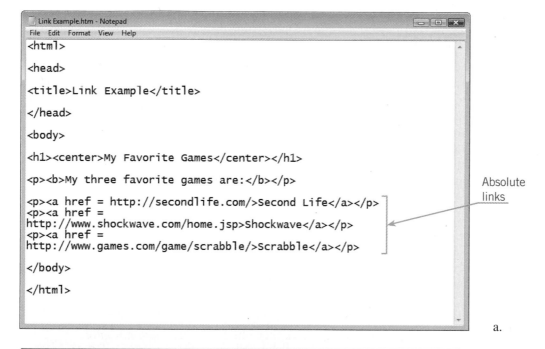

a.

b.

FIGURE 16–18   (a) Font tags specifying absolute links (b) Links displayed in the browser

▶ VOCABULARY
relative link

e-mail link

Relative Links

When all the files, including images and other related files, are saved in one folder or will be published on the same Web server, you can use relative links. A *relative link*, also called an *internal link*, gives the file location in relation to the current document. When you use relative links, you can move the folder and files that contain the hyperlink and maintain the destination of the link without breaking the path of the relative link.

The tags for a relative link are <a href = "filename"> </a>. Assume that Bryan Richard's Web page is located in a folder named BryanR. Bryan has two pages in the BryanR folder: Home_page and Bryan_Richard. He would like to link to his Home_page from his Bryan_Richard Web page. To do this, he creates a relative link. The link would look like the following: *<a href = "Home_page">Home Page </a>*.

E-Mail Links

Another type of link is an e-mail link. An *e-mail link* displays a blank e-mail form containing the recipient's address. It is a good idea to include your e-mail address on every page of your site. When the user clicks the e-mail link, the browser starts a mail program, and the e-mail address automatically is inserted in the address line. You use the <a> tag to create the link; for example: *<a href = "mailto:joesmith@ hotmail.com">Joe Smith</a>*.

In Step-by-Step 16.7, you add an absolute link to the name *Shakespeare*, then add your name, and then an e-mail link. You will need to substitute your name and e-mail address for those used in Step 3 of the exercise. You must be online and have Internet access to display the Shakespeare Web site to which you create your link.

Step-by-Step 16.7

1. Your home_page2.htm file should still be open. Click to the left of *Shakespeare* and type: **<a href= http://shakespeare.mit.edu/>**.

2. Click after the </font> tag at the end of *My favorite author is Shakespeare* and type **</a>**. Press **Enter** two times.

3. Type **<p><a href="mailto:BryanRichard@hotmail.com">Bryan Richard </a></p>**. (Substitute your name for *BryanRichard* and your e-mail address for *hotmail.com*.)

4. Save your file and display the Web page in your browser.

5. Click the **Shakespeare** link to display the Shakespeare Web page. Close your browser.

6. Click your linked name to display the New Message e-mail dialog box. In most instances, your screen should look similar to that shown in **Figure 16–19**. Some systems, however, may display a different e-mail client.

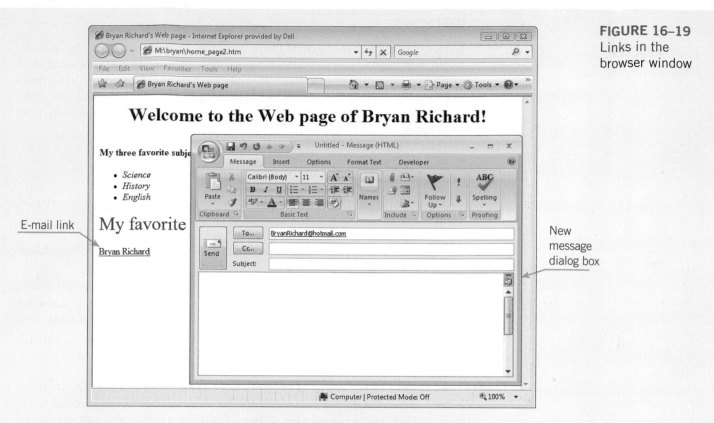

FIGURE 16–19
Links in the
browser window

7.   Send yourself an e-mail and then close your home_page2.htm file.

ETHICS IN TECHNOLOGY

Understanding E-mail Encryption

When you send an e-mail message, you might not realize that it can literally bounce all over the world before it reaches its final destination. As your e-mail message travels from computer to computer, it might encounter "sniffers," or software programs that are waiting to alter or tamper with your e-mail. Most of the time, the e-mail that you send is probably not that important. It could be a note to a friend or a request for information. On the other hand, it could contain your computer network user name and password or maybe even a credit card number.

Several companies have made programs available to encrypt your e-mail. In fact, there are literally hundreds of e-mail encryption programs. If you are using recent versions of Internet Explorer or Firefox, you have encryption options. Internet Explorer, for example, has two different types of certificates to protect your privacy: a personal certificate and a Web site certificate.

Encryption programs work with cryptographic types. The user provides a password, and the program turns the password into a cryptographic type. There is both a public type and a private type. The user retains the private type for decryption purposes.

Images

Images (also called *graphics*) add life to your Web site and make it exciting and fun. As much as they can add to a page, however, they also can slow the downloading of your Web page, especially for someone with slow access to the Internet. Many times when it takes too long to download a page, the person browsing the Web site clicks the browser's Stop button and moves on to another site. Keep this in mind when you are creating your pages.

Image Formats

Two popular image types (GIF and JPG) are supported by most browsers and are displayed on the Web:

- *GIF*: This is the most commonly used file type. It stands for Graphic Interchange Format and is pronounced "jif."

- *JPG* or *JPEG*: This is another commonly used file format that generally results in larger file sizes than GIF. This format is best used for photographs and other photo-quality images. JPEG stands for Joint Photographic Experts Group.

- *PNG*: This image type is native to Adobe Fireworks and is not as widely used as GIF and JPEG. *PNG* stands for Portable Network Graphics.

To add an image to your Web page, use the <img> tag. This is a single tag; that is, there is no end tag. However, many attributes are available that you can use within this tag. Table 16–1 contains a list of image attributes. Three of the most popular are as follows:

- *src*: This stands for *source*, and is mandatory. An example is: *<img src = "Bryan .gif">*.

- *alt*: This stands for *alternative*. Use this attribute to provide alternative text. Some people with slow Internet access turn off automatic image loading. Using the alt attribute provides them with an indication of the nature of the picture. For visually impaired users who use speech synthesizers with text-only browsers, the text in the alt tag is spoken out loud. In some browsers, this text also appears when the pointer is over the image. An example is: *<img src = "Bryan" alt = "Bryan_Richard picture">*.

- *align*: Use this attribute to align the image on the page—bottom, middle, right, left, or top. An example is: *<img src = "Bryan.gif" alt = "Bryan_Richard picture" align = left>*.

TABLE 16–1   Image attributes

ATTRIBUTE	FUNCTION
align	Controls alignment; options include bottom, middle, top, left, and right
alt	Alternative text is displayed when the user moves the mouse pointer over the image
border	Defines the border width
height	Defines the height of the image
hspace	Defines the horizontal space that separates the text from the image
src	Defines the location or URL of the image
vspace	Defines the vertical space that separates the text from the image
width	Defines the width of the image

When you look at a Web page with images, the images appear to be part of the page. In reality, however, if the browser displays three images, you have four separate files—the HTML file and the three image files. When the browser encounters the <img> tag, it knows to look for the src or source. The image could be located in the same folder as your HTML document, or it could be located on a totally different computer on the other side of the world. If the image is in a folder on your computer and the folder also contains the HTML file in which the image will appear, an example link would be *<img src = "racecar.gif">*. If it is an external link, you would specify the address of the image, just like you specify the address of an absolute link; for example: *<img src = "www.rockclimbing.com/rocks.gif">*.

You might wonder how the browser knows where to display the image on the page. The default is the left margin. You can, however, place images almost anywhere within the body of your Web page. They can be on a line by themselves, at the end of a paragraph, at the beginning of a line, in the middle of a line, and so on. Using the <align> tag and other attributes listed in Table 16-1, you can control to an extent where they are placed. **Figure 16–20a** shows how to enter image tags in an HTML document; **Figure 16–20b** shows how they appear in a browser.

a.

Code for image not aligned

Code for image aligned to the right

Code for image aligned to the left

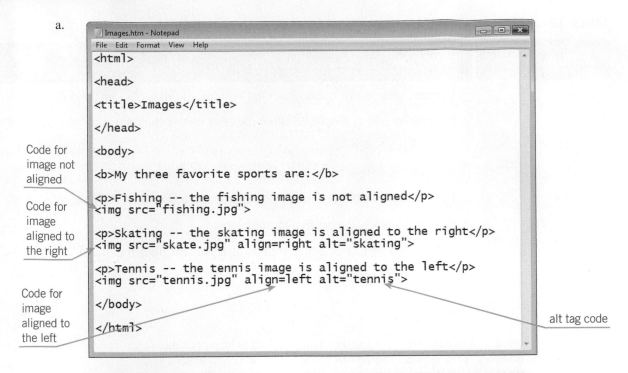

alt tag code

b.

Aligned to left by default

Aligned to the left

alt tag

Aligned to the right

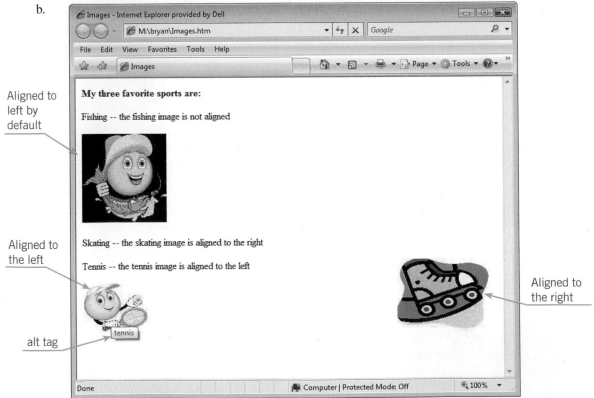

FIGURE 16–20   (a) Image tags (b) Alignment of images in the browser

Character Entities

Some characters have a special meaning in HTML, such as the less than sign (<) that defines the start of an HTML tag. In order for the browser to display these characters, you must insert *character entities* in the HTML document. A character entity has three parts: an ampersand (&), a # and an entity number, and a semicolon (;). The most common character entity in HTML is the nonbreaking space. If you press the Spacebar five times in your HTML document, for example, the browser only recognizes one. However, for each nonbreaking space entity you type, a space is added to the content when it appears in the browser. Table 16–2 lists some of the more common character entities.

TABLE 16–2   Character entities

CHARACTER	DESCRIPTION	ENTITY
&	ampersand	&
'	apostrophe	'
>	greater than	>
<	less than	<
	nonbreaking space	
"	quotation mark	"

▶ **VOCABULARY**
character entities

🔲 **EXTRA FOR EXPERTS**

Many places on the Web provide free images. Access the Ask search engine at *www.ask.com*, type an image name in the text box, and then click Images.

Horizontal Rules and Bulleted Lists

Many Web designers use horizontal rules (also called lines) to separate blocks of text. The horizontal rule <hr> is a single-entry tag that renders a thin line extending across the width of the browser window. Enter the tag to display the line. It does not require an ending tag.

Another option for separating blocks of text is to use some type of graphical divider. Many graphical dividers are available for download on the Web, or you can create your own with a paint or draw program such as Jasc Paint Shop Pro or Adobe PhotoShop. To add a graphical horizontal line to your Web page, go to the location within the document where you would like it to appear. Then use the <img src> tag to insert the line image; for example: *<img src = "graphical_line.gif">*.

Earlier in this lesson, you learned how to create and display bulleted lists. Suppose you prefer graphical bullets instead of the standard bullets. This also is accomplished easily with the <img src> tag. Place the tag and the image name before the line of text. **Figure 16–21a** shows how to enter rule, line, and bullet tags in an HTML document with a background color (backgrounds are covered in the next section); **Figure 16–21b** shows how they are displayed in a browser.

🔲 **EXTRA FOR EXPERTS**

If you are looking for backgrounds for your Web site, then one of the first places you should visit is Yahoo!'s Backgrounds for Web Pages. Here you will find an extensive list of links to many Web sites. Just go to *www.yahoo.com*, click the Images link, and search for Web page backgrounds.

Background color tag

Horizontal rule tag

Graphical bullet tags

Graphical line tags

Four nonbreaking space character entities

a.

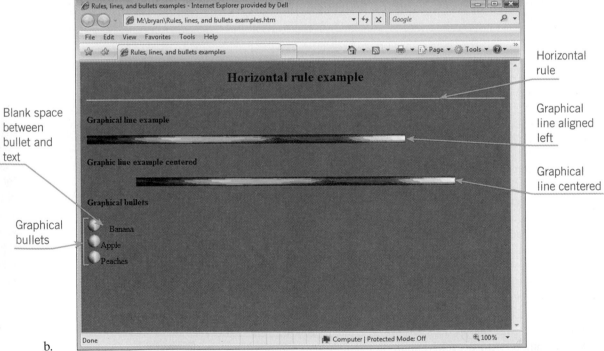

Horizontal rule

Blank space between bullet and text

Graphical line aligned left

Graphical line centered

Graphical bullets

b.

FIGURE 16–21   (a) Background color, nonbreaking space, rule, line, and bullet tags (b) Background color, nonbreaking space, rule, line, and bullet graphics in the browser

Backgrounds

As you surf the Web, you might notice the background color of many Web pages is either white or gray. Generally, the browser you are using determines the background color. You also might have noticed that many Web pages have color or an image for the ***background***. You, too, can add color or images to the background of your Web pages. To add a background color, include the bgcolor attribute in the <body> tag; for example: *<body bgcolor = "pink">*, as used in **Figure 16–21a**.

To add a background image to your Web page, specify the image name within the <body> tag; for example: *<body background = "image.gif">*, as used in **Figure 16–21a**.

In Step-by-Step 16.8, you add a background color, bullets, and a horizontal rule to your Web page.

▶ **VOCABULARY**
background

Step-by-Step 16.8

1. Open your template.htm document and then save it as **home_page3. htm**. Download the **pencil.jpg**, **rule.gif**, and **science.jpg** images and save them in the same folder as your home_page3.htm file.

2. Add the following title: **Lines, Bullets, and Images**. Press **Enter**.

3. In the home_page3.htm file, click to the right of the "y" in <body> and type **bgcolor = "green"**. Press **End** and then press **Enter** two times.

4. Add the following sentence: **This is a horizontal rule**. Add bold and paragraph tags to the sentence and then press **Enter** two times.

5. Add the horizontal rule tag (**<hr>**). Type **<p></p>** and then press Enter.

6. Add the following sentence: **This is a centered horizontal line image**. Change the font size to 5 and bold the sentence. Add paragraph tags as necessary.

7. Insert and center the **rule.gif** image.

8. Add the following sentence: **Science image center aligned**. Add paragraph tags as necessary.

9. Insert and center the **science.jpg** image. Add paragraph tags as necessary.

10. Add the following sentence: **Pencil image right aligned**. Add paragraph tags as necessary.

11. Insert and right-align the **pencil.jpg** image. Add pencil as the alt tag for the image.

12. Add paragraph tags and then add your name.

13. Save your file and then view it in your browser. It should look similar to **Figure 16–22**.

FIGURE 16–22
Home page with rules and images

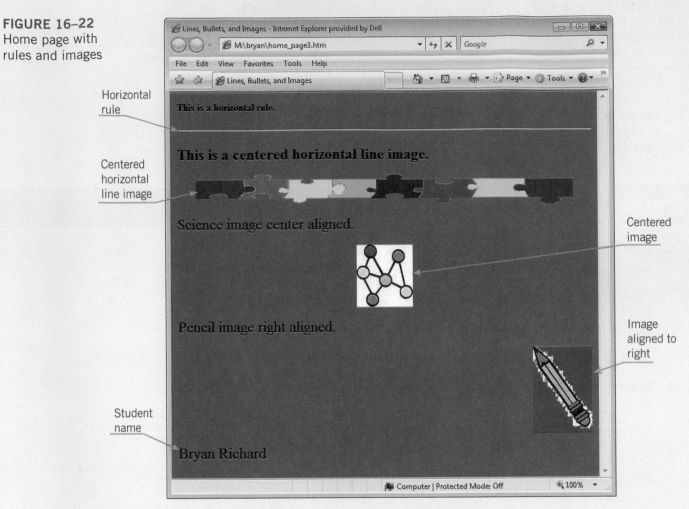

Horizontal rule

Centered horizontal line image

Centered image

Image aligned to right

Student name

Publishing Your Web Page

Your school might have its own Web server that you can use to publish your Web page creations. If not, do not be dismayed. Several Web sites on the Internet offer free space. Two of the more popular of these are Tripod, located at *www.tripod.lycos.com*, and Yahoo! GeoCities, located at *geocities.yahoo.com/home/*. See **Figure 16–23**.

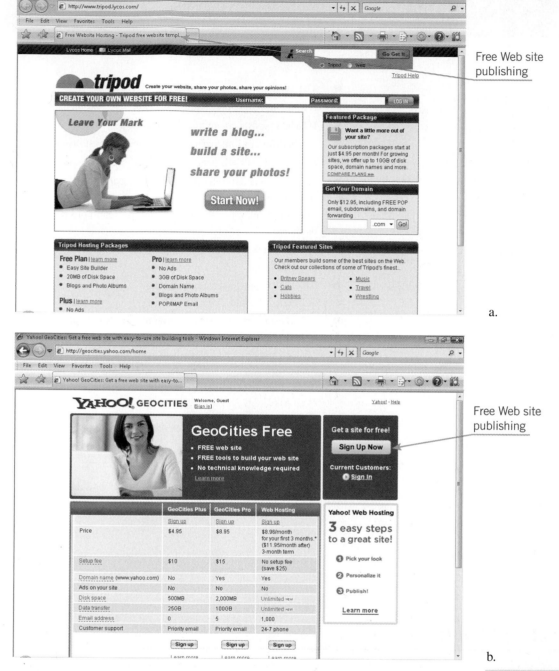

Free Web site
publishing

a.

Free Web site
publishing

b.

FIGURE 16–23 (a) Tripod free Web space (b) Yahoo! Geocities free
Web space

EXTRA FOR EXPERTS

Most of the sites that provide free
space also provide step-by-step
instructions on how to upload your
page. Find and click the "sign
up" link or the link indicating a
free home page or free space on
their server. If you wonder how an
organization can offer free space
for you to save your Web pages,
check out the advertising on the
Web site. These companies generate their income by selling banners
and other advertising space.

SUMMARY

In this lesson, you learned:

- A Web page is a document on the World Wide Web and is defined by a unique URL.

- HTML is the language of the Web.

- A Web browser is an application program that interprets the HTML tags within the page and then displays the text on the computer screen.

- A basic Web page has both page content and HTML tags.

- Some tags come in pairs, and others are single entities.

- Every Web page requires a particular set of tags structured in a particular format.

- Pressing the Enter key when creating a Web page has no effect on how the page is displayed.

- To start a new line in a Web page, use the break <br> tag.

- To insert a blank line in a Web page, use the paragraph <p> tag.

- HTML supports three types of lists that you can use to organize text on a Web page.

- The <center> tag is used to center text or graphics.

- HTML supports bold, italics, and underline text formatting.

- HTML supports changing of font size and font color.

- Seven different font sizes are supported by most browsers.

- Six levels of HTML headings are supported by most browsers.

- A link is an active reference to another part of the same document or to another document.

- A relative link gives the file location in relation to the current document.

- Absolute links are hyperlinks to other Web sites.

- One of the most common types of non-Web links is e-mail.

- Three different image types are supported by browsers—GIF, JPEG or JPG, and PNG.

- HTML supports the use of horizontal lines to separate blocks of text.

- HTML supports adding a background color or image to a Web page.

- Many Web sites provide free online space for publishing your Web page.

■ VOCABULARY REVIEW

Define the following terms:

absolute link	character entities	lists
attribute	e-mail link	mobile browser
background	headings	relative link
body	home page	style sheet
Cascading Style Sheets	images	title
		Web site

■ REVIEW QUESTIONS

MULTIPLE CHOICE

Select the best response for the following statements.

1. The _____ tag can contain information about the document.

   A. head   C. html

   B. end   D. http

2. The _____ of your Web page is what appears on the browser title bar.

   A. body   C. title

   B. heading   D. closing

3. To center a line of text, use the _____ tag.

   A. left side   C. all center

   B. center   D. right center

4. To leave a blank line on a Web page document, use the _____ tag.

   A.
                         C. <end>

   B. <p>   D. <start>

5. An ordered list generally is a _____ list.

   A. numbered   C. bulleted

   B. container   D. prefix

TRUE / FALSE

Circle T if the statement is true or F if the statement is false.

T F   **1.** All HTML documents contain three components.

T F   **2.** Within a Web page, you can change the background color.

T F   **3.** All Web page backgrounds are either white or gray.

T F   **4.** A relative link is also called an internal link.

T F   **5.** Every Web server has a unique Web address or URL.

FILL IN THE BLANK

Complete the following sentences by writing the correct word or words in the blanks provided.

1. A(n) _____ is a line that extends across the width of the browser.

2. _____ levels of HTML headings are available.

3. Use the _____ tag to create bold text.

4. A(n) _____ list generally is a bulleted list.

5. To center text or an image on a Web page, use the _____ tag.

■ PROJECTS

CROSS-CURRICULAR— MATHEMATICS

Create a Web page document for your mathematics class. Include within this document a heading, a numbered list, a background color, and absolute links to two mathematics-related Web sites. Add and center your name and apply a color to your name that matches your selected background.

CROSS-CURRICULAR—SCIENCE

Select a special science project on which you might be working or an area of science in which you are interested. Create two Web pages for this project. Include somewhere within these two pages an h1 heading, a definition list, a background color, relative links from one of the Web pages to the other, and absolute links to at least one other Web site on your selected topic. Include at least two images in one of your Web pages.

CROSS-CURRICULAR—SOCIAL STUDIES

Ask your social studies instructor for a list of topics that you will study in the next month, or select a social studies-related topic in which you have an interest. Create a Web page on your selected topic. Include a heading and a background color. Use *"Links to (name of topic)"* for the heading. Search the Web for Web sites related to the topics. Create a list of absolute links to the Web sites. List at least 10 Web sites and include a short description of what can be found at each Web site.

CROSS-CURRICULAR—LANGUAGE ARTS

Your instructor has asked you to write an article about your favorite school subject. After you write the article, convert it to a Web page document. Illustrate the page with images and graphical dividers.

WEB PROJECT

You are a member of a group learning about HTML and how to create and publish Web pages. Your instructor has asked you to put together a presentation on HTML commands not covered in this lesson. You are to research, report, and present an example of at least two linked Web pages and display the HTML code used to create the Web pages.

 TEAMWORK PROJECT

Now that you have the basic skills necessary to create a Web page, you want to create at least three pages identifying your favorite school activity. To extend your HTML knowledge, access the Web site *http://personalweb.about.com/cs/beginninghtml/a/basic_html.htm*. Include any additional HTML tags that you might find in one of these tutorials. Create the Web pages. Use as many tags as possible that were introduced in this lesson and any new tags you learned from the Web site, including at least one image per page. Create a link from each page to the other page.

 # CRITICAL THINKING

Investigate the possibility of publishing one of the Web pages you created in the preceding end-of-lesson projects. Review the information presented at the end of this lesson on the Tripod and GeoCities Web sites, which provide free Web site hosting. Then, use a search engine such as Google and search for and locate at least one other Web site that provides free Web site space. Compare the three Web sites and determine which one you would select to host your Web page. Explain why you selected the particular Web site to host your site.

 # EXPLORING GOOGLE

Google Groups, located at *http://groups.google.com*, provides an opportunity to "meet" with others and participate in discussion groups related to specific topics. Access the groups site and "Take the tour." If you were going to join a group, which group would you join? One of the options is to start your own group. Within your class or within a small group in your class, set up your own group and build a knowledge base around a particular topic related to your class. If instructed to do so, create a Web page within your group and share it with other group members.

LESSON 17

Technology, the Workplace, and Society

■ OBJECTIVES

Upon completion of this lesson, you should be able to:

- Describe the impact of technology on education.
- Describe the impact of technology on science and medicine.
- Describe the impact of technology on work and play.
- Identify types of computer crimes.
- Identify computer viruses.
- Identify various security measures.
- Identify computer-related laws.
- Identify the "work" of hackers.
- Describe how privacy is invaded with computer use.

As the age of innovation continues to blaze through the world of technology, changes are taking place in every aspect of life—from home to school to the workplace. These changes are swift and dramatic. As soon as we settle in and become comfortable with a new technological change, along comes something more innovative and different. As things look now, the world is in for a lot more of this type of change. Some of these changes have, unfortunately, introduced concerns over computer crimes, computer health-related issues, and even the need for laws to protect those injured by computer crimes and offenses.

■ VOCABULARY

artificial intelligence (AI)

biometric security measures

computer-based learning

computer crime

computer fraud

computer hacking

copyright

data diddling

digital cash

electronic commerce

genetic engineering

groupware

nanotechnology

online learning

optical computing

plagiarism

quantum computing

simulation

software piracy

time bomb

virtual reality (VR)

virus

worm

. . .

Education

Many similarities exist between today's schools and those of 40 or 50 years ago. In some classrooms, the students still sit in rows and the teacher stands at the front of the class, lecturing and using a chalkboard or whiteboard. However, in other classrooms, a technological revolution is taking place as educators are using computer technology to enhance their classrooms and curriculum.

Many people predict that technology will change the entire structure of education. Others believe the way most students receive education today—from a teacher in a traditional classroom—will remain the standard for many years. Regardless of who is right, technology is certainly having a tremendous impact on education in more classrooms around the world.

The Internet in Education

The Internet and the World Wide Web are the biggest factors affecting education today. Not long ago, if a science teacher gave a class a project to find out how a television works, the students would go to the library and do the research. In many of today's classrooms, the students most likely go to the Internet, and search sites such as the HowStuffWorks Web site to find this information (see **Figure 17–1**). Using the Internet is a fast and easy way to find the information you need.

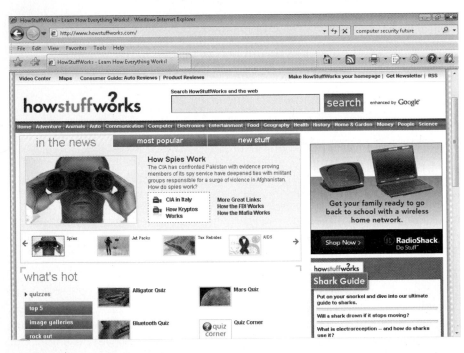

FIGURE 17–1   HowStuffWorks Web page

In addition to research, you can use the Internet to prepare for class. Perhaps you are having a quiz on the environment next week, and want to test your knowledge on the topic. You can use the Internet as your resource. One site you might visit is the National Geographic's Green Guide quiz page (*www.thegreenguide.com/quizzes/index.mhtml*), shown in **Figure 17–2**, or the CIA Game page (*https://www.cia.gov/kids-page/games/index.html*).

FIGURE 17-2 National Geographic Green Guide Web page

Perhaps you've had an opportunity to participate in or work with a WebQuest. This type of activity uses the Internet for investigation and problem solving. Bernie Dodge developed the WebQuest Model at San Diego State University. Since then, thousands of WebQuests have been developed by teachers and professors. Example WebQuests include exploring countries around the world, politics, learning about money, and so on. You can find a list and a link to some of these WebQuests at *http://webquest.sdsu.edu*. An example of one interesting WebQuest is titled Sensory Biology and the Plight of the Right Whales. See **Figure 17-3**.

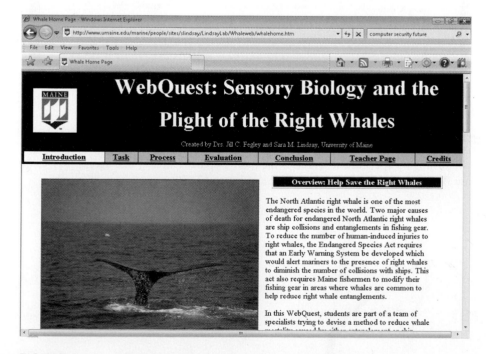

FIGURE 17-3 WebQuest Web site

Online Learning

For some time, people have been able to obtain their education via distance learning methods. Earlier non-traditional methods include television and correspondence courses that are completed through the mail. In the last few years, the Internet has become a way to deliver **online learning**. At the elementary and secondary school levels, the Department of Education supports an initiative called the Star Schools Program. This program provides online education learning to millions of learners annually.

Imagine being able to complete high school from home. This is possible in many states. For instance, any high school student who is a Florida resident can attend the Florida Virtual School online for free. This is a certified diploma-granting school, open any time—night or day. Students enroll, log on, and complete their work through the guidance of a certified Florida high school teacher. Several other states such as Utah provide similar programs. See **Figure 17–4**.

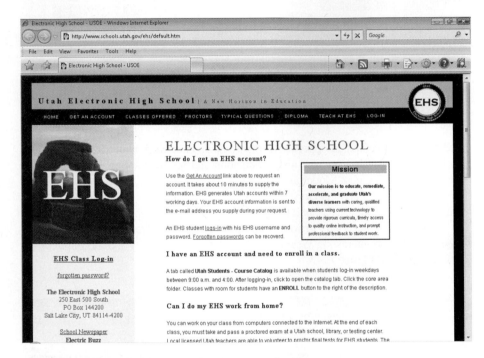

FIGURE 17–4   Utah electronic high school

Teachers use learning management systems to help deliver online courses. These programs are an integrated set of Web-based teaching tools that provide guidance and testing for the student. Three of the more popular learning management systems are Blackboard, Moodle, and Angel. See **Figure 17–5**.

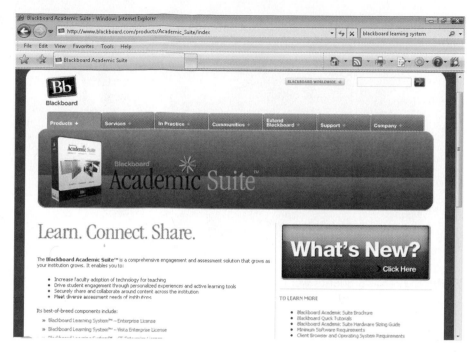

FIGURE 17–5   Blackboard online learning

Computer-Based Learning

Most likely, 20 or 30 students are in your class. These students (plus yourself) learn in different ways and at different rates. Likewise, information can be presented in many formats and at different levels. This can be through lectures, homework, group projects, movies, online tutorials, and so on. The more ways a teacher or system presents information, the more opportunities everyone has to use their own learning styles so they can master the particular topic.

You probably have heard the terms **computer-based learning** or computer-assisted instruction (CAI). These are examples of instructional methods for which the teacher uses the computer to deliver the instruction. Basically, this type of instruction uses a computer as a tutor. For many students this is one of the most effective ways to learn. For example, you might have difficulty understanding a specific mathematics concept, such as how to calculate percentages. Your teacher might suggest a special computer program to help reinforce that difficult concept. Using such a program provides you with the opportunity to master the idea by reviewing the concept as many times as necessary. See **Figure 17–6**. Instead of using live specimens for experiments in a biology class, you may complete all of your lab assignments using simulation software. These types of labs are called dry labs.

▶ **VOCABULARY**
computer-based learning

FIGURE 17–6   Students working in a computer lab

Simulations

Learning can be fun for everyone, especially if you use computer simulation. **Simulations** are models of real-world activities, designed to allow you to experiment and explore environments that might be dangerous, unavailable, or inaccessible. Using simulations, you can explore other worlds and settings without leaving your classroom. Simulations are fun and engaging and allow you and other learners to apply new skills in a risk-free environment. With this type of model, you learn by doing. You can find simulations on the Internet or on a DVD that you run from a local computer. The following sections describe some example simulations.

The Stock Market

Many of you probably have heard about fortunes being made and lost in the stock market. If you would like to see how good your investing skills are, you might want to try The Stock Market Game located at *www.smgww.org*. This simulation is for students of all ages—from middle school to adults. By playing this game, you learn about finance and the American economic system. To participate, you invest a hypothetical $100,000 in the stock market and follow your investments over a 10-week period. See **Figure 17–7**.

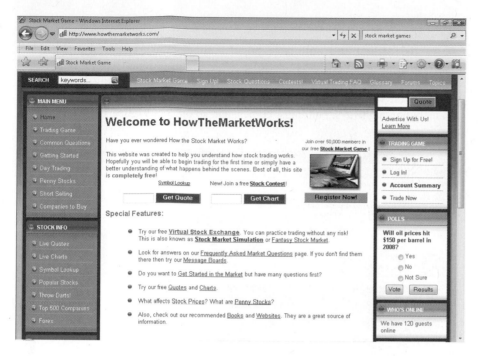

FIGURE 17–7 Stock Market simulation game

The Renaissance

Maybe you are interested in the Renaissance era and would like to explore and learn more about this historical period. You can do this through simulation. Try the Renaissance Connection located at *www.renaissanceconnection.org*. See **Figure 17–8**. You also will find links to several other simulations and resources from this site.

FIGURE 17–8 Renaissance Connection Web page

SimCity

One of the earliest and still most popular simulations is SimCity, located at (*http://simcitysocieties.ea.com*). Several versions of this program have been released, including one that runs on handheld computers. It is used extensively in schools throughout the world. This problem-solving software program allows you to create a city, including highways, buildings, homes, and so on. See **Figure 17–9**.

FIGURE 17–9   SimCity simulation game

Scientific Discovery and Technological Innovations

Our world is changing at an ever-increasing pace. Currently, people around the world can communicate with each other almost instantaneously. The amount of available information is increasing every day. In fact, it is continuing to increase faster than we can process it. On the positive side, the information and discoveries are contributing to a better lifestyle for many people. Predictions are that we will learn to cure many diseases and continue to increase our life span.

But there is another aspect to all of this. Within all of this change, other predictions are that an antitechnology backlash is possible. Many people feel technology is creating a world that is out of control. Moral and cultural dilemmas are becoming more common, and many people want to return to a simpler, slower way of life.

Whether society could and would return to something simpler is highly debatable. Even today, very few places in the world are not affected by technology. Many scientists say we are "only at the Model-T stage" of what is to come. Let's take a brief look at some of the predicted and possible scientific changes on the horizon.

Artificial Intelligence

If you enjoy science fiction, you might have read the book or seen the movie *2001: A Space Odyssey*. In the movie, originally released in the late 1960s, re-released in 2001, and now on DVD, a computer referred to as HAL controls a spaceship on its way to Mars. This computer has artificial intelligence, so it never makes a mistake. No computer such as HAL yet exists, though many have artificial intelligence. Computer scientists have made much advancement in this area.

The concept of **artificial intelligence (AI)** has been around for many years. In fact, the term was coined in 1956 by John McCarthy at the Massachusetts Institute of Technology. The goal for this software is to process information on its own without human intervention. Artificial intelligence applications are being developed and used today in many ways. Some examples are as follows:

- *Game playing*: The most advances have been made in this area.

- *Natural language*: This offers the greatest potential rewards by allowing people to interact easily with computers by talking to them.

- *Expert systems*: These are computer programs that help us make decisions. For instance, an expert system might help users determine the best type of insurance for their particular needs.

- *Robotics*: When you think of robotics, you might think of humanoid robots like those in *Star Wars*. In real life, however, you do not see this type of robot in our society. Robots, mostly used in assembly plants, are capable only of limited tasks. One of the newest types of virtual robots is called a *bot*, commonly used by search engines. Many universities throughout the world, such as Massachusetts Institute of Technology (*http://web.mit.edu*) and Iowa State University (*www.cs.iastate.edu*), have artificial intelligence research labs. See **Figure 17–10**.

> ▶ **VOCABULARY**
> **artificial intelligence (AI)**
> **genetic engineering**

FIGURE 17–10   MIT Web site for artificial intelligence

Genetic Engineering

The human life span has more than doubled in the last 200 years. We now can expect to live almost 80 years. Implications are that the average life span in the 21st century will continue to increase, possibly dramatically. One of the major factors contributing to this increase is **genetic engineering**, which refers to changing the DNA in a living organism. See **Figure 17–11**.

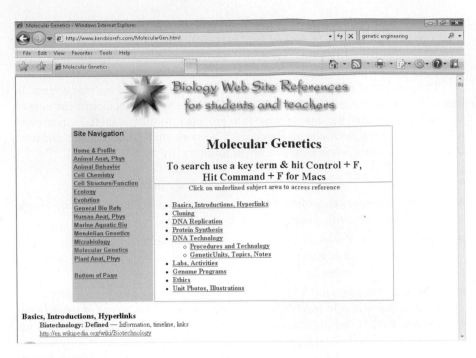

FIGURE 17–11   Genetic engineering

Many groups of people argue against this technology, including Greenpeace International. The supporters, however, point out many benefits. Here are some examples:

- Increasing resistance to disease
- Enabling a plant or animal to do something it would not typically do
- Enabling a fruit to ripen without getting overripe

One of the most widely known projects developed in this area is the Human Genome Project. Its goal was to identify all of the approximately 100,000 genes in human DNA, store and analyze this data, and address the ethical, legal, and social issues surrounding the project. The project was coordinated by the Department of Energy and the National Institute of Health. Because of the data and resources resulting from this project, some observers such as Bill Gates and former President Bill Clinton predict the 21st century will be the "biology century."

Virtual Reality

> **▶ VOCABULARY**
> virtual reality (VR)

The term **virtual reality (VR)** means different things to different people. A general definition is an artificial environment that feels like a real environment. This environment is created with computer hardware and software. Virtual reality and simulation share some common characteristics. Simulation sometimes is referred to as desktop VR. However, virtual reality provides more sensations of being in the actual environment—of using all or almost all of the five senses. You are immersed completely inside the virtual world, generally through a head-mounted display. This helmet contains virtual and auditory displays. Virtual reality is used in many different ways and areas. Some examples are as follows:

- *Education*: Virtual environments can help students develop a better understanding of history. Imagine experiencing World War II as though you were really there. Or maybe you would like to experience what it would be like to live during the age of dinosaurs. With a virtual world, you feel as though you are part of the environment. See **Figure 17–12**. One popular VR Web site is Second Life (*www.secondlife.com*). Many businesses, schools, and nonprofit organizations use this site for training and amusement.

FIGURE 17–12　Virtual reality

■　*Training*: If you have played a virtual game, you might have felt you were part of the action. You could control much of the environment and make choices about your next move. A variation of this type of virtual reality is being used to train pilots, navigators, and even astronauts. These people are put into virtual life and death situations where they must make decisions. This helps prepare them for similar situations in real life.

- *Medicine*: The Virtual Reality Medical Center in San Diego, California is using virtual reality in combination with physiological monitoring and feedback to treat anxiety disorders, such as fear of flying, fear of heights, fear of public speaking, claustrophobia, panic disorders, and so on.

Computing Trends

Nanotechnology, quantum computing, and optical computing are predicted to be technologies of the future.

Nanotechnology relates to creating computer components that are less than 100 nanometers in size. To put the concept of nanotechnology into perspective, consider the following: The width of a single grain of sand is about 900,000 nanometers! Many scientists predict that nanotechnology will make possible the production of ever-smaller computers that can process data considerably faster than today's computers and can store vastly greater amounts of information.

Optical computing uses light beams for the internal circuits instead of electricity. Thus, it has the advantage of small size and high speed. This type of computing has definite advantages—light beams are much faster than electricity and can cross each other, providing for even faster speeds. Researchers working on this technology indicate that optical computers could do in a second what now takes days or weeks. Enormous hurdles must still be overcome before a true optical computer exists.

Quantum computing uses the laws of quantum mechanics and the way that atoms can be in more than one state at once to do computational tasks. Quantum computing is still in the pioneer stage, but shows great promise. Its strong point is in the areas of encryption and code-breaking.

These are just a few examples of activities taking place today. As in the past, it is certain that scientific discovery and technological innovation will greatly affect our economic and military developments in the future. Predictions are that science and technology will continue to advance and become more widely available and used around the world. Some people forecast, however, that the benefits derived from these advancements will not be evenly distributed.

▶ **VOCABULARY**
nanotechnology
optical computing
quantum computing

EXTRA FOR EXPERTS

Nanoparticles are expected to be so inexpensive that they can be integrated into fabrics and other materials, creating, for example, military uniforms that defend against bullets and germ warfare.

ETHICS IN TECHNOLOGY

Who Is Responsible?

Increasingly, computers participate in decisions that affect human lives. Consider medical safety, for instance, and consider that just about everything in a hospital is tied to a computer. So what happens if these machines do not produce the expected results? What happens if they have been incorrectly programmed?

When programmers write a program, they check for as many conditions as possible. But there always is a chance they might miss one. So what happens if a computer malfunctions and applies a high dosage of radiation? Or what happens if two medications are prescribed to an individual and the computer does not indicate that the medications are incompatible? Or what happens when someone calls for an ambulance and the system does not work and there is no backup?

Then the question becomes: Who is responsible for these mishaps? Is it the programmer? Is it the company? Is it the person who administered the radiation treatment?

The incidents described here actually happened. These are ethical issues that are being decided in court.

Work and Play

How will technology affect us as individuals in our work and social life? Although no one knows what the future will bring, predictions are numerous. Many people predict that with high-skilled work in greater demand, semi-skilled work will start to disappear. Discussed previously was how some of the changes already are taking place in education and how genetic engineering is helping increase life expectancy. As a result of these advances, what types of changes can we expect in the economy and in our personal lives?

Global Economy

One thing is certain about the new economy: Knowledge is the greatest asset. However, knowledge is limited by time—it can be incredibly valuable one moment and worthless the next. The spread and sharing of knowledge, the development of new technologies, and an increased recognition of common world problems present unlimited opportunities for economic growth.

Consider banking, finance, and commerce. Electronic technology is having a dramatic effect on these industries. Think about currency. Will it become obsolete? Most likely it will. Already, huge amounts of money zip around the globe at the speed of light. Technology is affecting the way information and money are transmitted. You no longer have to go to the bank to do your banking; you can do it in the comfort of your home using online banking. Online banking allows you to transfer money electronically, which makes it possible for you to pay your bills online and check your account balances. This can be done from anywhere in the world!

Electronic Commerce

You probably have read about the Industrial Revolution and how it affected our world. The Internet economy is being compared to the Industrial Revolution. **Electronic commerce**, or e-commerce, which means having an online business, is changing the way our world does business.

We find e-commerce in every corner of the modern business world. Statistics indicate that over a billion people are connected to the Internet. Connection speed continues to increase as more people add fiber optics, cable modems, and digital subscriber lines (DSLs). All of this activity and high-speed connections indicate more online businesses. Some analysts predict that within the next 10 years, Internet-based business will account for up to 10 percent or more of the world's consumer sales.

Within this electronic business, one can buy and sell products through the Internet. When it comes to buying online, many people hesitate because they fear someone will steal their credit card numbers. However, **digital cash** is a technology that might ease some of those fears. The digital cash system allows someone to pay by transmitting a number from one computer to another. The digital cash numbers are issued by a bank and represent a specified sum of real money; each number is unique. When you use digital cash, no one can obtain information about you. Some credit card companies have a virtual account option that works like digital cash.

As you read about electronic commerce, you might wonder about the effects it will have on you personally. You or someone in your family might have already made a purchase online. Buying online will become much more common in the future, and you might find it becomes a way of life. You also could continue to see an increase in spam—junk mail sent to your e-mail address. Some online businesses use spam to sell their products or entice you to return to their Web sites. Several states already are looking at ways to legislate against this electronic junk mail.

▶ **VOCABULARY**
electronic commerce
digital cash

The introduction of electronic commerce also has generated a number of new jobs and categories of jobs. This might be something you want to consider as you look toward a future career. Some examples include Webmasters, programmers, network managers, graphic designers, Web developers, and so on. You also might think about going into an online business for yourself. Individuals with imagination and ambition will discover that the greatest source of wealth is their ideas.

The Workplace

The computer has created many changes in the workplace. The way information is managed has changed. Instead of file cabinets and paper file folders, electronic copies of documents are created and stored.

> **VOCABULARY**
> groupware

Computers also are used to improve communication in a business. A computer network can be a vital tool for helping work run more smoothly. One category of software that assists in communicating over a network is called groupware. **Groupware** refers to programs and software that help people work together even if they are located far from each other. One of the more common types of groupware is e-mail. E-mail is an easy and cost-effective way for users to communicate across short or long distances. E-mail allows users to keep documentation of correspondence about a particular topic, something that is lacking with telephone communication.

Groupware also includes electronic calendars and daily, weekly, or monthly planners. With this software, users enter their appointments that become available across the network. All meetings are scheduled in the electronic calendar system, which then checks to see that everyone invited can attend. This software can also check the electronic room scheduling system and find a conference room for the meeting.

Collaborative writing software is another form of groupware. This software allows different users to add their own parts, comments, and changes to a single common document, such as a report. The software keeps track of the additions from each user. The changes can be accepted or rejected in the final document. Database software can also be used collaboratively, with different departments providing their own data, such as product specifications or due dates, in the database for the whole company to see and use.

A related type of groupware is project management software. This software allows users to track time lines and processes for complicated projects that involve many workers and departments. Every department can contribute to the information and track its parts of the project, ensuring that everything is accomplished correctly and on time.

Another type of groupware is video conferencing. This allows users at different locations to hold a virtual meeting without traveling to a central location. Cameras and microphones connected to each person's computer allow users to see and talk to each other.

Many employers allow their employees to work from home. This arrangement is called telecommuting. It involves using communications technology to keep the employee connected to the office. Telecommuting has many advantages for both the employer and the employee. It saves traveling time and expense, and it allows the employee to work at a time that is convenient.

Personal Lives

Computers play such an important part in our lives. Sometimes we take for granted the role they play because they work "behind the scenes." When you order a pizza, the order is transmitted through a computer. When you get money out of an ATM, the transaction is completed by a computer. Many late-model cars have features such as wipers that turn on automatically, directions available at a moment's notice, automatic parallel parking, and brake systems that slow down the car if it gets too close to an object in front of it!

Will our personal lives become almost like *Star Trek*? Many people predict this will happen. Just as technology is affecting our work environment, it also is affecting our personal lives.

In the 20th century, society witnessed all types of changes in the places people lived. They moved from the farms to the cities and then to the suburbs. The 21st century also will witness changes as the home becomes the center for work, entertainment, learning, and possibly even health care. More people will telecommute or run businesses from their homes. As a result, they will have to manage their own lives in a world of uncertainty. This will be a great change for many people. They will have to make decisions about how to separate their business and personal lives.

Following are some examples of potential technological advances that could affect our personal lives:

- *Clothes that fight odor and bacteria*: Some clothing companies are manufacturing clothes that keep you comfortable and smelling good. For example, you can find jackets that grow warmer as the temperature drops, and sweat socks that resist bacteria and odors. Or, how would you like clothing that kills mosquitoes on contact?

- *The flying car*: This has long been a fantasy of the American public, but the question is: How long will it be before we all have flying cars? It probably will be a few more years before we are flying around like the Jetsons, but possibilities are on the horizon. Moller International has developed a personal vertical takeoff and landing vehicle (VTOL). The Skycar can operate in a much less restrictive area than a helicopter or airplane and is less expensive and safer than both. These factors allow this type of future transportation to be addressed and investigated for the first time. See **Figure 17–13**.

FIGURE 17–13   Moller Web site with flying car

- *Nonlethal weapons*: A company in San Diego is working on a nonlethal weapon that uses two ultraviolet laser beams. These two beams of UV radiation ionize paths in the air to create "wires" in the atmosphere. This device is harmless, but can immobilize people and animals at a distance.

- *Smart shoes and smart seats*: When we think of technology, not too many of us consider our shoes. No matter how expensive our shoes are, they can still become uncomfortable after wearing them for long hours. A technology called expansive polymer gel uses a micro voltage to expand or contract the gel. Weight can be evenly distributed and heat dissipated. This technology also is being applied to car seats.

- *Medical needs*: Consider that you could meet with your doctor from your home and get a checkup online. In the not-too-distant future, doctors will be able to make "computer" calls. Using audio chat, Webcams, and medical hardware attachments, you could convert your computer into a portable home medical station. Test results can be processed through your computer and transmitted to the physician's computer at home or work. This will be especially significant for seniors with limited mobility or people with limited transportation access.

Technological Issues

It is true that computers have made a positive impact in our lives. They have made our daily lives much easier, our work more efficient, learning more interesting and convenient, and even our game playing more exciting. However, computer users should be aware of problems, such as misuse of information, computer crimes, risks of using hardware and software, health issues, privacy, and security.

Misuse of Information

Use of the Internet has grown at an astounding rate. Users are able to access a multitude of information in a very short amount of time. Putting together a report is a snap with the ability to access information on almost any topic with just a few clicks. This is causing a rise in plagiarism and violation of copyright laws. **Plagiarism** is presenting someone else's ideas or work as your own, without authorization. **Copyright** is the legal protection for authors of creative works. It guards against the unlawful copying or using of someone else's original work. Some specific examples of plagiarism include:

▶ **VOCABULARY**
plagiarism
copyright
computer crime

- Buying a report from a "free term paper" Web site
- Paraphrasing information from a source, but not indicating that the information is taken directly from that source
- Having someone else write a report for you

Types of Computer Crimes

What is **computer crime**? It is a criminal act committed through the use of a computer; for example, getting into someone else's system and changing information or creating a computer virus and causing damage to information on others' computers. Computer crime is a bigger problem than most people realize. Billions of dollars every year are lost to corporations because of this often undetected, and therefore unpunished, crime. Computer crimes have increased since data communications and computer networks have become popular. Many computer crimes consist of stealing and damaging information and stealing actual computer equipment. Other types of computer crimes include:

- Unauthorized use of a computer
- Infection of a computer by a malicious program (a virus)
- Harassment and stalking on the computer
- Copyright violations of software
- Copyright violations of information found on the Internet

Computer Fraud

Computer fraud is a type of computer crime that involves the manipulation of a computer or computer data in order to obtain money, property, or value dishonestly or to cause loss. Examples of computer fraud include stealing money from bank accounts or stealing information from other people's computers for gain.

Computer Hacking

Computer hacking involves invading someone else's computer, usually for personal gain or just the satisfaction of doing it. Hackers usually are computer experts who enjoy having the power to invade someone else's privacy. They can steal money or they can change or damage data stored on a computer.

Computer Viruses

A **virus** is a program that has been written, usually by a hacker, to cause the corruption of data on a computer. The virus generally is attached to an executable file (like a program file) and spreads from one file to another once the program is executed. A virus might cause major damage to a computer's data, or it might do something as minor as display messages on your screen. There are different variations of viruses:

- A **worm** makes many copies of itself, resulting in the consumption of system resources that slows down or actually halts tasks. Worms do not have to attach themselves to other files.
- A **time bomb** is a virus that does not cause its damage until a certain date or until the system has been booted a certain number of times.
- A Trojan horse is harmful software that does something different from what it is expected to do. It might look like it is performing a useful task, while in actuality it is doing something different (usually something disastrous).
- An e-mail virus consists of e-mail messages to carry the virus and software to automatically send itself to hundreds and/or thousands of people.

To protect your computer against virus damage:

- Use antivirus software. This software should always run on your computer and should be updated regularly.
- Be careful when opening e-mail attachments. It is a good idea to save attached files to disk so you can scan them before reading their contents. It is also a good idea to open messages only from people you know.

▶ **VOCABULARY**

computer fraud

computer hacking

virus

worm

time bomb

EXTRA FOR EXPERTS

The FBI's National Crime Information Center has a division for computer crime.

- Do not access files copied from disks or downloaded from the Internet without scanning them first. **Figure 17–14** shows online security scan and virus detection options.

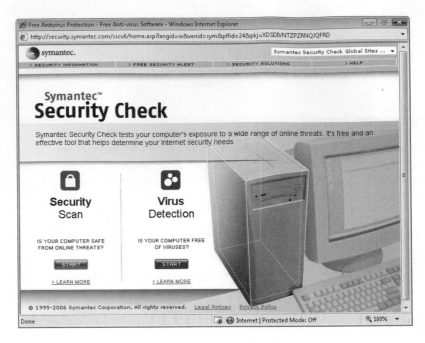

FIGURE 17–14   Security scan and virus detection

Other Computer Crimes

Theft of computer time also is a crime committed regularly in the workplace. This crime is committed when an employee uses a company's computer for personal use, such as running a small side business, keeping records of an outside organization, or keeping personal records. When you are engaged in these types of activities on the job, you are not being as productive as you could be for your employer.

Using the information you see on someone else's computer screen or on a printout to profit unfairly is theft of output.

Changing data before it is entered into the computer or after it has been entered into the computer is called **data diddling**. Anyone who is involved with creating, recording, encoding, and checking data can change data.

Risks of Using Computer Hardware and Software

Computer equipment as well as data stored on computers are subject to various types of hazards. These include damage caused by improper use, damage caused by improper configurations, fire, flood, and even electrical outages or storms. Many of these conditions can be prevented by proper planning, such as providing users with appropriate training to safeguard the equipment. Computers should be equipped with surge protectors and other types of protection to prevent outages. When flooding is a possibility, it is a good idea to locate computers above the first floor of a building.

Illegally copying and using software is called **software piracy**. This has become a major problem because it is so easy to copy software. Software piracy costs software companies millions of dollars in sales each year. Many persons are misusing shareware as well. Shareware is software you can use for free for a specified period of time to try it out. If you decide you like the software and it meets your needs, you are supposed to pay for it.

Health Issues

Working on computers for long periods of time can cause various types of health problems and concerns. These are referred to as ergonomic-related concerns and usually are caused by repetitive motions that result in wear and tear on the body, such as rapid hand and wrist movement. A very common disorder caused by using a keyboard on a consistent basis is carpal tunnel syndrome. One remedy to reduce this condition is to replace a regular keyboard with an ergonomic keyboard. This type of keyboard will take the stress off the wrists and reduce injury. Problems also can occur because of poor lighting or inappropriate furniture and equipment such as the type of monitor. It is the responsibility of the employer or educational institution to provide a safe working environment, which will result in a healthy and productive workforce. **Figure 17–15** shows an example of an ergonomically designed workstation.

Eyes looking at top part of screen

Screen a comfortable reading distance away

Adjustable chair with adequate lumbar support

Desk at elbow level

Thighs parallel to the floor

Mouse in close, next to keyboard

Feet flat on floor or on footrest

(Photography by Hader Goren)

FIGURE 17–15 Workstation ergonomics

Privacy

The amount of personal information electronically available on each of us is astonishing. Most individuals would be surprised to know the extent to which this information is accessible and to whom it is available. Many companies gather information to create databases and sell or trade this information to others.

Any time you submit information on the Internet, it is possible for this information to be used for various situations. Information also can be gathered from online data regarding school, banking, hospitals, insurance companies, and any other information supplied for such everyday activities.

Much of the information gathered and sold can result in your name being added to mailing lists. Companies use these lists for marketing purposes. Information regarding one's credit history also is available for purchase. Using credit cards to purchase merchandise on the Internet can be risky. Some sites are advertised as being secure. If the sites are not secure, your credit card number can be stolen and used by others.

Security

Computer security is necessary to keep hardware, software, and data safe from harm or destruction. Some risks to computers are natural causes, some are accidents, and some are intentional. It is not always evident that some type of computer crime or intrusion has occurred. Therefore, it is necessary that safeguards for each type of risk be put into place. It is the responsibility of companies or individuals to protect their data.

The best way to protect data is to control access to the data. The most common form of restricting access to data is the use of passwords. Passwords are used to protect against unauthorized use. Users must have a password in order to log into a system. Companies sometimes restrict access to certain computers. Passwords usually are changed periodically.

Other security measures include the following:

- Making security a priority by maintaining and enforcing security measures
- Using electronic identification cards to gain access to certain areas within a building or department
- Protecting schools and company networks from external networks by using firewalls—special hardware and software that allow users inside the organization to access computers outside the organization while keeping outside users from accessing their computers
- Using antivirus software to protect data

TECHNOLOGY CAREERS

Simulation Analyst

Simulation analysts and consultants work with all types of companies of any size. Their primary job is to investigate different options to determine which would be the best for a particular situation. For instance, health care company administrators might want to implement a new system for filing and processing insurance claims. Before spending a huge amount of money, they might hire a simulation analyst to determine which system would best meet their needs. Or a bank is going to bring in a new system to process checks. It hires an analyst to do simulation modeling of what the system might and might not do.

Some necessary skills include the ability to see detail in a system and to be a good technical writer. The person should be a logical thinker and have good analytical skills. A good memory is an additional asset. Opportunities and the need for simulation analysts are increasing. One of the reasons for the increase is that more and more companies are applying simulation to a larger variety of problems.

As a consultant, you would probably do some traveling. Consulting fees are usually quite generous, with some simulation analysts making as much as $75,000 or more per year. You might find some analysts with only a two-year degree, but generally you need at least a bachelor's degree in computer information systems or computer engineering.

- Instituting a selective hiring process that includes careful screening of potential employees, and dismissal of employees who refuse to follow security rules
- Regularly backing up data and storing it off site
- Employing **biometric security measures**, which examine a fingerprint, a voice pattern, or the iris or retina of the eye and compare them against employee records; this method of security is usually used when high-level security is required (see **Figure 17–16**).

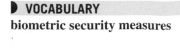

▶ **VOCABULARY**
biometric security measures

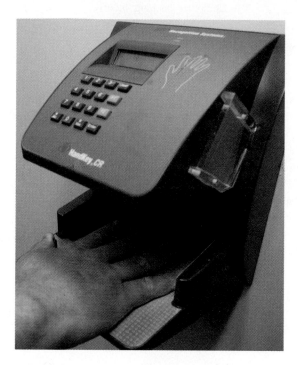

FIGURE 17–16 Biometric security measures

As computer piracy and code breaking becomes sophisticated, many individual users will choose biological security. Hackers cannot duplicate individual fingerprints and voice-activated algorithms.

Protection for Technology Injuries

Many laws have been passed in an effort to assist those injured by computer crimes and other technology issues. However, most of the offenses are difficult to prove. A list of some of the laws that protect users follows:

- Copyright Act of 1976—protects the developers of software
- Software Piracy and Counterfeiting Amendment of 1983—protects software development companies from the copying and use of their software programs
- Electronic Communication Privacy Act of 1986—prohibits the interception of data communications
- Computer Fraud and Abuse Act of 1986—prohibits individuals without authorization from knowingly accessing a company computer to obtain records from financial communications

In addition, many states have individual laws governing computer crimes that happen within their states.

SUMMARY

In this lesson, you learned:

- Technology is having a tremendous impact on education. Many people predict that technology will change the entire structure of education.

- The Internet and the World Wide Web are the biggest factors affecting education today.

- Some people predict an antitechnology backlash.

- Electronic commerce is the buying and selling of goods and services using the Internet.

- Digital cash allows someone to pay online by transmitting a number from one computer to another.

- New jobs and new job categories are being developed because of the Internet and electronic commerce.

- Some technological advances are voice recognition, nonlethal weapons, space travel, flying cars, smart shoes and smart seats, clothes that fight odors, and electronic shopping.

- Computer crime has become a major problem, costing companies billions of dollars annually.

- Computer fraud is conduct that involves the manipulation of a computer or computer data for dishonest profit.

- Computer hacking involves invading someone else's computer. Sometimes it is done for financial gain and sometimes just as a prank.

- A computer virus is a program that has been written to cause corruption of data on a computer.

- To protect against viruses, install and keep an antivirus program running on your computer. Be sure to update it regularly.

- Computer security is necessary to keep hardware, software, and data safe from harm or destruction.

- The most common way to control access to data is to use passwords.

- Illegally copying and using software is called software piracy. It has cost companies millions of dollars in lost sales.

- Laws have been passed in an effort to assist those who have been injured by computer crimes and offenses. Many computer crimes are difficult to prove and prosecute.

◼ VOCABULARY REVIEW

Define the following terms:

artificial intelligence (AI)
biometric security measures
computer-based learning
computer crime
computer fraud
computer hacking
copyright
data diddling

digital cash
electronic commerce
genetic engineering
groupware
nanotechnology
online learning
optical computing
plagiarism

quantum computing
simulation
software piracy
time bomb
virtual reality (VR)
virus
worm

◼ REVIEW QUESTIONS

MULTIPLE CHOICE

Select the best response for the following statements.

1. _____ invade other people's computers.

   A. Hackers   C. Software pirates

   B. Programmers   D. System analysts

2. When high-level security is required, a company most likely would use _____ security measures.

   A. biometric   C. password

   B. hunt and share   D. simulation

3. A type of virus that makes copies of itself is called a _____.

    A. snake   C. worm

    B. pig   D. nanoparticle

4. _____ is the delivery of education over the Internet.

    A. Simulation   C. Virtual reality

    B. Online learning   D. none of the above

5. The buying and selling of goods on the Internet is called _____ _____.

    A. economic commerce   C. on-hand business

    B. electronic commerce   D. local commerce

TRUE / FALSE

Circle T if the statement is true or F if the statement is false.

T F   **1.** With digital cash, you can pay someone by transmitting data from one computer to another.

T F   **2.** Worms, time bombs, and Trojan horses are variations of viruses.

T F   **3.** Hackers only attack other people's computers for fun.

T F   **4.** A WebQuest activity requires the use of the Internet for investigation and problem solving.

T F   **5.** It is not possible to enroll in an online high school.

FILL IN THE BLANK

Complete the following sentences by writing the correct word or words in the blanks provided.

1. Computer _____ is necessary to keep hardware, software, and data safe from harm or destruction.

2. Using _____, which are models of real-world activities, you learn by doing.

3. _____ language allows people to interact easily with computers by talking to them.

4. _____ relates to creating computer components that are less than 100 nanometers in size.

5. _____ refers to an online business.

■ PROJECTS

CROSS-CURRICULAR— MATHEMATICS

The development of the microprocessor has not only changed the world, but it also has changed lives. Some people have been more affected than others. Visit the Intel Education Web site at *www.intel.com/education/makingchips/index.htm* and complete the 12-page lesson. Prepare a report on what you learned and share this information with the class.

CROSS-CURRICULAR—SCIENCE

A firewall was discussed briefly in this lesson. Visit the Microsoft site at *www.microsoft.com*, search for *firewall faq*, and then select the Firewall: FAQ link. Review at least six of the questions and answers listed on this page. Then write a short overview of what you learned and how you can apply it to computer security.

CROSS-CURRICULAR—SOCIAL STUDIES

Viruses have been around for quite a while. Use the Internet and other resources to research the history of early computer viruses. Prepare a report to share with your classmates on the types of viruses and the damage they caused. Also, include any information you might find on the person who programmed the virus, if possible. Use a search engine and the keywords *computer viruses* or *early computer viruses*.

CROSS-CURRICULAR—LANGUAGE ARTS

The year is 2070. You were born in 2055. Use your word-processing program to write a letter to someone who was born at the beginning of the century and tell him or her about your life and your community.

WEB PROJECT

Most dentists today use computers in one way or another. For instance, instead of obtaining a film of an X-ray, it can be sent to a computer screen. Some dentists use a sonic device to clean teeth. Use search engines such as *www.google.com* and *www.altavista.com* to see what you can discover about how dentists are using computers. Prepare a presentation and share it with the class.

 ## TEAMWORK PROJECT

Your instructor has assigned to you and a team member a project relating to the global economy and electronic commerce. You and your partner are to prepare a report on what information you would need to know before setting up an e-commerce Web site. Create a PowerPoint presentation and present it to your class.

CRITICAL THINKING

Congratulations on your new job at Bank International. Assume that your supervisor has asked you to research and prepare a report on biometric security measures. After you thoroughly research this project, create a report listing each item you selected and explain why you selected that particular item. Submit your report to your instructor.

EXPLORING GOOGLE

As you have learned so far, Google offers a wealth of services. Consider now how convenient it would be to access many of these services from your cell phone. Thanks to Google Mobile, you can use your cell phone to send and receive Gmail, get driving instructions, search online for text and/or images, view a calendar, display a location map or a satellite map, and read Google news. Visit the Google Mobile Help Center located at *www.google.com/support/mobile* and review the Help topics. If you have a cell phone, locate your phone model and then create a list of services applicable for your particular phone. Write a short overview of which service or services you most likely would use. If your cell phone is not listed, select one that you would purchase.

UNIT III REVIEW

Computers and Society

■ REVIEW QUESTIONS

FILL IN THE BLANK

Complete the following sentences by writing the correct word or words in the blanks provided.

1. A(n) _____ is an attempt to deceive an audience into believing that something false is real.

2. The main page or index page of most Web sites is referred to as the _____.

3. Some people predict a(n) _____ backlash.

4. _____ are a popular way to arrange and organize text on a Web page; examples are ordered and unordered.

5. _____ is the exclusive right, granted by law for a certain number of years, to make and dispose of literary, musical, or artistic work.

6. _____ different font sizes are supported by most browsers.

7. A basic Web page contains both page content and _____ tags.

8. Computer _____ is necessary to keep hardware, software, and data safe from harm or destruction.

9. _____ is the language of the Web.

10. When citing electronic references, the _____ style is widely used.

MULTIPLE CHOICE

Select the best response for the following statements.

1. _____ is the ability to move through a Web site.

   A. Surfing   C. Citing

   B. Navigation   D. Sharing

2. A Web page is a document on the World Wide Web and is defined by a unique _____.

   A. CPU   C. HTML

   B. URL   D. JPEG

3. Google, AltaVista, Excite, and Yahoo are examples of _____.

   A. domains   C. electronic resources

   B. search engines   D. shareware

4. _____ is the unauthorized use of software.

   A. Software piracy   C. Copyright violation

   B. Stemming   D. Data diddling

5. _____ refers to changing the DNA in a living organism.

   A. Simulated games   C. Genetic engineering

   B. Artificial intelligence   D. Format management

6. Computer _____ is conduct that involves the manipulation of a computer or computer data for dishonest profit.

   A. accounting   C. commerce

   B. fraud   D. mismanagement

7. All of the following are examples of groupware except _____.

   A. project management software   C. video conferencing

   B. collaborative writing software   D. desktop publishing

8. A _____ is a program that has been written to cause corruption of data on a computer.

   A. Web quest   C. hacker

   B. computer virus   D. simulation

9. Defining features of any Web page are the _____.

   A. links (or hyperlinks)   C. font sizes

   B. headings   D. formatting styles

10. All of the following are examples of lists you can use to organize information or data in a Web page *except* _____.

   A. numeric   C. unordered

   B. ordered   D. definition

TRUE / FALSE

Circle T if the statement is true or F if the statement is false.

T   F   **1.** Many Web sites provide free space online for publishing Web pages.

T   F   **2.** An antivirus program always should be installed and running on your computer.

T   F   **3.** Passwords are useless in controlling access to data.

T   F   **4.** HTML is a protocol that controls how Web pages are formatted and displayed.

T   F   **5.** The goal of artificial intelligence software is to process information on its own without human intervention.

T   F   **6.** Information is only as good as the source.

T   F   **7.** HTML supports five types of lists.

T   F   **8.** When creating a Web page, the <center> tag is used to center data.

T   F   **9.** HTML does not support adding a Web page background color.

T   F   **10.** A character entity that is inserted into an HTML document has four parts.

■ PROJECTS

CROSS-CURRICULAR—MATHEMATICS

Computer crimes have been responsible for the loss of millions of dollars. Some crimes result in more loss than others. Use the Internet and other resources to locate information on lost revenue due to the top five computer crimes. If you have access to spreadsheet software, prepare this information in a spreadsheet and write formulas that will add the totals for each crime and the percentage of each crime's portion of the overall total. Some keywords that might be helpful are *computer crimes*, *computer crime costs*, *hackers*, and *software piracy*. Use various search engines.

CROSS-CURRICULAR—SOCIAL STUDIES

Professional journals are available for many areas of science. Many of these journals have a related Web site—*Popular Science*, *Smithsonian*, *Discover*, and *Scientific American* to name a few. Use the Internet to locate the Web sites for at least two science magazines. The Web site address generally is the name of the journal in lowercase letters, followed by *.com*. Use the information in Lesson 15 to evaluate these sites.

CROSS-CURRICULAR—SOCIAL STUDIES

The typewriter was probably the first "technology" device used in the workplace. Use the Internet and other resources to research other technology devices used in the workplace in the "early" days of technology. Use word-processing software to present your findings in a table. Include the name of the device, a brief description of the device, and an explanation of how it impacted the workplace.

CROSS-CURRICULAR—LANGUAGE ARTS

Prepare a handout that identifies electronic sources and how to cite these sources when using them in a report or other research. Include samples in your report.

WEB PROJECT

Technology has changed considerably the way instruction is delivered in recent years. Use the Internet and other resources to research how technology will continue to change education. Prepare a report identifying and describing at least two new educational technologies that will affect education in the future.

TEAMWORK PROJECT

It is time to elect a new mayor in your hometown and two candidates are running for the position. You are one candidate. Select a partner to be your "opponent" for the mayor's position. Each of you is to create three to four Web pages for your campaign that will provide information for potential voters. Use as many of the tags as possible to make your Web pages useful and attractive. Remember, you want to be mayor!

■ CRITICAL THINKING

Many companies are allowing their employees to work from home. This is another example of how technology has changed the workplace. The trend will increase over the next 10 years or so. There are many advantages and disadvantages for both the employee and the employer. After conducting research, prepare a report that discusses the advantages and disadvantages. Include at the end of your report whether or not you would consider working from home. Explain your choice.

VIDEO PROJECT

Visit the Online Companion Web page for this book, and then click the link for the Unit 3 Review to watch a video. According to the video, what innovations does Zeno, the robot toy, introduce? What role does artificial intelligence play in the robot's performance and responses? If necessary, search the Web to find additional information regarding Zeno the robot. Although it is currently a toy, what practical applications do you imagine for Zeno? Prepare a report in the form of a written document, electronic presentation, or Web page to describe what you learned.

■ SIMULATION

JOB 3–1

You and your partner have decided that a Web page would be very beneficial for advertising your Computer Help OnCall business. Computer Help OnCall offers the following services: computer setup, network support, virus detection and removal, software installation, laptop computer repair, printer services, data backup and restore, and wireless network setup. Design two to three Web pages advertising your business. Include elements that will make the pages appealing and user friendly.

JOB 3–2

You have noticed that many students in your computer classes are having difficulty selecting appropriate electronic resources for their term papers and citing the selected sources. They are spending hours surfing the Internet to locate legitimate information. As a result, you have asked your instructor if you could develop and give a presentation on the criteria for evaluating electronic resources. Use the information in this unit and other sources to develop a five- to six-slide presentation.

■ PORTFOLIO CHECKLIST

Include the following activities from this unit in your portfolio:

_____	Lesson 15	Mathematics Cross-Curricular Report
_____	Lesson 16	Language Arts Cross-Curricular Web Page
_____	Lesson 17	Exploring Google Project
_____	Unit 3 Review	Mathematics Cross-Curricular Spreadsheet
_____	Unit 3 Review	Social Studies Cross-Curricular Report
_____	Unit 3 Review	Job 3–1 Business Web Site

APPENDIX

Keyboarding

■ OBJECTIVES

Upon completion of this lesson, you should be able to:

- Define keyboarding.
- Identify the parts of the standard keyboard.
- Identify the home row keys.
- Identify correct keyboarding techniques.
- Type text without watching the keys.

■ VOCABULARY

bump keys

carpal tunnel syndrome (CTS)

ergonomic keyboard

home row keys

insertion point

keyboarding

QWERTY

timed writings

virtual keyboard

...

Introduction to Keyboarding

The computer has become a part of our daily life—at work, at home, and at play. Increasingly, we use the computer to complete a variety of everyday tasks, such as composing letters, sending e-mails, managing our finances, and so on. To effectively use the computer requires good keyboarding skills. **Keyboarding** (also called *touch typing*) is the ability to input data by touch using the alphabetic and numeric keys on a computer and/or typewriter keyboard. Using the proper touch system of keyboarding is most important since it determines our speed and accuracy.

Developing good keyboarding skills requires practice and time. Once you have developed your keyboarding skills, you can use word application software programs more productively. In addition, proper keyboarding techniques can help reduce the risk of **carpal tunnel syndrome (CTS)**. This condition occurs due to an expansion of tendons in the wrist, resulting in pain and/or numbness in the hand and arm.

Keyboard History

The first "writing machine" was developed in the 1800s. These early writing machines came in various sizes and shapes. Many attempts were made to design a

APPENDIX   Keyboarding

keyboard that would allow a typist to type quickly and accurately. **Figure A-1** shows examples of two of these early writing machines.

FIGURE A-1   Early writing machines

The **QWERTY** keyboard was the work of inventor Christopher L. Sholes, who developed the prototype for the first commercial typewriter in a Milwaukee machine shop in the 1860s. Pronounced *KWER-tee*, it is named after the first six letters on the top row of alphabetic keys on the standard English computer keyboard. Today, the QWERTY layout is still the most widely used keyboard format for computers. **Figure A-2** shows a typical QWERTY keyboard.

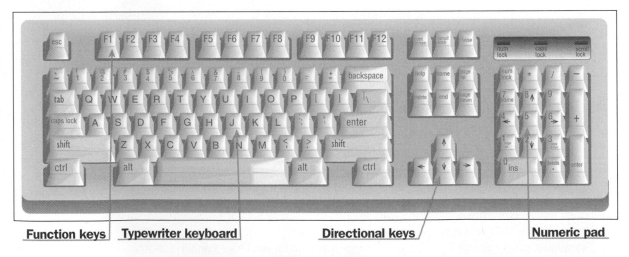

Function keys **Typewriter keyboard** **Directional keys** **Numeric pad**

FIGURE A-2   QWERTY keyboard

Some keyboards are designed to relieve stress that can result from repeated and/or longtime use on a keyboard. These are called **ergonomic keyboards**. The newest type of keyboard is a **virtual keyboard**. **Figure A-3 (A)** shows an example of an ergonomic keyboard and **Figure A-3 (B)** shows an example of a virtual wireless keyboard.

(A)

(B)

FIGURE A-3   (A) Ergonomic keyboard (B) Virtual wireless keyboard

Even though there are different types of keyboards, they all have the same basic parts. These are identified in **Figure A-4** and described in the following text.

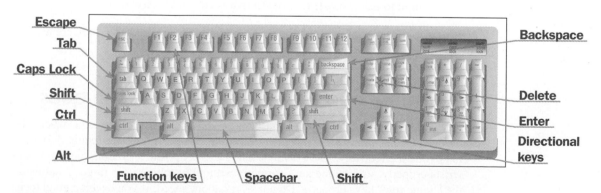

FIGURE A-4   Computer keyboard parts

1. The **Spacebar** is used to insert a space between words and at the end of a sentence. You press the Spacebar with the left or right thumb.

2. The **Alt** (alternate) key can be used alone, or in combination with other keys to do common tasks. Its function is dependent on the specific software program. It is considered a modifier key.

3. The **Ctrl** (control) key, also a modifier key, can be used alone, or in conjunction with other keys to do common tasks. Its function is dependent on the specific software program.

4. Use the **Shift** key to capitalize letters and to type the symbols above the number keys. Hold down the Shift key while you hit the letter you want capitalized. The keyboard contains two Shift keys, usually located on either side and below the home row. Use the right Shift key to capitalize letters that you type with your left hand and vice versa. Use your little fingers to operate the Shift key.

5. Use the **Caps Lock** key to capitalize a series of letters. The Caps Lock key is on the left side of your keyboard. When you press the Caps Lock key, all letters you type will be capitals until you press the key again. It only affects letters, not punctuation symbols or numbers.

6. Use the **Tab** key to move the **insertion point** to the next tab marker in your document. One of the more common uses of the Tab key is to indent the first line of a paragraph.

7. The **Escape** (Esc) key usually is located to the left of the top row of letter keys on the keyboard. Generally, this key is used to interrupt or cancel an operation. It can be used for other functions, depending on the software program.

8. **Function** keys are a set of programmable keys on a keyboard. They generally are positioned across the top of the keyboard, and labeled F1 through F12. These keys perform different tasks, determined by the software program.

9. Pressing the **Enter** key moves the insertion point to the next line and starts a new line of text.

10. The **Backspace** key removes the character to the left of the insertion point.

11. The **Delete** key removes the character to the right of the insertion point. It also is used to delete any text or object that is currently selected.

12. The **directional keys** are the four keys with arrows on them. They are used to control movement of the insertion point on the screen.

Learning Correct Keyboarding Techniques

Keyboarding is much like playing a piano or other musical instrument, where the brain and fingers must work together. Several basic techniques are required to learn to keyboard effectively. These include using correct posture, holding the hands and wrists properly, striking the keys correctly without watching your fingers, and using the "home row" keys properly. Do not worry about speed; if you develop good techniques, the speed will come.

▶ **VOCABULARY**
insertion point

Position

The correct keyboarding position refers to your posture. See **Figure A-5**.

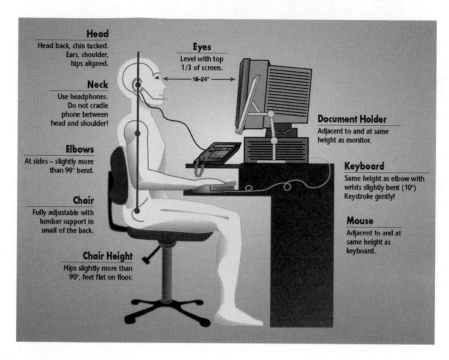

FIGURE A-5   Correct keyboarding position

- Sit up straight and lean forward slightly from the waist. Your body should be about a hand's length from the front of the keyboard and centered with the keyboard.
- Keep both feet flat on the floor.
- Let your elbows hang naturally at your sides.
- Rest your fingers lightly on the keys.
- Focus your eyes on the book or reference resources unless you are composing at the keyboard; in that case, keep your eyes on the computer screen.

Keystroking

You must use the correct finger to stroke each key you type. Learning the location of each key and which finger to use to press the key may be the most challenging aspect of learning to keyboard. Keep your fingers curved over the home row. The **home row keys** include *A, S, D, F,* and *J, K, L, ;*. These keys are called the home row because they are the keys to which you return your fingers after you press a key.

On most keyboards, the home row has **bump keys** to assist you in correct placement of your fingers. The bump keys have a small, raised dot in the center of the key or a raised dash at the bottom of the key. They are placed differently on different keyboards and might be on the two index-finger keys or on the middle-finger keys. These keys provide a physical clue to correct finger placement on the home row. Memorizing the location of the keys will help you to develop your keyboarding skill. Do not look at your hands or the keys as you type. See **Figure A-6**.

> **VOCABULARY**
> **home row keys**
> **bump keys**

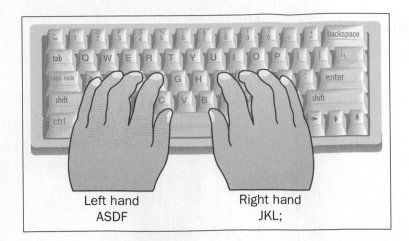

FIGURE A-6   Correct finger position

Your fingers are named for the home row keys on which they rest: *A* finger, *S* finger, *J* finger, and so on. Assigning your fingers names will assist you in making proper moves when reaching for keys. To type the letter "r," for example, you will press the key with the *F* finger, and to type the letter "n," you will press the key with the *J* finger. **Figure A-7** provides a closer look at the fingers you use to press the different keys.

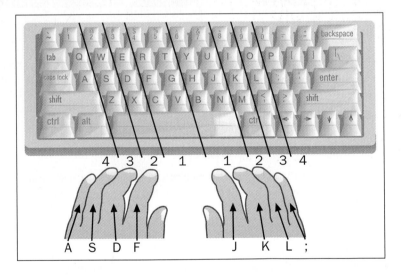

FIGURE A-7   Fingers you use to press various keys

Following are some guidelines for stroking keys:

■   Rest your fingertips lightly on the keys.

■   Keep your fingers slightly curved and upright. Make sure that the palm of your hand does not touch the keyboard or the desk.

■   Press the key with a quick, snappy stroke and return the finger to the home row.

Two additional keys you will learn to use are the Enter key and the Spacebar. **Figure A-8** shows the proper finger position for these keys.

You use the Enter key to move down to the next line. Use the finger on the semicolon key to press the Enter key.

You use the Spacebar to insert spaces between words, punctuation marks, and so on. Use the right or left thumb to press the Spacebar.

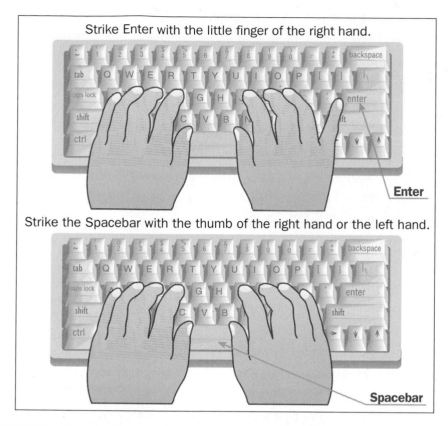

FIGURE A-8   Finger positions for the Enter key and Spacebar

Your Workstation

An organized workstation, which includes your desk, chair, computer, printer, supplies, and reference materials, enhances your productivity. Place reference materials on the right side of the computer and supplies on the left side. Remove any items you are not using.

Developing Beginning Keyboarding Skills

Now that you are familiar with the keyboard layout, you are ready to begin developing keyboarding skills. The most important factor in mastering keyboarding skills is good technique. You build speed and accuracy by applying good technique. At this point, however, do not concern yourself with speed. Concentrate on being accurate, and the speed will come later.

Learning to type all of the keys and to develop accuracy and speed will take several weeks of concentrated study. This lesson does not provide you with comprehensive keyboarding instruction. It introduces you to keyboarding concepts and provides practice drills to help you learn the location of the keys. Additional keyboarding drills can be downloaded from the Web page for this book.

Start your word-processing program and practice typing the home row keys in Step-by-Step A.1.

Step-by-Step A.1

1. Organize your workstation.

2. Start your word-processing program.

3. Check your posture to be sure you are following the guidelines listed earlier in this lesson.

4. Place your fingers on the home row keys. Curve your fingers so the tips of your fingers are resting on the home row keys. Remember, your fingers are "named" for the home row keys on which they rest: *A* finger, *S* finger, *D* finger, and so on.

5. Press the **Spacebar** to enter a space between words. Practice using the Spacebar. Tap the **Spacebar** once (with your right or left thumb); tap it twice; tap it once; tap it twice.

6. Press the **Enter** key to move to the next line. This is called a *hard return*. To press the Enter key, extend the "semi" (for semicolon) finger to the Enter key and press lightly. Practice using the Enter key. Reach and press **Enter**. (Remember to return the semi finger to the ; key.) Press the **Spacebar** once, twice, once, twice. Press **Enter**.

7. Type the following home row keys. Press **Enter** two times after each line. (If time allows, repeat this step several times to get more practice with these keys.)

    ff jj dd kk ss ll aa ;; f j d k s l a ;

    ff jj dd kk ss ll aa ;; f j d k s l a ;

    jj ff kk dd ll ss ;; aa fj a; fj a;

    jj ff kk dd ll ss ;; aa fj a; fj a;

    jk fk kl ds l; sa fj kd sl a; fj a;

    jk fk kl ds l; sa fj kd sl a; fj a;

    aaa lll lll all all sss aaa ddd sad sad

    aaa lll lll all all sss aaa ddd sad sad

    sad sad fad fad ask ask lad lad dad dad

    sad sad fad fad ask ask lad lad dad dad

8. Press **Enter** again and keep the document open for Step-by-Step A.2.

Most keyboarding courses use the same method to teach the rest of the alphabetic keys. After learning the location of the alphabetic keys, you complete drills on the number and symbol keys and begin drills focusing on accuracy and then speed. In Step-by-Step A.2, you will practice new key reaches.

Step-by-Step A.2

1. The E key is typed using the *D* finger, and the H key is typed using the *J* finger. Type the following lines. Press **Enter** two times after each line. (If time allows, repeat this step several times to get more practice with these keys.)

    ddd ddd eee eee ded ded ede ede

    ddd ddd eee eee ded ded ede ede

    hhh hhh jjj jjj jhj jhj hjh hjh

    hhh hhh jjj jjj jhj jhj hjh hjh

    he he she she shed shed held held

    he he she she shed shed held held

    he asked; she has; a shed; he has ash

    he asked; she has; a shed; he has ash

2. Type the following lines to practice using the Shift, Caps Lock, Tab, and Backspace keys. Press **Enter** two times after each line. (If time allows, repeat this step several times to get more practice with these keys.)

    [left Shift] j [Spacebar] [left Shift] j [Spacebar]

    Jade Jade Jade Jas Jas Jas Jeff Jeff Jeff

    [right Shift] e [Spacebar] [right Shift] e [Spacebar]

    Ed Ed Ed Ada Ada Ada Dale Dale Dale

    [Caps Lock] SEE JAMES EAT

    JEFF JEFF AL AL ASA ASA [Caps Lock]

    [Tab] Jake Jake safe safe Half Half

    [Tab] She She He He feed feed all all

    she had a lead; shed [Backspace] [Spacebar] had a lead;

    she asked a lade [Backspace] [Spacebar]

3. Complete the following steps to save your work.

    a. In Microsoft Office Word, click the **Office Button** and then point to **Save As**.

    b. Click **Word Document** and select the drive where you save your work.

    c. In the File name box, type **Practice** as the name of the document.

    d. Click the **Save** button.

Drills used to develop speed and accuracy are called **timed writings**. These types of drills and timed writings are beyond the scope of this book.

▶ **VOCABULARY**
timed writings

Printing and Closing

To print a file, complete the following steps:

- Click the Office Button and then click Print.
- In the Print dialog box, click the OK button.
- You are returned to your screen while the document is printing.

    To close a document, click the Office button and then click Close. When you finish working in a program, you should close the program. To do so, click the Office Button and then click Exit Word.

Retrieving a File

After you save a file, you can open that file to review it, add or delete information, or make other changes.
    To open a file:

- Click the Office Button and then click Open.
- In the Open dialog box, select the drive and folder where your file is located.
- Click the name of the file you want to open.
- Click the Open button. A copy of the file is displayed on your screen.

Keyboarding Software

Many different keyboarding software programs are available for learning to keyboard. These programs provide instruction, drills, and testing for developing keyboarding skills. Some of the more popular of these keyboarding software programs include Mavis Beacon, Typing Instructor Deluxe, and Typing Tutor.
    Some of these programs are designed for persons with special needs, such as those who have poor vision or who can use only one hand. Some programs have voice instructions. When using one of these programs, it is important to use appropriate techniques as discussed previously in this lesson.

Speech Recognition Software and Other Input Devices

Several software programs now support speech recognition. You speak through a microphone that is connected to your computer, and the information is displayed on your screen. You will need to train your computer to recognize your voice. This might take some time, but the result of this new skill will be that you can get your work done faster. Studies have shown that voice input easily can exceed 100 words per minute and with practice, 130 words per minute. The average typist can type 40 to 50 words per minute.
    Additional input devices include handwriting recognition software, scanners, mobile tablet PCs, personal digital assistants (PDAs), digital pens, and touch screens.

SUMMARY

In this lesson, you learned:

- Keyboarding (or touch typing) is the process of inputting text by touch into a device such as a computer by pressing keys on a keyboard.

- The home row of a keyboard consists of the following keys: *A S D F J K L* and *;*.

- Bump keys are located on selected keys on some keyboards to assist in the correct placement of your fingers.

- Using correct techniques is important in developing keyboarding skills. These techniques include posture, keystroking, and the organization of your workstation.

- You can retrieve files that have been saved.

- Keyboarding software is available for learning to keyboard.

- Speech recognition software allows you to "talk" to your computer to enter data.

- Digital pens, PDAs, handwriting recognition, mobile tablet PCs, and touch screens are other tools that can be used to input data.

■ VOCABULARY REVIEW

Define the following terms:

bump keys	home row keys	QWERTY
carpal tunnel syndrome (CTS)	insertion point	timed writings
ergonomic keyboard	keyboarding	virtual keyboard

■ REVIEW QUESTIONS

MULTIPLE CHOICE

Select the best response for the following statements.

1. Standard keyboards have the _____ layout.

   A. QWARKY   C. QWAZXY

   B. QWYTRE   D. QWERTY

2. _____ is the ability to input data by touch.

   A. Counting   C. Reading

   B. Writing   D. Keyboarding

3. Proper keyboarding techniques can help reduce the risk of _____.

   A. touch typing   C. blind keys

   B. carpal tunnel syndrome   D. timed writing drills

4. The home row keys include _____.

   A. a, b, c, d, k, l, ; ,   C. q, w, e, r, t, y

   B. a, s, d, f, j, k, l, ;   D. y, r, t, q, k l, j

5. You press the _____ key to move the insertion point to the next line.

   A. Backspace   C. Spacebar

   B. Enter   D. Tab

TRUE / FALSE

Circle T if the statement is true or F if the statement is false.

T   F   **1.**   Keyboarding is much like playing a piano, where the brain and fingers work together.

T   F   **2.**   The first "writing machine" was developed in the 1900s.

T   F   **3.**   Bump keys are located at the very top of the keyboard.

T   F   **4.**   Slouching in the chair while keyboarding affects your keyboarding skills in a positive way.

T   F   **5.**   Ergonomic keyboards relieve stress that can be incurred from repeated and/or longtime use on a keyboard.

FILL IN THE BLANK

1. Keyboarding is sometimes referred to as _____ typing.

2. PDAs, digital pens, and voice recognition software are examples of _____ devices.

3. Use the _____ key to capitalize a series of letters.

4. Your fingers should rest _____ on the keys.

5. The _____ is used to insert spaces between words and punctuation marks.

■ PROJECTS

CROSS-CURRICULAR— MATHEMATICS

Access the Web site at *http://en.wikipedia.org/wiki/Typing*. This article describes four different input or typing methods: touch typing, hunt and peck, buffering, and thumbing. Create a chart listing each of the methods and rank each method using a scale from one to five, with one representing an advantage and five representing a disadvantage. After your chart is complete, add a paragraph explaining which method you prefer and why.

CROSS-CURRICULAR—SCIENCE

This lesson described several electronic devices used for inputting data. Use the Internet and other resources to research some of the electronic devices identified in this lesson. Prepare a report describing these devices, how they are used, and the approximate cost of each. Which device would you prefer for inputting data? Explain why.

CROSS-CURRICULAR—SOCIAL STUDIES

You learned in this lesson that Christopher Sholes is given credit for designing the first typewriter. However, there were many attempts to invent a writing machine in the early 1800s. Use the Internet and other resources and write a two-page report on the history of three of these early writing machines. Include the name of each early machine you discover, a description, the date, the inventor, and the cost.

CROSS-CURRICULAR—LANGUAGE ARTS

The author of a book on technology careers is visiting your facility in two weeks. Prepare a list of five technology-related questions that you would like to ask the author at the reception following the presentation. Some of your questions should focus on the importance of knowing how to type, and the minimum skill level.

WEB PROJECT

Many jobs require keyboarding skills. Some examples include administrative assistant, data-entry technician, receptionist, newspaper reporter, author, and secretary. Access *www.hotbot.com*, *www.google.com*, and other Internet sites to locate information regarding these and other jobs and careers that involve or require keyboarding skills. Prepare a report on two of these careers. Include the duties performed, the level of skill required, and the starting salary.

 ## TEAMWORK PROJECT

Ergonomics is a growing concern for persons using computers. Users can develop physical discomforts and conditions. Partner with a classmate to research ergonomics as it relates to computer users. Prepare a report to define ergonomics, identify at least five specific problems for computer users, identify causes of each, and propose solutions for each.

CRITICAL THINKING

This lesson discussed the development of the QWERTY keyboard and the layout of the keys on the keyboard. Other keyboard layouts have been developed over the years, one of the more popular being the Dvorak keyboard. Proponents of the Dvorak keyboard argue that the layout is much more efficient and easier to learn, and that the user can type faster. More recently, Microsoft released the Microsoft Keyboard Layout Creator (MSKLC) program, which lets the user define his or her own keyboard layout. This program (for Windows Vista) is free to download from the Web at *www.microsoft.com/ globaldev/tools/msklc.mspx* (or visit *www.microsoft.com* and search

for *MSKLC*). Earlier versions of this program are located at *www. microsoft.com* by searching for "Dvorak keyboard."

Consider these alternatives to the traditional QWERTY keyboard. Do you think another keyboard layout eventually will replace the QWERTY keyboard? Do you think the MSKLC program will become widely used? Would you prefer to stay with the traditional QWERTY keyboard or try something new? Explain your answers in a one-page report.

 # EXPLORING GOOGLE

Google participates in the Open Directory Project. The project, which is a human-edited directory of the World Wide Web, is maintained by a group of volunteers. This is a directory and not a search engine. Within this directory project, Google maintains a variety of links to many topics. One of those topics is typing and contains a variety of links to a number of typing programs and typing tutorials. Some of the programs are commercial programs for sale, and a number of others are free downloads. To access these programs, you start at

www.google.com/dirhp. This is the Google Directory home page. Click Computers and then click Software. This brings you a page with a list of software programs. Click Educational and then click Typing. A list of 40 or more programs is displayed. Select two or three of the free programs and complete the practice exercises. After you complete the exercises, use your word-processing program to list the programs you used and the skills you learn to apply.

GLOSSARY

802.11 A family of standards governing wireless transmissions.

A

absolute cell reference In a worksheet, cell contents that will not change when copied or moved to another cell.

active cell Currently selected cell in a worksheet.

adapter card A circuit board that enhances the functions of a system component and/or provides connections to peripheral devices.

Address bar The space in a window that displays the name of the open folder or object.

alignment The placement of text between the left and right margins; text can be aligned at the left, at the right, or in the center.

American Standard Code for Information Interchange (ASCII) A coding scheme used to represent data.

animation Adds movement to text, graphics, and other objects on a PowerPoint slide or a Web page.

application software Software that helps you perform a specific task, such as word processing, desktop publishing, and so on; also called productivity software.

arithmetic/logic unit (ALU) A component of the microprocessor; performs arithmetic, comparison, and logical operations.

Arrange in Groups Allows you to group files by any detail of the file, such as name, size, type, or date modified.

artificial intelligence (AI) Software that can process information on its own without human intervention.

attachments Documents, images, figures, and other files that you can attach to an e-mail message.

audio input The process of inputting sound into the computer.

AutoFormats Customized preset styles that come with Excel.

AutoSearch An Internet Explorer feature; used to view a list of likely matches in the Search bar, and display the most likely Web page in the main window

B

background The part of Web pages that have color or an image.

bandwidth The transmission capacity of a communications channel.

baseband Low bandwidth.

basic input/output system (BIOS) Contains the code that controls the most common devices connected to a computer.

binary Machine language, which is ones and zeros.

biometric security measures Security measures that examine a fingerprint, a voice pattern, or the iris or retina of the eye.

Biometrics An authentication technique using automated methods of recognizing a person based on a physiological or behavioral characteristic.

BIOS ROM A chip that contains nonvolatile memory.

bit A zero or one in computer code.

blog A short form for weblog, a personal journal published on the Web.

Bluetooth Uses radio waves to connect mobile devices such as cell phones, PDAs, and notebook computers.

body Web page content.

Boolean logic Boolean logic used to search Web site databases; consists of three logical operators: AND, OR, and NOT.

booting The process of starting a computer.

border Lines and outlines that can add emphasis to a document and call out important information.

broadband High bandwidth.

browser   Software program used to retrieve documents from the Internet.

bump keys   Keys with a small dot in the center or a dash at the bottom to assist in correct finger position.

bus topology   In a network, all devices are connected to and share a master cable.

byte   Made up of eight bits; a byte represents a single character, such as the letter A.

C

cable modem   Uses coaxial cable to send and receive data.

cache memory   High-speed RAM that is used to increase the speed of the processing cycle.

Campus Area Network (CAN)   A collection of local area networks within a limited geographical space, such as a university campus or a military base.

Cascading Style Sheets   A collection of formatting rules that control the appearance of content in a Web page.

cathode ray tube   Used for computer monitor; large sealed glass tube; screen is coated with dots of red, green, and blue phosphor material.

cell reference   The name or address of a spreadsheet cell.

cell   Point at which a column and row meet in a spreadsheet.

central processing unit (CPU)   Also called the microprocessor, the processor, or central processor, it is the brains of the computer.

channel   The media that carries or transports the message; this could be telephone wire, coaxial cable, microwave signal, or fiber optic.

character entities   A code in HTML that has three parts: an ampersand (&), a # and an entity number, and a semicolon (;).

chart   Graphical representation of worksheet or table data.

chat room   An area online where you can chat with other members in real-time.

circuit board   A thin plate or board that contains electronic components.

client/server network   A type of architecture in which one or more computers on the network acts as a server.

clients   Computers on a network that are not acting as a server.

coaxial cable   The primary type of cabling used by the cable television industry; also widely used for computer networks.

collapse   The minus sign button in the Folders pane of Windows Explorer, which hides additional levels of folders within the selected folder.

communication devices   Facilitate the transmitting and receiving of data, instructions, and information.

communications channel   The link through which data is transmitted.

computer crime   A criminal act committed through the use of a computer.

computer fraud   Conduct that involves the manipulation of a computer or computer data in order to obtain money, property, or value dishonestly or to cause loss.

computer hacking   Invading someone else's computer, usually for personal gain or just the satisfaction of doing it.

computer system   Input, output, and processing devices grouped together.

computer   Electronic device that receives data, processes data, stores data, and produces information.

computer-based learning   Instructional methods where the teacher uses the computer to deliver the instruction.

concept searching   Used for Web site searching; the search engine tries to determine what you mean and displays links to Web sites that relate to the keywords.

contacts folder   A folder designed to store information about business and personal contacts with whom you often communicate.

contacts   Information on friends, family, and other individuals with whom you work or communicate with on a regular basis; stored in an address book.

container application   The program that will contain a linked or embedded object.

Content Advisor   A filtering program developed by Microsoft that is part of the Internet Explorer Web browser.

Contents pane   In Windows Explorer, the right pane that displays the folders and files that are contained in the folder or disk selected in the Folders pane.

control unit   Coordinates all of the CPU's activities.

controller   A device that controls the transfer of data from the computer to a peripheral device and vice versa.

copyright   The exclusive right, granted by law for a certain number of years, to make and dispose of literary, musical, or artistic work.

currency   Refers to the age of the information, how long it has been posted, and how often it is updated.

D

data communications The transmission of data from one location to another.

data diddling Changing data before it is entered in the computer or after it has been entered in the computer.

data projector Output device that projects the image from a computer screen onto a larger screen; primarily used for presentations.

data Information entered into the computer to be processed. Consists of text, numbers, sounds, video, and images.

database management system (DBMS) A software program that is used to create, maintain, and provide controlled accesses to data.

Database window The command center for working with Access objects.

database A collection of related information organized in a manner that provides for rapid search and retrieval.

datasheet In a database, a row-and-column table view of the data in tables, forms, and queries.

Datasheet view In a database, a row-and-column view of data in a table, form, or query.

decoding Part of the machine cycle; the process of translating the instruction into signals the computer can execute.

decryption Using a key to unscramble information and return it to the original text.

Deep Web See *Invisible Web*.

design templates Predesigned formats containing color schemes, styled fonts, background graphics, and so on, that can be applied to a presentation.

Design view In a database, used to create a table, form, query, and report.

desktop computer Computer that fits on a desktop.

destination program The program that will contain a linked or embedded object.

destination Location where a copied file or folder will reside.

Details view Displays the name of the file or folder, along with information on the file size, the file type, and the date the file was created or last modified.

dial-up modem Enables a computer to transmit data over analog telephone lines.

digital camera A camera using digital technology.

digital cash Allows someone to pay by transmitting a number from one computer to another; the digital cash numbers are issued by a bank and represent a specified sum of real money; each number is unique.

digital pen Pen-like writing instrument that allows the user to input information by writing on a PDA or other mobile device or to use the pen as a pointer.

disk cache A portion of RAM set aside for temporarily holding information read from a disk.

domain name The unique name that identifies an Internet site.

dot matrix printer An impact printer; prints by transferring ink to the paper by striking a ribbon with pins.

download To transfer (data or programs) from a server or host computer to one's own computer or device.

DSL Uses a digital subscriber line (DSL) to connect a computer to the Internet.

dual-core processor A single chip that contains two separate processors.

E

editing Changing the text in an existing document.

electronic commerce Conducting business and business transactions online.

electronic communication Communication using computers.

electronic mail (E-mail) The transmission of files and data using a computer network.

e-mail address Consists of three parts—user name of the individual, the "@" symbol, and the user's domain name.

e-mail link A hyperlink that displays a blank e-mail form containing the recipient's address.

embedded computer Computer that performs specific tasks and are usually found in a device such as an MP3 player.

embedded object A static object; if changes are made to the object in the source program, those changes are not reflected in the object in the destination program.

embedded operating system System that includes technologies and tools that enable developers to create a broad range of devices. This operating system, which resides on a ROM chip, is used on small handheld computers and wireless communication devices.

encrypting Scrambling a message so that it can only be read by someone with the key.

ergonomic keyboard A keyboard designed to relieve stress on the hands and wrists that can result from repeated and/or longtime keying.

Ethernet Was the first approved industry standard protocol; one of the more popular LAN protocols.

executing Part of the machine cycle; the process of carrying out the processor commands.

execution cycle (E-cycle) Amount of time it takes the central processing unit to execute an instruction and store the results in RAM; also called instruction cycle (I-cycle).

expand The plus sign button in the Folders pane of Windows Explorer, which displays all folders and subfolders on a disk.

expansion board Enhances functions of a component of the system unit and/or provides connections through a port to peripheral devices.

expansion slot Openings on the motherboard where an expansion board, also called an adapter card, can be inserted.

Explorer windows File managers including the Documents Explorer, Pictures Explorer, Music Explorer, Videos Explorers, and Downloads.

Extended Binary Coded Decimal Interchange Code (EBCDIC) Standard computer code used mostly in very large computers.

extranet Network that allows outside organizations, such as suppliers and vendors, to access internal company Web sites.

F

Favorites A method of storing individual Web pages or Web locations on your computer.

fax machine An input/output device; transmits and receives documents over a telephone line.

fax modem An input/output device; transmits and receives documents through a computer.

fetching Part of the machine cycle; the process of obtaining a program instruction or data item from RAM.

fiber-optic cable Physical media; used to transfer data; made from thin, flexible glass tubing.

fields A column in a database table. Each field contains a specific piece of information for a record.

file allocation table (FAT) A special log on the disk that keeps track of the data storage location.

file management The process of organizing and keeping track of files.

File Transfer Protocol (FTP) An Internet standard that allows users to download and upload files to and from other computers on the Internet.

file The instructions the computer needs to operate (called program files or executable files); it may contain a text document you can read (often referred to as a document file); or a file may contain an image or other media.

Filmstrip view Available in Windows Explorer picture folders; displays pictures in a single row of thumbnail images.

FireWire A type of external bus; also known as IEEE 1394 and IEEE 1394b.

Flag Status column Column in the Outlook window to which you can assign a flag that can be used to identify a message. Flags can be used as reminder notices or to identify the importance of a message.

floppy disk A storage device; flat circles of iron oxide-coated plastic enclosed in a hard plastic case.

folder Used to organize files into manageable groups.

Folders pane Left pane in Windows Explorer that displays a hierarchy of disks, folders, and files on the computer.

font style Attributes, such as bold, italics, and underlining, that are applied to a font.

font The design of a typeface.

footer Information that appears at the bottom of every page in a document in Office documents.

Format Painter Formatting tool that allows you to copy the formatting on selected text and apply it to other text.

formatting a) The process of preparing a disk so you can write data to and read data from the disk; b) applying certain attributes to text, specifying margins, spacing, and so on; enhancing the text in a document.

form In a database, the object used to enter data in a table.

formula prefix The equal sign (=) that is entered before a formula in a worksheet cell.

formula A statement that performs a calculation in a spreadsheet.

function A built-in formula that is a shortcut for common calculations, such as summing and finding the average.

G

gateway A combination of software and hardware that links two different types of networks that use different protocols.

genetic engineering Refers to changing the DNA in a living organism.

graphical user interface (GUI) An interface that displays a symbolic desktop.

graphics tablet A flat drawing surface on which the user can draw figures or write something freehand.

groupware Refers to programs and software that help people work together even if they are located in different physical locations.

H

hard copy   A printout; printed information.

hard disk   Primarily used to store data inside of the computer, although removable hard disks also are available.

hard return   Moves the insertion point to the next line of type; pressing the ENTER key.

hardware   The tangible, physical computer equipment that can be seen and touched.

header   Information that appears at the top of every page in a document or at the top of every page in a worksheet.

heading   On a Web page, the typeface, size, and the extra space above or below the heading.

hits   The number of returns or hyperlinked Web sites addresses displayed based on your keyword Web search; also called results.

hoax   An attempt to deceive an audience into believing that something false is real.

Home Area Network (HAN)   A network contained within a user's home.

home page   The main page or index page of a Web site.

home row keys   Keys on the keyboard from which all keystrokes are made. These keys are a, s, d, f, j, k, l, and ;.

host computer   A computer to which other computers are connected so that the host can manage time-intensive computing tasks.

host node   A node where a host processor is located.

hot plugging   The ability to add and remove devices to a computer while the computer is running and have the operating system automatically recognize the change.

hyperlink   Object on a Web page that, when clicked, takes you to another location on the same Web page or to other Web pages.

hypertext markup language (HTML)   A text-based program used to create documents to display in a browser; a series of tags that are integrated into a text document and describe how the text should be formatted.

hypertext transfer protocol (HTTP)   Communication protocol used to connect to servers on the World Wide Web. The primary function of HTTP is to establish a connection with a Web server and transmit HTML pages to the user's browser.

I

IBM AIX   An IBM variation of UNIX.

icon   Small image that represents a file, command, or another computer function.

Icons view   Displays a small icon identifying the type of file with the filename or folder name beneath. These are typically arranged in horizontal rows in Windows Explorer.

identify theft   The unlawful gathering of personal information, acquire credit, and conduct transactions using false identities.

IEEE 1394   See *FireWire*.

image   A graphic, such as a picture, photo, or drawing.

impact printer   Uses a mechanism that actually strikes the paper to form letters and images.

index   The third part of a search engine; when the spider finds a page, it feeds the data to the index; also called the Indexer.

indexer   See *index*.

information processing cycle   Series of input, process, output, and storage activities performed using a computer.

information   Data that has been organized and processed so that it is meaningful and useful.

inkjet printer   Output device where the color is sprayed onto the paper.

input   Data entered in a computer to be processed.

input devices   Devices used to input data into the computer.

insertion point   A blinking vertical line that shows your current position in a document.

instant messaging   E-mail feature that allows you to send and receive messages while you and the contact are both logged on to the Internet.

instruction cycle (I-cycle)   See *execution cycle*.

Internet service provider (ISP)   A company that provides an Internet connection.

Internet   The largest network, used as a communication tool.

interoperability   The ability of software and hardware on multiple machines from multiple vendors to communicate meaningfully.

intranet   A network used exclusively by the members of an organization for distributing company information.

Invisible Web   Searchable databases; not available through traditional search engines; also called Deep Web.

IrDA   The sending of signals using infrared light waves.

ISDN (Integrated Services Digital Network)   Modems that connect your computer to the Internet.

item   A particular piece of information stored in an Outlook folder.

J

joystick A type of input device primarily used for games; a plastic or metal rod mounted on a base.

K

keyboard The most common input device for entering numeric and alphabetic data into a computer.

keyboarding The ability to key text by using the correct fingers without looking at the keys.

keyword A descriptive word within a Web document.

L

label printer Output device; prints labels.

label Alphabetic text or data that will not be used in a formula in a spreadsheet.

language translators Convert English-like software programs into machine language that the computer can understand.

large format printer Output device; used for drawings and drafting output.

laser printer Output device; produces images using the same technology as copier machines.

leaders Characters that fill in blank spaces between columns of text and/or numbers.

line printer A high speed impact printer.

line spacing Controls the amount of space between lines of text in a document.

linked object An object that retains a connection to the original file; the source document displays a representation of the linked data.

Linux An open-source operating system program that is free and one that programmers and developers can use or modify as they wish.

List view Provides a list of file and folder names with small icons identifying the type beside each name. These typically are arranged vertically.

lists On a Web page, a popular way to arrange and organize text on a Web page, and suit the way people read Web pages.

LISTSERVs A mailing list software program that automatically distributes mailing lists on a particular subject.

local area network (LAN) Connects personal computers, workstations, and other devices such as printers, scanners, or other devices.

M

Mac OS Operating system designed for Apple's Macintosh computers and Macintosh clones.

machine cycle A combination of the instruction cycle and one or more execution cycles.

magnetic tape Storage media; mostly used for making backup copies of large volumes of data.

mailing list A group of e-mail addresses that are used for easy and fast distribution of information to multiple e-mail addresses simultaneously.

main memory See *random access memory*.

mainframe computer Large and powerful computers used for centralized storage, processing, and management of large amounts of data.

margins White space around the edge of a page that frames a document.

math symbols Used with search engine math.

memory On the computer's motherboard; where the data is stored.

menu bar Displays a list of commands.

Metropolitan Area Network (MAN) A network that interconnects users with computer resources in a designated geographic area.

microwave A signal that is sent through space in the form of electromagnetic waves.

mid-range server A computer on a network that manages network resources.

mobile browser A browser designed for use with mobile devices.

mobile computers Personal computers such as notebook computers and tablet PCs.

mobile devices Electronic devices that fit into the palm of your hand, such as PDAs and smart phones.

mobile printer A small, battery-powered printer; primarily used to print from a notebook computer.

modem An acronym for modulate-demodulate; a communications hardware device that facilitates the transmission of data by converting analog signals to digital and vice versa.

modifier keys Keyboard keys that are used in conjunction with other keys; Ctrl, Alt, and Shift.

modulate-demodulate Converts analog signals to digital and vice versa.

monitor Output device; produces soft copy.

motherboard Circuit board that contains components such as the central processing unit, memory, controllers, and expansion ports and slots.

mouse The most common pointing device for personal computers.

MP3   A file format that allows audio compression at near-CD quality.

MS-DOS   A command-line interface for microcomputers.

multi-core processor   An expansion chip that provides for more than two separate processors.

multifunctional device   Output device that provides the functionality of a printer, a scanner, a copier, and a fax machine.

multimedia   The use of text, graphics, audio, and video in some combination to create an effective means of communication and interaction.

multitasking   Allows a single user to work on two or more applications that reside in computer memory at the same time.

N

nanotechnology   Technology that relates to creating computer components that are less than 100 nanometers in size.

navigation   The ability to use links to move through a Web site.

Neighborhood Area Network (NAN)   Generally consists of access points, in which networking services are shared among neighboring businesses and residences.

network interface card (NIC)   Enables and controls the sending and receiving of data between the computers in a network.

network operating system   Resides on a network server and is designed specifically to support a network.

network   A group of two or more computers linked together; connects one computer to other computers and to peripheral devices such as printers.

newsgroup   An online discussion group where participants exchange messages on a specific topic.

nodes   Computers and other peripheral devices on a network.

nonimpact printer   Forms characters without striking the paper; examples are ink jet and laser printers.

Normal view   In PowerPoint, the default view that contains the Outline and Slides tabs, the Slide pane, the Notes pane, and the View buttons.

Notes pane   Used to enter information that the presenter may refer to as the presentation is being delivered.

O

objects   The components in a database; objects include tables, forms, queries, and reports.

object linking and embedding (OLE)   A technology developed by Microsoft that lets you create a document or object in one program and then link or embed the data into another program.

Office Fluent   Part of the Microsoft Office user interface that groups tools by task.

online conferencing   Also called Web conferencing; is used to hold group meetings or live presentations over the Internet.

online learning   Education delivered online.

online service provider (OSP)   An online service provider is an entity that provides a service online.

operating system   Provides an interface between the user or application program and the computer hardware.

optical computing   Uses light beams for the computer's internal circuits instead of electricity.

optical storage   Uses laser technology to read and write data on silver platters.

order of evaluation   The sequence by which mathematical operations in a formula are performed.

Outline tab   Organizes the content of the presentation.

output devices   Devices that display processed data or information.

output   Data processed by a computer.

P

packets   The small chunks of data that an e-mail message is broken into when it is sent; automatically reassembled into their original format when they reach their destination.

Palm OS   A competing operating system with Windows Mobile; runs on Palm handhelds and other third-party devices.

parallel port   Computer port that can that transfer data eight bits at a time.

patent   Guarantees the inventor exclusive rights to the process or method for a certain period of time.

PC-DOS   IBM's version of MS-DOS.

peer-to-peer network   A network configuration where all of the computers on a network are equal.

peripheral devices   Devices such as keyboards, monitors, printers, and the mouse.

Personal Area Network (PAN)   The interconnection of personal digital devices within the range of about 30 feet.

personal computers   Computers designed for use by an individual.

personal information management (PIM)   A program that you can use to organize your schedule, keep track of your contacts, and manage e-mail.

placeholder   A box with dotted borders that reside within a slide layout and are displayed when you create a new slide.

plagiarism   Presenting someone else's ideas or work as your own, without authorization.

plotter   An output device generally used by architects and engineers.

Plug and Play   Refers to the ability of a computer system to automatically configure expansion boards and other devices.

pointer   The object on the screen that is controlled by an input device.

pointing device   An input device that allows a user to position the pointer on the screen.

pointing stick   A pressure-sensitive device that looks like a pencil eraser. It is located on some keyboards, generally between the G, H and B keys.

points   The standard measurement unit for fonts, approximately 1/72 of an inch; the higher the point size, the larger the font.

port   The point at which a peripheral device attaches to a system unit so it can send data or receive information from the computer.

presentation software   A computer program used to organized and present information in the form of a slide show.

Preview pane   A pane in an Explorer window that lets you preview the content of documents, pictures, and so on without opening the individual file.

primary key   Assigned to a field, it uniquely identifies each record in a database table.

printhead   The mechanism inside the printer that prints.

printout   A printed copy of a document.

processor   Also called the microprocessor, central processor, or the central process unit, is the brains of the computer.

protocol   An agreed-upon format for transmitting data between two devices.

public domain   Material on which copyright protection has lapsed, thereby making it available for anyone to copy.

Q

quantum computing   Uses the laws of quantum mechanics and the way that atoms can be in more than one state at once to do computational tasks.

query   Database object that lets you specify criteria by which you search the data stored in a table.

Quick Click Flat Status column   Located to the right of the message heading in the Microsoft Office Outlook Inbox, the column contains flags that can be used as reminder notices or other indicators that are needed for your personal or business use.

QWERTY   The arrangement of the alphanumeric keys on a standard keyboard; refers to the first six keys on the top row of letters.

R

random access memory (RAM)   A type of computer chip; short-term, volatile memory.

range   A contiguous group of cells.

read-only memory (ROM)   A type of computer chip that stores specific instructions to manage the computer's operations; non-volatile.

receiver   A computer receiving a message.

records   Rows in a database table that consist of a group of related fields.

related search   Preprogrammed queries or questions suggested by the search engine.

relative cell reference   In a worksheet, cell contents that change relative to the cell to which they are copied or moved.

relative link   A link in HTML that gives the file location in relation to the current document.

report   Database object used for presenting data in an attractive format, and used primarily for printing.

results   See *hits*.

ring topology   A type of architecture where the network devices are connected in a circle.

router   Directs network traffic.

ruler   The area on the screen that is used to change paragraph indentations and margin settings in Microsoft Word.

S

sans serif   Fonts that do not have lines at the ends of the strokes of each letter.

satellite   Wireless media; contains equipment that receives data transmission, amplifies it, and sends it back to earth.

scanner   Input device used to make digital copy of pictures or other documents.

SCSI   See *Small Computer System Interface*.

search engine math   A method of searching the Internet using math symbols.

search engine   A software program that enables the user to search the Internet using keywords.

section break A break that lets you format a section differently from the rest of the pages in the document.

section A portion of a document that is separated from the rest of the document.

selecting Identifying text by clicking and dragging the I-beam across the text to highlight it.

sender A computer sending a message.

serial port Computer port that can transfer data one bit at a time; generally used by the modem and mouse.

serif Fonts that have lines at the ends of the strokes of each letter.

server A computer on a network that manages the network resources.

shareware Software that is free for an evaluation period but requires payment if you continue to use it beyond the evaluation period.

signature Consists of text and/or pictures that you create that automatically is added to the end of outgoing e-mail messages.

simulation Models of real-world activities, designed to allow the user to experiment and explore environments that may be dangerous, inaccessible, or unavailable.

sizing handles The small squares surrounding a selected image or piece of art that you drag to resize the image or art.

slide layout In Microsoft PowerPoint, refers to the way text and objects are arranged on a slide.

Slide pane In Microsoft PowerPoint, displays the currently selected slide, on which you can enter and edit text, insert graphics, images, or audio and video clips, apply formats, and so forth.

Slide Show view The current slide fills the computer screen; in this view, you can click to progress through your slides and see the PowerPoint presentation as your audience will see it.

Slide Sorter view Displays thumbnails or miniature images of all slides in a PowerPoint presentation.

Slides tab Displays thumbnail images of each slide in a PowerPoint presentation. Click an image to display that slide in the Slide pane.

Small Computer System Interface A standard interface for connecting peripherals such as disk drives and printers.

soft copy Information displayed on a monitor.

software license Agreement between a software developer and the buyer that gives the buyer the right to use the program.

software piracy The unauthorized copying of software.

software Intangible set of instructions that tells the computer what to do; program or instructions that give directions to the computer.

solid-state storage A nonvolatile, removable medium that uses integrated circuits.

source program The program used to create an object that is later embedded.

source The file to be copied.

spam Unsolicited e-mail.

speakers Output device; produces sound.

spider A search engine robot that searches the Internet for keywords.

sponsored site A site that has paid a search engine a fee in exchange for being listed in the "sponsored sites" section.

spreadsheet A row and column arrangement of data.

star topology A type of architecture in which all devices are connected to a central hub or computer.

status bar Area on the screen that displays information about the document including current page number, total pages in the document, location of the insertion point, and the status of some of the specialized keys.

stemming Used with search engines, when you search for a word, the search engine also includes the "stem" of the word; also called truncation.

storage media Devices including magnetic disks, optical discs, PC cards, tape, microfilm and microfiche, and mobile storage media such as Flash memory cards, USB flash drives, and smart cards.

storing Part of the machine cycle; means writing the processed result to memory.

styles Pre-designed formatting options that have been saved.

style sheet A collection of formatting rules that control the appearance of content in a Web page.

stylus Pen-like writing instrument that allows the user to input information by writing on a PDA or other mobile device or to use the pen as a pointer.

subject directories A search tool where data is organized by subject categories.

supercomputer Fastest type of computer; used for specialized applications requiring immense amounts of mathematical calculations.

switch   A device located at the telephone company's central office that establishes a link between a sender and receiver of data communications.

system software   A group of programs that coordinate and control the resources and operations of a computer system.

T

tab stop   Location on the Microsoft Word horizontal ruler that tells the insertion point to stop when the Tab key is pressed.

table   An arrangement of information in rows and columns; primary object in a database that contains the raw data.

telephony   Technology associated with the electronic transmission of voice, fax, or other information between distant parties.

text area   The area on the screen that will contain the information that you type.

theme   A predesigned set of fonts, colors, lines, fill effects, and other formatting that can be applied to a presentation to maintain consistency and to give the presentation a professional, finished look.

thermal printer   Output device; forms characters by heating paper.

Thumbnails view   In Windows Explorer, displays the files and folders within a folder as small images, with the filename or folder name displayed beneath it.

Tiles view   In Windows Explorer, displays a large icon identifying the type of file with the filename or folder name, the type of file, and the size of the file displayed beneath.

time bomb   A virus that does not cause its damage until a certain date or until the system has been booted a certain number of times.

timed writings   Keyboarding drills used to develop speed and accuracy.

title bar   Area of the window that displays the name of the document you are working on as well as the name of the software program you are using.

title   The first heading on a Web page.

token ring   A LAN protocol where all of the computers are arranged in a circle.

toolbar   Row of buttons at the top of the browser or other software programs; area of the screen that displays icons (little pictures) of commonly used commands.

topology   The geometric arrangement of how a network is set up and connected.

touch display   Input device; a special screen with pictures or shapes.

touch typing   Entering text by using the correct fingers without look at the keys.

touchpad   An input device commonly used on laptop computers. To move the pointer, slide your fingertip across the surface of the pad.

trackball   A pointing device that works like a mechanical mouse turned upside down.

tracks   A circle on a magnetic media storage device; where data is stored.

trademark   Legal protection for a company's logo or other graphic information.

transitions   In PowerPoint, determine how slides move in and out of view in a presentation; you can attach special visual and sound effects to them.

Transmission Control Protocol and Internet Protocol (TCP/IP)   The protocol used by LANs and WANs that has been adopted as a standard to connect hosts on the Internet.

transmission media   Physical or wireless media used to transmit data.

truncation   See *stemming*.

twisted-pair cable   A type of inexpensive physical media used to transmit data.

U

Uniform Resource Locator (URL)   An address for a resource or site on the World Wide Web. Browsers use this address to located files and other remote services.

Universal Serial Bus (USB)   A port that that supports data transfer rates of up to 480 million bits per second (Mbps); replacing the standard serial and parallel ports on newer computers.

UNIX   An open-source operating system.

urban legends   Stories which may at one time have been partially true and that have grown from constant retelling into a mythical yarn.

USB flash drive   A small removable data storage device that uses flash memory.

Usenet   A collection of news or discussion groups.

user interface   The part of the operating system with which we interact when using our computer.

users   The people who use computers.

utility programs   Programs designed to complete specialized tasks related to managing the computer's resources, file management, and so forth.

V

value   Numeric data, or data that will be used in a formula, in a spreadsheet.

video input   The process of capturing full-motion images with a type of video camera.

views   Format in which you can display and work with the various objects in a database.

virtual reality (VR)   An artificial environment that feels like a real environment.

virus   A program that has been written, usually by a hacker, to cause the corruption of data on a computer.

voice input   The process of using a microphone to input voice; a category of audio input.

voice recognition   The computer's capability of distinguishing spoken words.

W

watermark   Ghosted text or image behind the page content and often is used to indicate that a document is confidential.

Web 2.0   Web sites where users can modify the content, including a new generation of Web-based services.

Web page   A document written in HTML that can be accessed on the Internet. Every Web page has a unique address called a URL.

Web server   A computer that delivers (serves up) Web pages. Every Web server has an IP address and possibly a domain name.

Web site   A group of related Web pages.

WebQuest   Educational activity; uses the Internet for investigation and problem solving.

wheel   A steering-wheel type of device used with games to simulate driving a vehicle.

wide area network (WAN)   Covers a large geographical area.

Wi-Fi (wireless fidelity)   This technology identifies any network based on the 802.11 family of standards.

wildcard character   The asterisk character, which can be used to search the Internet when you do not know the complete spelling of a word.

Windows Embedded CE   A scaled-down Windows operating system, designed for including or embedding in mobile and other devices with limited functionality.

Windows Mail   The e-mail software included with Microsoft Windows Vista.

Windows Mobile   An operating system that works on specific types of PDAs such as Pocket PC and Smartphones.

Windows   Microsoft's graphical user interface operating system.

wireless access point   A mechanism that connects wireless communication devices together to create a wireless network.

word wrap   Word-processing feature that wraps text to the next line when it reaches the right margin.

WordArt   Microsoft Office tool for adding special effects to text.

workbook   Excel file that contains individual worksheets.

worksheet   Sheet within an Excel workbook file that contains a row-and-column grid of cells.

World Wide Web   A network of servers linked together by a common protocol, allowing access to millions of hypertext resources.

worm   A virus that makes copies of itself.

Z

zoom Slider   A device on a keyboard that makes it easy to zoom in for a closer look at documents, spreadsheets, pictures, maps, and Web pages.

INDEX

PHOTO CREDITS